Population
and Progress
in the
Far East

Population
and Progress
in the
Far East

By WARREN S. THOMPSON

The University of Chicago Press

Library of Congress Catalog Number: 59-10428

THE UNIVERSITY OF CHICAGO PRESS, CHICAGO 37
Cambridge University Press, London, N.W. 1, England
The University of Toronto Press, Toronto 5, Canada

PREFACE

This is my third attempt in the past thirty years to examine population changes and their relations to the development of population pressures. I have been particularly interested in those portions of the world where the growth of population pressures seemed likely to contribute significantly to political tensions. The second of my major efforts and the present one were both actually begun as revisions of the preceding essays in the expectation that mere revision would be sufficient to enable me to contribute to a more realistic discussion of the role of population changes in creating such pressures. In both cases it became clear as work progressed that so many significant changes— demographic, economic, political, and social—had taken place that an essentially new essay was needed, even though the central theme remained much the same—the theme being that population changes are intimately and organically related to numerous other *social changes* (using this latter phrase broadly) which tend to determine the intensity of the feeling of population pressure.

I realize, however, that what may appear to me the natural development, over time, of this central theme may appear to others as the virtual abandonment of it and the substitution for it of a theme that economic development is the most significant variable in the situation treated in this essay. I do not believe this is the case. However, I am not much interested in discussing this point, since it seems largely a problem in semantics. Actually it became apparent as the work proceeded that the mere addition of up-to-date materials would not be sufficient. A complete rewriting of the essay was necessary, placing much more emphasis on factors which seemed of lesser importance in the past. When the completed manuscript was submitted to the publisher, it was recognized at once that this was essentially a new book. Hence, the present title, which I must admit is more descriptive of the contents of this essay than the title of its predecessor (*Population and Peace in the Pacific*) would have been.

It will be in order to mention here the four principal changes since World War II which made this new essay necessary. They and several others of much significance are described in the introductory chapter. Besides, these and other changes of lesser importance appear again

and again in the course of the discussion as factors of critical significance in determining the success or failure of the efforts being made
to advance the welfare of the people and, by so doing, to keep in
abeyance the increase of the feeling of population pressure.

The four principal changes as I see them are: (1) More effective
health work is throwing the increasingly heavy burden of a rapidly
growing population on the economies of most of these countries. (2)
The political independence which has come so quickly to most of the
colonial and semicolonial peoples of the Far East has, in most cases,
given great impetus to indigenous efforts both to build strong states
and to make the political state also a welfare state. (3) The emer-
gence of the Communists in China as a strong totalitarian government
is an event of great significance for the whole of Asia. (4) The recognition by the leaders of Japan, China and India that population control should become an operating policy if their peoples are to make
rapid economic progress, or even maintain their present economic
status, is also of the highest significance.

If population pressure in any country is thought of as the feeling of
the people that they are being in some way deprived of opportunity
to improve their living conditions, then this essay may be regarded as
an attempt to throw light on the question: Is population pressure now
growing in these countries of Asia, and is this feeling likely to increase
in the foreseeable future? If it is growing, what are some of the consequences to be expected as population pressure becomes more intense?

I do not claim that these questions are answered, only that after long
study they are given the most careful consideration of which I am
capable. Naturally, I hope that this discussion will contribute to the
better understanding of the relation of population changes to those
other social changes being encouraged in the hope of improving the
welfare of the peoples of the Far East.

It is quite impossible for me to acknowledge my greatest obligations.
They often have not been specific, and many times I did not know at
the time what I was learning from a particular contact—from the Japanese farmer and his wife who told me what they did to keep the
yields of rice and wheat at a high level; from the group of Mysore
farmers making sugar (jaggery), with whom information regarding
agriculture in the United States and in Mysore was exchanged; from
the harigan women in a village in Madras who specified in no uncertain terms the handicaps under which they suffered as compared with

the caste groups in the same village. Hundreds of other personal contacts with many types of people over a period of many years have left their impress, though I cannot acknowledge them more precisely. It is the same with a great number of the articles and books I have read in the course of pursuing my interest in this field.

I can, however, acknowledge with gratitude the service rendered me by Mrs. Ruth W. Smith in preparing the tables, in organizing the bibliography, and in preparing the index; also the aid of Mrs. Jeannette Lewis in patiently converting successive revisions of almost illegible manuscript into one that could be submitted to the publisher without too much trepidation. I am also grateful to the Population Council for financial aid and to the Scripps Foundation for the use of facilities which made my task lighter. Finally, I wish to express here, in addition to the formal acknowledgment on each map, my indebtedness to the authors and publishers who so graciously granted permission to use their maps.

WARREN S. THOMPSON

TABLE OF CONTENTS

CHAPTER I

INTRODUCTION

The main points on which this essay focuses attention may be stated very briefly and, in consequence, rather dogmatically as follows: (1) In much of the area being considered here population is already quite dense, and it is now beginning to grow at an unprecedented rate in most of these countries. Moreover, it is likely to grow still faster in the near future if even the present near-subsistence levels of living can be maintained. (2) In several of the larger and more important of these countries the agricultural resources needed to provide a decent living for the people are so meager, and their more efficient exploitation is so difficult, that pressure on these resources will grow rapidly. (3) Although the nonagricultural resources in the Far East as a whole have proved to be more abundant than formerly believed, the exploitation of these resources is, for many reasons, a difficult and slow process and does not promise as rapid an improvement in living conditions in the next two or three decades as is widely expected, since a large proportion of the products of the new nonagricultural enterprises will be devoted for some time to the production of capital goods. (4) While this situation is putting more actual pressure on agricultural resources in some countries the feeling of pressure will probably grow even more rapidly, and the need for larger mineral resources will quickly expand in a number of these countries once nonagricultural development really gets under way. This is because the people are steadily becoming more aware of the significance of all types of resources for the improvement of the economy, i.e., they are being educated to understand the relation between the opportunity to work effectively (the possession of adequate resources) and the level of living. (5) It is questionable whether the rate of economic development in several of the larger and more important of these countries can reasonably be expected to provide any substantial improvement in living conditions in the near future unless the rate of population growth can be reduced considerably in the next few years. (6) World

1

peace, as well as internal peace, is essential to the development of an efficient economy in all countries, and both will be endangered by this growing feeling of pressure on resources as the population continues to increase rapidly.

CHANGES SINCE WORLD WAR II

It has been noted in the Preface to this edition that certain important changes which have taken place quite recently, chiefly since the beginning of World War II, need to be evaluated with care if we are to assess usefully the effects of changes in the population on the economic and political development of the Far East. A few of these changes are so fundamental in character, and have such a far-reaching influence not only on the welfare of the peoples of Asia but of the whole world, that they should be enumerated and described briefly prior to the more specific discussion of the relationship between population growth and economic change in the several countries. At this point only seven of the more important of these recent changes will be considered, and the discussion will be brief and in rather general terms.

POLITICAL INDEPENDENCE

The attainment of political independence by a number of the countries in the Far East has thus far had quite different effects in the individual countries. In those former colonies where reasonably strong governments could be established rather quickly, the upsurge of economic and welfare activity has been quite amazing. Making this statement does not, however, commit one to the belief that all of the many economic enterprises being undertaken will yield large net gains in better living in the near future, nor does it mean that these enterprises will have the permanent effects hoped for by those who bear chief responsibility for their initiation and direction. But I believe that the gaining of independence has given a great psychological lift to the activity of large numbers of the better-educated people in a number of these countries and has thus insured more intensive and devoted efforts toward the improvement of living conditions than could have been expected had they remained in colonial status. The feeling of a number of the better-educated people that they are now working for their own country rather than for an alien ruling class is a potent stimulus to many who are in positions of responsibility and power. In addition, it seems reasonable to assume that these responsible leaders have enough influence, through their example, to encourage many of their associates in less important positions to also give their best efforts to national development.

On the other hand, the very beliefs and slogans which have been used to arouse the people and to gain their support for the independence movement have led many people to expect the impossible. As a result, the leaders in countries which are trying to follow democratic processes in their political and economic evolution often find themselves in political difficulties when circumstances make impossible the fulfilment of the hopes which the leaders themselves had encouraged during the struggle for independence. Furthermore, the gaining of independence has been such a disturbing and costly process in some countries that even leaders of great ability and high integrity have not yet had opportunity to prove the quality of their leadership in constructive social and economic development. It is also likely that some very good leaders in an independence movement may not be the best leaders for a period of reconstruction. In still other countries the "struggle for independence" seems to have been directed by a ruling clique which hoped to perpetuate its own powers of exploitation without the restraint of the "colonial masters."

It must also be recognized that some of these countries were not yet ready for any substantial degree of self-government, and that premature independence (as compared with enlightened and steadily diminishing colonial control) is endangering their economic development and may possibly lead them into a new form of colonial control such as exists in Poland, Hungary, and other countries in central Europe. Finally, independence has made the leaders in a number of countries more conscious of the need for defense against aggression than they were under colonial control and, as a consequence, has led to relatively larger expenditures on defense than had been expected. It is impossible, of course, to say whether defense now consumes a larger proportion of a country's national production than it did when the country was a colony or, if it does, whether the increase in proportion is due to the conditions associated with the upsetting of the balance of power in the world, and in South and East Asia in particular, by the war. In several of these countries the defense services are absorbing so much of the national income that the use of capital for economic development is being seriously curtailed. This situation again emphasizes the fact that peace is necessary to the progress of economic development.

COMMUNIST CHINA

The second change I would stress is the establishment of a strong communist government over the whole mainland of China. Not only has this affected the social and economic development of China, but it has also exerted, and will continue to exert, a powerful influence over the thinking of the Asian peoples. If China attains fairly substantial economic success under communist control within the next few years—if, for example, she achieves more than India does in the same period under a democratic form of government—China's influence in Asia will be increased still further.

While India's government is avowedly socialistic, great effort is being made to maintain a democratic form of political control which allows a large amount of personal and political freedom, and India's "mixed" economy also provides a great deal of economic freedom as compared with the almost complete governmental control operating in China. The relative efficiency of these two systems in providing for the welfare of their people is being watched closely by many Indians, as well as by people in other countries in the Far East, and their relative economic success may have a big part in determining which of the two systems will be most widely imitated. It is very important to realize that China's propaganda regarding her economic successes has a tremendous impact on the thinking of these Asian peoples. Many of the young intellectuals, in particular, feel that their countries could also achieve the economic miracles the Chinese so loudly proclaim if they were to adopt the communist pattern of economic and political organization. The more mature men, especially those who have had an opportunity to see things for themselves, are much less impressed by the economic developments they observe.

TECHNICAL ASSISTANCE

Technical assistance helps those new nations to develop their economies and to establish such social services as health and education faster than would otherwise be possible. Such assistance is a new feature in the relations between nations. It is not only a gesture of good will; it is a very practical contribution to the building of a more productive economy, which, after self-determination, is the chief aim of those countries which have attained enough internal security to be able to devote both thought and effort to the improvement of their living conditions.

Technical aid programs are making available to these underdeveloped countries much useful knowledge and practical experience concerning production in a shorter time than would be possible without such aid. At present the technical men who are sent out constitute a very substantial supplement to the relatively small corps of experienced native technicians, even in the most advanced of these underdeveloped countries. In some of these countries, unfortunately, these outside technical men are almost the only well-trained men available for consultation in working out practical plans for the development of the country's natural resources. In addition, some of the technical assistants, and some of the students who are being sent abroad for special training under various student aid plans, are helping considerably to develop native training programs in science, in technology, and in a variety of social services.

Technical aid at times involves a certain amount of direct economic aid toward establishing various types of services such as malaria control, the training of extension workers in agriculture and community organization, research in plant-breeding, etc., but it does not, in general, provide for financing specific productive enterprises. Thus there is comparatively little objection to technical aid on the basis that it may be used indirectly for political purposes. However, it must be recognized that many technical assistants, although fully competent in their specialized fields, are not highly competent in the field of human relations and, therefore, do not get on well with the people with whom they must work. This lack of understanding can sometimes render the technician almost useless, because it creates personal antagonisms which make close co-operative effort impossible. All too often, moreover, the technical assistant's term of service is so short that just about the time he is becoming highly useful he leaves the country; then a new assistant has to be broken in, or, worse yet, the continuity of the service is disrupted by the lack of a replacement. The more serious defects in the technical assistance programs are quite generally recognized today, and constant improvement is undoubtedly taking place. It is greatly to be hoped that this type of service can be continued on a fairly large scale, until these peoples have developed their own training programs and no longer need such assistance.

PUBLIC HEALTH WORK

Since the war, public health work has expanded very rapidly in the underdeveloped countries of South and East Asia. Increasingly efficient mass controls over many of the contagious and infectious diseases have already been established and, as a consequence, death rates are falling rapidly in most of these countries, though at widely differing rates.

Because Japan already had a large corps of medical men, some of whom were well trained in public health, and because of the substantial aid rendered by the medical services of the occupation forces of the United States, the decline in her death rate was almost unbelievably rapid during the five years following the war. In Ceylon the decline was even more astonishing (chap. ii). But it should be pointed out that in Japan there had been a long period of preparation for this concentrated attack on the contagious and infectious diseases, and that Japan also had a uniformity of culture which made it relatively easy to organize a health service well suited to the entire country. Ceylon also possessed these advantages and, in addition, is a very small country in which it was rather easy to organize an attack on the most important causes of death. In the larger countries, and in those which previously had little or no public health service and only a small personnel available, the reduction of death rates will be much slower. But the decline in the death rate will be very rapid even in these countries, compared with its rate of reduction in the Western world between 1800 and 1920 (see chap. ii). In fact, this control over the death rate is proceeding so rapidly that the historian of one hundred years from now may regard it as having been the most important factor in preventing a faster and more enduring rise in the level of living of these Asian peoples.

BIRTH CONTROL IN ASIA

The approval of birth control by the leaders of India and China, and its rapid spread in Japan since the war, are events of the very highest significance. There is wide recognition among educated people in India not only of the hardships suffered by families, and particularly by mothers, because of too frequent births, but also of the relation between the improvement of the national economy and the absolute size and rate of increase of the population. That there is as yet no perceptible change in India's birth rate, except in the relatively small educated class, is one of the most important facts that must be faced in considering the likelihood of substantial improvement in India's level of living in the foreseeable future.

The conversion of China's top leaders to a belief in the need for birth control is so recent that it is impossible to determine with certainty whether it represents a genuine departure from the conventional communist doctrine that there can be no economic problem involved in caring for the population under a communist regime no matter how fast the population may grow, or whether this about-face is merely a temporary tactical move adopted to effectuate some political or economic policy that is not yet apparent. Some of the most important Chinese writers who discuss the ideology of communism are going to great pains to explain that birth control is being advocated as a health measure for mothers and children and as a way to insure the better education and training of young adults for work in the reconstruction of China, but not as a means for effecting the slower growth of population—in other words, that the advocacy of birth control by the communist leaders does not signify their acceptance of the Malthusian point of view. The nature of these explanations leads some people to believe that the public discussion of birth control may soon be stopped and the official sanction and encouragement of contraception reversed. On the other hand, such explanations may also be interpreted as a deliberate attempt to persuade the rank and file of Communists that the orthodox Marxian and Leninist view—that the size of a population can never be a cause of poverty and hardship under communism—does not conflict with whatever temporary adjustments of population policy are needed to meet particular situations, e.g., the need to strengthen the country's economy, which has long been kept weak and inefficient by malicious capitalist control. But it also seems quite reasonable to assume that the 1953 census results (583 million on the mainland), and an annual population increase of 12 million or more, have given the leaders of Communist China such a severe shock that they are ready to promote vigorously the only means in sight that gives any promise of lowering the rate of population increase in the foreseeable future.

The rapid acceptance of birth control by the Japanese people in the past few years is one of the most encouraging events of recent times. It leads one to hope that other countries will follow Japan's example in attempting to make a rational adjustment of population to the resources available for its support (see chap. iv).

In any event, I believe the prospects are good today that voluntary control of family size will spread much more rapidly among the peoples of the Far East than seemed likely fifteen years ago, although I remain less sanguine than some regarding the time it will take to bring about a reduction large enough to keep the population approximately stationary.

SPREAD OF EDUCATION

The spread of education in most of these Asian countries is proceeding much more rapidly than could have been anticipated before the war. All the countries with definite development plans are earmarking substantial funds for education of all grades, from kindergarten to institutes of higher studies, with a strong emphasis on scientific and technical education. This rapid intensifying of educational effort must be taken into account in attempting to assess the significance of all social, economic, and political developments in their relation to population change. It should also be noted in this connection that the spread of education, in its broadest meaning, is greatly complicated in some of these countries by the existence of several languages. Such a situation makes the effort to develop a ready means of communication between different language groups a formidable political task, as well as a difficult educational problem, and is almost certain to retard the spread of education in some countries.

THE DRIVE FOR A MORE EFFICIENT ECONOMY

Finally, a seventh factor that should be noted is the intensive drive to make the economy more efficient, an effort several of these countries have initiated as the chief means of enhancing the general welfare. In fact, in some respects a more efficient economy may fairly be regarded as the goal of all other efforts, since it alone can provide the means by which a nation can become strong enough to insure the maintenance of its independence and a supply of the goods essential to an improved level of living for the masses.

Some of the changes just noted merely represent an increase in the amount of effort being made to attain a certain specific end, e.g., the extension of education and health services; others, such as political independence and technical assistance, must be regarded as relatively new factors in the social, economic, and political development most of these countries consider essential to a better way of life.

THE GENERAL PLAN OF THE BOOK

The real problem of population pressure in these Asian countries, as it bears on the maintenance of peace, centers around two questions:

(1) What will be the probable growth of population in these countries during the next generation? (2) Keeping in mind this probable population growth, is per capita income likely to increase fast enough in those countries which will develop substantial military power during the next generation to prevent any significant increase in the feeling of need for larger resources? Of course, such questions can be answered only in terms of probability, i.e., in terms of a personal assessment of the significance of the many variable factors in a very complex situation. In spite of this limitation, the attempt seems a worthwhile one.

The first step toward answering these questions will be a discussion, in broad terms, of the patterns of population change over a considerable period of time; it is hoped that this will yield a fairly clear picture of the factors which are most active in effecting population changes in this region today and will thus provide a basis for judging what changes in population growth are most probable during the next two to four decades. This discussion will be followed by a sketch of certain social and economic conditions, under the heading "Prerequisites for Rapid Economic Development." In general terms, these prerequisites may be described as preparations for the cultural acceptance of new knowledge—preparations for the development of new attitudes toward the changes taking place in many of the old established patterns of living and toward certain important conditions that favor the growth of those new organizations and institutions essential to the creation of a more dynamic economy. The degree to which these prerequisites exist in the different countries varies greatly, and there is no method by which this degree can be judged with any precision. Furthermore, although several countries may appear to have much the same degree of preparation for economic change, each may achieve quite different results because of cultural variations which, in the course of time, have led to the acceptance of somewhat different value systems.

The statement of these general considerations is followed by an attempt to assess the probable population changes and the probable improvements in production in the several countries. This effort constitutes the body of our study and centers around developments in Japan, India, and China. Japan is a country which has rather recently accomplished the transition from a traditional agricultural economy to a relatively highly developed dynamic economy, and her experience should provide valuable data for the assessment of progress in the underdeveloped countries of today. India and China are great countries which probably contain nearly two-fifths of the world's population and which, in order to put all their resources to better use, are now trying strenuously to make the same transition Japan has achieved. The smaller countries of South and East Asia are also struggling to make this transition to a more dynamic economy. Unfortunately, the developments taking place in these latter countries can be considered only briefly. Finally, the concluding chapters undertake to draw together the several threads of the discussion and to indicate the significance of the findings as they bear on international tensions and the likelihood of war arising out of these tensions.

CHAPTER II

PATTERNS OF

HUMAN POPULATION GROWTH

WORLD POPULATION IN MODERN TIMES

Comparatively little is known about definite population changes in particular areas of the world prior to A.D. 1750, when specific data concerning certain parts of Scandinavia became available. In spite of this fact, it will be of interest to note the best available estimates of population growth in the world as a whole, and in the continents, since 1650. Table 1 gives the figures arrived at by Willcox and by Carr-Saunders regarding world population from 1650 to 1900. Almost the whole difference between their figures for 1650 is found in those for Asia. When one examines their data more closely than can be done here, one finds that practically all of this latter difference is in the population of China. These differences continued to be substantial (except for 1800) up to 1900. During this period (1650 to 1900) the population of the world increased about 3.3 times according to Willcox, and somewhat less than 3 times according to Carr-Saunders.

According to both authors, however, the growth rates of Asia and Europe were quite different. The population of Europe, about which there was no difference of opinion, increased more than fourfold between 1650 and 1900, while Asia's population increased only 3.3 times in the same period according to Willcox, but only 2.8 times according to Carr-Saunders. Moreover, population in the area of European settlement (including Europe) increased about 5 times during this two and a half centuries. There can be no reasonable doubt that Asia and Europe, but particularly Asia and the area of European settlement, differed substantially in their rates of population growth during this rather long period, even though no great reliance can be placed on the figures for Asia. As a result of these differential rates of growth in Asia and Europe, the proportion of the world's population living in Asia declined from 54.6 per cent in 1650 to 53.3 per cent in 1900 according to Willcox, and from 60.0 per cent to 56.9 per cent according to Carr-Saunders. During this same period the proportion living in Europe rose from 21.9 per cent to 26.9 per cent according to Willcox, and from 19.0 per cent to 26.4 per cent according to Carr-Saunders. The proportion of the world's population living in the areas of European settlement, including Europe, rose from 24 per cent in 1650 to 36.4 per cent in 1900 according to Willcox, and from 21.6 per cent to 35.6 per cent according to Carr-Saunders.

Since 1900 the proportion of the world's population living in Asia has been increasing, according to the estimates of the United Nations,

TABLE 1

ESTIMATES OF WORLD POPULATION (IN MILLIONS)
BY REGIONS, 1650–1955

Series of Estimates and Date	World Total	Africa	North-ern Ameri-ca*	Latin Ameri-ca†	Asia Exclud-ing U.S.S.R.‡	Europe and Asiatic U.S.S.R.	Oce-ania	Area of European Settle-ment§
Willcox' estimates:‖								
1650.....	470	100	1	7	257	103	2	113
1750.....	694	100	1	10	437	144	2	157
1800.....	919	100	6	23	595	193	2	224
1850.....	1,091	100	26	33	656	274	2	335
1900.....	1,571	141	81	63	857	423	6	573
Carr-Saunders' estimates:#								
1650.....	545	100	1	12	327	103	2	118
1750.....	728	95	1	11	475	144	2	158
1800.....	906	90	6	19	597	192	2	219
1850.....	1,171	95	26	33	741	274	2	335
1900.....	1,608	120	81	63	915	423	6	573
United Nations' estimates:**								
1920.....	1,810	140	117	91	967	486	9	703
1930.....	2,013	155	135	109	1,073	531	10	785
1940.....	2,246	172	146	131	1,213	572	11	860
1950.....	2,476	199	168	162	1,360	574	13	917
1955.....	2,691	223	183	183	1,481	606	15	987

* United States, Canada, Alaska, Saint Pierre and Miquelon.

† Central and South America and Caribbean Islands.

‡ Estimates for Asia and Europe in Willcox' and Carr-Saunders' series have been adjusted to include the population of the Asiatic U.S.S.R. with that of Europe rather than Asia. For this purpose, the following approximate estimates of the population of the Asiatic U.S.S.R. were used: 1650, 3 million; 1750, 4 million; 1800, 5 million; 1850, 8 million; 1900, 22 million.

§ Includes Northern America, Latin America, Europe and the Asiatic U.S.S.R., and Oceania.

‖ Source: 343, p. 45. Estimates for America have been divided between Northern America and Latin America by means of detailed figures presented, *ibid.*, pp. 37–44.

Source: 51, p. 42.

** Source: 293, 1956, p. 151.

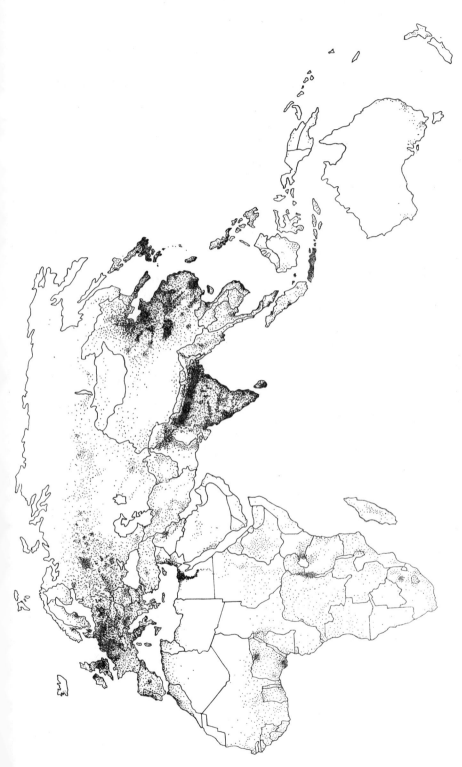

Map 1.—Distribution of population in the Eastern Hemisphere. (Adapted from map compiled and drawn by the U. S. Department of State, Division of Geography and Cartography. Population distribution by Clarence B. Odell. Redrawn and reproduced by permission of Clarence B. Odell and *Encyclopaedia Britannica World Atlas.*)

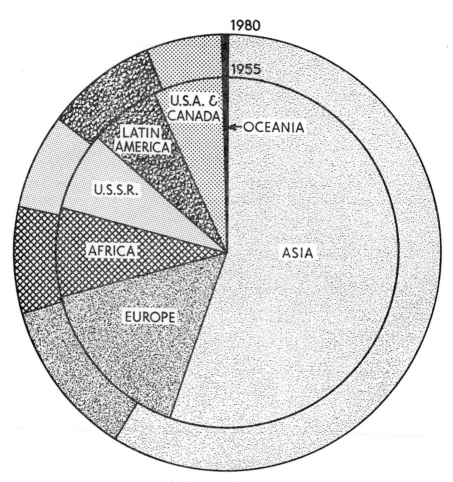

Fig. 1.—Per cent distribution of the world's population by regions, 1955 and estimated 1980.

and in 1955 it amounted to 55.3 per cent; the proportion living in Europe has been declining, and in 1955 constituted only 15.2 per cent of the world's total. The projection of population to 1980 shown in Figure 1 indicates that, proportionally, Asia and Latin America will grow much faster than the other parts of the world shown in the figure, and that Europe, the United States, and Canada combined will have a substantially smaller proportion of the total than they do now. While such projections cannot be exact, they indicate the most probable direction of the changes likely to result from the trends that now prevail. The chief factors involved in these changing trends will be discussed below.

PATTERNS OF POPULATION GROWTH IN
PREINDUSTRIAL CULTURES

Although we have few exact data showing changes in the size of populations before about 1800, history and anthropology lend considerable support to certain general conclusions, now rather widely accepted, regarding patterns of population growth in preindustrial cultures. Our knowledge of these earlier patterns will also help us understand the population changes that have taken place in the world during the past two or three centuries and those that are now in process. These general conclusions regarding the pattern of population growth in the past will be stated rather dogmatically here, since there is space for only a very brief discussion of the reasons for believing they are sound.

1. Most human groups have had high birth rates until quite recently.[1] The term "high birth rate" can be made a little more precise if we say that most population groups numbering more than a few thousand have probably had birth rates in the vicinity of 40 per 1,000 per year until rather recently. This may be compared with a 1955 birth rate in the United States of 24.9 per 1,000. High birth rates are still found in most of the underdeveloped areas of the world, and

---

[1] Exceptions have been found, chiefly in tribal or other small groups whose customs and institutions (e.g., abortion, segregation of females for long periods after childbirth, and prolonged nursing of children) have kept the birth rate far below the physiological capacity to conceive. Polyandry would also result in a relatively low birth rate, even if every woman had a large number of children. At times, particular classes in different societies have resorted to practices, chiefly abortion, which kept their birth rates low. The upper classes in Rome at the time of Augustus are supposed to have practiced abortion rather widely. Some societies have also encouraged celibacy on a large scale.

rates in excess of 50 per 1,000 have been recorded for several groups within the past few years.

2. With comparatively few exceptions in averages over fairly long periods, but with numerous exceptions in particular years, the death rates of all peoples have been high until quite recently, i.e., until two or three centuries ago, almost equaling their birth rates in most years and occasionally exceeding them.

3. In the past the birth rates of most peoples have fluctuated considerably less from year to year than their death rates. Hence, it can be said quite properly that in the past the rate of population growth of most peoples has depended primarily upon the fluctuations in their relatively high death rates.

4. On the whole, the growth in numbers of most human groups until about two or three centuries ago was slow and rather highly variable from year to year or from one relatively short period to another.

The reasons for these conclusions can be stated here only briefly.

We know that in the Western countries where reliable vital records first became available, between 1750 and 1850, the birth and death rates were relatively high. But even then they were lower than the rates in many parts of the world today. Thus in a number of countries which have only recently achieved fairly reliable registration of births, the birth rates are still very high (Ceylon, Egypt, Taiwan, Singapore, Ecuador, Venezuela, Mexico). We also know from an occasional intensive study of birth rates and death rates in Chinese and Indian communities that their rates are high, probably higher than those of most European communities were for several decades immediately preceding the development of reliable registration of births and deaths. As will be shown below, death rates are now declining in both India and China.

There is mathematical proof that birth and death rates must have been at about the same level, on the average, throughout most of human history. This proof is quite simple. If population grows steadily at any given rate, even a very low rate, it will double in a given period of time, just as money drawing a fixed rate of interest compounded annually will double in a certain number of years. Thus if the population of the entire world numbered 100 million at the time of Christ's birth (it was probably considerably larger), and if it had grown steadily at a rate of 1.9 persons per 1,000 per year (a birth rate of 40 and a death rate of 38.1 would yield this rate of increase), the total population of the world would now be about twice as large as it actually is. Expressed in terms of percentage, this would be a rate of increase of 0.19 per cent per year, or 2 per cent in ten years, a rate so low that the increase would scarcely be noticed during his lifetime by an interested and informed observer living to a ripe old age. Such a low rate of increase would even be missed frequently by a decennial census if it were not taken with considerably greater care than is customary today even in the more advanced countries. At a rate of increase of 4 per 1,000 per year, which would be considered a very low rate today, 100 million people at the time of Christ would have doubled more than eleven times by now; the present population of the world would be about 288 billion, or about 110 times as large as it actually is. Clearly, before about A.D. 1700 rates of growth noticeable to contemporary observers were few and far between, and affected relatively few people during a few relatively short periods, and in a few places.

The reasons for high birth rates in the past have been, in general, biological—the nature of man's sexual life. The actual birth rate, however, has seldom if ever risen to the physiological maximum, because it has always been dampened by man's institutions and traditions. But until recently, and among only a few peoples, these social controls over the birth rate have not kept it below the *high* level referred to above.

Man has had a high death rate until rather recently because of what Malthus (1798) called the positive checks to population growth —disease, famine, and war. Disease needs little comment. Records of two or three centuries ago often show one-half or more of the children born in certain areas dying before they reached ten, or even five, years of age. There are also histories of epidemics and plagues that carried off one-quarter to one-half of the population in a few months or within a year or two, e.g., the Black Death in Europe (1347–50), and of many other epidemics that were less deadly but that still decimated the populations of many areas from time to time. But the toll taken by recognized epidemics of great magnitude is probably insignificant compared with the regular annual loss of life from diseases like tuberculosis, typhoid, dysentery, and smallpox, to say nothing of the lesser infectious and contagious diseases. It is only about seventy-five years since the bacterial cause of the most deadly contagious and infectious diseases was discovered (Pasteur made his most important announcement of the results of his studies in 1878). Jenner made public his results concerning vaccination against smallpox in the same year (1798) that Malthus published his first *Essay*.

Famines, like great epidemics, are often spectacular causes of death; until quite recently they were very frequent and very deadly, because it was usually impossible to move food into the stricken areas. The effect of famine on population growth, however, like the effect of the great and widely recognized epidemics, was probably quite small compared with the effects of prolonged undernourishment. But neither disease nor hunger operated independently. A great epidemic was almost certain to disrupt the production of food, and a famine was equally certain to contribute to the spread of many diseases. A starving wretch was an easy prey to dysentery, etc., and a malaria-ridden man who could not tend his crops properly was likely to be the victim of hunger.

War has also had an active part in keeping man's death rate high, but it has caused far more deaths by reducing the food supply and spreading disease than by the actual killing of people in battle or during an invasion. Of these three great killers, hunger and undernourishment probably would rate first, with disease in second place and war a long third, except in some rather small tribal societies.

But it has never been merely the date that determined the intensity with which these *positive* checks to population growth operated; it has been, rather, the relation between population growth and the production of the necessities of life which determined the death rate. When man extended his co-operation with nature to the cultivation of plants, he greatly increased his control over the necessities of life both as regards the quantity available to the local community and the certainty of their availability. Likewise, when man domesticated animals, he not only directly increased his food supply and increased its certainty but also, in the course of time, obtained animal power to aid in cultivation. One may say that any invention connected with agricultural practices or with the use of tools (improvement in technology) probably brought about a temporary relaxation of the positive checks to population growth; such inventions, therefore, reduced the death rate at least temporarily and led to some increase in man's numbers. The same results followed the development of every invention that reduced the incidence of disease; these inventions appear to have been relatively unimportant in decreasing the death rate, however, until the discovery of vaccination against smallpox. In fact, rapid progress in controlling specific diseases has been highly concentrated in the very short period of human history since about 1875.

The expansion of the food supply and the acquisition of more adequate clothing has resulted chiefly from the improvement of agriculture and from the extension of the agricultural area. As probable examples of the effect of such changes on population growth, one may mention two rather widely accepted cases, although there is no exact knowledge about them. It is quite generally believed that (1) there was a relatively rapid growth of population in the Roman Empire during the two centuries following Augustus (112a, Vol. I, chaps. i and ii, *passim;* 180a, chap. iv, pp. 55–85), and that (2) a rapid growth in China's population began around the time peace was established after the Manchu conquest in the middle of the seventeenth century and lasted through the ensuing century and a half or two centuries (63, chap. i; 51, chaps. ii and iii; 342, II, Part I, pp. 35–52). In both cases these particular periods were relatively peaceful, and agriculture is supposed to have been greatly extended and to have improved in productiveness. The tremendously rapid growth of population in the United States from the early days of settlement until about 1860 was very obviously based largely on the extension of the agricultural area rather than on the improvement of agricultural practices, and war did little to interfere with this agricultural expansion. Advances in scientific medicine had comparatively little effect on the death rate before about 1900, while economic improvements became mildly operative in the West around A.D. 1700.

From the little we do know about the growth of particular populations in more distant times, and from such simple calculations as those given above, it seems reasonable to conclude that until recent times man's growth in numbers in the world as a whole must have been very slow over long periods of time, that in most groups and areas it must have been highly irregular, and that the level of the death rate was the chief factor in determining the rate of population growth.

The general pattern of population growth until quite recently in human history may be fairly adequately portrayed by a zig-zag curve whose direction and position, in relation to a straight line representing a stationary population, was determined at any given time chiefly by the variations in the death rate. The general trend of this curve for some centuries past has probably been upward, but for relatively long periods, and in particular areas or even continents, there may have been little or no change which could have been noticed by contemporaries, or even by historians who might have been interested in such changes.

Although a brief statement of the probable pattern of population growth in the more distant past has value, we are much more interested here in the population changes which have taken place since about 1700. Fortunately, we know a great deal more about what has happened during the past two and a half centuries, and we also have some information about the more important economic and social conditions associated with these demographic changes. We are able, therefore, to analyze the relations between these factors with greater assurance. This analysis, in turn, helps us to project probable population growth into the future and to relate them to probable economic and social developments. However, we must recognize that even now we have comparatively little power to foresee social and economic changes and the demographic developments likely to accompany them.

About 1700, certain changes began to take place, especially in Western Europe and in the areas then being settled by Western Europeans, which enabled these peoples to alleviate the hardships determining their death rates. Perhaps the most important factor in the growth of Europe's population during the eighteenth century was the improvement of agriculture.

Agricultural practices which would maintain and improve the fertility of the soil were being discovered, and the better practices already in use in some areas were being introduced in other areas. More efficient tillage, which gave the crops an earlier start in the spring and reduced their competition with weeds, was becoming more common. Better varieties of seeds were being more widely distributed and used, and certain crops that had been grown only in rather restricted areas were found to thrive elsewhere and to increase the productivity of agricultural labor. Livestock was being improved through the efforts of men interested in animal husbandry. The advance of agriculture during the eighteenth century was substantial. It led to significant increases in tilled land, which directly affected total yields, to increases in acre yields, and to increases in meat and milk and power from farm animals. These agricultural advances also reduced somewhat the year-to-year variations in yields, thus modifying some of those uncertainties which arose from variations in the weather.

By the middle of the eighteenth century the Industrial Revolution was also beginning to affect man's productive power in certain Western countries, particularly in England. From this time onward agriculture and industry both advanced slowly, but these advances had a profound effect on population growth in Europe because they increased the productivity of human labor. In recently opened countries like America the abundance of new and fertile land made possible an extremely rapid increase in total agricultural production, even though the agricultural practices in many of these new areas were not improving as fast as the practices in parts of Western and Central Europe. It may also be noted, in passing, that during the second quarter of the nineteenth century transportation became so cheap and speedy that Europe could import bulky foods from the new countries across the sea in payment for the manufactured goods sent them and the capital loaned them; this arrangement, in effect, greatly extended the agricultural area of Europe.

It will be impossible to dwell at any length on the way these revolutions in man's productive power affected population growth. A brief description of population changes in Sweden during the past two centuries will illustrate the general pattern that probably prevailed in most of Western Europe during much of this time, although these changes did not occur simultaneously in all countries nor were they always of the same magnitude. Sweden has been chosen as an example because both its population figures and its vital statistics are generally believed to be quite reliable from 1750 on.

Figure 2 shows that during the decade 1751–60 Sweden's birth rate averaged a little over 35 per 1,000 and its death rate averaged about 27, leaving a natural increase of about 8 per 1,000 per year. This was a relatively high rate of growth for that time. Since economic conditions (principally agricultural production) were not so good during the ensuing thirty years, 1761–91, the death rate rose slightly; the birth rate declined a little, probably because of the postponement of marriages, and the natural increase averaged only about 5 per 1,000. In the last decade of the century, 1791–1800, economic conditions again improved; the death rate fell to about 25 and the birth rate averaged about 33, hence the natural increase rose again to about what it had been forty years earlier, although both birth and death rates were somewhat lower. Then came a succession of bad crop years accompanied by war, with the result that the decade 1801–10 witnessed a rise in the death rate to an average above 28 and a decline in the birth rate to about 31. The natural increase in Sweden during this decade (2.6) was the lowest it had been since records became reliable. From this decade (1801–10) onward Sweden's death rate fell fairly steadily, although not uniformly, decade after decade, except for an increase of about 1 per 1,000 during the decade 1851–60. During the decades 1811–20 and 1821–30 the birth rate rose, and in the latter decade it was only about one point below that of 1751–60.

It is difficult to see any secular trend in Sweden's birth rate during the eighty years from 1751 to 1830, and until after 1851–60 the down-

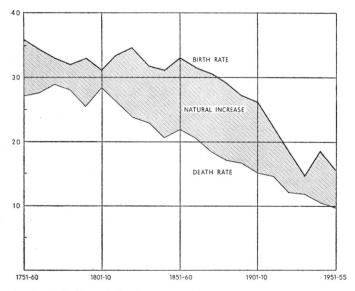

Fig. 2.—Crude birth and death rates and natural increase, Sweden, 1751–1955 (ten-year averages).

ward trend was certainly slight. On the other hand, although there was no significant secular trend in Sweden's death rate between 1751–60 and 1801–10, the downward trend of the death rate after the latter decade was much more rapid than the downward trend of the birth rate until after 1851–60. In the fifty years 1851–60 to 1901–10, both the birth rate and the death rate declined steadily and fairly rapidly, the decline in the birth rate slightly exceeding that in the death rate. Thus the significant and rather steady decline in Sweden's birth rate lagged about fifty years behind the equally significant decline in her death rate; for another fifty years the declines in the two rates were so nearly the same that from 1821–30 to 1901–10 there was only a rather small variation in the rate of natural increase.

It is quite important to realize that very little of the decline in the death rate before 1850, in Sweden or in any other Western country, can be attributed to specific improvements in medical practices—in spite of Jenner's discovery of the vaccine against smallpox in 1798. The practical significance of Pasteur's and Koch's work on bacteria was not widely realized even in the medical profession until about the end of the nineteenth century. In spite of the lack of organized public health work, and in spite of the lack of knowledge about how most contagious and infectious diseases could be prevented, the decline in the death rate was very great during the nineteenth century in most Western countries. In some of them, this decline certainly began during the latter part of the eighteenth century or earlier. These earlier declines in death rates must be attributed largely to the improvement in man's productive capacity and to the availability of new land. This made possible a more adequate and certain food supply and an increasing cleanliness—clean water, sanitary sewage disposal, soap for personal and home use, etc. It also made available cheaper and better transportation, which meant that local food shortages could be relieved by food from abroad or by the moving of food from areas of surplus to areas of deficit within the same country. In Malthusian terms, one can say that in Western Europe and in the lands being settled by Europeans during the eighteenth and nineteenth centuries people were learning to lessen the hardships of life by producing many kinds of goods, including agricultural products, more efficiently, and/or by extending the agricultural area.

In sum, the increasing productivity of man's work and his enterprise in bringing new land into use made life a little easier and soon led to a slow decline in the death rate, with little or no decline in the birth rate for several decades. This was followed by a period, of varying duration in different Western countries, during which both death rates and birth rates declined substantially and almost equally, with the result that the rate of natural increase remained fairly high and relatively constant for several decades. This period was followed, in turn, by one in which the birth rate declined more rapidly than the death rate, which resulted in a lower rate of natural increase. In a few countries the natural increase almost disappeared, so that the population became practically stationary. In France for several years after World

War I, the number of deaths exceeded the number of births, but both rates were at a fairly low level.

In new countries like the United States and Canada, where living was relatively easy because of the abundance of fertile land, the growth of population was unusually rapid until about 1860, and in Australia and New Zealand for several decades after that. The fact that only a small proportion of the people lived in cities, where death rates until quite recently were higher than in rural areas, also helped to keep the death rate low. Benjamin Franklin noted the rapid population growth in this country in the middle of the eighteenth century and attributed it chiefly "to the Ease and Convenience of Supporting a Family" and to earlier marriage. By the time of the first United States census (1790) it was clear that population was growing at an amazing rate in North America and that, although immigration was important, most of this growth resulted from the excess of births over deaths.

The chief reason the decline in the birth rate lagged behind that in the death rate is that cultural patterns largely determine the birth rate, and these patterns change rather slowly. This change depends on a personal acceptance of new values and patterns concerning marital relations and the functions of the family. On the other hand, environmental changes that require very little change in personal behavior, beyond a passive acceptance of new conditions of which people are scarcely aware, may almost automatically reduce the death rate. Thus public sanitation (a pure water supply and effective sewage disposal) benefits everyone in the community, although very few people have any active part in providing it. Again, most people are anxious to provide for themselves a more adequate diet and better housing, which will almost automatically reduce the death rate when the conditions of life are difficult. And almost anyone who is ill will gladly accept professional advice and care.

But while the birth rate does not change as automatically in response to environmental changes as does the death rate, many environmental factors do operate to change the cultural patterns which determine the birth rate. Thus in the relatively recent period with which we are most concerned here, the Industrial Revolution led vast numbers of people to leave rural communities for urban communities. This industrialization and urbanization of the population has had a profound effect upon the entire pattern of living, but it took time for these cultural changes to alter the behavior patterns determining the birth rate. They did affect these patterns, however, in the course of several decades.

The length of time between the onset of a decline in the death rate and an equally significant decline in the birth rate varied greatly from one country to another and from one part of the same country to another part. The lag in Sweden has already been noted. In England and Wales good data on births and deaths were not available until 1838; in the five years 1838–42 the average death rate there was 22.1 per 1,000, about the same as the rate in Sweden at that time. This was a very low death rate for that period. By 1838 England's birth rate may already have fallen some, just as Sweden's may have fallen some before 1750. There is no evidence of any decline in England's birth rate below the 1838 level (36 per 1,000) until about 1880. It is highly probable, therefore, that after the decline in the death rate became significant, it was a century or more before a similar decline took place in the birth rate. In Germany the lag in the decline of the birth rate was only about forty years.

These differences among Western countries with respect to the interval between the decline in their death rates and the decline in their birth rates can probably be explained primarily by differences in the rapidity with which industrialization and urbanization took place; but there can be no reasonable doubt that, although these countries all belonged within the same broad cultural pattern, the cultural differences between them were also important in determining the speed of the changes in their birth rates.

Those countries settled by European peoples during this modern period showed a pattern of growth somewhat different from that of the older countries of Europe. The areas settled were chiefly in the temperate zones, to which Europeans were fully acclimatized and in which most of the European crops could be grown by the methods used in Europe. The difficulties the earliest colonists experienced in establishing themselves should not be overlooked; but once they had established a few settlements and had learned how to till the customary European grain crops and the more important native crops in their new environment, lack of food and clothing and housing ceased to be positive checks on population growth. Moreover, in most of these areas the indigenous inhabitants were few, and because they were poorly equipped against men using gunpowder they could be pushed back almost at will. For all practical purposes, therefore, the land available for settlement by Western Europeans was unlimited for about two centuries. The one significant *positive* restriction on population growth was disease, and even its deadliness was somewhat mitigated by the widely dispersed settlements and the difficulty of communications. Even so, it is doubtful whether death rates in the United States were as low as those in Scandinavia and England until about 1900.

On the other hand, birth rates were extremely high in the United States (and Canada), as Franklin had noted. The rate of natural increase, therefore, was very high and quite steady. It seems highly probable that in the United States, for the two centuries from 1660 to 1860, the rate of natural increase (allowance being made for immigration) was sufficient to double the population in thirty years or less. The French-Canadians apparently grew with about equal rapidity for approximately two centuries.

In the United States rapid urbanization and industrialization began only after the Civil War (1861–65). A fairly rapid decline in the birth rate also began at about that time, although there is evidence that as early as 1800 the birth rate of New England, then the most urbanized part of the country, was well below that of the rest of the country. Even as late as 1900 some regions of the United States still had high birth rates.

In the Western countries as a group, the birth rate began to decline first among the more comfortable classes in the cities, who also enjoyed relatively low death rates; the decline gradually spread to other groups or classes in the cities and then to the rural areas. In the rural areas also, the decline in the birth rate began first among the more comfortable classes and gradually spread to the poorer classes—the people who were also the most isolated and the least educated. France deviated somewhat from this pattern of decline in the birth rate, in that the French peasants seem to have had rather small families during most of the nineteenth century.

Toward the end of the nineteenth century, and in the early years of the twentieth, the increasing knowledge of the role of bacteria in causing infectious and contagious diseases led to much greater emphasis on sanitation, both public and private, as a health factor. Once such knowledge was put into use, the improvements in sanitation were startling in their effects on the death rates of infants and young children. Over most of the Western world these rates were cut by half, or even more, in the course of the first two or three decades of this century. Today they are only about one-fourth of what they were in 1900.

This by no means ends the story of the decline of the death rate in the more industrialized nations since the time of Pasteur. The increasing funds made available for medical research in the past twenty to thirty years, because of a more productive economy, have produced almost incredible results, and there can be no doubt that they will continue to yield knowledge which will increase our control over those viruses and organic diseases that have become more important now that the well-known contagious and infectious diseases are no longer significant causes of death. However, the more effective control of the organic diseases does not promise such spectacular declines in the crude death rate in the foreseeable future as have already taken place. Nevertheless, control of these diseases will make possible a much more satisfactory life for vast numbers of people and will also add to the effectiveness of their economic activities until a later age.

Control over the death rate in the more economically developed countries has now increased to the point where large and violent fluctuations in this rate do not seem likely to occur. This conclusion may be overoptimistic, but it seems reasonable if we assume that great man-made catastrophes such as nuclear war do not take place. For this reason, always bearing in mind the qualification just made, future changes in the size of the populations of the economically advanced countries will result from changes in the birth rate, rather than from changes in the death rate as has usually been the case in the past. Since there is indisputable evidence that the decline of the birth rate in these more developed countries is voluntary and is effected primarily by contraceptive practices, it can be assumed that significant changes in the birth rate in the foreseeable future will be a result of changes in social values and will be recognized as such. This does not mean that wide variations in the birth rate may not occur, but it does mean that if they occur they will be the result of people's voluntary action and not merely an accidental result of unknown and uncontrollable conditions.

We dare not assume, however, without careful examination, that the pattern of population change just described will be repeated by the populations in all of South and East Asia and in other underdeveloped areas of the world during the next several decades. In fact we already know that in certain respects they are not following the same patterns.[2]

[2] Many details concerning changes in death rates in the several countries will be found in the appropriate chapters below.

In the first place, a very large part of the decline in the death rate in most Western countries took place rather slowly, over a period of a century or more. A very significant portion of the decline also occurred before there was any precise knowledge of the causes of those contagious and infectious diseases which, always and everywhere, have been the great killers of mankind. The basic cause of this decline during the hundred to the hundred and fifty years preceding 1900 was the improvement in living conditions. In 1900 the death rates in the most advanced industrialized countries in the West were still 15–17 per 1,000 per year. The increasingly intensive application of scientific knowledge since 1900 has caused the death rates in these countries to fall to 9–11 per 1,000, and even below 9 per 1,000 in a few cases.

Today the virtual elimination of these very deadly contagious and infectious diseases can be achieved without the improvement in living conditions which was such an important factor in the West. The economic cost of controlling these diseases is also quite low when mass methods requiring almost no individual care are applicable, e.g., ridding an area of the mosquitoes which spread malaria and yellow fever, and carrying out mass inoculations against typhoid, dysentery, cholera, smallpox, etc. Even though the small amount of money available for health work in most underdeveloped countries retards the reduction of the death rate, it is still being reduced at a speed that would have seemed incredible only a few years ago.

The point to be noted here is that the process by which the death rate was reduced in the West is being reversed. Instead of declining slowly and as a consequence of improved living conditions, the death rate in the underdeveloped countries is being reduced by the scientific control of disease; and this reduction is being effected largely without any consideration of the changes needed in the economy to provide a living for the increased numbers resulting from this control over the death rate.

Although most of the evidence showing the sudden and rapid decline in the death rate in underdeveloped countries will be presented in the following chapters, some data are needed here to make the point that these declines are associated only tenuously with an improvement in economic conditions.

THE EFFECTS OF RECENT HEALTH WORK IN CEYLON

Ceylon has had some public (civil) health service since 1859, but as late as the decade 1921–30 the death rate averaged 26.5 per 1,000 per year (53, p. 61), which was approximately the same as the rate in some of the Western countries a century and a half or two centuries ago. The death rate in Ceylon declined to 23.0 in the decade 1931–40 and averaged 20.4 in the six years 1941–46 (293, 1948, p. 315). Clearly, health services were even then becoming more effective. The death rate then dropped suddenly by about one-third, to 13.8, in the years 1947–48, and to 10.6 in the years 1953–54 (293, 1956, p. 639). Thus the decline in the death rate in Ceylon between 1931–40 and the present, i.e., in less than twenty years, has been of much the same magnitude as it was in most Western countries in the seventy-five to one hundred years preceding 1950 (89).

An examination of the death rates from particular causes shows that certain diseases—plague, cholera, and smallpox—which Westerners tend to think of as the most important causes of death in Asia have not been very significant as causes of death in Ceylon within the period of about a century for which records are available, and that they are now practically eliminated. The elimination of these particular diseases played only a negligible role in the very great decline in the death rate (from about 26 per 1,000 to 10 per 1,000) that has taken place during the past twenty years. Malaria, on the other hand, has always been widely prevalent in Ceylon and in very bad years has attacked more than one-half of the population; its morbidity rate fell from an average of 402 cases per 1,000 of the total population in the years 1945 and 1946 to 152 per 1,000 in 1947 and 1948 and to 9 per 1,000 in 1953 and 1954. Malaria only occasionally kills its victims outright, but its death rate per 100,000 of the total population fell from 16 in 1945–46 to 5.7 in 1947–48, to 1.1 in 1952–53, and to 0.7 in 1953–54. This decline in malarial morbidity and death rates probably gives a grossly inadequate idea of the effect the tremendous decrease in the incidence of malaria had on the general health of the people. A person weakened by malaria more easily becomes a victim of many other diseases, e.g., the intestinal diseases, and malaria often, perhaps generally, renders a person unable to perform his usual tasks effectively. This great reduction in malaria was due largely to the intensive campaign through which most of the breeding places of the anopheles mosquito were sprayed with DDT.[3]

[3] The great successes thus far achieved in the control of malaria by the use of DDT should not lead us to overlook the fact that when DDT is used to control flies, some strains which appear to be immune to it soon begin to multiply rapidly. New and more powerful sprays are then required to prevent their breeding. This may also prove to be the case in the control of mosquitoes that carry malaria. At the

Other diseases that have long been important causes of death in Ceylon are also being rapidly eliminated, and their death rates have decreased as follows: typhoid fever from 21.1 per 100,000 in 1945–46 to 5.9 in 1952–53; ankylostomiosis (lockjaw, or tetanus) from 24.0 to 9.3 during the same period; dysentery from 28.5 to 10.0; diarrhea and enteritis from 108.6 to 43.0; and tuberculosis from 52.2 to 31.2 (89). These declines testify to a remarkable achievement in the control of the contagious and infectious diseases in Ceylon, in a small fraction of the time required to secure similar declines in most Western countries. One of the simplest but most significant indexes of this control is the decline in infant mortality (deaths of babies under one year of age per 1,000 live births in the same year). In Ceylon this rate fell from 140 in the years 1945–46 to 71 in the years 1953–54, i.e., by one-half in seven years. It took most Western countries from thirty to forty years to achieve a similar reduction.

The provisional data on the birth rate of Ceylon in 1956 (the latest available at the time of writing) show a decline of only 2.8 (to 36.4) from the average rate of the preceding five years (39.2). This cannot be considered valid evidence of any permanent decline in the birth rate, although it may be the beginning of such a decline (see Ceylon, chap. xiv). Up to the present, therefore, the most significant effect of the very remarkable decline in Ceylon's death rate has been a rise in the rate of natural increase. Ceylon's population is now growing at a rate which will lead to its doubling in about twenty-five years or less.

RECENT HEALTH WORK IN JAPAN

The history of Japan's health situation is very different from that of Ceylon but it is no less interesting and informative. Data on the death rate in Japan first became available in 1872, but these early data are quite defective (150, 1924, p. 11). The recorded average death rate for the decade 1881–90 was about 20 per 1,000. It rose by almost one point during the ensuing twenty years (1891–1910), dropped back to the 1881–90 level in 1911–13, and then rose by a little more than two points in the decade 1914–23. It seems highly probable that this in-

---

moment, therefore, we cannot be sure that the conquest of malaria by DDT is not a temporary achievement. It may prove to be far more costly to maintain control over malaria than to achieve control in the first place. Furthermore, it may well be that large countries like India, China, and Indonesia, in which it will take some years to achieve control of malaria, may never gain such complete control as that in Ceylon. In Ceylon control was effected quickly, before strains of mosquitoes immune to DDT had a chance to become numerous.

crease in the death rate between 1881–90 and 1914–23 was apparent rather than real—that it is to be explained by the increasing completeness of the registration of deaths and by the inadequacy of the population base used in the calculations before 1920 when the first real census was taken. There can be little doubt, however, that after 1920 the death rate fell slowly but steadily, and that in the four years preceding Japan's heavy involvement in China (1937) it averaged a little over 17 per 1,000—about what it had been in the United States and several other Western countries thirty to fifty years earlier. At that time (about 1937) this was a very low death rate for any country in Asia, and it showed clearly that in the preceding two decades Japan had made reasonably good use of the knowledge then available for the improvement of health. However, the most significant part of Japan's experience in health work was yet to come.

After World War II the occupation authorities of the United States took a prominent part in Japan's intensive efforts to promote public health; this led to a decline in the death rate which was almost as remarkable as that in Ceylon. By 1946 the high death rates of the later war years had been reduced to the prewar level of about 17. By 1947 the more intensive public health work, which included the use of the sulpha drugs, the antibiotics, the BCG antituberculosis treatment, and the DDT sprays against insects and flies (even before the war Japan had comparatively little malaria), had reduced the death rate to 14.6. By 1955 the death rate had fallen to 7.8 (293, 1956, p. 641). Thus the death rate of 17.4 immediately prior to the war had again been attained by 1946, but was cut by more than one-half in the period 1947 to 1955, giving Japan one of the lowest crude death rates in the world.

The very rapid reduction of the death rate in 1947, 1948, and 1949, coupled with the postwar increase in the birth rate in those years (32–34 per 1,000), led to the most rapid rate of population increase Japan had ever recorded (20–21 per 1,000 per year). The high postwar birth rate began to decline in 1949, however; by 1956 it had fallen to 18.5 per 1,000, and the rate of natural increase to about 10.0 per 1,000. In Japan, unlike Ceylon, the recent extremely rapid decline in the death rate has been accompanied, with a lag of only three or four years, by an even more remarkable decline in the birth rate. But, even so, the *rate* of Japan's population growth is now but little below what it was about 1900–1920. It has now been about ninety years since Japan began to modernize her economy, and her annual increase in numbers still amounts to about 900,000 a year. By October of 1958 the total population was about 92 million, which is more than two and one-half times its size at the time of the Restoration in 1868 (see chap. iv).

The preceding discussion is intended to provide a general background which, in conjunction with the more detailed population data on the several countries, will help us arrive at reasonable conclusions concerning how fast death rates are likely to decline, how soon birth rates are likely to follow death rates, and what the probable population growth will be during the next three or four decades. We are dealing in probabilities, of course, and no precise predictions about any of these points are possible. However, the data that are available will be helpful in making useful projections and will be presented in due course.

CHAPTER III

SOME PREREQUISITES FOR
RAPID ECONOMIC DEVELOPMENT

Since our study is quite largely concerned with the problems involved in raising the level of living among the masses of the people in the Far East, whose numbers are now increasing more rapidly than ever before, it is essential that some attention be given to the cultural conditions—the social prerequisites—which must be present before economic development can progress rapidly. This does not mean that there are no economic prerequisites; there are some very important ones, and they will not be ignored in the discussion, but the emphasis at this point is on the cultural changes that must be in process before any rapid economic development can go forward. Other things being equal, the degree to which these cultural changes have become effective will determine the speed with which economic development can reasonably be expected to take place. Our present discussion will be in rather general terms; the more specific data and illustrations will be reserved for later chapters.

The underdeveloped countries in the Far East have only recently (within the past three or four decades) begun to give much attention to the problems involved in developing a social and economic system calculated to increase the welfare of the masses of their people. Except in Japan, the more intensive efforts toward economic development began only about a decade ago. This is not surprising. The cultures of these peoples have been, and still are, highly traditional. The values that are most respected by the masses, and the practices that have developed to give effect to these values, are accepted largely without question by the great majority directly engaged in tilling the land (a proportion varying perhaps from 65–70 per cent in the more advanced of these countries and amounting to 80–85 per cent in the least advanced). Only the small educated class and a few workers in modern industries may be said to be more or less emancipated from the traditional cultural values.

POWER OF TRADITION

Speaking generally, no economic changes of much significance can take place in a society as long as the power of tradition remains firm, i.e., until traditional behavior begins to give way to more rational economic conduct. There has probably never been a society which did not accept some changes or innovations over considerable periods of time. Times of crisis, when tradition and custom provided no solutions for urgent problems, have always weakened the resistance to change. No doubt the failure of the customary food supply has often forced groups to choose between starvation and the breaking of taboos against eating certain foods they have traditionally avoided. But in India devout Hindus will starve before they will eat beef. Again, conquerors have often been able to "convert" great masses of people to their religion as the alternative to annihilation. Likewise, important inventions like the wheel, the making of fire, the use of copper and iron, and the use of animal power to pull carts or plows, have eventually found a place in most cultures, although it may have taken centuries for some societies to accept certain of these innovations. Most societies have been very reluctant to accept new ideas or new ways of doing things, especially if these changes seemed likely to affect adversely the conditions of survival. Thus, any changes in family life which might affect the number of children born, any new agricultural practices which seemed likely to endanger the food supply, or any innovations in behavior which might draw the wrath of the deity in the form of pestilence and famine would be accepted only slowly and with great reluctance as they proved beneficial or necessary.

For our purposes, this broad generalization regarding the difficulty of weakening the power of tradition might be stated more concretely somewhat as follows: *the more unquestioned the power of tradition over conduct the slower will be the change in the death rate and the birth rate, and the slower will be the increase in the productivity of the economy—in other words, the slower will be the development of a new set of cultural values.* As a practical matter, the degree of traditional resistance to specific types of change will determine the speed with which such change will take place. It should also be remembered that there is a unity—an integrity—in the culture of a people which often makes it difficult to make changes in one direction if complementary changes in certain other directions are not taking place simultaneously. Some aspects of a culture may lag behind others in their adaptation to new conditions, and this specific lag will put a brake on the society's entire process of cultural adaptation to a newly developing social situation. Thus, it is possible for underdeveloped countries to achieve rather rapid success in adopting new types of community activity which do not run counter to cherished beliefs and traditional practices, while other types of activity are rejected for long periods because they require the acceptance of new values.

An illustration from the field of health work will make this point clear. Much of the work that must be done to eliminate malaria consists in spraying damp and swampy areas that are of little or no agricultural value at the present time and that serve as breeding places for mosquitoes. This does not interfere in any visible way with the customary use of the land, nor does it threaten cherished cultural values. Besides, it requires no positive aid from the people themselves and, quite probably, no new tax of which they are aware. Thus a truly vast improvement in health may be achieved at low cost and with very little opposition, and without any conscious acceptance of new values. However, if more intensive antimalarial work requires that the village as a social unit consent to the spraying of the ditches alongside its streets and that the householders approve the spraying of portions of their own homes, such positive co-operation may not be forthcoming because it involves the introduction of a new "medicine" which might anger the protecting deity. Other aspects of health work, e.g., mass inoculations against smallpox, typhoid, cholera, dysentery, etc., may meet such resistance in some communities that they must be abandoned unless the authorities feel they are strong enough to meet this resistance with force, and unless the use of force for such purposes is consistent with the cultural values of the community. On the whole, however, health work encounters relatively mild resistance from traditional cultural attitudes.

On the other hand, the active resistance, or the indifference, to efforts introducing changes in patterns of behavior in the family and in the status of women—changes which might pave the way for the widespread adoption of the voluntary control of family size—may prevent any rapid change in the birth rate. Changes in these traditional patterns of family relationships involve the personal acceptance of new values regarding the number of children considered desirable to insure family survival, the marital relations of husband and wife, the attitude

of the community toward the couples who follow patterns of reproduction that are not consistent with traditional practices, etc. One concrete example may be of interest.

In both India and China the wife's status in the family is altered so
little when she becomes a widow that she is unlikely to remarry. This
situation has been changing very slowly. But in both countries at present there is a large deficit of young adult women; hence a fairly rapid
abandonment of the traditional family pattern would make millions of
young widows eligible for remarriage. This might very well lead to a
substantial increase in the birth rate, at a time when the governments
of both India and China are making strong efforts to introduce widespread contraception in order to reduce the rate of population growth.[1]

Changes in the field of economic development also encounter varying degrees of resistance; some of these changes will affect economic
development as a whole, while others involve only specific economic
sectors. In general, there is comparatively little resistance to the development and use of new types of transportation, because these innovations do not seem to imperil traditional cultural values. The real
difficulties of improving transportation, therefore, would appear at first
glance to be economic and technical. In a sense, this is the case; but if
raising the capital for railway improvement involves imposing new
taxes or the shunting of students from the traditional type of education into engineering schools which, in turn, require higher taxes,
it becomes clear that the power of tradition is an important factor in
particular economic developments.

One example of this kind of circumstance may be stated rather
briefly. Rapid economic development in underdeveloped countries depends in large measure on the agricultural surplus that can be made
available over and above the necessary consumption of the agricultural
population. Since the productivity of agricultural labor is very low in
most of the underdeveloped countries of South and East Asia, it is clear
that a rapid increase in investment, i.e., in capital, depends chiefly on
the increase in such productivity. In these countries the behavior of the
farmers as a class is very largely determined by custom, and in the
villages where most of the farmers live the weakening of the power of
tradition has made little headway. Furthermore, for ages the farmer's
contacts with officials have taught him to beware of the government at

---

[1] It seems likely that the traditional family will break up more slowly in India
than in China, because the Chinese government is making a strong and deliberate
effort to destroy it.

all times. The farmers have always been taken advantage of in such contacts, and it has become traditional for them to resist official suggestions until they know exactly what the changes involve. If the government proposes to sell a better variety of seed rice, or wheat, or any other important crop at a low price in order to help introduce it, the farmer is likely to think some trick is involved and to refuse to co-operate. Then, too, some risk of failure is always involved in the planting of a new variety of seed, and the failure of the crop may mean starvation.

There is the same kind of strong resistance to the adoption of a new method of cultivation, even when its superiority has been demonstrated to farmers whose education enables them to understand such demonstrations. A change in the system of land tenure, a change in taxes, a change in village organization, and many other changes which might be highly beneficial to the farmers will be passively opposed by lack of co-operation, because they involve accepting new ideas and practices which conflict with custom at the level where it is still deeply revered.

Because the increasing of agricultural productivity is so important a factor in the provision of greater funds for industry and for basic services like transportation, generation of electric power, an adequate educational system, etc., failure to engage the active interest of the farmers in increased production may mean that many plans for economic development can be realized only slowly. Although the agricultural problems of different countries will be discussed more fully in later chapters, it is important to realize at the outset that traditionalism gives way slowly in an illiterate agricultural population, and that this situation needs the most careful attention if rapid economic development is to be achieved.

It is my personal conviction that far too little attention is being given to the cultural obstacles to economic development, and that too much attention is centered on the financial obstacles which are often only the symptoms of more deep-seated cultural difficulties. Careful study of those sectors of their culture which interpose serious obstacles to economic development would enable these countries to form more feasible plans for economic development. The failure to search out and remove these cultural obstacles to economic development and to adapt plans to what is culturally feasible may very well retard economic development in the long run more than the lack of capital and competent technicians.

THE TRADITIONAL USES OF SURPLUSES

In every society where traditionalism largely determines conduct, the uses of the economic surplus—defined as the margin between actual production and the bare subsistence needed by the agricultural population—are largely determined by long-standing customs.

At times religious institutions have absorbed a large portion of all the surplus goods of the community and have used these funds to build temples, to support a large body of ecclesiastics, to provide elaborate festivals, etc. At other times, most of this surplus has gone to the princes, enabling them to build monuments commemorating themselves and their families, to support an elaborate court life, or to undertake conquests. Among the mass of the population any surplus above subsistence has generally been very small and has been spent largely on providing dowries for daughters, on wedding feasts, funerals, and other ceremonies highly valued by the community. Thus the rather meager funds which might have been used for capital were consumed regularly in the types of conspicuous expenditure required by the cultural values of the society.

In addition, the few people who had large incomes which they did not dissipate through conspicuous expenditure either hoarded them in the form of gold, jewels, etc., or bought up land which was already being cultivated instead of bringing new land into cultivation, experimenting with improvements in agriculture, or trying to improve other types of production. Moreover, in many of these cultures the people who actually used their savings for economic purposes were despised and considered inferior both to the agriculturists and to the people who spent lavishly in the customary manner. And often such severe restrictions were put on the use of capital by these economic developers that all incentive to engage in productive enterprise was destroyed. Such attitudes made it difficult both to accumulate savings for investment and to use savings to increase production. They also discouraged the wealthier and better-educated classes from giving thought to trade, manufacturing, and other enterprises which might have strengthened the economy. This attitude toward economic motivation effectively closed a whole field of thought and endeavor to the men who might have become leaders in economic development.

SOCIAL MOBILITY

In traditional societies the social and economic status of every individual is determined to a large extent by birth. A person is born into a farm family, a weaver's family, or a ruler's family, and this accident of birth determines his occupation and his social status. Actually, there is usually some movement from occupation to occupation and from class to class (social mobility) in most societies, but it does not become a significant social force for human betterment until the power of tradition has been sufficiently weakened to permit an increasing measure of personal freedom. This inheritance of occupational and social status makes it difficult to reorganize an economy into a new pattern that demands personal qualities and types of training which have little or no relation to birth status.

A rigid class structure also intensifies the difficulty of finding incentives which will induce workers to apply their efforts effectively in the many new types of work essential to the development of a revolutionary economy. The problems of developing adequate incentives and of providing adequate technical training are closely associated with the inability to effect the necessary cultural changes.

THE EDUCATIONAL TASK

It is generally recognized today that the efficient operation of a modern economy depends largely upon the knowledge, the skills, and the experience of the workers of all types and grades. From the purely economic standpoint, underdeveloped countries will remain under a heavy handicap as long as their formal educational systems provide only the traditional "classical" training. It is not enough to learn to read the "classical" works. The great mass of the people needs to acquire new knowledge which will prepare it to receive the training a rapidly changing economy demands. Learning to read about the world in which they live and work must become an essential part of elementary and secondary education. This will help weaken the power of tradition and will encourage an increasing number of young people to undertake scientific and technical training in institutions of higher learning. Unfortunately, much of the formal education in most underdeveloped countries teaches the students to be rather disdainful of the practical aspects of education, e.g., engineering and technical training; hence, much of the education that follows the acquirement of reading ability will have to be changed in its orientation before the educated people of these countries consider it respectable for a boy or girl with a secondary education to study mathematics and science with a view to becoming an engineer or a technician. It is not yet customary in Asia for an "educated" person to soil his hands in the course of his daily work, as many engineers, technicians, and laboratory workers must regularly do.

It is quite obvious that it will be very costly for these countries to make the broad educational effort which is a critical prerequisite to the rapid development of their economies, but much of the cost will be wasted if education is not used to hasten the erosion of the traditional patterns of conduct obstructing the application of knowledge to practical problems. Unfortunately, as a competitor with agriculture, manufacturing, transportation, public utilities, housing, and many other types of enterprise, for the meager savings of underdeveloped countries, education is not faring very well in many of these countries of Asia. Under these circumstances, it is by no means certain that enough people will be properly educated to insure the development of a more productive economy at anywhere near the speed these countries seem to expect.

Thus far the cultural prerequisites to rapid economic development have been treated in rather general terms. It will be well at this point to consider briefly some concrete factors which are important, even critical, in their effect upon economic development and to indicate how the speed of their operation depends on the extent to which traditionalism is weakened.

TECHNICAL AID

The educational difficulties noted above are being mitigated to some extent by outside aid in the form of technical personnel who are brought in for specific purposes. This kind of aid should not be disparaged, but at best it is small in quantity, uncertain in duration, and often ineffective because of the inability of the technical assistant to adjust himself to the conditions, both physical and cultural, under which he must work. The most that technical assistance can offer is a small measure of temporary compensation for the lack of an adequate educational system.

A second way in which these underdeveloped countries are being aided in their attempt to secure more technical personnel is by the sending of students abroad to good technical schools. Such trainees constitute a valuable addition to the corps of well-trained workers in their countries, but this form of assistance also has its drawbacks. The technical man trained abroad often encounters rather serious social and economic difficulties when he returns home. Most of his training and experience have been acquired in a much more advanced technical setting than is available at home, and because he himself is better educated than many of the men with whom he works at home he is apt to overestimate his own capacities and to be rather contemptuous of his fellows. This attitude does not make for harmony in the corps of technically trained men who must work together in every enterprise of any size. Besides, the foreign-trained scientist or engineer often demands the same expensive and elaborate equipment he has become accustomed to abroad, although such equipment may not be suited to the conditions in which he must work at home.

Also, the foreign-trained technician frequently finds a serious conflict arising between what is required of him as a member of a family which has a definite social position with established obligations and what he must do to function effectively in his new position in the economy. That is to say, the work he must perform in order to improve the economic efficiency of the enterprise in which he is engaged often conflicts with certain cultural patterns to which he is expected to conform by his family and his class. In the course of time such conflicts will disappear, but the adjustment may take some years; in the meantime, the foreign-trained technician may be able to contribute less than has been hoped for to the improvement of the economy. In any event, it must be recognized that these additions to the supply of technical personnel through outside aid do not, and never can, supply any considerable part of the total need for trained men. Education for the operation of a modern economy is a huge undertaking; it must remain the task of the country itself, and for years it will make large demands upon the small surplus production of every underdeveloped country and will encounter serious cultural obstacles.

THE FORMATION AND ACCUMULATION OF CAPITAL

The rate at which capital can be accumulated and *invested effectively* in production and in basic services will determine in large measure the rate at which the national income of an underdeveloped country can be increased, other conditions remaining the same. In all underdeveloped countries the proportion of the national income that can be saved for capital in the early days of modern economic development is necessarily small because: (1) the productivity of simple hand labor, both in agricultural and nonagricultural tasks, is so low that there is only a small margin between what is produced and what is needed by the producer for subsistence, and (2) certain essential services such as the maintenance of civil order, the provision of some education, the distribution of goods, the support of religious institutions, etc., must be kept operating if economic development is to make any headway at all. The margin that can be converted to capital undoubtedly varies from one underdeveloped country to another, but many students think that it is around 4–5 per cent in the poorer countries, although they recognize that this figure is, at best, only an informed guess. For purposes of comparison, it may be helpful to know that some of the more highly industrialized countries, e.g., the United States, can save as much as 15–20 per cent of their annual national income for investment while they are spending an even larger proportion of it for military equipment and personnel, and can still produce enough to provide for the improvement of an already high level of living among the mass of the population.

In the countries which are more highly developed economically, the ratio of the growth of capital to the growth of national income seems to be about three or four to one—that is, $100 of new investment will yield $25.00 to $33.00 in new income (175, pp. 201–2). Whether the ratio for capital investment is different in underdeveloped countries is not known, and the theoretical arguments about whether capital is more or less productive in such countries than in the more developed countries seem to me quite inconclusive. Lewis (175, pp. 203–7) seems to think that there is probably not much difference between the capital-income ratios of the more developed and the less developed countries. Assuming that this is the case, a country such as India, which probably invests 7–10 per cent of its national income annually, can do little more than maintain the present level of living among a population that is probably growing at a rate of 1.5–1.7 per cent a year. In order to raise the level of living by 1 per cent a year, India would have to raise the proportion of the national income that is used effectively as capital by another 3–4 per cent. Since in a number of the underdeveloped countries the rates of population growth are now 1.5–2.0 per cent per year, or even higher, it appears that these countries would need to invest effectively every year new capital amounting to approximately 8–10 per cent of their national incomes merely to maintain their present levels of living.

The history of Japan's development of a more productive economy since about 1880 gives some substance to the hope that the present underdeveloped countries of South and East Asia will find it possible to increase the proportion of their national incomes which is available for investment fast enough to enable them to do more than merely maintain their growing populations at the current low levels of living. Japan was able to increase her agricultural productivity quite rapidly between 1880 and 1920 without any considerable use of new capital, thus leaving a slowly increasing surplus available for industrial investment. At the same time, however, Japan's population was increasing at a rate of only 1–1.2 per cent per year. The increase in her agricultural productivity came largely from the adoption of better farm practices—the use of seeds from improved varieties of the principal crops, rice, wheat, and barley, the adoption of better tillage practices, the use of more fertilizer, the more efficient use of water, the improvement of the simple implements already in use, and, of course, from research in scientific agriculture accompanied by the development of a system of extension education which taught the farmers how to make use of these improvements. However, during this period Japan also increased the amount of land being tilled by about one-third; this was of great importance in increasing total yields, although it may have tended to retard the increase in acre yields (see chap. v).

It appears that in the course of about three decades (1885–1915) the productivity of the Japanese agricultural laborer almost doubled. Since the government took a considerable portion of this increase in taxes, it was able to support a growing proportion of the population in nonagricultural tasks (see chap. vi).

The underdeveloped countries of South and East Asia now have very large proportions of their workers engaged in agriculture (65–80 per cent), as Japan had seven or eight decades ago, and a great part of their total national income derives from agriculture. Therefore, since Japan's experience proved that a substantial increase in agricultural productivity is possible without the expenditure of much capital, it would seem that if effective taxation policies are followed, the improvement of agricultural productivity offers these countries the quickest and surest way to a more rapid accumulation of the capital they need for national economic development. In this way they could employ much of the increased productivity of agricultural labor to support workers engaged in the creation of capital goods of many kinds and in the construction of basic services. This means, of course, that the agricultural population, which constitutes the great mass of the people, will gain improvements in their living conditions only slowly in the early years of economic development.

In the process of capital accumulation during the early stages of modern economic development, *construction*—i.e., housing, public buildings (schools, post offices, etc.), transportation facilities (roads, railways, etc.), factory buildings, and public utilities (water, electricity, sewer systems, and irrigation works)—bulks very large and absorbs perhaps 60 per cent or more of all investment. Much of this construction can be carried out by unskilled laborers who need be paid little more than the scanty subsistence wage they are accustomed to and who can use materials which are relatively inexpensive because they can be provided locally and, to a large extent, by unskilled labor. This means that by careful planning, and a considerable degree of indifference to the *immediate improvement* of the welfare of the masses (the agricultural population), any substantial increase in agricultural productivity can be made to provide not only for the increase in population and for some slight rise in the level of living but can also contribute more of the investment which must be made if a country is to employ an increasing proportion of its total population in works that directly help to set in motion the upward spiral of economic development (for further discussion see chap. vi).

The other domestic sources from which capital might be accumulated—chiefly the profits of industries and businesses already in operation and the personal incomes of the salaried and professional classes—will also have to be taxed heavily; but because these are underdeveloped countries, such sources of capital will be rather small in absolute amount for some time, even when they are fully exploited. I would not underrate the amount of capital that can be raised even now from nonagricultural sources, nor the psychological advantage these governments can gain by effecting a more just distribution of the national income through taxation; but I seriously question whether any of these underdeveloped countries will be able to accumulate a very large proportion of the capital they need from nonagricultural sources in the near future. Furthermore, as regards increased production that can be turned into capital in the early stages of economic development in countries where land is scarce, the chief hope lies in the adoption of agricultural practices which will lead to larger yields. On the other hand, in countries where land is relatively abundant the extension of the tilled area will probably give better results, temporarily, than the improvement of agricultural practices.

The point I would make is that the rapid accumulation and the efficient use of capital are *critical* elements in rapid economic development, but that traditionalism must be weakened quite extensively before any significant amount of capital can be accumulated and before what is accumulated can be used to good advantage. I would also emphasize the point that the production of food and fibers beyond subsistence needs will almost certainly be the chief source of capital in most underdeveloped countries for some years after the development of a more efficient economy is actively undertaken. This fact does not seem to be fully appreciated in many quarters. The concentration of attention on the money aspects of capital accumulation tends to make people forget that in poverty-stricken underdeveloped countries most food above subsistence can be turned directly into capital with the proper management and, hence, that the quickest and surest way to accumulate capital is to improve agriculture, at which two-thirds to three-fourths of all the people work.

Foreign sources of capital.—Up to this point, capital accumulation has been discussed as a domestic problem. This has been done deliberately to emphasize how critically important it is for these underdeveloped countries to stimulate the production of the goods they already know how to produce—chiefly agricultural products and the products of home industry. Also, this emphasis calls attention to the relatively small role which foreign loans and grants play in the economic development of underdeveloped countries. By far the greatest proportion of all capital used in the economic development of underdeveloped countries must come from their own production. Under present conditions the amount of capital that can be borrowed by any such country is small when compared with its total needs, and even when compared with the actual amounts it is already saving domestically. This is not to say that foreign borrowing, even on the present limited scale, is not an extremely important addition to domestic savings in a number of these countries. But if India were to borrow each year an amount equal to about 4 per cent of her national income, i.e., enough to provide the capital for a rise of about 1 per cent in the level of living of her present population, or for a 1 per cent increase in population at the present level of living, the carrying charges on a debt accumulating by a billion dollars per year would soon become a serious drain upon her foreign exchange, unless the interest were allowed to accumulate indefinitely. Furthermore, unless the entire economy is managed with more skill and understanding than can reasonably be expected in the early years of modern economic development, foreign borrowing on a large scale is likely to lead to serious inflation.

There is always the question of whether any strings are tied to the granting of these loans which limit the independence of the borrower. Such strings may not be readily apparent; but the purposes for which the loans are granted may in themselves involve political obligations, while the terms of repayment may often seriously impair freedom of economic action by the borrowing government. When the loans come from private or semipublic institutions in the "free" countries which must raise their funds from private sources, there is much uncertainty about whether large amounts can be counted on regularly for long-time projects. This uncertainty arises, in part, from the fact that small private investors in most Western countries are not accustomed to buying bonds issued by an international bank and secured by the assets of foreign corporations or even by the promises of a foreign government. Also, insurance companies and other institutional investors disposing of large funds gathered from the public are often not permitted by law to buy foreign securities. A number of other factors make it doubtful whether relatively large funds could be raised from private sources for the economic development of underdeveloped countries, but only one can even be mentioned here.

When governments are the borrowers, and when they are avowedly working toward a socialist state, they hesitate to accept loans from other governments that might interfere with the accomplishment of these long-time aims or to allow private borrowers to accept loans that might make the achievement of a socialist economy more difficult. Naturally, borrowing by private enterprises in underdeveloped countries from private sources in other countries will be quite limited under these circumstances. For these reasons it does not seem likely that foreign loans will be able to supply more than a small proportion of the capital needed by any of the underdeveloped countries in the near future. However, this small proportion may be *critical*.

Deficit financing.—Because of their urgent need for capital, all underdeveloped countries are greatly tempted to resort to borrowing from a central bank to meet some of the costs of the enterprises they are undertaking. This kind of borrowing always carries with it the risk that the currency it creates and puts into circulation may exceed the increase in the need for money generated by the increase in population and by the increase in the goods available for consumption. The inflation which this situation brings about may easily become "runaway" and may make sound economic development well-nigh impossible.

POLITICAL STABILITY

Another prerequisite of critical importance for economic development is political stability. Since its importance is generally recognized, I will not discuss it here, other than to say that it is often threatened by the cultural changes inevitably involved in the sloughing-off of traditional patterns of conduct. It is extremely difficult to maintain political stability at a time of great social and economic change, and yet such stability is essential if these other changes are to be effected smoothly and rapidly.

EFFICIENT GOVERNMENTAL ADMINISTRATION

It must be remembered that most underdeveloped countries in the Far East have only recently gained political independence or passed through a revolution, and that even those whose political stability seems quite secure have not yet had time to establish as efficient an administration of governmental affairs as now exists in most of the more developed countries. Hence, even in those governments whose higher officials are rendering devoted service there is still much waste and confusion. Often the actual governmental policies are not clearly defined, and many policies which are well defined are not carried out efficiently. This situation has many causes: (1) There has not yet been time to train a large body of civil servants in the arts of public administration. (2) The methods by which personnel is selected for technical work, as well as for administration, are still in a formative stage. (3) The functions of the different agencies of government are not clearly differentiated, and the methods by which these agencies can co-operate effectively have not yet been worked out. (4) The traditional cultural patterns of behavior in these countries still have great compulsive force, and these patterns sometimes conflict with the kind of conduct needed for efficient administration; for example, the age-long tradition of responsibility to one's family often requires that an official provide members of his family with jobs regardless of whether they are as well fitted for these jobs as other people who might be found. (5) In many of these countries public servants have traditionally enjoyed certain perquisites of office, the acceptance of which we consider improper because it implies that the official accepting them is obligated to the persons or organizations giving them—a situation which is inconsistent with disinterested public service.

As time passes, these underdeveloped countries will undoubtedly improve the efficiency with which they administer their public services, but in the early stages of economic development the inefficiency of their public administration certainly inhibits the progress of such development. The quality of public administration is even more important in these underdeveloped countries than it is in most of the free countries, because the governments of most of the former are undertaking many economic tasks which previously had not fallen within the province of public administration.

NATURAL RESOURCES

It is a truism to say that the economic development of any country is vitally affected by the physical resources it possesses. The relationship is so obvious in the case of agriculture that we need only note that the area of tillable land, the quality of the soil, the rainfall, and the length of the growing season are all critical factors in agricultural production.

We know that some countries have been able to achieve a considerable degree of industrialization without possessing any significant mineral resources, but we also know that the possession of good mineral resources is of great advantage to any country hoping to develop a high degree of industrialization and to achieve a high standard of living among its people. Whether or not the lack of particular mineral resources will be critical will depend upon the circumstances prevailing in each nation at a given time and upon the political and economic relations existing between the several nations.

The essential point in this discussion of the prerequisites of rapid economic development in underdeveloped countries is that although many factors may be *critical* in economic development—in the sense that a particular enterprise cannot be built quickly and made to operate efficiently if certain economic conditions are not met—the basic reason these conditions are not met is often to be found in the culture of a people. The cultural patterns which seem, on the surface, to be only remotely related to the specific difficulty of the moment may in fact be its cause. For example, no one would deny that the building of a steel mill may, at a particular moment, be delayed or prevented if the capital is not forthcoming. In a particular case this difficulty may be overcome by borrowing abroad, by borrowing from a central bank, or by imposing higher taxes to enable the government to raise funds. But it should be clear that this process cannot be repeated indefinitely, because there is a limit on the amount of capital that can be borrowed abroad, because there is great probability that destructive inflation at home will accompany heavy borrowing from a central bank, and because the tax base is too restricted. The real difficulty lies in the very small margin of production above subsistence; the underlying critical factor in the early years of economic development is the low productive capacity of the great mass of the population, which has its roots in the cultural patterns according to which they live. Moreover, although it is of the utmost importance to establish institutions for assembling the small amounts of savings which the farmers, laborers, professional men, and small businessmen may be able to put by, it is much more important to change the cultural patterns that determine and limit the productive capacity of the masses and to devise ways of using much of this increased production as capital. This effort may make it necessary to think of food and fibers as capital, to collect taxes in kind, to have food banks and fiber banks as well as money banks, and to study how incentives can be provided which will induce the mass of the people to work harder and more effectively.

Basic cultural changes of this kind may bring about economic development much faster in underdeveloped countries than would the establishment of all the conventional financial institutions now operating in the more developed countries; furthermore, such changes might make it unnecessary for underdeveloped countries to borrow on a large scale from other countries. I am not saying that capital does not beget capital, nor am I saying that foreign loans are not important in getting economic development started; but I am saying that the mass of the people must be provided with incentives to increase their own productivity, and that much of the resulting increase can be used as capital if proper attention is given to changing the traditional cultural patterns. If there is *a* basic prerequisite to rapid economic development, it is this modification of cultural patterns, or the wiser use of these patterns, so that the great mass of the people—the agricultural population—may be induced to increase their production, and that ways may be found to use much of this increased product as capital in projects where labor can be employed with comparatively little capital beyond that needed to provide food and shelter.

Finally, the limitation of population growth should be included in this discussion of prerequisites to rapid economic development. In fact, the chief argument of this essay is that rapid population growth is an important factor in retarding such development in practically all of these countries of South and East Asia, and that in some of them it must be counted among the critical factors. There can be no reasonable doubt that the growth of population will add to the feeling of economic pressure which is building up in several of these countries and thus will become a factor of increasing importance in determining not only the political relations between these Asian nations but also their relations to nations in other parts of the world.

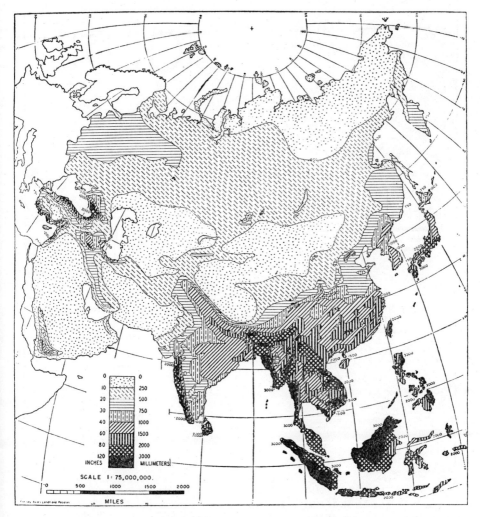

Map 2.—Annual rainfall in Asia. Asia's rainfall varies from over 450 inches to an inch or less, according to wind systems and mountain barriers. The heaviest precipitation occurs on mountains in the path of prevailing winds, as in India and southeastern Asia, while the driest areas are behind mountains, as in western China. (Reprinted by permission from *Asia's Lands and Peoples,* by George B. Cressey. ©, 2d ed., 1951, by McGraw-Hill Book Co.)

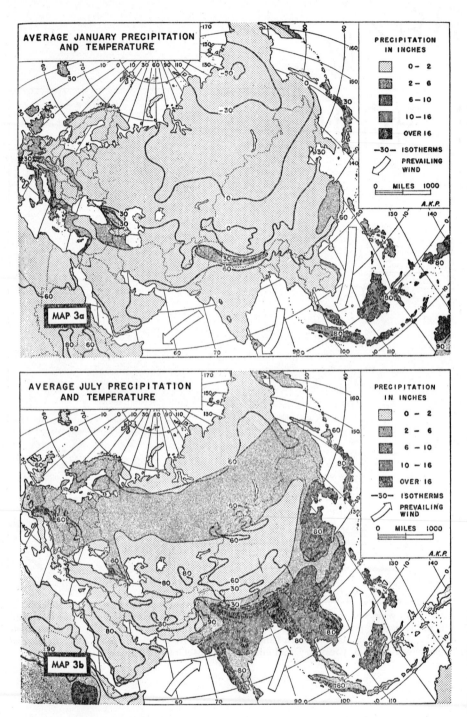

Maps 3a and 3b.—January and July precipitation and temperature in Asia. (From *The Pattern of Asia*, ed. Norton S. Ginsburg. © 1958 by Prentice-Hall, Inc., Englewood Cliffs, N.J. Reproduced by permission. Maps by Allen K. Philbrick.)

CHAPTER IV

JAPAN:

POPULATION

The first census was taken in Japan in 1920. The data in Table 2 give the figures based on censuses for 1920 and later years, as well as the figures quite generally used for 1872–1910 which were derived from registration rolls maintained in local administrative areas. Different official publications do not always use the same figures, nor, as a rule, do they offer any explanation for the differences between them. The data given here for 1920–55 refer to the postwar territory of Japan and are somewhat smaller than those found in most official publications for 1920–40. However, these differences are so small as to be of negligible significance for our discussion.

In 1920 the census showed a population of 55,391,000 (158, 1927, p. 44) as of October 1, but the "legal" population at the end of that year, presumably based on the registration rolls, is given elsewhere in official publications as 57,919,000. This latter figure is not adjusted to the postwar area and may be 400,000 to 500,000 larger than the proper comparable figure. In any event, it is about 2 million more than the census population, after allowance is made for the difference in territory and in date. Since this "legal" population was determined at various dates, beginning in 1872, by adding the numbers found on the local registers in which, according to the law of that time, all persons belonging in a particular area were supposed to be enrolled, and since it is probable that the number of people moving about within the country increased with the development of modern transport facilities, it is also highly probable that the local registers contained an increasing number of duplications and also of persons who had died but whose names had not yet been removed from the rolls, while the census was based on the resident (*de facto*) population.

If it is assumed that an increasing error crept into the "legal" sum-

53

mations between 1872 and 1920, the figure of 35 million for 1872, which is now very commonly used, seems quite reasonable. Just how the reported "legal" population at different dates between 1872 and 1920 should be adjusted to show the probable growth of Japan's population during the first fifty years of her modern development will be determined in large measure by one's judgment regarding the pattern her population changes most likely followed during this period. If Japan's population was 35 million in 1872 and 55,391,000 in 1920, the increase amounted to almost 60 per cent in forty-eight years. This

TABLE 2

POPULATION (IN THOUSANDS) AND PER CENT CHANGE, JAPAN, 1872–1955*

Year	Population	Per Cent Change	Year	Population	Per Cent Change
1955........	89,276	7.3	1920........	55,391	12.6
1950........	83,200	14.7	1910........	49,184	12.2
1945†.......	71,998	....	1900........	43,847	9.9
1940........	72,540	5.6	1890........	39,902	8.9
1935........	68,662	7.5	1880........	36,649	5.3
1930........	63,872	7.9	1872........	34,806	....
1925........	59,179	6.8			

* Source: 1920–55 from 151, I, 20–21; 1872–1910 from 157, 1953, p. 20. Figures given exclude Okinawa-ken.

† The figure for 1945 is taken from the special census of November 1, 1945, which was taken shortly after the Occupation was established and before any considerable amount of repatriation had taken place. It also excludes the population of certain areas (Karafuto and the Ryukus) over which Japan previously held control. The population of the colonies (Taiwan and Korea) has always been reported separately, although it had been added to that of Japan to show the population of the empire. We are not concerned with the empire here.

NOTE.—Since this book was sent to press Dr. Irene B. Taeuber's book *The Population of Japan* (263a) has appeared. It is an exhaustive study which will undoubtedly become the standard reference of the future.

would be an *average* annual increase of about 1 per cent. It is quite unlikely, however, that the rate of increase was uniform throughout this period.

BEFORE 1872, AND 1872 TO 1920

In 1872 Japan was just entering upon her modern social and economic development. The old feudalism had been slowly disintegrating for some decades. Thus, in spite of many survivals of feudalism that continued to exert an important influence on Japan's social and economic development, the leaders were becoming less and less bound by the feudal cultural patterns and were more open-minded toward new ideas.

Such information as is available regarding Japan's population changes in the century and a half preceding 1872 is highly conjectural, but the commonly accepted picture shows a population fluctuating

within the rather narrow limits of around 26–28 million during much
of the eighteenth century and growing rather steadily after 1800 to
about 30 million by the middle of the nineteenth century. Whether
the population grew or declined during any particular period appears
to have depended primarily on the level of the death rate, as it did
over most of the world at that time. If crops were good and there were
no unusually severe epidemics or other natural disasters, population
increased somewhat. When such an increase put more intense pressure
on subsistence, in a situation where neither the tilled area nor the
techniques of agriculture were changing—or were changing very slowly—abortion and infanticide were resorted to on a somewhat larger
scale than usual as additional deterrents to population growth. But
the factors chiefly responsible for raising the death rate, and thus for
reducing the population, probably were bad crop seasons and epidemics of more than usual severity. Rebellion against the shogun and
war between feudal lords were also disastrous in particular areas at
times and resulted in higher death rates.

It appears that some small economic improvement, consisting largely in a slow increase in agricultural production, began about the early
part of the nineteenth century and that it was accompanied by some
increase in numbers. If the population amounted to about 30 million
in 1846, as seems to be rather widely believed, and to 35 million in
1872, then the increase was in the vicinity of 16 per cent in twenty-six
years, or at the rate of approximately 6 per 1,000 (0.6 per cent) per
year. This is much the same rate of increase shown by several European countries as they began to emerge from a strongly traditional
social and economic system into a more dynamic system which resulted in the slow breakup of many social institutions and in the
gradual development of a more efficient economy. An increase from
35 million in 1872 to 44 million in 1900 (see Table 2) would give an
average annual rate of increase for this period of 8 to 9 per 1,000
(0.8–0.9 per cent). If the population was 44 million in 1900 and rose
to 55,391,000 by 1920 (census), the average rate of increase during
this twenty years was about 11 per 1,000 (1.1 per cent) per year.

Frankly, these conjectures regarding Japan's probable rates of population growth from 1872 to 1900 and from 1900 to 1920 are based
in part on observations of the pattern of growth in some Western
countries (see chap. ii) as these countries began their modern periods
of development, as well as on the interpretation of the Japanese data.

It is of considerable interest that if Japan's population did increase from 30 million to 35 million in the period 1846–50 to 1872, it means that Japan attained a moderate rate of growth, averaging about 6 per 1,000 per year, in a fairly short period, at a time when public sanitary measures and health services cannot have had any significant effect on the death rate. The decline in the death rate that would have made such growth possible must have come chiefly from some slight improvement in the living conditions of the mass of the people due to the expansion of the tilled area and improvements in agricultural practices. This improvement no doubt led to somewhat more sanitary home conditions, just as it did in most Western countries.[1] There is a strong probability, however, that if accurate annual data were available, the average rate of increase of 6 per 1,000 that may have prevailed between 1846 and 1872 would resolve into a series of yearly rates of increase that fluctuated rather widely but had a definite, though slight, upward trend. There is a much sounder basis for accepting the data regarding the growth of population after 1872, although, as noted above, these data are by no means satisfactory. The assumption that population increased from 35 million in 1872 to 55.4 million in 1920 is probably not much in error. Furthermore, the assumption of a pattern of decreasing fluctuations in the death rate from year to year during this period is also consistent with what we know about changes in the pattern of population growth under slowly improving economic conditions in other countries. The economic changes chiefly responsible for the decline in the death rate from 1872 to 1920 will be discussed in following sections.

FROM 1920 TO 1955

Although somewhat different figures would be arrived at by using other official sources for the years 1920–40, it is believed that the data in Table 2 based on the censuses are substantially accurate for the postwar area. Since more reliable vital statistics also became available about 1920, it will be well to consider them at this point.

Death rates.—The death rates before 1920 are based on the "legal" population referred to above. Hence, any error in the population base would be reflected in the rate. If the population base were too large, a given number of deaths would yield a rate lower than the actual

---

[1] It is also possible that the small improvement in agriculture at this time slightly reduced the hardships felt by the family and thus led to a decrease in the practices of abortion and infanticide. Any significant decline in abortion would naturally lead to some rise in the birth rate. In the past abortion appears to have become less frequent when the pressure of population on subsistence had been temporarily eased.

rate. But the error in the death rate before 1920 probably came chiefly from the failure to secure the registration of all deaths. The data appearing in the official reports indicate a rather steady increase in the death rate, from 20.7 in the period 1886–90 to 23.6 in 1916–20. There is good reason to doubt the reliability of these figures. In the first place, it is highly probable that a slowly increasing proportion of deaths was being registered during much of this period, since such an improvement in accuracy is usual for some years after death registration begins. Thus, what appears to be a rise in the death rate is in part the result of an increasingly accurate registration. If the deficiency in registration was quite large at the earlier date, there may even have been a significant decline in the death rate during the period when the registration figures were showing an increase. The use of a "legal" population, which was probably increasingly larger than the actual population, as a base for calculating death rates during this period would also have concealed some of the improvement in registration.

In support of the view that the death rate actually declined during this period, there exists what seems to be fairly conclusive evidence that living conditions improved during most of the period 1886–90 to 1920 and that this improvement became more substantial after 1900 (see chaps. v and vi). There is also evidence that medical practice was being slowly modernized (especially after 1900) and that health work was beginning to reduce the incidence of some of the contagious and infectious diseases. It also seems reasonably certain that infanticide was diminishing, probably chiefly as a result of improving economic conditions. Since an infant death which occurred naturally would be more likely to be registered than one due to infanticide, a rather steady reduction in infanticide might be expected to increase the proportion of all deaths registered and thus to raise the registered death rate. This probably would not be a very significant factor.

By 1916–20 the registration of deaths had probably become fairly accurate, and the rate for the three years 1920–22, using the census population and estimating the annual increase for 1921 and 1922 as the base for calculation, was 23.8. Such a rate seems reasonable for a people who had already begun to make substantial progress toward a more efficient economy but who had not yet made much progress in public health work. After 1920–22 the death rate fell rather steadily, to 19.8 in 1925–29, and to 18.1 in 1930–34 (293, 1955, p. 657), and in

1937–39 it averaged 17.5. Death rates in the war and postwar periods will be discussed below.

Birth rates.—The registration of births, like that of deaths, undoubtedly improved during the thirty-five years preceding 1920. This will no doubt explain most of the rise in the birth rate from 28.5 in 1886–90 to 35.0 in 1920–24. Any reduction in the abortion rate would probably have been a minor factor in this rise in the birth rate. This rise was fairly steady except for the Russo-Japanese War period and the later years of World War I, when there were significant declines. This pattern is consistent with what would be expected to result from a rather slow and steady improvement in registration and the use of a relatively smaller population base for the calculation of the birth rate after the census of 1920. If the reported birth rate of 35.0 per 1,000 for 1920–24 (293, 1955, p. 615) is substantially correct, it is reasonably certain that a somewhat higher rate prevailed in earlier years, since several important changes almost certain to have had a depressing effect on the birth rate had already taken place in parts of Japan by that time.

By 1920 Japan (see chaps. v and vi) was industrializing at a fairly rapid rate, and her cities were growing fast. Her farming population had become almost stationary because of migration to the cities. It is not surprising, therefore, that the birth rate for the country as a whole declined rather steadily after 1920–24. In the period 1925–29 the birth rate fell slightly, to 34.0. In 1930–34 it was 31.8, and in 1936–37 (before the China war) it was 30.4. Such a decline is a substantial one in a period of about fifteen years, a much larger decline than would be expected to result from the use of contraceptive practices by the upper classes in the cities. It suggests that important social changes, closely related to industrialization and urbanization, were beginning to affect family life rather widely.

Natural increase.—When these data on birth and death rates from 1920 to World War II are brought together, they show a natural increase of 12.0 per 1,000 in 1920–24, of 14.2 in 1925–29, of 13.7 in 1930–34, and of 13.1 in 1936–37. These rates are somewhat lower than the growth shown by the censuses. This difference suggests several possibilities: (1) as late as 1930, at least, more births than deaths remained unregistered; (2) up to and including 1930, the censuses may have been increasing in accuracy of coverage, thus raising the population count; (3) the difference may have been due, in part, to net immigration, chiefly of Koreans, who were brought in as unskilled laborers. The chief point of interest here is that, up to 1930, Japan's rate of natural increase was rising. After 1930 this rate declined slowly because the birth rate was beginning to decline faster than the death rate. However, the decline in rate of natural increase was very slow between 1930 and 1940.

The war and postwar periods.—During the war the death rate (of persons living in Japan) declined from 17.8 in 1939 to 16.4 in 1940, and then to 15.7 in 1941. It remained at about that level until 1944, when it rose to about the prewar level—17.4. In 1945 it skyrocketed to an estimated 29.2 (293, 1948, pp. 314–15). The birth rate fell rather rapidly after 1937 and averaged only 27.7 in 1938–40. It then recovered to about 30 and stayed there until 1945, when it fell to an estimated 23.2 (*ibid.*, pp. 262–63). For the eight years 1938–45 the death rate (of persons living in Japan) averaged 18.3 and the birth rate 28.4; thus the natural increase averaged only 10.0. This was a very substantial decline in natural increase, but smaller than might have been expected in a country as heavily involved in war as Japan was from 1941 to 1945. In 1945 an excess of deaths over births of almost 430,000 was reported (*ibid.*, pp. 255, 307). Such an excess is by no means improbable, but there may be serious errors in the registration data for this year; great destruction had been caused by bombing, and a very large movement of people from the bombed areas—chiefly cities—to rural areas had taken place in the year preceding Japan's surrender. This movement must have been accompanied by much confusion in the registration of births and deaths. Data on births and deaths in 1946 are lacking, except for the last three months of that year. Because of these uncertainties it will not pay to try to reconstruct here the registration data for these two years. For our purposes it will be sufficient to arrive at an approximate figure for the net change in the size of Japan's population in 1940 and in 1950, and for the relative importance of the components of this change. (For the distribution of Japan's population in 1950 see Map 4.[2])

The total population enumerated in Japan in 1950 was 83.2 million. That enumerated in 1940 in the same area was 72.54 million. The in-

[2] Most of the large island of Hokkaido is not shown on Map 4. This island contains only 5–6 per cent of Japan's total population. It also is quite mountainous, so that most of the land is untillable. The tillable land is better adapted to growing wheat and potatoes than rice, and none of it can be double-cropped. Hokkaido can never be expected to contribute more than a very small proportion of the extra food needed by the 94–95 per cent of the population living on the other three large islands (see Map 5).

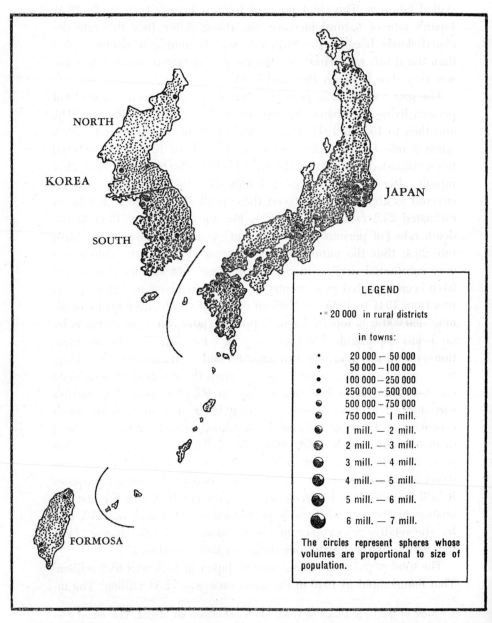

LEGEND

' = 20 000 in rural districts

in towns:

•	20 000 — 50 000
•	50 000 — 100 000
•	100 000 — 250 000
◑	250 000 — 500 000
◓	500 000 — 750 000
◓	750 000 — 1 mill.
◕	1 mill. — 2 mill.
◉	2 mill. — 3 mill.
●	3 mill. — 4 mill.
●	4 mill. — 5 mill.
●	5 mill. — 6 mill.
●	6 mill. — 7 mill.

The circles represent spheres whose volumes are proportional to size of population.

MAP 4.—Population distribution in Japan, Korea, and Taiwan. (Adapted by permission of Dr. Friedrich Burgdörfer and the Heidelberger Akademie der Wissenschaften from *The World Atlas of Population* [Hamburg: Falk-Verlag], copyright 1957 by Heidelberger Akademie der Wissenschaften, Heidelberg, Germany.)

crease was 10.66 million, or 14.7 per cent. This figure for net increase between 1940 and 1950 does not show the nature of the impact of the war on Japan's population, nor can we take space here to go into detail about the role of the different components which make up this net figure; however, a few words are needed. In the first place the vast majority of the Japanese living abroad in 1940 and not included in the census of Japan were repatriated. The survivors of this group together with their children born after 1940 and surviving through repatriation to 1950, as well as their children born after repatriation and surviving to the 1950 census, would constitute a net addition to Japan's 1940 population at the census of 1950. This group probably numbered 1.6 to 1.8 million persons. Nearly all the remaining repatriates (about 4.5 million) probably were included in the 1940 census, since they were the survivors of military and civilian personnel sent abroad in connection with the war. They do not constitute any net addition to Japan's 1940 population. In the second place Japan suffered military losses of about 2 million. In addition, after the war about 1.2 million migrants left Japan. The great majority of these were Koreans who were resident in Japan in 1940 and who were enumerated in the 1940 census. Thus, of Japan's 1940 population about 3.3 million were lost to the 1950 population as either war deaths or emigrants. Since the immigration of persons living abroad in 1940 compensated for these losses only to the extent of about 1.8 million, the total excess of births over deaths during this decade (including military deaths) must have been about 12.2 million—10.66 million, the actual gain, plus 1.5 million net loss arising from military deaths and emigration combined. (For a detailed discussion of these matters see 265a, Part VII.)

This rather large excess of births over nonmilitary deaths can be explained to a significant extent by the fact that in Japan the number of marriages rose rapidly during the war years up to 1944—from 1,740,000 in the three years 1938–40 (the early war years) to 2,192,000 in the three years 1941–43, i.e., by 26.0 per cent (293, 1948, pp. 458–59). The number of marriages rose even more rapidly after the war as the repatriation of military personnel and civilians gained in volume. In the three years 1947–49 the number rose to 2,730,000, about 1 million more than in 1938–40—an increase of 57 per cent (293, 1955, p. 730). In 1947 the birth rate rose to 34.3, about what it had been in the mid-1920's. It dropped only to 33.7 in 1948, and to 32.8 in 1949. It then fell very rapidly to 28.2 in 1950.

This postwar increase in marriages and in the birth rate was not particularly surprising; but it was surprising that by 1947 the death rate (14.6) had fallen about three points below the lowest prewar death rate and by 1950 had fallen to 10.9. The natural increase in the three years 1947–49 averaged almost 21 per 1,000 and was higher by almost one-half than Japan had ever experienced in prewar years. In 1950, in spite of the sharp decline in the birth rate, the natural increase was still 17.3 (293, 1956, pp. 615, 657). In three years and nine months (1947 to October 1, 1950) the total number of births registered was 9,810,000, and the total number of deaths was 3,719,000.

TABLE 3

REPATRIATION AND EMIGRATION FROM JAPAN, 1945–49*

DATE	MIGRATION (IN THOUSANDS)†		
	To Japan	From Japan	Net to Japan
Total.........................	6,215	1,190	5,025
Oct. 1, 1945–Nov. 1, 1945........	273	187	86
Nov. 1, 1945–Apr. 26, 1946........	2,308	762	1,546
Apr. 26, 1946–Oct. 1, 1946........	2,013	88	1,925
Oct. 1, 1946–Oct. 1, 1947.........	1,136	135	1,001
Oct. 1, 1947–Oct. 1, 1948.........	329	11	318
Oct. 1, 1948–Oct. 1, 1949.........	156	7	149

* Source: 157, 1950, p. 97.

† Between the census of 1940 and the special census of 1945 there had been a vast movement of military personnel abroad and also a considerable movement of civilians to organize and manage the "co-prosperity sphere." Most of these were still abroad on November 1, 1945. This table gives the official estimates of the migration movements from October 1, 1945, to October 1, 1949, which go far to explain the extremely rapid increase in population between 1945 and 1950.

Thus there was a net natural increase of 6,091,000 in this postwar period of three and three-quarter years. This includes, of course, the natural increase of the repatriates, who did not live in Japan in 1940. Even so, it appears probable that approximately 60 per cent of the natural increase in Japan's population between 1940 and 1950 was supplied by the 1940 population in the three and three-quarter post-war years (1947 to October 1, 1950). As was shown above, this great natural increase was due to a large rise in the birth rate accompanied by a very rapid decline in the death rate. In the light of this unusually large postwar natural increase, the total natural increase of Japan's population between 1940 and 1950 does not appear unreasonable.

Since 1950 both the birth rate and the death rate have continued to decline in a surprising manner. The death rate, which was 10.9 in 1950, fell to 8.9 in 1953 and averaged only 8.0 in 1954–56 (227, July,

1957, p. 280), about 1.3 points below that of the United States in the same years. At the same time, the birth rate fell from 28.2 in 1950 to 21.5 in 1953 (293, 1956, p. 617) and continued downward to 18.4 in 1956 (*ibid.*, p. 278). Thus the birth rate has been declining more rapidly than the death rate, and the natural increase has been falling— from 17.3 in 1950, to 12.6 in 1953, and to 10.4 in 1956. But even so, in the last year for which data are available Japan's population had a natural increase of about 900,000.

At the present time, any further decline in Japan's crude death rate seems highly improbable. In fact, the rate of about 8 per 1,000 is possible only because Japan has a relatively young population. In a few years it may be expected to begin to rise slowly, even if fairly good economic conditions prevail and if the death rates at most ages decline somewhat further. On the other hand, for reasons which will be given below, the birth rate also may be expected to decline still further; this will reduce the natural increase below the level of 1956, which, incidentally, is only a little below the probable rate of growth around 1890–1900, as far as one can judge from the available data.

Urbanization.—In 1921 the reported birth rate for Japan as a whole was 35.0 per 1,000; for communities of 50,000 or more it was only 28.1 per 1,000 (150, 1921, pp. 4, 8). Since only about 16 per cent of the population then lived in such cities, a birth rate of 36.0 would have been sufficient in the other 84 per cent of the population to yield a birth rate of 35.0 for the total population. This differential between city and noncity birth rates may be somewhat exaggerated, because it was not unusual for Japanese women who were actually living in the cities to return to their "homes" in rural areas to give birth to their children. However, there can be no reasonable doubt that a significant rural-urban differential in birth rates existed as early as 1921. Moreover, this differential was largest between "cities" and the more remote rural areas from which there had been comparatively little urban migration.

Taeuber and Beal, using reproduction rates, find a decline in gross rates from 1920 to 1935, most of which took place between 1925 and 1930. The net reproduction rate rose slightly between 1920 and 1925 and then declined rapidly until 1930, but rose very slightly between 1930 and 1935 as a result of the more rapid decline in the death rate than in the birth rate. There was a substantial urban-rural differential during the entire period from 1920 to 1935, and it changed comparatively little (265, pp. 248–50).

Education.—By 1920 elementary education was widespread in Japan, and a large proportion of the population aged ten to forty could read and write. A larger proportion of the urban population was literate than of the rural population, and a larger proportion of males than of females. The spread of education and the increasing number of students in secondary schools and in institutions of higher learning no doubt had some effect on age at marriage and probably hastened the spread of knowledge concerning family limitation. In 1923 I was told by people whom I considered well informed that a significant proportion of the upper economic groups and of the better-educated middle class was already practicing contraception.

The birth control movement.—This movement had gained only a little momentum by the early 1920's, but the knowledge that contraception was possible was unintentionally given wide publicity by the government when it prevented Margaret Sanger from speaking on the subject during her visit in 1923. The publicity resulting from this action may very well have been greater than her speeches would have received.

It is quite probable that the points just mentioned should be regarded merely as conditions that made people more conscious of the relation between the size of their families and their economic and social welfare, rather than as true *causes* of a decline in the birth rate. But that does not make them less significant as changes that are intimately associated with such a decline and that make more likely the spread of contraceptive practices once people become aware that the number of children reaching adulthood increases as the death rate declines with no corresponding drop in the birth rate.

THE JAPANESE AS COLONISTS

Thus far nothing has been said about migration as it affected the growth of Japan's population. It has seemed best to treat this subject in connection with the expansion of Japan into her colonies and into Manchuria and Manchoukuo.

Japan acquired Taiwan as a result of her successful war with China, 1894–95. The exploitation of Taiwan as a Japanese colony was begun almost at once. Ten years later, in 1905, there were 60,000 Japanese living there (155, 1934, p. 508). By 1920 there were 167,000 Japanese on Taiwan, and by 1930 there were 232,000 (149, 1925, p. 148). At the end of 1938 there were 309,000 (114, p. 25). Clearly, there had been no significant migration from Japan to Taiwan, since the yearly average could not have much exceeded 7,000 when the excess of births over deaths in the immigrant population is taken into account. The relief provided by such an amount of migration was negligible. In the meantime, the native (Chinese) population of Taiwan grew from a little under 3 million in 1905 (29, p. 13) to 5.6 million in 1940 (267, pp. 2, 3), almost doubling in thirty-five years. The rate of increase in the last five years before the war (1933–37) rose to 25 per 1,000 per year (see chap. xvii).

As regards relief for Japan through migration, the situation was even less favorable in Korea than in Taiwan, although the number of Japanese living in Korea in 1937 (630,000) was about twice as large as the

TABLE 4

OCCUPATIONAL DISTRIBUTION OF JAPANESE
IN KOREA, 1938*

Occupation	Per Cent Distribution
Total.	100.0
Agriculture.	5.3
Fishing.	1.5
Mining.	2.3
Industry.	16.6
Commerce.	23.4
Communications.	5.9
Public and professional services. . . .	38.1
Other occupations.	2.9
No occupation.	4.0

*Source: 115, p. 79.

number in Taiwan (155, 1940, p. 504). The reason Korea provided no relief to Japan was that about 800,000 Koreans were living in Japan in 1939, and more than 1 million were living there by 1940 (115, p. 81). Japan actually drew a considerable unskilled labor force from Korea, while she sent to Korea a smaller number of trained administrators, experienced managers, and skilled workers, as Table 4 shows (see also chap. xvii).

Only a small group of the Japanese employed in Korea were engaged in agriculture (5.3 per cent), and many of these were managing estates, irrigation works, and forests, where they did not come into direct competition with the Korean peasants. More than 80 per cent of the Japanese—those engaged in industry, commerce, communications, and public and professional services—scarcely came into competition with the Koreans at all. This occupational pattern was very similar to that found in Taiwan. The Japanese farmer lived at a substantially higher level than the Korean farmer and could not replace him on the land without lowering his level of living. Likewise, for the least skilled and poorest paid jobs the Japanese unskilled worker was underbid by the unskilled Korean worker. This is quite the usual result of such a situation. People with a higher standard of living cannot compete in farming and in unskilled work with those who have a lower standard. This is the basic reason why relatively few Japanese went to these colonies.

In Manchuria, with variations in details, the story was the same. As Japan's industrial and commercial interests expanded, the number of Japanese immigrants increased. But in 1914, about ten years after the Russo-Japanese War, there were only 100,000 Japanese living in Manchuria, and in 1931 (when Japan seized complete control of Manchuria and established Manchoukuo) this number had only increased to 233,000 (155, 1934, p. 816). At this time the occupational make-up of Japanese immigrants was about the same as it was in Korea. They were trained administrators and skilled workers of various types who encountered no serious competition from the Chinese.

After Japan seized Manchuria and undertook its industrial development in earnest, the Japanese population grew rapidly, to about 593,-000 in 1937 (155, 1940, p. 604), and had increased to 642,000 by December of 1939 (187, 1942, p. 121). It was said that there were a number of agricultural settlers among these Japanese immigrants. In 1939 there were said to be 9,900 households to which about 500,000 acres had been allotted (155, 1940, pp. 607–9). Even so, the occupational composition of the Japanese population in Manchuria at that time was very little different from that of the Japanese in Korea and Taiwan. In their League of Nations mandate in the Pacific (830 square miles) they took better advantage of the agricultural opportunities available, because there they met no competition from the natives. About 70,000 Japanese, most of them farmers, were living there in 1940. The total number of Japanese in these areas was about 1.6 million by 1940, or a little less than the natural increase of one and three-quarter years based on the average annual increase in 1931–35. Clearly, the colonies and Manchoukuo after 1931 had not provided any significant outlet for Japan's population in the forty-five years up to 1940. Moreover, this 1.6 million included the children of migrants as well as the migrants themselves. Thus this total number probably represented but little more than one year's increase of population in Japan.

The reason relatively few Japanese migrated to their colonies can be found in the situation which always arises when people who have different levels of living come into contact with each other. If the contact is initiated by people with a higher level of living than those among whom they are settling, the migrants find very few opportunities through which they can better their economic situation. This was clearly what happened when Japanese migrants went into the colonies and into Manchuria. All governmental jobs of any importance were reserved for the Japanese, of course, as is generally the case in colonies. Besides, business openings requiring capital, jobs requiring technical knowledge and experience, and even jobs requiring skill were monopolized by the Japanese—chiefly because very few natives had the necessary experience and training. But if Japanese farmers and unskilled laborers had migrated to their colonies, they would have come at once into direct competition with the natives. They would not have been able to make as good a living as they had been accustomed to in Japan. The native laborers were accustomed to working for smaller wages, and the native farmers sold their produce for lower prices than the farmers in Japan. Under these circumstances comparatively few Japanese had any incentive to move to the colonies. The Japanese who did migrate to their colonies, like the Europeans who migrated to theirs, were in superior economic positions. Their salaries and wages and their incomes from business were much higher than all but a very few of the natives could command.

The Japanese did go to their colonies (including Manchuria) in considerably larger proportions than Europeans went to theirs in Asia. Moreover, many of them took types of jobs which Eurpeans would not have taken. But, even so, the jobs they were willing to take were not numerous, and mass migration never occurred. On the other hand, it is interesting to note that once the migration of Japanese to Hawaii and California began, it increased rapidly and bid fair to become a mass movement. The belief in the United States that the immigration of the Japanese would assume large proportions was what led to its prohibition. As had been true of the Chinese at an earlier time, the Japanese who came to the United States had the lower level of living; they could compete with and displace our citizens in many types of farming and gardening, because they were willing to work harder for smaller wages and to sell their produce at lower prices. It is not surprising that they soon incurred the enmity of those who suffered in status and income by competing with them. It was not basically the unwillingness of the Japanese to migrate that kept them from going to their colonies in larger numbers but their unwillingness to migrate when they could not see a chance to live better in a new home than they were living in Japan.

Although the Japanese colonies did not provide a large outlet for migrants from Japan, it would be a mistake to assume that they did not contribute substantially to Japan's economic development (see chaps. v and vii). Japan obtained large amounts of rice and soybeans from Korea and most of her sugar and pineapples as well as rice from Taiwan. Korea also supplied her with considerable amounts of minerals. These were not gifts, but they were procurable within the Empire and within the yen block, and they aided substantially in the support of Japan's growing population and industry. Manchoukuo (which was about 60 per cent larger than Manchuria) promised to be much more valuable to Japan than Korea and Taiwan, both as an outlet for population and as a provider of food and minerals, even during the relatively short period between 1931, when Japan seized complete control, and 1940, when she became so involved in Asia that she had no chance to undertake further development. All reasonable expectations of large returns from Manchoukuo evaporated on December 7, 1941, with the attack on Pearl Harbor.

BIRTH CONTROL TODAY

The rapid decline of the birth rate in Japan since 1949 has been, in large measure, a voluntary one. When the more influential people in Japan fully recognized what the loss of their colonies and Manchoukuo meant to their economy and realized that the rapid reduction in the death rate was increasing their numbers faster than ever before, they were not long in coming to the conclusion that only by reducing the birth rate quickly could they save the nation from economic disaster. As early as 1948 it was clear that only continued aid from the United States for the next few years would enable Japan to feed her people, revive production, and develop the trade necessary to enable her to purchase those critical raw materials on which so many of her industries depended. Thoughtful Japanese were finding it increasingly difficult to see any substantial hope for an improvement in living conditions unless Japan made a great effort to adjust her population growth to the resources which would be available to meet the needs of her people. These needs were rapidly becoming more urgent, with the population increasing by 1.5 to 1.7 million a year (1947, 1948, 1949,

1950). The military leaders, who had done all they could for some years to stop the practice of contraception and to encourage the expansion of the empire, were badly discredited.

For these reasons, and also because of increasing freedom of speech and press, there began to be more and more public discussion of Japan's population problems. The newspapers gave these discussions wide publicity, and after the Occupation the birth control movement was revived rapidly. Several influential new groups were organized to study the economic problems involved in supporting a rapidly growing population. Surveys were made to ascertain the attitudes of people toward family planning and toward the idea of controlling population growth. It will be impossible here to make more than a few general statements about the development of public opinion regarding the need for family limitation and the achievement of those legal changes which made such limitation easier and more respectable.

In 1948 a Eugenics Protection Law was passed which, with amendments in 1949, legalized abortion and sterilization for *medical, social,* and *economic* reasons. This law also enabled the local governments to disseminate information about family limitation and to set up eugenic marriage consultation offices in all prefectures. By the end of 1950 there were 704 health centers in operation, but in only 247 of them had marriage consultation offices been established (11, p. 10). Both funds and personnel were lacking to extend these offices more rapidly. The number of *legal* abortions increased from about 250,000 in 1949 to 1,143,000 in 1954. In addition, there were also many illegal abortions. In 1954 (168, p. 282) Dr. Koya wrote: "The recent figure [for abortions] would probably reach some one million several hundred thousand, if the 'unreported, secretly performed' abortions were included." In a personal interview in late 1955, Dr. Koya confirmed his belief that the total number of abortions was still increasing, but expressed the hope that it would soon begin to decline. He said that surveys then being made showed that the proportion of the population practicing contraception was increasing and that this would reduce the need for abortion. Further amendments to the Eugenics Protection Law were also expected to reduce the number of illegal abortions and, hence, to mitigate their harmful effects.

The Population Problem Council was established as a government advisory board in 1949. In 1954 it recommended that the government become more active in promoting contraception and that physicians performing abortions be required to give contraceptive service later.

These recommendations were made in the hope that illegal abortions could be abolished and that the total number of abortions would decline rapidly as reliable contraceptive information spread and as the people gained experience that would make the use of contraceptives more effective.

Active efforts to make family limitation safer and easier have been multiplying. By the end of 1952 about 18,000 nurses and midwives had been trained in contraceptive work and had received certificates. Several surveys of public opinion showed that the Japanese people were becoming better informed about the need for family limitation and that a goodly proportion approved of it. In 1950 the *Mainichi Press* made a survey which showed that over 60 per cent of those replying believed that family limitation would be a good thing for Japan and that 44 per cent of those who practiced it did so for economic reasons. Another public opinion survey showed that 87 per cent believed Japan was overpopulated and that family limitation was needed (11, p. 9). In spite of the wide prevalence of abortion, it appears that most of the people who are asked for their opinion about it believe it is a bad thing. It seems fair to infer that if more effective, more practicable, safer, and cheaper methods of contraception were available, the practice of abortion would decline rapidly.

In addition to widespread abortion and the increasing practice of contraception, a growing number of women are being sterilized. This operation is generally done following childbirth or when an abortion is performed. The reported number of sterilizations in 1950 was 11,403, and it had increased to 32,552 in 1953 (169, p. 368). There is good reason to assume that the number is continuing to increase rapidly. Each sterilization performed at thirty years of age reduces the number of births per woman by about two under the prevailing conditions; thus a continued increase in sterilization at the present rate would, in the course of a few years, have a substantial effect on the birth rate. If, as the authors referred to above suggest, actual sterilizations are five to ten times as numerous as reported, they are already beginning to have a significant effect on the birth rate.

The decline in the birth rate noted above is ample proof that all these efforts combined have been highly effective. That they have not reduced the absolute increase in the population far more is due, as we have seen, to the very remarkable decline in the death rate. Since the crude death rate of approximately 8 per 1,000 cannot fall significantly —although specific death rates at certain ages will no doubt decline still more—any further decline in the birth rate will be accompanied by an almost equal decline in the rate of natural increase. It is now widely recognized in Japan that the outlook for a better level of living would be much improved if Japan's birth rate would continue its rapid decline for several years, until it reached a level of 12–14 per 1,000. This would give just about the number of births needed to offset the deaths likely to take place a few years hence, when the population will have a larger proportion of persons forty years of age and over.

The general outlook for an improvement in Japan's living conditions will emerge more clearly as Japan's past economic development and her present economic situation are sketched in succeeding chapters, but it can be said that the reasonable hope of an almost stationary population in Japan in the near future is very encouraging.

CHAPTER V

JAPAN:

AGRICULTURAL DEVELOPMENT

INTRODUCTORY

As a result of losing the war, Japan has again been reduced in size to approximately the same territory she occupied at the time of the Restoration (1868). Japan now consists of four rather large islands and a great number of small islands of which only a few are large enough to be of any economic significance. The total area is approximately 142,000 square miles, a little less than that of California (1, p. 1). The territory lost by Japan—Korea, Taiwan, and the southern half of Sakhalin—was only a little smaller than that left to her. If Manchoukuo is included in her losses (for economic purposes it was a part of the empire from 1931 to 1945), she lost another 500,000 square miles. By 1940 Manchoukuo had come to supply substantial amounts of several essential raw materials (coking coal, iron ore, and a few other minerals) and also of food and fertilizers (wheat, soybeans, and soybean cake).

Today Japan is a relatively small country, with a population of about 92 million (1958)—probably over two and one-half times as large as it was in 1870. Because of its geographic location between latitudes 24° 15′ and 46° 20′ north, and because of the moderating effects of ocean currents, one-half or a little more of Japan has a subtropical climate which provides a long growing season. Japan also has a rainfall which is generally adequate, in those regions where the growing season is long enough, for good crops in both summer and winter (see Maps 2, 3a, and 3b). Since Japan is a very mountainous country, however, only a small proportion of the land is tillable—14–15 per cent (see Map 5). This figure may possibly be increased to 17 per cent (1, p. 1). Most of Japan's tilled land is found near the coast, and about one-third of it is double-cropped. Far and away the most important summer crop is rice, even on the northern island of Hokkaido. The winter grain crop is generally

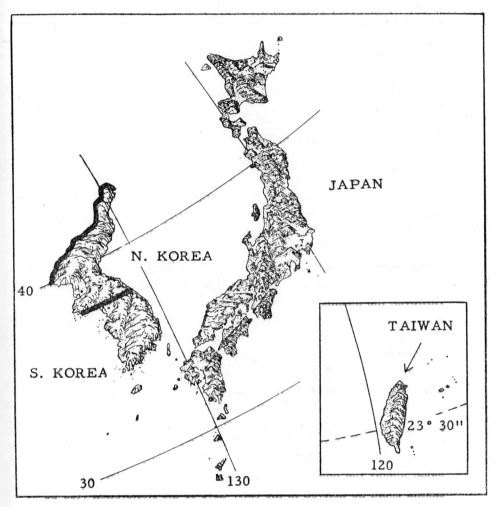

MAP 5.—Physiographic map of Japan, Korea, and Taiwan. (Base map a section of the Physiographic Diagram of Asia, © by A. K. Lobeck, reproduced with permission from the Geographical Press, a division of C. S. Hammond & Co.)

wheat or barley; many vegetables are also grown, especially in the southern half of the country. In only a few small areas can a second (winter) crop of rice be grown. Altogether, the cultivated area is about 14.5 to 15.0 million acres, of which about 5 million acres is double-cropped, so the total area cropped annually is about 20 million acres. If Japan were entirely dependent on her own land for her food, each cropped acre would now have to support approximately four and one-half persons, as compared with two acres to each person in the United States.

AGRICULTURE AT THE RESTORATION

It is probable that the per capita production of Japan's agricultural workers in 1870 was about the same as that of most of the underdeveloped countries in Asia today. Agriculture was carried on largely by hand, only a small amount of animal power being used in the preparation of the seed bed. The implements and tools were few and simple; they were made in village shops and in the homes of the farmers themselves. Some slight progress toward higher production appears to have been made in the three or four decades preceding the Restoration. However, the tenants on the feudal estates had neither the knowledge needed to insure much improvement in farm practices nor the incentive to invest in improvements on the land—and few of them possessed the financial means to undertake such improvements even if they had desired to do so. It is estimated that, preceding the Restoration, about 40 per cent of the total agricultural product went to the feudal lords and their retainers, who, altogether, numbered about 2 million (180, p. 4), or less than 6 per cent of the total population. Very little of this product found its way back to the farms for the improvement of agriculture. This estimated 40 per cent of the agricultural product provided almost the only source from which any substantial amount of capital could be derived in the early days of the Restoration (see below).

THE AGRICULTURAL POPULATION

At the time of the Restoration, Japan was overwhelmingly agricultural. Nasu estimated that 78.9 per cent of the population was engaged in agriculture in 1872 (205, p. 7). Taeuber believes that the *population* of all households engaged in agriculture declined from 71 per cent in 1884 to 60 per cent in 1909, and to 58 per cent in 1919 (173, p. 321). The first actual census, taken in 1920, listed 52.4 per cent of the *oc-*

cupied persons as engaged in agriculture and forestry. By 1930 this proportion had declined to 47.7 per cent (157, 1949, p. 71). Johnston believes that not only the proportion of the population, but also the actual number of persons, engaged in agriculture decreased by about 2 million between the decades 1881–90 and 1911–20 (159, p. 499). Lockwood finds a decrease of somewhat more than 2 million in the number of workers engaged in agriculture, fishing, and mining between 1900 and 1920 (180, p. 462). From 1920 to 1940 there appears to have been no significant change in the number of workers thus employed—approximately 15 million; but by 1940 the proportion so employed had fallen to about 44 per cent. Furthermore, it is probable that both the number and the proportion employed in agriculture in the years immediately preceding 1940 are somewhat exaggerated, since an increasing proportion of farm families contained one or more members who, although principally occupied with agriculture, had subsidiary part-time work in other industries.

GROWTH OF CULTIVATED AND CROPPED AREAS

The estimates of cultivated land prior to about 1903 are not very reliable, but Nasu estimated that between 10.1 and 11.0 million acres were being cultivated in 1877 (205, p. 68).[1] If the average of these two figures (10.5 million acres) is accepted as the area of cultivated land in 1877, then it appears that the cultivated area increased by about 38 per cent, or to 14.5 million acres, by 1920. After that, there was no significant increase, and there may even have been a slight decrease by 1940 (155, 1940, p. 286).

The fact that the cultivated area did not increase after 1920 is of great significance, for very considerable efforts were made to enlarge it. All these efforts seem to have been counterbalanced by the use of farm land in the extension of cities, in the building of new roads and airfields, in the expansion of railroad yards, and in other ways which contributed to industrial and/or military power. There had also been some destruction of farm land by earthquakes. Altogether, it appeared that the expansion of the cultivated area, except in the northern island of Hokkaido, could be achieved only at a cost which was prohibitive in comparison with the cost of imported food. In Hokkaido the

[1] In Japan the cultivated area is substantially less than the crop area because a significant proportion—somewhat more than one-third—of the land is cropped twice each year.

amount of land suitable for rice is quite limited, but the area suitable for other grains and for white potatoes can be expanded considerably.

There is no clear evidence regarding any increase in the proportion of cultivated land which was irrigated during the period 1877–1940, but I am inclined to believe that it remained rather stationary at 52 to 53 per cent.[2] On the other hand, there probably was some increase in the proportion of the irrigated land which was double-cropped between 1903, when it was given as 37 per cent (158, 1907, p. 324), and 1939, when it was given by Nasu as 43 per cent (205, p. 94).[3]

Although these data on cultivated area, irrigated area, and crop area leave much to be desired, especially the data available concerning these different types of areas before 1903, there can be little doubt that the increase in each of these categories fell within the range of 35–45 per cent between 1872 and 1940. It likewise seems reasonably certain that practically all of the increase had taken place by 1920.

AGRICULTURAL PRODUCTION

These changes in the land used for agriculture and in the agricultural labor force were accompanied by large increases in total production and in yields per acre. According to figures given by Allen, the index for the physical volume of agricultural production in 1873 was 28.6 (1921–25 = 100) (9, p. 169). This rose to 37.2 in 1880, or by about 30 per cent, and averaged about 110.0 for the period 1927–34. Johnston gives three series of indexes, 1881–1920, showing changes in area of cultivated land, in yields per acre, and in total agricultural production which are of much interest here (159, p. 499). When the decade 1881–90 is used as the base (100), the index for the area in the six major crops of Japan in the decade 1911–20 was 121; the index for the yield per acre of these same crops was 146, and that for total production was 177. Johnston further estimates that if total agricultural production increased in the same manner as the output of these six major crops, and if the labor force engaged in agriculture declined by about 14 per cent between 1881–90 and 1911–20, as was noted above, the output per farm worker increased by about 106 per cent during this period (159, p. 500).

Lockwood reports a very substantial increase—about 21 per cent—

[2] Estimates for the late 1930's are found in the following references: 242, p. 119; 104, Part 1, p. 114; and 116, p. 19.

[3] Comparatively little unirrigated land is double-cropped.

in rice production from 1878–82 to 1888–92 (180, p. 18) and at a later point (p. 87) gives indexes (1910–14 = 100) which would indicate an increase in the physical volume of agricultural production of about 60 per cent from 1885–89 to 1905–9. Clark's international units, the equivalent of indexes, indicate that the real product per man in agriculture and fishing rose rapidly, from 64 in 1897 to 118 in 1914, to 125 in 1925, and to 148 in 1934 (78, p. 213).

All these men caution the reader to regard the indexes for the early years as only approximate. But, even so, there can be no reasonable doubt that before about 1910 the increase in the area of cultivated land was fairly rapid, while the increase in total agricultural production, in acreage yields, and in production per worker was even more rapid during much of the period from 1870 to 1920. Moreover, total production, yield per acre, and product per worker continued to increase up to the war (1937), although at a much slower rate after 1920. Lockwood gives indexes (1910–14 = 100) for total food production, including fisheries, which show an increase from 125 in 1920–24 to 161 in 1935–39—an increase of about 29 per cent during a period in which population was increasing about 24 per cent (180, p. 86).

There is good reason to think that this more rapid increase in food production than in population began shortly after the Restoration and lasted until Japan became deeply involved in the war in China. However, the margin of difference in these rates of increase became substantially smaller after 1920; the population grew somewhat faster after 1920, while agricultural production grew more slowly.

One very interesting point in connection with these rates of increase in food production and population growth is that practically all careful students of Japan's economic development believe that there was comparatively little improvement in the level of living of the masses of the Japanese people up to about 1880, or even somewhat later. Lockwood thinks that real wages of employed industrial workers may have risen by one-third between 1897 and 1914, and by about two-thirds, or possibly more, between 1914 and 1935–39 (180, p. 144). In general, it seems probable that the agricultural workers did not fare as well as the nonagricultural workers from the very beginning of Japan's economic revolution, in spite of the fact that for a decade or two practically all of the increase in the physical volume of production came from agriculture.

HOW AGRICULTURE WAS IMPROVED

The most significant aspects of this truly remarkable agricultural revolution in Japan may be summed up as follows: (1) It was accomplished with almost no increase in the use of mechanical power. (Agriculture in Japan is still carried on largely by handwork applied intensively to small areas and without any significant amount of mechanical aid, although there has been some increase in the use of draft animals.) (2) Consequently, the amount of capital used in effecting this agricultural revolution, in addition to the improvements on the land due to the labor of the farmers themselves, amounted to a very small part of the increased product. Moreover, most of this capital was devoted to agricultural research, to education in the agricultural schools, and to extension work, rather than to increasing farm equipment. Some of this increased production was used as capital to extend the cultivated area and to improve irrigation works, but the amount thus employed was not large compared with that used as capital for nonagricultural development. (3) The chief factors in bringing about this increase in agricultural production in Japan were: (*a*) the development and use of improved strains of rice and other grains; (*b*) the use of better methods of planting and cultivation, even though agriculture still depended on hand labor and simple hand tools; (*c*) the more efficient use of water in irrigation; (*d*) the employment of better methods of handling compost and night soil to prevent the loss of their fertilizing qualities (commercial fertilizers contributed little to increased production before World War I but became increasingly important thereafter); and (*e*) the increase in the cultivated area, amounting to perhaps 35–38 per cent, most of which had taken place by 1915–19 (180, p. 86).

In spite of the very large growth in agricultural production, it became necessary after 1914 to import small but increasing amounts of food to sustain the rise in the level of living, which was by then proceeding at a somewhat faster pace. The amount of food imports began to increase more rapidly after 1920 and shortly before World War II amounted to approximately one-fifth of the total needs of the country. After 1920, these imports included increasing amounts of food which added variety to, and improved the quality of, the diet of the masses.

PRESENT FOOD SITUATION

As a result of the loss of Korea, Taiwan, and Manchoukuo, and the elimination of her foreign trade, Japan's food situation since the war would have been desperate without the aid given by the United States. There can be no doubt that the total volume of agricultural production after the war remained substantially below that of the years 1933–35 until 1950, when the index was 98.9 (1933–35 = 100). In 1953 the index fell to 97.6. On a new base (1951 and 1952 = 100) the index for 1953 was only 96 (317, Part 1, No. 56–15, p. 4). It would appear that this new base, including the very good year 1952, was slightly higher than the 1933–35 base. On this new base the index was 106 for 1954, and for 1955, the best crop year Japan has ever had, it was 120. It would probably have been two or three points higher on the 1933–35 base. Preliminary reports indicated that agricultural production for 1956 "would be substantially above normal . . . but that it . . . was not expected to equal the 1955 record crop" (*ibid.*, No. 57-1D, p. 2). If *normal* means the 1951–52 base, which was probably two to three points above the 1933–35 base, it would appear that by about 1954 total agricultural production surpassed prewar production by several points and that it has remained above the prewar level. But it is reasonably certain that, even with the inclusion of the record crop of 1955, the average index for the three years 1954–55–56 would not have exceeded 110.

This recent improvement in agricultural production must be viewed in the light of two other facts if we are to see its true significance: (1) The population of Japan increased approximately 30 per cent between 1935 and 1955 (see chap. iv). (2) The agricultural labor force increased about one-fifth during this same period (303, 1955, p. 132). Thus the increase in population is steadily outstripping the gain in total agricultural production; per capita agricultural production remains substantially below its prewar level, while yields are now changing but little.

The extent to which Japan depended on imports of certain important crops in 1954 was as follows: rice, 13.6 per cent; wheat, 60.6 per cent; barley, 38.0 per cent; sugar, 95.2 per cent; and soybeans, 57.4 per cent.[4] The degree of dependence on imports varies considerably from year to year, both as a total and for particular foodstuffs. Thus a relatively small amount of rice was imported in 1956 following the bumper rice crop of 1955, while the quantities of other leading foodstuffs imported in 1956 declined very little.

[4] *Degree of dependence on imports* is the ratio between the quantity imported and the total quantity supplied, i.e., production plus import (303, 1955, p. 127),

OUTLOOK FOR AGRICULTURE

It is the experience of all highly industrialized countries that the need for land for nonagricultural purposes increases steadily. Cities are growing and need more land for dwellings and factories; transportation needs more and wider roads, larger marshaling yards for railroads, and large areas of level land for airfields. In Japan, far more than in the United States, much of this land needed for nonagricultural purposes must come from the better land now used for agriculture. This is one reason why, between 1920 and 1940, there was no increase in Japan's cultivated land.

Some of the land taken out of agricultural use before and during the war has since been reclaimed for such use. But one cannot wander through the cities of Japan today without being impressed by the way they are spreading into the surrounding rural areas, in spite of the fact that comparatively few families have automobiles. Although some of the land which was used for military airfields, depots, and other installations is being returned to cultivation, the improvement of roads and the development of other nonagricultural projects continue to demand land at an even more rapid rate than before the war. Moreover, in spite of the great decline in the birth rate since 1950, the numerical increase of population in Japan today is greater than it was in most years before 1940, and almost all of this increase accrues to the cities.

In 1947 the Ministry of Agriculture and Forestry in Japan estimated that approximately 3.8 million acres could be reclaimed for agricultural purposes under a ten-year program. This amount, added to the cultivated area of 1945, would give Japan a total cultivated area of about 17.8 million acres in 1957 or 1958 (1, pp. 378–79).[5]

Of the 3.8 million acres mentioned above, over one-third was in Hokkaido, and 94 per cent of the remainder could not be irrigated. Altogether, about 96 per cent of this reclaimable land could yield only one crop annually. Since much of this was rough land in the mountains and a great deal of the remainder was in the relatively cold north (Hokkaido), it is highly probable that the crops it would yield would be significantly smaller than the customary winter crops raised on the better land already in use (see Map 5). Furthermore, almost no reclamation work has yet been done, and, in early 1958, the total area of cul-

[5] No explanation is given of the decline in cultivated area from almost 15 million acres in 1940 to 14 million acres in 1945. Presumably some of this land had been converted to military use during the war and was in need of reclamation before it would again be suitable for agriculture.

tivated land in Japan still appears to be somewhat smaller than it was in 1940. Regarding the probability of an increase in cultivated land in the near future, therefore, the most reasonable conclusions seem to be that such an increase will be small, that it can be achieved only at a high cost, and that the production contributed by the reclaimed land will be offset to a considerable extent by the loss of better land near the cities for nonagricultural uses.

This scarcity of new land for agriculture seems to indicate that any considerable increase in domestic food production in the near future must come chiefly from the more intensive use of fertilizer and from the wider use of root crops (potatoes and yams) on the new land when, and if, it is reclaimed. In general, the Japanese people would regard a wider use of these root crops as a deterioration of their level of living. If Japan is to bring the general standard of living back to what it was in the mid-1930's, she will have to increase her food imports greatly during the next few years—in spite of the fact that the decline in the birth rate seems likely to continue. It may very well be several years, perhaps a decade, before the annual population increase falls substantially below one-half million. The seriousness of Japan's present food situation will become increasingly apparent as other aspects of Japan's modern economic development are reviewed.

AGRICULTURE AND ECONOMIC DEVELOPMENT

At this point, it will be well to note briefly the role agriculture has played in Japan's modern industrial development.

At the time Japan's modern economic development was undertaken, comparatively little capital was available. The only significant source of capital was the margin of agricultural, fishing, and forestry production that remained after the subsistence requirements of the people who produced these goods and of those who were engaged in civil administration and military service had been taken care of.

The general character of the problems involved in securing the capital needed to inaugurate modern economic development has been sketched in chapter iii. Here it will be sufficient to note how Japan met her problems of capital accumulation in the early years of her modern economic development. In the first place, attention should be called to the fact that even when a society is as predominantly agricultural as Japan was at the time of the Restoration (75–80 per cent of the population was engaged in agriculture), a substantial amount of capital is regularly invested in maintaining and increasing agricultural production if the population is growing regularly. It is obvious that even simple hand tools, as well as homemade plows and harrows, wear out and have to be repaired or replaced, and that cows, bullocks, and buffaloes grow old, sicken and die, and have to be replaced. In addition, although it is not so generally recognized, much of the productive quality of all land is due to the investment the farmer makes in irrigation, in drainage, in soil conservation works and practices, and in other types of improvements whose cost is a constant charge on the crops. Although it consists chiefly of the farmer's own labor, this investment is not an insignificant portion of the margin between his production and his actual and necessary consumption, even in an economy in which most people live close to the subsistence level.

During the early years of modern economic development in Japan, as in most underdeveloped countries, agriculture was almost the only significant source from which domestic capital could be accumulated. The exports needed to pay for essential capital goods and for training new types of workers had to come from agricultural production. The leaders of the Restoration deliberately tried to divert as much as possible of this margin from the conspicuous expenditure of the feudal lords and their retainers into the strengthening of the state through taxes and to see that as much of it as possible got into the hands of people who would invest it in new enterprises. Many of these enterprises were founded and operated by the state in the beginning, and those undertaken by individuals were partly supported by subsidies until they became profitable.

Any state deliberately entering upon a program of economic development, and having a very limited amount of capital at its disposal, must gather capital assiduously and use it with great care. In Japan, for political as well as economic reasons, very little capital could be raised by borrowing abroad. Since practically all imports of every type had to be paid for by agricultural exports, except for the export of a small amount of specie, the early developmental projects had to be confined largely to those which could be carried out by taking the agricultural margin from the producers and using it to support workers engaged in those types of construction involving neither large expenditures abroad for machinery and equipment nor the import of any considerable number of specialized technicians. Hence, the Japanese relied heavily on: (1) an increase in agricultural production requiring only small use of capital, and (2) the use of this capital, whenever possible, in those types of enterprise calling for domestic materials and labor rather than a considerable amount of expensive machinery. In this way the need for foreign exchange was kept at a minimum, and foreign loans, which Japan neither wanted nor would have been able to obtain, were avoided for some years. Thus Japan's economic development during the twenty years following the Restoration, i.e., up to about 1890, consisted largely of construction in which Japanese labor was by far the chief element of cost and which was paid for mainly by taxes on agriculture. Shortly after the Restoration, the tax system was reformed so that the growing agricultural margin could be used to the best advantage of the national economy.

In 1873 the feudal dues, which had been payable in kind, were transmuted into a land tax payable in money. This tax provided 94 per cent of the ordinary revenue of the government (180, p. 98). Smith found that during the entire period from 1867 to 1881, approximately 80 per cent of the ordinary revenue of the government came from this source (249, p. 74). Smith's data on expenditures from ordinary revenue during 1867–81 seem to indicate that about 42 million yen (or almost 10 per cent of the revenue from the land tax) can be definitely identified as having been used for economic development. In addition, it is highly probable that a considerable proportion of the relatively large expenditure on the army and navy during this period should be charged to economic development, because it was used to build navy yards, arsenals, foundries, machine shops, etc. (249, pp. 71, 72). Since nearly all defense expenditures were made with what was raised by the land tax, this capital also came from agricultural production.

Lockwood gives his views on the importance of the land tax in early economic development as follows: "The land tax, a heavy burden on small peasants, furnished over 90 per cent of State tax revenues in the early seventies. Twenty years later it still accounted for as much as 60 per cent. Together with exorbitant rents and usurious debt charges, it continued for another generation or more to sluice off large amounts of agricultural income for the support of State enterprise and industrial investment" (180, p. 17).

Johnston points out that the new tax laws of 1873 placed a heavy burden, amounting to one-fourth or more of the annual crop, on the owners of land until about 1879 (159, pp. 501–2). It was somewhat lighter thereafter, but Lockwood says that even in 1908 the land tax and the other taxes placed on the farmer were estimated to amount to 28 per cent of his income, as compared with the estimated 14 per cent of the incomes of merchants and industrialists that was gathered in taxes (180, p. 26).

In sum, the increase in agricultural production provided by far the larger part of the funds Japan had available for getting development started in the nonagricultural sectors of her economy during the first three decades after the Restoration. At the same time, the increased efficiency of agricultural labor made possible the use of an increasing proportion of the total labor force in nonagricultural work and also provided a slowly rising level of living for a population which was one-fourth to one-third larger in 1900 than it had been in 1872.

It is important to note that although Japan established some modern factories, hired some hundreds of foreign technicians, and sent many students abroad before 1900, her most significant achievement during that period undoubtedly was the improvement of agriculture. This improvement would almost certainly not have taken place if, in spite of the high taxes on agriculture, enough of the increase in production had not been left in the hands of the agricultural population to provide a strong incentive for more efficient production. This improvement not only provided nearly all the foreign exchange required by the modern projects being undertaken, but, above all, it enabled the government to direct relatively large amounts of labor into works which would later make possible the rapid increase of the industrial capacity of the nation.

It seems to me that a number of the countries that are now striving so hard to develop a more productive economy would do well to study more carefully how Japan managed to make her agriculture increasingly productive and how she was able to draw from it the sustenance to initiate progress in the nonagricultural sectors of her economy.

CHAPTER VI

JAPAN:

MODERN INDUSTRIAL DEVELOPMENT

INTRODUCTORY

One motive has long been recognized as probably having provided the chief driving force in the early years of Japan's modernization of her economy: the conviction of her leaders that political independence was contingent largely on Japan's becoming strong enough economically to support a military establishment that would command the respect of the Western powers. Without doubt, this same political motive had also been powerful in giving purpose and drive to the revolt which overthrew the shogun and resulted in the Restoration. As is true of all highly significant social revolutions, the reasons for the overthrow of the existing government (the shogunate) and for the social and economic developments following the establishment of a new government at the Restoration are to be found in changes that had been in process for some years. While these changes were making an increasing number of people aware of the abuses and the inadequacies of the existing government and were thus encouraging revolution, they were also providing the knowledge and experience from which reforms would later sprout.

Politically, the shogunate had for some years been failing to provide the leadership Japan needed to meet the problems raised by her increasing contacts with the Western world. Economically, the country had been falling to pieces. The shogunate system had deprived a large part of the retainer class, especially the warriors (samurai), of most of its traditional functions, leaving it impoverished and embittered. The positive efforts being made to improve the economy by introducing a few Western-style enterprises were so feeble, and were so largely confined to providing better military materiel, that they had no significant effect in strengthening the economy of the nation as a whole; nor did they much increase its ability to defend itself against Western encroachments. Moreover, the economic activities of all the unemployed groups were still hedged about with most of the traditional feudal restrictions regarding occupation, freedom of movement, legal status of individuals, etc. Under these conditions, efforts to introduce a new economy could not appear as more than a gesture to the people who had lost their status under feudalism and who were suffering most from these restrictions as they tried to adjust to a new system which apparently had no purpose and, therefore, no drive. The feeble efforts made to improve the economy could do no more than focus the attention of these functionless people on the weaknesses of the shogunate.

Although the growing ineffectiveness of the shogunate in coping with changing social and economic conditions probably provided the chief motive to most of those who wanted to overthrow it, certain of its actions had inadvertently helped to develop a feeling of nationalism and thus to make possible the new national government which replaced it. Without this new national government, the relatively rapid economic development that took place in Japan during the following decades would have been impossible. The shogun required the feudal lords and their more important retainers to spend alternate years in Tokyo, where they were under the surveillance of his officials, and also to leave hostages there when they went to their fiefs; this requirement had one important incidental effect which probably had not been foreseen. It led to some improvement in the roads and in the means of travel between Tokyo and the castle towns of the feudal lords (daimyo). This improvement in transportation and communication, together with the concentration of such a large part of the spending power of the nobles and their retainers in Tokyo, led to some manufacturing of luxury goods which were traded beyond the bounds of the village or the city, as well as to the development of a national market in rice. Thus it fostered some economic development of a national character.

However, in spite of these small steps toward a national economy, Japan's industry and commerce, like her agriculture, was still essentially parochial at the time of the Restoration. Most manufactured goods used by the agricultural population—tools and implements, household wares, textiles and clothing, etc.—were made in the villages or in the homes by hand. The mines and forges operated by the producers of metals were small, crude, and inefficient, although some of the workers were quite skilled. Even the producers of the luxury goods used by the upper class operated only small workshops and sold their goods to the large merchants or their agents, who disposed of them chiefly in the court city—Tokyo. The shogun and a few of the daimyos owned small arsenals and several small semimodern textile factories. These were almost the only efforts that had been made to modernize Japan's manufacturing. Industrially, the Japan of 1870 had had far less experience in the use of the power machinery then available in the West than any of today's underdeveloped countries have had. But Japan did have a considerable body of skilled workmen who were producing luxury goods and metal products in the workshops.

ECONOMIC AND SOCIAL REFORMS OF THE RESTORATION

The new leaders of Japan seem to have clearly realized that the political revolution had been possible largely because of a wide demand for social and economic reforms. They realized that such reforms had to attempt not only to redress past wrongs but particularly to release the unused energy of certain classes of feudal retainers—chiefly the warrior class. This class had lost a large part of its reason for existence in the last decades of the shogunate and had played an important part in the political revolution.

In the first place, the special privileges and rights which affected personal freedom and participation in economic activity had to be abolished. Feudal rights in land and feudal claims to service had to be done away with; restrictions on the freedom of movement from place to place of certain groups and classes had to be abrogated; restrictions on the right to engage in certain professions, occupations, and trades had to be removed; foreign trade could no longer be prohibited; the farmer could no longer be forbidden to grow certain crops merely to assure local self-sufficiency for the fief of the daimyo; all special privileges before the law had to be suppressed; barriers to travel and communication needed to be removed. There were also many minor practices of a traditional character that could not be immediately suppressed by law but whose disappearance was inherent in the new rights granted to the mass of the people.

On the positive side, it may be noted that every restriction removed constituted a new right conferred; thus the removal of the restrictions on the purchase of land conferred the right to buy land and to use it as one saw fit. In addition, new rights resulted from the establishment of new institutions, e.g., the right to attend school and the right to vote (at first on quite a limited scale). In a very real sense, all that is said below about Japan's modern economic development in nonagricultural sectors merely shows how the new legal rights conferred at the Restoration were gradually realized.

Although at first mention these reforms may not appear highly significant from the standpoint of the release of economic energy, a little thought will show that they were fundamental. They meant the breaking-away from traditions that had long throttled the freedom of action of a large part of the population and had prevented them from trying to better their economic life and enlarge their sphere of personal development; they constitute clear evidence that the power of tradition had begun to disintegrate and that Japan was ready, culturally, to undertake the modernization of her economy.

GOVERNMENT IN THE ECONOMY

The situation out of which a national government developed in Japan at the time of the Restoration made it inevitable that this government, in the years immediately following its accession, would assume the leading role in the development of the nonagricultural areas of the economy. No other organization, and no one class, could provide leadership in the development of a national economy. The feudal lords, as a group, had lost much of their economic power when their fiefs were transferred to the state. Those few who had the training and experience that would have fitted them for economic leadership could find scope for their activities only within the government. The rich merchants who had some capital had had no experience in establishing modern industries or in conducting foreign trade. Moreover, even if they had been competent to introduce a new type of economy, they could not have been counted on to pursue the economic aim of a national government. Under the new system of government, most of the national income which was not consumed directly by the agricultural population and by the people dealing in agricultural products could now be taken in taxes, and only a relatively small part of the tax receipts was required to pension off the feudal lords. As a consequence of these reforms the government was the only agency in a position to accumulate any considerable "chunks" of capital and to direct their investment in the national interest. Even the rich merchants, when they had funds to spare, preferred to act as bankers and to lend such funds to the government rather than to assume the role of entrepreneur.

Besides, it should be remembered that a great deal of the investment in a modern economy, especially in the early years of its development, consists in providing many services which yield no immediate return, e.g., transportation and communication, certain types of financial services, diplomatic and consular services, health services, education, etc. Furthermore, in the early days of development most industrial enterprises involved great risks—greater than the few capitalists, inexperienced in modern industry, were willing to take.

It does not appear, however, that the government assumed most of its economic functions for ideological reasons. It was simply forced, in the furtherance of national interests, to undertake the establishment of new enterprises and to assume the connected risks. Thus, during the 1870's the government acted as entrepreneur in building and operating cotton-spinning mills, took over the economic enterprises of the shogunate and the daimyos and re-equipped them (chiefly arsenals), imported textile machinery and sold it to private interests on the installment plan, and established silk-reeling mills, tile and cement works, shipyards, powder mills, and other industries (9, pp. 27–30). As early as "1872 there were at least 200 foreign technical experts in the employment of the Government" (9, p. 28).

As fast as these enterprises (except those primarily of military importance) became self-supporting they were sold on favorable terms to private interests, often with guarantees of income on investment until the enterprise became profitable. Even though the government was continually selling enterprises to private interests, in 1880 it still owned 3 shipyards, 51 merchant ships, 5 munitions works, 52 other factories, 10 mines, 75 miles of railways, and a telegraph system (9, p. 30). Up to 1900, in fact, almost all the Western-type enterprises were established by the government and, generally, were operated by it until the risks were so reduced that private interests were willing and anxious to take them over at bargain prices.

The government also aided actively in the development of those financial institutions needed by a modern economy. The operation of these institutions, like that of industrial enterprises, was soon placed in the hands of private interests; but the government retained sufficient control over them to insure that national interests, as it interpreted them, would be adequately served. Allen considers that the "financial foundations" laid during the period 1881–1914 were of vital importance to Japan's rapid economic development after that time. Many other students of Japan's modern economic development also regard the astute handling of her financial affairs, both those of the government and those of private interests, as a factor of prime importance in Japan's economic growth. It seems almost certain that if the government had not assumed leadership and control in the development of her financial institutions, they would have contributed much less to the country's economic development than they actually did.

Another way in which the government aided economic development was to allow, and even to encourage, many types of business organizations which were more or less monopolistic. Some of these may have kept the prices of certain goods at artificial levels, but on the whole they probably contributed substantially to Japan's rapid economic growth. For example, the export associations which were organized prevented competition between Japanese producers in foreign markets and also established standards of quality so that Japanese goods would not come into disrepute. Besides, they often made it possible for many small producers to market some of their products abroad.

Thus, the government of Japan has been closely associated with all aspects of the development of the economy from the time of the Restoration, but, except for certain important military enterprises, railways, communications, and a few other services, it has not continued to operate the enterprises it established for any length of time. It continued somewhat longer to take risks and to pay subsidies in certain enterprises it considered essential to national interests, and it has never ceased to exercise considerable control over the economy as a whole.

This close relationship between the government and the economy should be borne in mind, for it has been, and still is, very important. It may be regarded as marking the chief difference between the locus of control in Japan's economy and that of most Western peoples prior to the rise of fascism and nazism. This control of the economy by the government also made it relatively easy for the military to take over economic control when it reached a position of great political influence.

WEAKENING OF TRADITION

The reforms which were carried through in the first few years after the Restoration have been referred to as proof that there was already a substantial weakening of the power of tradition at the time of the Restoration. However, traditionalism was probably as strong in Japan at that time as it is now in most of the underdeveloped countries of Asia, and possibly even stronger. Even so, it was not until about thirty years later that Japan's economy began to expand rather rapidly. Moreover, the intellectual ferment at work in Japan in the few decades preceding the overthrow of the shogunate had centered around the study of Japanese history. While this had helped, no doubt, to develop the feeling of national pride and national unity, it had not been as favorable to the preparation of a background of thought, or a climate of opinion, which would be receptive to rapid economic change as the long period of enlightenment in Europe preceding 1750. In addition, there had been no indigenous development of science. The speed with which traditionalism could be weakened sufficiently to permit rapid economic development depended also in part on the ability of the new leaders themselves and on their skill in making better use of the energy of former feudal retainers by providing them with opportunities to regain a new and satisfactory social status. The masses of the people, the farmers, were not expected to accept new and strange ideas quickly; in fact, it was considered that they would be most helpful if allowed to proceed in their accustomed ways —except for being encouraged to improve their production—since they could be taxed more heavily if they did not acquire unreasonable ideas about better living too soon.

EDUCATION

The revival of interest in Japanese history noted above helped not only to revive pride in things Japanese but also to gain respect for the man of learning. This latter result was of great benefit when a national system of education was established. The very fact that Japan, at the Restoration, had nothing that could properly be called a national system of education meant that it was not necessary to graft education in modern knowledge onto a traditional system that scorned such knowledge. The acquiring of a modern education could easily be presented as a patriotic endeavor on the part of the individual and as a service to the Emperor. Supplying the means for acquiring such an education became a patriotic duty of the new government. It was not long before many elementary and secondary schools were established and the system was rapidly extended. Technical schools and universities were soon added. Many students were sent abroad, both to prepare for work in the new educational institutions of Japan and to acquire knowledge and experience in Western industry and business. Many of these institutions were given the prefix "Imperial," to indicate their national character and also to show that they were a manifestation of the Emperor's desire for the people to make use of them. The rapid spread of modern education in Japan was one of the remarkable achievements of the Restoration and a basic factor in the rapid economic development of the country.

TRANSPORTATION AND COMMUNICATION

As we have seen, the requirement that the feudal lords live much of the time in Tokyo had made necessary a considerable amount of travel for them and their retainers, and the transportation of considerable amounts of goods to the capital. This had led to some improvement of the roads, especially those leading to Tokyo. It had also led to some improvement in the water transport of certain bulky goods, chiefly food and raw materials. But land transport remained very slow and costly; water transport was also slow (though less costly), for the shogun's prohibition against building sailing ships large enough to engage in foreign commerce had also had a harmful effect on domestic trade. Allen says that in 1870 the tonnage of the mercantile marine was only 1,500 (9, p. 30). This probably does not include the small sailing ships and fishing boats that existed in every coastal village. In any event, it is clear that in 1870 Japan had no transportation adequate for any substantial amount of domestic commerce, and no ships suitable for foreign commerce. She was entirely dependent upon foreign vessels for her foreign trade, the total of which (exports and imports) was valued at only 26 million silver yen in 1868. Communications, of course, were in the same undeveloped state as transport. It is not exaggerating to say that the building of a modern system of transport and communications had to start from scratch.

HEALTH CONDITIONS

Very little is known definitely about the health conditions prevailing in Japan in 1870. What little evidence is available is indirect. It appears, as was noted above, that Japan's population had been increasing rather slowly during the three or four decades preceding the overthrow of the shogunate. In general, this would lead the student of population to believe that the death rate had been slightly declining during this period. This seems reasonable, since, as mentioned in the preceding chapter, it is likely that some slight improvements in agriculture were taking place. It is possible, of course, that there had been some increase in the birth rate, but this is less likely. There can be no doubt that between 1872 and 1910 the population grew fairly steadily and at a slowly increasing rate. But it was not until the decade 1910–20 that what we think of today as public health work really began to take hold, and even then the progress in reducing the death rate was quite slow until after World War II.

The points of most interest here regarding health work in Japan are: (1) There was no public health service at the time of the Restoration, and apparently there was little demand for such service for the next three or four decades. (2) The death rate remained quite high and declined but slowly, so that the growth of population was slow and probably did not exceed 1 per cent per year (10 per 1,000) until after 1900. (3) By the time the health services began to supplement the effects of the rising level of living, i.e., around 1920, the birth rate had begun to decline. Thus, even when Japan's population was growing fairly rapidly during the two decades preceding World War II, the rate was substantially lower than it now is in a number of the underdeveloped countries of South and East Asia.

The relatively slow growth of Japan's population during the first four or five decades of her modern economic development was a distinct advantage to her in building a modern economy. If Japan had had a 50 per cent to 100 per cent higher rate of population growth, it would have interfered seriously with her ability to accumulate capital, to expand her educational facilities for training an adequate personnel for the new economy, to meet her needs for foreign exchange, and to develop the financial institutions and agencies essential to the efficient operation of a modern economy. It is possible, therefore, that the slower rate of population growth in Japan, from 1870 to 1910 or thereabouts, as compared with the rate in India, and perhaps China, today, more than offset certain advantages these latter countries may now possess favoring the rapid development of their economies.

TECHNICAL ASSISTANCE

When Japan began her economic modernization, there was no such thing as free technical aid to underdeveloped countries. On the contrary, there was a rather widespread feeling in the more developed countries that knowledge about methods of production and forms of business organization should not be shared with the less developed countries. It was necessary for Japan not only to finance the development of a new educational system in order to train a body of men in science and engineering, but also to meet *all* expenses connected with bringing in foreign experts and teachers as well as *all* the costs of sending her own people abroad for study. Providing the technical personnel that was needed—both to start a number of new enterprises and to train the Japanese to take over such work—was a severe drain on the small amount of foreign exchange Japan earned through foreign trade during the early years of her economic revolution. Japan was at a considerable disadvantage in this respect compared with the underdeveloped countries today.

NATURAL RESOURCES

A Western-style economic development in any country depends to a significant degree upon the natural resources available. Japan's agricultural resources have been discussed above. Here we are concerned with mineral, water power, and forestry resources.

For a small country, Japan contains a large variety of minerals. However, only three of modern industry's major minerals—coal, copper, and sulphur—are found in relatively self-sufficient quantities.

As regards coal, an important reservation is required. For metallurgical uses requiring coke, Japanese coal must be mixed about one-half with imported coal of better quality. Japan's coal reserves are estimated at about 20,000 million tons or more, while her present production is only about 43 million tons annually. There are also considerable reserves of lignite, for which there is little demand as yet. Thus for all purposes except those requiring metallurgical coke, Japan appears to have adequate coal to last for several decades. On the other hand, Japan has comparatively little petroleum and depends largely on imports for liquid fuels and for oils.

Iron ore.—Of the most important of all metals, iron ore, Japan has only small amounts which are now usable. Most of the ore she possesses is of such poor quality that comparatively little is mined except under pressure of necessity. About 80 per cent of all the iron ore used at present is being imported.

Nonferrous metals.—Japan has rather large reserves of copper, and at present exports of copper are of considerable importance. However, it probably will not be long, perhaps fifteen to twenty-five years, before significant imports of copper will be needed. Zinc and chromite, although of small importance compared with copper, appear to be adequate for Japan's own uses for some years to come. Gold and silver are also probably adequate for industrial uses, but these uses are relatively unimportant. On the other hand, Japan must depend on imports for a large part of her lead, bauxite, manganese, molyb-

denum, nickel, platinum, tin, tungsten, cobalt, vanadium, and magnesium. The alternative, possible in a few cases, is to produce these
metals from inferior ores at a very high cost.

Water power.—Fortunately, Japan has a relatively large amount of
dependable water power because of the favorable distribution of
the annual rainfall (see Maps 3*a* and 3*b*). It is said to amount to about
20 million kilowatts (337, p. 8). About 8 million kilowatts are already
developed. This constitutes more than three-fifths of the total generating capacity of the country. Since the hydroplants already in operation are those cheapest to install, it is probable that the increase
in generating capacity in the future will come more from thermal
plants and, on the whole, will be more expensive. But, even so, Japan
should have no shortage of power in the near future.

Atomic power.—No official information seems to have been made
public yet regarding the availability of the raw materials needed for
the development of atomic power. From time to time, however, newspaper items hint that significant amounts of uranium have been
discovered.

Building materials.—The minerals commonly used for construction,
aside from iron, are relatively abundant in Japan, as they are in most
countries. The supplies of limestone, clay, and gypsum are adequate
to meet the needs for brick, cement, and building stone for an indefinite time, while sand and gravel are abundant everywhere.

From the standpoint of her mineral resources Japan must be regarded, on the whole, as a have-not country, although she is not as
badly off as some countries in this respect.

Forests.—Japan's forests occupy about four times the area of her
cultivated land—over 61 million acres—and furnish a very large share
of her building material, especially for houses. They also supply large
quantities of charcoal, which is used chiefly in the home for cooking
and, by those who can afford it, for some heat in the winter months.
Very little of the land that is now forested can be brought into
tillage, since it is mostly rough and mountainous (see Map 5). The
forests also supply large amounts of the wood pulp used in making
paper and rayon fiber, although Japan has imported substantial quantities of pulp for some years.

ACCUMULATION OF CAPITAL

It is believed that at the Restoration approximately 40 per cent of
the agricultural produce came into the hands of about 5 to 6 per cent

of the population, chiefly the feudal lords and their retainers, and that it was almost the only source of savings and investment in the early days of Japan's modern development. This 40 per cent constituted almost all the recurrent income which could be taxed. Indeed, if one can judge from the taxes imposed on nonagricultural economic activities, it was almost twenty-five years after the Restoration—about 1890–95—before Japanese industry and commerce became productive enough to make a substantial contribution to investment funds. The government was probably lenient in taxing industry, both because of favoritism and because business profits, as a rule, were quickly reinvested. The government also borrowed some specie from the rich merchants and exported it to help cover the foreign-exchange deficits, part of which had been incurred through the purchase of capital goods abroad (9, p. 32). No considerable foreign borrowings were made until after the war with China (1894–95), which proved to the Japanese leaders and to the world at large that Japan now had a fairly efficient modern army. As a result, she felt more secure in borrowing rather heavily abroad. These borrowings added appreciably to Japan's industrial capital at that time.

At about this time, 1890–95, private savings also appear to have become significant as a source of funds that could be used for economic investment. Lockwood gives figures showing a partial estimate of gross private savings for the period 1893–1937 (180, p. 252). For the first ten years of this period (1893–1902), the annual average, in millions of yen, was 103; in the second ten years, 315; in the third ten years (1913–22), 1,518; in the fourth ten years, 1,263; and in the final five years (1933–37), 3,355. It is clear that even in the mid-1890's private savings were sufficient to contribute substantially to industrial investment and that they were rapidly gaining in importance. For the twenty-five years 1913–37, according to these partial estimates, private savings averaged about 15.3 per cent of the total national income. Thus it was about forty years from the time the modernization of Japan began before a rather high rate of private savings (15 per cent of the annual national income) became effective. Lockwood is careful to point out that gross private savings is by no means the same as investment in economic development, and that the evidence turned up by all efforts to ascertain the capital accumulated and invested in Japan must remain inconclusive, both as regards the actual amount of money available for investment and the proportion of the national income invested at different periods (180, pp. 252, 264).

It is quite possible that the relatively slow rate at which investment capital accumulated from 1872 to about 1910 resulted in a more efficient use of capital than would have followed a faster and easier accumulation. The relatively slow accumulation allowed time for other critical factors in economic development—the education and training of scientists and technicians, the building of a reasonably adequate transportation system, and, above all, the weakening of traditionalism—to become effective and thus to contribute more fully to the efficient use of capital.

SOME OTHER FACTORS OF IMPORTANCE

Allen mentions several other factors characteristic of Japan at the time of the Restoration and of importance in her economic development (9, pp. 156–57). Though some of these are implicit in what has been said above, they will bear repeating. He stresses the unity in national feeling which made for a relatively easy acceptance of the national aims of the Restoration government. This no doubt derived in large measure from the traditional reverence felt for the Emperor by all the people, a feeling cultivated assiduously by the new national government. Allen also points out that the unity in language and culture contributed importantly to national unity. The ready acquiescence of the people to governmental requests and directives also facilitated national economic development. Then, too, Japan had a considerable number of skilled workers who, although they were not trained in the use of machines, were careful and disciplined workmen who could learn rapidly to use and to maintain the new power equipment. In addition, certain accidents, such as the outbreak of serious silkworm disease among the silk producers of Europe and a rapidly increased demand for silk in the United States, helped Japan at a time when she greatly needed foreign exchange.

Almost every student of modern Japan's economy calls attention not only to her development of modern large-scale production enterprises but also to the truly vast number of small-scale, and even tiny, enterprises which were so organized as to contribute substantially to the new economy. Even as late as 1930 these small industries still employed over one-half of all the workers whose chief occupation was manufacturing, although it is reasonably certain that many of these workers did not work full time as did those in larger factories, and, because they worked with small capital equipment, they were much less productive. The workers in these small factories contributed only

8.5 per cent of the national income, as compared with 18.7 per cent contributed by the smaller number of workers in the larger factories. But the fact is that Japan, by integrating small-scale production into the economy, has been able to keep a very large number of persons employed in industry with a comparatively small capital expenditure. These workers probably live better than those engaged in agriculture, forestry, and fishing, though not as well as those in the more highly capitalized enterprises. The maintenance of these small-scale factories has been a stabilizing and strengthening element in the Japanese economy throughout its modern development. This fact should be given far more attention by the underdeveloped countries of Asia that are now striving to make better use of their resources, both human and natural, and that have very limited amounts of capital available.

EVIDENCES OF ECONOMIC PROGRESS

Industrial employment.—Obviously, the decline in the proportion of the population engaged in agriculture (see chap. v) was accompanied by an increase in the proportion engaged in industry ("industry" being used to include all nonagricultural employment except forestry and fishing). When the first census was taken in 1920, 45.1 per cent of the gainfully occupied persons were engaged in industry. This is probably about twice the proportion so engaged in 1872 (22–25 per cent). By 1930 the nonagricultural workers constituted 50 per cent of all the gainfully employed, and by 1940 their proportion had risen to 56 per cent (180, p. 465). This last increase was due to the rapid expansion of war industries and to the growth in the military forces that removed great numbers of men from the "gainfully occupied" class.

In the 1920 census industrial employment, in the broad sense, was broken into several categories. Mining at that time employed only 1.6 per cent of all occupied persons; it fell to 1.1 per cent in 1930, but rose to 1.8 per cent in 1940 when Japan found it necessary to produce more raw materials at home from inferior natural resources. By 1920 the largest of the nonagricultural categories was manufacturing and construction, which gave principal employment to 19.0 per cent of all occupied persons. This proportion increased slightly to 20.0 per cent in 1930; then, under the stimulus of war needs, it leaped to 25.0 in 1940. Commerce, transportation, and communication, combined, employed 17.1, 19.9, and 19.2 per cent in these same years. Government and professional workers accounted for 4.6 per cent, 6.0 per cent, and

6.8 per cent; service workers constituted 2.4 per cent in 1920, 2.7 per cent in 1930, but only 0.2 per cent in 1940 (180, p. 465). These figures on industrial employment give a general picture of the industrial changes which took place in Japan from 1920 to 1940. But they also emphasize the fact that by 1920 Japan had already laid the foundation for a rapid development of manufacturing and commerce.

Increase in production.—The increase in the number of workers in manufacturing was accompanied by a much more rapid increase in the volume of production of manufactures. The index of manufacturing production in 1896–1900 was 35 (1913 = 100). It rose to 64 in the years 1906–10, to 205 in 1921–25, to 410 in 1931–35, and to 631 in 1936–38 (180, p. 117). The increase after 1906–10 is quite remarkable. In certain types of manufactures and services, the rate of growth was even more remarkable than that for the total of manufactures. Thus, in the twenty years 1910–14 to 1930–34, the production of metals and machinery rose from an index of 100 in the earlier period to 410 in the later period (180, p. 115). In chemicals the increase was from 100 to 643, in electricity and gas from 100 to 1,002. Clearly, the big industries which needed large capital investment were going forward by leaps and bounds after 1914 and were not slowed up appreciably by the depression of the 1930's.

This rapid progress in the large-scale heavy industries is also shown very clearly by changes in the relative importance of certain kinds of manufactured goods between 1920 and 1938. In 1920 textiles accounted for 41.2 per cent of the value of all manufactures, while in 1938 they accounted for only 20.3 per cent. Metallics, machines, tools, and chemicals, which accounted for only 32.3 per cent of the value of all manufactures in 1920, contributed 60.8 per cent of the total in 1938 (102, 1943, p. 119; 155, p. 362; 202, pp. 552–53). This change in the relative importance of different types of manufactures in Japan closely resembles the pattern most of the industrialized Western countries followed at an earlier period. But, as a few figures will show, the speed with which Japan accomplished this change was quite remarkable. In 1896 only 26,000 metric tons of pig iron were produced; by 1913 over nine times that amount (243,000 metric tons) was produced. This was more than doubled in the next seven years; this, in turn, was doubled by 1929, and again by 1936. The increase in the production of finished steel was even more impressive: from 69,000 metric tons in 1906 to more than 500,000 in 1920, and a doubling in each following five-year period to 4.5 million in 1936 (9, p. 177).

Coal production rose from 5.0 million metric tons in 1895 to 21.3 in 1913, to 31.5 in 1925, and to 45.3 in 1937. The generating capacity for electricity (in thousands of kilowatts) was only 504 in 1913, but rose to 2,768 in 1925 and to 7,276 in 1937.

In transport, the story is the same—a relatively slow growth until about 1895–1900, and then a very rapid growth. There were no railways in 1870. By 1887 there were only 640 miles. This figure was more than tripled (2,100 miles) by 1894. In each of the next four decades the increase averaged about 3,000 miles, bringing the total in 1934 to 14-500 miles. The gross tonnage of steamships and motor ships (in thousands of tons) rose from 26 in 1872 to 143 in 1890, to 657 in 1904, to 1,514 in 1913, to 3,496 in 1925, and to 3,812 in 1934 (9, p. 178).

In a very real sense, all of Japan's industrial development up to 1940 has been summed up by Colin Clark in terms of real product per man-year (78, pp. 136–37). In 1887 this product was 100, and there was almost no change up to 1897 (101). By 1908, however, it had risen to 134, by 1918 to 168, by 1928 to 386, and by 1940 to 600. Clark also finds a fairly close relationship between this increased productivity per man and the savings per head for persons-in-work, which increased from 89 international units of fixed value in 1913–19 to 155 in 1938. This is very significant from the standpoint of capital formation and confirms the indirect evidence of rapid capital growth found in the rapid increase of heavy industry and services after 1920.

Level of living.—There is much uncertainty regarding improvement in the level of living of the mass of the Japanese people before about 1914. This is especially true with respect to the agricultural population. Allen gives data on the production and consumption of rice from 1880–84 to 1935–37 which show a rapid increase in total production, and in production per acre, up to 1915–19 (9, p. 171). At the same time, there was a fairly steady increase in per capita consumption, from about 4 bushels (0.80 koku) in 1880–84 to about 5.6 bushels in 1915–19; this consumption declined a little after 1925–29, in spite of a rapid increase in imports after 1920–24. Lockwood thinks that between 1914 and 1919 "the evidence indicates a 13 per cent rise in per capita food supply from home production and imports, as well as some diversification and improvement in diet, clothing, and minor items in family budgets" (180, p. 41). Allen finds that the real income of industrial workers in 1929 was 50 to 60 per cent above that in 1914 (9, pp. 106 ff.), and Lockwood thinks that real civilian consumption rose about 20 per cent from 1930 to 1936 (180, p. 74). Since population grew only about 9 per cent in this interval, it would appear that the level of living rose substantially during that time also.

The increase in the real income of the agricultural population remains obscure. Most writers agree, however, that the increase was not as large as it was among industrial workers. Allen thinks, nevertheless, that "even the peasants, especially those in the neighborhood of the industrial centres, were better off [in 1930] than they had been in 1914, except in bad years" (9, p. 106).

Another evidence of substantial improvement in the level of living is indirect, but highly convincing. After 1870 the rate of population growth increased slowly for forty or fifty years, and this must have been due chiefly to a decline in the death rate. This decline, in turn, must have resulted from better economic conditions, since public health services and Western medicine had not yet reached any significant proportion of the people. Improved health services spread slowly over Japan after about 1920, but did not become strikingly effective until after 1946 (see chap. iv).

CHAPTER VII

JAPAN: MODERN INDUSTRIAL
DEVELOPMENT—Continued

FOREIGN TRADE

Japan's foreign trade was very small at the time of the Restoration, as was noted above. The decision to modernize her industry made it necessary, almost at once, to secure an increasing amount of foreign exchange with which to buy machinery, to hire experts, and to send students abroad. Some of it could be borrowed from the rich merchants in the form of specie, but this could provide only a small part of what was needed, even in the first few years. Besides, the development of the textile industry soon made the import of cotton necessary, and every forward step in industrial development increased the need for machinery and trained technicians. These growing needs served as a strong spur to the expansion of foreign trade. At the same time, increasing foreign trade presented many serious difficulties to a relatively late comer in the field. A brief statement of Japan's trade accomplishments will assist in understanding how she became an important industrial power and how she became increasingly dependent on this trade.

Foreign trade, 1870–1900.—During the thirty years between 1870 and 1900, the character of Japan's foreign trade was about what would be expected of an industrially backward country compelled to allow imports to enter practically free of duty under the terms of its early treaties with the Western powers. In the early 1870's tea and silk products (raw silk predominating) accounted for almost two-thirds of Japan's total exports. These agricultural products required a comparatively small amount of processing, which could be carried on near the place of production in small units. In 1870–71, Japan's exports were valued at only 16.3 million yen, and her imports at 27.8 million yen (Table 5). In 1880 the same products still predominated, although fish and seaweed, camphor, copper, and coal had become of some importance; in 1880–81, the value of exports had grown to 29.7 million yen, while imports had increased to 33.9 million yen. In the next twenty years, 1880–1900, silk held its own and tea dropped into a minor position, but most of the other agricultural products and raw materials increased proportionally; thus, although the same groups of products still accounted for almost three-fourths of all exports, in 1900 the proportions were somewhat different. Between 1880 and 1900 the total value of both exports and imports increased over sevenfold.

During this period Japan imported chiefly manufactured and semi-manufactured goods. The only important raw material imported in the early 1870's was raw cotton, which constituted only 3 to 4 per cent of all imports. In 1880 the situation was practically unaltered. By 1900,

TABLE 5

AVERAGE ANNUAL VALUE (IN MILLIONS OF YEN) OF EXPORT
AND IMPORT TRADE, JAPAN, 1870–1938

Year	Total	Exports	Imports
1938*................	5,353.0	2,690.0	2,663.0
1937†................	6,958.0	3,175.0	3,783.0
1930–31†...........	2,699.3	1,308.4	1,390.9
1920–21†...........	3,575.8	1,600.6	1,975.2
1910–11‡...........	941.9	452.9	489.0
1900–1901§.........	499.9	228.4	271.5
1890–91§...........	140.4	68.1	72.3
1880–81§...........	63.6	29.7	33.9
1870–71§...........	44.1	16.3	27.8

* Source: 155, 1940, p. 450.   ‡ Source: 152, 1916, p. 86.
† Source: 148, 1937, p. 76.   § Source: 154, 1904, pp. 448–49.

however, a definite change had set in. In that year, raw cotton constituted one-fifth of all the imports, and iron goods, of which a considerable proportion was for use in construction, amounted to almost 10 per cent of the total. By that time cotton goods imports had ceased to be of much importance, but a large variety of manufactured and partly manufactured goods, including machinery, constituted well over one-third of all imports in 1903–4. If allowance is made for the fact that the imports of foodstuffs in 1903–4 were unusually large because of poor crops, the proportion of all imports which consisted of manufactured and partly manufactured goods was about 47 per cent, and the proportion of raw materials was about 40 per cent.

Foreign trade, 1900–1938.—After 1900, Japan's foreign trade increased rapidly. Both exports and imports practically doubled in value between 1900 and 1910 and, because the price level was quite stable at that time, it may be assumed that the volume increased at about the same rate. In the decade including World War I, from 1910–11 to 1920–21, Japan's foreign trade more than tripled in value, but rising prices account for a substantial portion of this increase. After allowance is made for price changes, it appears probable that exports increased in volume by about 60 per cent and imports by about 90 per cent. The gain in volume of exports was made almost entirely in the years 1910–15; the gain in imports continued throughout the decade, but was faster in the years 1915–20 (see Table 5).

During the next decade, 1919–21 to 1929–31, the volume of trade again rose rapidly, exports by about 77 per cent and imports by almost 50 per cent. In the case of imports, most of this increase took place before 1925, while exports increased rather steadily throughout the decade. Due to the great decline in prices, however, the value of both exports and imports dropped sharply.

The changing character of foreign trade.—Japan's growing dependence on foreign trade is also shown clearly by the increase in the proportions of the total textile production which were exported. In the years between 1920–22 and 1935–36 the proportion of raw silk exported rose from about 57 per cent to 73 per cent, and of cotton fabrics from 34 per cent to 55 per cent (242, pp. 220–21). The proportions of other exported textiles, although lower, were high enough in most cases to be of great importance to the Japanese economy. A rather large proportion of the Japanese production of bicycles and tires, electric light bulbs, toys, rubber shoes, and light metal wares was also exported, although no exact figures are available. Clearly, a number of Japan's important industries were becoming more and more dependent on foreign markets. In 1935 Japan's total industrial production was valued at 15,255 million yen, and her total exports were valued at 2,499 million yen, or about 16 per cent of the total. By 1937 the effects of the trade war (see below) and the increasing preparations for war had reduced the percentage of exports to 14.9.

The change in the general character of the goods involved in Japan's foreign trade after 1900 is shown in Table 6. In 1903–4 Japan's exports consisted chiefly (47 per cent) of partly manufactured goods, with raw silk and cotton yarn predominating. Wholly manufactured goods intended largely for consumption constituted only about 30 per cent of her exports, while raw materials and foodstuffs constituted about 9 and 12 per cent, respectively. Between 1903–4 and 1910–11 (1911 is the year in which Japan finally achieved complete tariff autonomy) there was not much change in these proportions, although the Russo-Japanese War had intervened. By 1920–21, however, a marked shift had taken place. Partly manufactured goods constituted a little less than 40 per cent; wholly manufactured goods had risen to first place and amounted to almost 46 per cent, while raw materials and foodstuffs together had declined to 13.6 per cent and were of decreasing importance. This trend, with some minor fluctuations, continued until the

TABLE 6

PER CENT DISTRIBUTION OF FOREIGN TRADE, BY CLASSES OF
COMMODITIES, JAPAN, 1903–37 (ANNUAL AVERAGE)*

YEAR	TOTAL	FOOD-STUFFS	RAW MATERIALS	GOODS PARTLY MANUFAC-TURED	GOODS WHOLLY MANUFAC-TURED	MISCEL-LANEOUS
			Exports			
1936–37........	100.0	7.7	4.4	26.2	58.9	2.8
1930–31........	100.0	8.8	4.2	36.2	46.8	4.0
1926–27........	100.0	7.2	6.9	43.0	41.7	1.2
1920–21........	100.0	6.8	6.8	39.4	45.6	1.4
1917–18........	100.0	10.7	5.2	41.6	40.4	2.1
1913–14........	100.0	10.3	7.9	51.9	28.8	1.1
1910–11........	100.0	11.4	8.9	48.4	30.3	1.0
1903–4.........	100.0	11.8	9.2	47.0	29.6	2.4
			Imports			
1936–37........	100.0	7.5	57.8	23.1	10.8	0.8
1930–31........	100.0	13.2	54.5	15.0	16.2	1.1
1926–27........	100.0	14.8	55.8	15.5	13.3	0.6
1920–21........	100.0	11.2	50.4	21.0	16.7	0.8
1917–18........	100.0	7.9	52.5	28.8	10.1	0.7
1913–14........	100.0	15.0	51.5	16.8	16.0	0.7
1910–11........	100.0	9.9	47.4	18.7	23.4	0.6
1903–4.........	100.0	31.3	31.0	13.6	22.7	1.4

* Source: 1920–37 from 148, 1937, p. 77; 1903–18 from 350, pp. 5–6. These percentages may not be exactly comparable because it was necessary to use these two different sources to complete the series, but, even so, there is no doubt of the trend.

attack on China (1937). In 1936–37 the proportion of wholly manufactured goods had risen to almost 59 per cent of all exports, and partly manufactured goods had fallen to 26 per cent. At that time, raw materials had declined to about 4.4 per cent, and although foodstuffs were slightly above the level of 1920–21 (7.7 per cent), these two classes together had declined to 12.1 per cent of the total. The change in the character of imports during this period is equally marked and clearly indicates a growing industrial maturity.

Japan's imports of foodstuffs, as a proportion of all her imports, have fluctuated rather widely in the past, depending considerably on the size of the home harvest in any given year. Thus, in 1903–4 foodstuffs constituted over 31 per cent of all imports, while in 1910–11 the percentage dropped to 10. Such fluctuations affect the proportions of other types of imports from year to year, but, even so, the data in Table 6 show that the proportion of imports consisting of raw materials increased rather consistently from possibly 40 per cent in 1903–4 (allowing for normal food imports of about 11 per cent) to almost 58 per cent in 1936–37. Except for 1936–37, the proportion of partly manufactured goods declined after 1917–18, and the proportion of wholly manufactured imports showed no clear trend after 1913–14.

This brief description of the development of Japan's foreign trade up to World War II clearly shows not only that it was becoming a more important factor in the total economy, but that Japan was becoming more and more dependent on the import of raw materials and the export of wholly maufactured products. It is important to realize that, because of the scarcity and/or poor quality of her own natural resources, the increasing volume and proportion of wholly manufactured goods which Japan exported depended in large measure upon her ability to import an increasing quantity and variety of raw materials.

Conditions favoring foreign trade.—In the development of foreign trade, as in the development of industry, the Japanese government played an important role. In the organization of the banking system special facilities were provided for the financing of foreign trade, which made it possible for Japanese exporters to meet the credit needs of their customers. At the same time, these financial institutions provided much valuable knowledge regarding possible new markets and the financial needs for operation in these markets. Without such specialized services, a newcomer in international trade would make headway but slowly in the face of competition with well-established firms which already had this experienced financial service. But this was only one of the aids to foreign trade established by, or with the encouragement of, the government.

Sometimes an industry was encouraged to form an association of producers, or of distributors, or of buyers of raw materials, or of exporters, or of all these; such associations were not only officially sanctioned but were given broad powers of control over the industry as a whole. Obviously, a buying agency of this character had a great advantage in bargaining with a large number of independent sellers—

for example, dealers in cotton, scattered all over the globe. Or, if it were a selling agency, it could cut the costs of distributing the goods below the level likely to be attained by any individual producer, even a large one. Such organizations could also help enforce standards of quality, allot export quotas to the several manufacturers, and furnish much useful trade information. They also could assemble the products of the many small producers without sufficient products to justify seeking a market on their own account, or those who produced only particular parts for a finished product, e.g., bicycles. The size and monopolistic structure of these organizations enabled them, in many cases, to bypass the usual selling agencies in the customer countries and thus establish a system of distribution not burdened with the heavy costs and the traditional inertia of the existing system.

Actually, the organization and operation of trade associations, and their relation to the government, were not so simple as these statements may seem to imply. Although these relationships between the government and business varied greatly from industry to industry, there was in general a very effective working relationship of a kind which had not existed in the West since the days of the monopolies of the great trading companies. The advantage of this Japanese organization for foreign trade lay chiefly in the military-like rapidity with which it could adjust itself to new conditions arising in foreign markets.

No close examination of the differences in business organization between Japan and the United States and Europe is needed to show that the semimonopolistic character of much Japanese business, and the semigovernmental authority granted to the trade associations, gave Japanese business certain important advantages in the development of foreign trade. But many other factors were also important.

In addition to mere proximity, the Japanese had a cultural affinity with the other peoples of Asia, as the British had to Europeans and to the peoples from Europe who had gone to America and elsewhere. This cultural affinity became increasingly important as Japanese exports came more and more to be those products of industry destined for personal consumption. The Japanese were in a better position than were the Europeans to adapt their goods to the needs of the other peoples of Asia. They realized that most Orientals could not buy high-priced Western goods, and that they must have cheaper cotton cloth, bicycles, electric lamps, shoes, and a hundred other items if they were to buy any such goods at all. Japan's businessmen saw that there was a new market, with a broader base, to be opened up if these goods could be supplied at prices within the means of larger and larger groups of people in Asia. They understood this market because it was developing in much the same way that their home market had developed, and they were equipped psychologically and industrially to supply it with the kinds of goods it could absorb.

The abundance and docility of Japan's labor supply were also important factors in the growth of her foreign trade. It has been shown above (chap. iv) that Japan's population was growing, although rather slowly, for several decades before the Restoration, at a somewhat increasing rate up to about 1920, and at a somewhat higher and fairly steady rate thereafter until World War II. This meant that by 1910 and thereafter several hundred thousand young workers were entering the labor market each year, in excess of the number of older workers who were leaving it by death or retirement (19, p. 192). This number of younger workers was increasing steadily. Until 1920 or a little later, the great majority of these workers had been raised on farms and were available for many types of nonagricultural work at approximately the standards of return to which farmers and their families were accustomed. Unlike European peasants during most of the nineteenth century, when their numbers were growing fairly rapidly, they had little opportunity to emigrate to America or, indeed, to go anywhere else in any considerable numbers. They could stay on the farm, making at best a very meager living, or they could go into nonagricultural occupations where they did a little better. The latter was naturally the alternative chosen by a great many of them.

The reader should also bear in mind that even as late as 1930 more than one-half of the persons employed in manufacturing in Japan were employed in factories having fewer than five workers. Since many of these small factories were located in small cities and towns in the agricultural areas, the wages paid, while generally better than those earned by agricultural workers, were lower than wages in the larger industrial establishments in the cities. In this situation real wages, although rising, remained low as compared with European wages. Hence goods which could be produced with fair efficiency in small factories could be produced quite cheaply—especially if labor costs constituted a high proportion of the total cost of production. This was of great advantage, of course, in the expansion of Japan's foreign trade.

Another of Japan's advantages in foreign trade was her development of trained personnel. From 1880 onward, Japan had been educating an increasing number of scientists, engineers, and technicians. At the same time, the number of experienced managers had been growing steadily. Once a few thousand experienced engineers and managers and a few hundred thousand skilled industrial workers were available, the job of adding to these numbers as needed became comparatively easy. By about 1914 Japan had reached the point where the industrial personnel of the country could be increased as rapidly as needed, even for the quick development of heavy industry and chemicals. This made possible a rapid increase in the variety of goods Japan could produce to meet the needs of foreign trade as well as her own increasing need for steel and other heavy goods. But even with the increase of heavy industry in large factories, the small factory held its own in a remarkable manner, and the wages of trained workers in many kinds of manufacturing remained relatively low, although the level of living was rising.

Finally, Japan was in an excellent position to trade with most Asiatic countries to their great mutual advantage. She needed iron ore, coking coal, tin, cotton, rubber, soybeans (for food and fertilizer), the alloy minerals, petroleum and its products, bauxite, potash and phosphates (fertilizers), and a hundred other essentials. Many of the Asiatic countries possessed some of these raw materials and were anxious to trade them for manufactured goods, which they were still either not producing at all or were producing in inadequate amounts. In many cases, European countries either did not need these raw materials from Asia, or could buy them nearer home and thus keep transportation costs lower. Hence, the Japanese market for raw materials was a boon to other Asian countries, just as their need for new and cheap types of manufactured goods was a boon to Japan. Japan's exploitation of these Asian markets needs a little further explanation. Japan expanded her foreign trade in Asia during the period 1920–35 not merely by taking markets away from the European countries; she also developed markets for new types of manufactured items by supplying goods that could be sold at prices which made them available to people with very low incomes. Such articles as rubber shoes, cheap cotton and rayon goods, light electrical goods, bicycles, and a variety of light metal articles and toys, found a wider market than might have been anticipated, because the Japanese were able to price them so that a growing number of urban workers all over Asia could afford them. The growing export of such articles goes far to explain the increase in the volume of Japan's exports, from 120 in 1916 (1913 = 100) to 233 in 1929 (9, p. 180); at the same time, to be sure, Japan was expanding her trade in heavier types of goods, and in goods of higher quality, in competition with other countries.

The trade war of the 1930's.—The depression of the 1930's brought a severe drop in the value of Japanese exports, but the volume continued to increase (Table 5). However, the value of imports fell even more than did the value of exports, while the volume of imports, which did not change much between 1925 and 1930, did not increase nearly as fast after 1930 as did the volume of exports. From the standpoint of our interest here, the chief effect of the depression was to intensify the struggle for foreign markets among those countries which were highly dependent upon trade. This struggle set off a real trade war, which was waged with political weapons as much as with economic weapons —political weapons which were made possible, as the Japanese saw it, only because much of South and East Asia, with which they had a large trade, was under the political control of Europe. The European colonial authorities, on the other hand, believed, quite naturally, that their own use of political control to maintain trade with the home country, or with other European countries, was justified by the fact that Japanese industry and commerce had long had close ties with the government, which gave them an "unfair" advantage. Thus the colonial authorities, in their view, were only meeting political action with political action, in order to maintain the economic status quo.

In the trade war which followed, many new forms of trade restriction were developed, and many of those already in use were applied more stringently. Trade restrictions were no longer confined largely to import duties. The great colonial powers generally claimed that the new restrictions they imposed were necessitated by the forms of business organization which, though they had long prevailed in Japan, had become increasingly effective as Japan's industrial efficiency increased. The colonial powers felt that the combination of business and government for economic ends was so much more powerful, and was so different from that available to private business enterprises in the West, that private business, unless it were also aided by political measures, could not compete with it.

The chief measures adopted to curb Japanese trade were preferential tariffs and bilateral trade treaties; closely related to these were reciprocity agreements, import quotas, special import duties levied on the goods of countries which had devalued their currencies more than had the receiving country, and a variety of exchange control measures. It is obvious that any or all of these devices could be used to discriminate against the trade of any country, if this were desired, since very few countries can completely balance their trade with any particular country and still get the goods they need; consequently, bilateral treaties, import quotas, and reciprocity agreements can easily be used to curb trade with one country and encourage it with another.

More important than bilateral agreements, however, were trade quotas. Any country or colony could very easily make these quotas operate against Japan by choosing those years, in calculating Japan's quotas, when Japan's trade with the country had not yet become important. This was done by British Malaya (195, pp. 150–51) and the Netherlands East Indies (93, p. 183). India also used a quota system, but coupled it with a variation of the balancing agreement by which the permissible imports of cotton goods were increased in proportion to the increase in the exports of raw cotton to Japan (104, Part II, p. 119). Like the rest of the British Empire, India also gave tariff preference to Empire goods.

Australia used preferential tariffs, import licenses, and quotas to restrict the import of certain types of Japanese goods and, at the same time, tried to maintain exports to Japan at several times the value of her purchases from Japan (*ibid.*, pp. 122–23). Quite naturally, this effort was not successful for any length of time. Australia could not retain the trade advantages of being a member of the British Empire while selling her surplus food and wool in any considerable amounts on the Japanese market.

Most European countries, and the United States, relied chiefly on tariffs to curb imports in the interests of home industry. But the United States was not above juggling specifications in its reciprocity treaties in order to exclude Japanese goods (*ibid.*, pp. 147–48). Both the United States and Great Britain also resorted occasionally to quotas, which were generally arranged through gentlemen's agreements between trade organizations in the two countries rather than by governmental action (*ibid.*, pp. 120–22).

In spite of the restrictions on her trade, Japan managed to maintain a rapid growth in volume of exports through 1935. The increase became slower after 1935; it was clear that Japan was going to have further trouble in the future and that her trade might not only be less profitable but might diminish in value. This inevitably raised serious questions regarding her ability to continue to buy the raw materials she needed. Moreover, several Asiatic countries were increasingly interested in developing their own manufactures.

THE DEVELOPING ECONOMY AND POLITICS

There seems to be no reasonable doubt that Japan's expanding economy, with its growing dependence on foreign trade, and her increasing difficulties in expanding this trade, had a profound influence on her international policies. A very brief description of the three most important steps Japan took to expand her territory will be helpful in understanding the relationship between her modern economic development and her policies of expansion.

The war with China, 1894–95.—Japan's first step in expanding the empire was the war with China, in 1894–95. The outcome proved that Japan had an army strong enough to protect herself and to conquer territory from neighbors who did not have modern armies. Taiwan came immediately under Japanese control, and its economic development was begun almost at once. The area of tilled land was soon increased and better agriculture was introduced, so that by 1905 Taiwan was sending more than 3 million bushels of rice to Japan; in the next thirty years this amount rose to about 23 million, and by 1935–36 about 50 per cent of Taiwan's entire rice crop was exported to Japan (114, p. 55). Sugar production was developed quite rapidly; exports to Japan increased to almost 200 thousand tons in 1909–14 and to an annual average of about 1 million tons by 1937 (155, 1940, p. 537; 174, 1928, p. 70). Other important exports from Taiwan to Japan were sweet potatoes, bananas, and pineapples.

Although Korea came under a measure of Japanese control at the close of the war with China in 1895, it was not closely integrated with Japan as a colony until after the war with Russia in 1904–5. In 1907 Japan's control was substantially extended, and in 1910 it became so complete that Korea was henceforth a colony, in fact if not in law. Under Japanese administration, the crop area was slowly extended, especially the irrigated area; also, the crop yields were improved (115, pp. 94–97), though not to the same extent as those of Japan. By 1920 about 20 per cent of Korea's rice was being sent to Japan, i.e., about 14 to 15 million bushels. By 1936 the amount sent had risen to over 40 per cent of the total crop, or about 35 million bushels. Korea also produced and sent to Japan substantial amounts of cotton and soybeans. In addition, Korea possessed considerable mineral resources—iron ore, coal, sulphur, bauxite, magnesite, graphite, lead, and zinc—and substantial amounts of the alloy minerals molybdenum and tungsten. The exploitation of these resources was only well begun before World War II.

The war with Russia, 1904-5.—The war with Russia was much more costly than the Chinese war had been. However, it left Japan in almost complete control of Korea and with a strong foothold in Manchuria, so that she was able to expand her economic interests in that quarter rather steadily up to 1931, when she took over complete political control.

The seizure of Manchuria.—The seizure of Manchuria by the Japanese military clique in September of 1931 and the establishment of Manchoukuo represented a truly great expansion. About 500,000 square miles were added to its territory, and this additional area was rich both agriculturally and in mineral resources. Although the Japanese had been exploiting a portion of this area to some extent since the war with Russia, their control was limited to a rather narrow zone along the South Manchurian Railway and a leased area in the Kuangtung peninsula including Dairen and Port Arthur. Outside of these areas there was so much banditry and guerilla activity that it was not feasible to exploit the mineral resources by investing heavily in enterprises which could not be easily defended. The reasons for the seizure of Manchuria were, without doubt, many and complex. Some of these reasons probably had little or nothing to do with the economic situation developing in Japan; however, an enumeration of some of the conditions that did have direct economic implications will be useful in understanding the way in which many Japanese looked upon this expansion. Even Japanese who were much opposed to the power which the military clique had acquired over the government were very seriously concerned about Japan's economic future. The chief reasons for this concern were as follows:

1. Japan's population had been gaining steadily for several decades, and by 1930 it had grown to 63.9 million—an increase of approximately 83 per cent since the Restoration. Between 1920 and 1930 it grew faster than it had at any previous time, and there was a strong probability that it would grow even faster in the near future.

2. Japan's agricultural area had ceased to expand about 1920, and it seemed clear that very little future expansion could be expected. Moreover, any expansion would be costly if the land were irrigated for rice, and if it were located in the uplands the yields would be relatively small. Diminishing returns in agriculture had clearly set in.

3. Korea and Taiwan could not long continue to send Japan even

the amounts of foodstuffs they were then sending, because of their limited areas and the rapid growth of their own populations, especially Taiwan's.

4. Japan herself had meager mineral resources, especially for steel making, and those of Korea, while of considerable value, were far from being able to make the empire self-sufficient in heavy industry.

5. Japan was becoming increasingly dependent on foreign trade, and on a kind of trade which demanded the import of more and more raw materials from abroad—cotton, coal, iron ore, etc.

6. There was no international organization which, through the processes of trade, could guarantee Japan—or any other nation—access to the raw materials she needed.

7. Japan had been notably successful in her wars. Korea and Taiwan had cost very little either in lives or money. The foothold in Manchuria had cost more, but the cost still had not been large. This fact was calculated to make the military leaders, at least, more ready to take Manchuria by force from the Chinese, who were quite unable to maintain law and order in this area.

It was quite clear that these conditions were exercising much influence on Japan's policies during the late 1920's and that her economic problems were not unlikely to lead her to undertake the conquest of new territory in the fairly near future (275).

All told, it seemed quite probable that the acquisition of Manchuria would relieve the population pressure that had been building up and would make it possible for the living conditions of the masses to continue to improve, as they had been during the preceding two decades.

THE POSTWAR SITUATION

Industry since World War II.—The industry of Japan suffered greatly during the war. Much of her manufacturing capacity was destroyed by bombing. The whole structure required for foreign trade was wiped out when the financial and diplomatic services abroad were eliminated and her fleet, both military and merchant, was sunk. She had no means of securing the raw materials essential to many of her industries, except as United States policy found it expedient to finance such imports. How essential these imports were, even before the war, has been shown above; but after the war, with no colonies and with Manchuria restored to China, there was no yen bloc within which Japan could operate even if she had had a completely free hand in commercial relations with other nations. In 1954 Japan imported 100 per cent of the cotton she needed (she had done this almost from the beginning of her industrial development), 100 per cent of the wool, 81.9 per cent of the iron ore, 28.4 per cent of the coking coal, 95.2 per cent of the crude oil, 100 per cent of the rubber, 27.3 per cent of the rayon pulp, 100 per cent of the phosphate and potassium (fertilizer) compounds, and 80.2 per cent of the salt (303, 1955, p. 127).

In spite of this extreme and increased dependence on imports of raw materials, Japan has been making a rapid recovery during the past several years. On the basis of prewar production (1934–36 = 100), the index for all manufactures had risen to 189.4 by 1955, for production of electrical energy it had risen to 255.0, and for all industrial activity to 187.9; coal and copper production were about the same as they had been in 1936 (153, 1956, sec. II, p. 6). Part of this recovery resulted from the Korean war and from the very great need of the underdeveloped countries of South and East Asia for capital goods and light consumers' goods which Japan could supply in return for raw materials and food. The rather large reparations which were to be paid to the countries that suffered from Japanese occupation during the war also played a part in this recovery. A big shipbuilding boom has contributed substantially to the recovery of the steel industry. Japan's industrial recovery is again bringing her into competition with the prewar suppliers of manufactured goods to Asia. How much of her present market Japan can retain during the next few years cannot be foretold. But, at best, such great dependence on foreign trade makes for great uncertainties in the national economy and may very easily set off trade wars that will embitter international relations in the years ahead.

Japan may be able, for a few years, to increase her exports sufficiently to pay for her absolutely indispensable imports. However, the latest data seem to indicate that Japan's level of living has not yet returned to the prewar standard, and there is serious question whether it can be brought back to this standard in the near future. Furthermore, even in these years of very rapidly increasing industrial production the number of unemployed workers has been large. The average monthly number of totally unemployed rose from 580,000 in 1954 to 659,000 for the January to October period of 1955 (317, Part I, No. 56-15, p. 4). Unemployment fell a little during the first nine months of 1956, but remained above the 1954 level even though 1956 was a truly *boom* year for Japanese industry (*ibid.*, No. 57-10, pp. 3–4.).

Economic plans being worked out in Japan indicate that even if a rapid growth in industrial production is maintained for the next several years, there will be a growing surplus of labor; more new laborers will be coming on the market each year than can find jobs, to say nothing of the present large excess of workers in agriculture, many of whom are underemployed.

THE FUTURE

As a result of World War II, Japan's area has been reduced to about what it was in 1872. Thus she has lost control over the resources of Korea, Taiwan, and Manchoukuo. Perhaps 1.8 million Japanese who had found homes abroad (in the colonies or in foreign countries) during the seven decades 1870–1940 were repatriated to Japan. Her total population had risen to 89 million in 1955 and is now (1958) about 92 million. Her commerce, which had become increasingly important up to the outbreak of World War II, not only was completely wiped out, but the whole network of organization which had built it up—banking and credit facilities, trade organizations of many kinds, merchant shipping, consular services, etc.—was destroyed and the personnel widely scattered. These changes made Japan much more dependent on imported raw materials—fertilizers to maintain crop yields, iron ore, coking coal, nonferrous ores and metals, fibers, rubber, wood pulp, oil, and many other materials of lesser importance. To pay for these she had to rebuild her export trade and enlarge it as compared with prewar years. Clearly, Japan was in a much tighter box after World War II than she had been in 1931, even before the acquisition of Manchoukuo.

Shortly after the war, fortunately, the serious character of Japan's population problem gained wide recognition among thoughtful Japanese (see chap. iv), and there was relatively free access to the knowledge needed for the rapid spread of birth control; a little later, the government took positive action in the encouragement of family planning. The demographic results are seen in the remarkable decline in the birth rate. However, there was also a remarkable decline in the death rate; hence, in spite of the fact that Japan's birth rate is only about 75 per cent as high as that of the United States, Japan's population is still increasing by about 900,000 per year. Furthermore, the latest data on production and employment show that increase in employment is lagging far behind, while the calculations of the people who are making the over-all plans for the next few years indicate that this situation will become increasingly grave later and will remain so for several years after the very large number of children born in the years 1947–51 begin to enter the labor force.

The outlook for restoring the living conditions of Japan's people to prewar level in the near future is quite discouraging, to say nothing of the outlook for improvement beyond that level. This holds in spite of the rapid decline in the birth rate, in spite of the very rapid increase in the efficiency of Japanese industry, and in spite of the large expansion of exports in the past few years (258, pp. 34–36). The chief reason for this is her great and increasing dependence on foreign commerce. At present she is enjoying large "windfall" gains in commerce, which began when the United States made large purchases for the Korean war, and which are continuing in the form of large orders for ships from Europe and large reparations payments to countries occupied during the war. Furthermore, China wants Japan's capital goods and Japan must have raw materials, many of which—particularly coal and iron ore—China can supply. However, a growing dependence on trade with China involves some very serious risks. It will give Communist China the power to disrupt, by sudden shifts in policy, Japan's entire economy at any moment.

On the other hand, there is good reason to believe that for some years nearly all the other Asian countries will be needing many types of capital goods, in addition to those involved in reparations, which Japan can supply more cheaply than other countries, and that trade agreements can be made which will be of mutual benefit for some years after the reparations agreements have been fulfilled. Furthermore, the machinery sent out under the reparations agreements will tie the expanding economies of these countries to Japan for some time. There is also reason to believe that Japan can supply much technical aid at a lower cost than the Western countries can. Japanese technicians will almost certainly find it easier to make adjustments to the living conditions in these countries than will Westerners and will understand better the problems peculiar to the economy of Asian nations. But in all of these relations Japan will find herself more and more dependent on the good will of the communist regimes in China and the Soviet Union. If they decide that it would be to their advantage *in any way* to disrupt Japan's economy by sending out exports below cost or by rendering technical aid without cost, much of Japan's foreign commerce might vanish almost overnight.

But quite apart from the dangerous dependence on foreign commerce, which may be cut off at any time by communist political action rather than by economic competition, there is going to be an increasing amount of competition of a bona fide economic character from India and China as their industries expand. For some time they will have cheaper labor than Japan, and they also are desperately in need of foreign exchange. In fact these countries are already beginning to compete with Japan in the export of textiles and of a few other types of light consumption goods. It is only reasonable to assume that such competition will become more difficult for Japan within the next few years. Moreover, it should not be forgotten for a moment that the communist countries always regard foreign trade as a weapon in the cold war rather than as a normal feature of international economic relations.

When all the circumstances that determine Japan's economic future are considered, it seems almost certain that population pressure will increase rather rapidly within the next two or three decades. Therefore it seems to me that we must ask ourselves whether we can reasonably expect the Japanese to tamely accept either the failure to improve living conditions, which seems highly probable, or their deterioration, which seems quite possible. Since it seems highly improbable that Japan will be able to expand onto the continent—even into the territory of Indonesia or of the other Asian countries in the foreseeable future—without the permission of China, she would seem to have only one alternative: to move into the Pacific islands now controlled by Australia, which contain, including the eastern half of New Guinea, a large part of the inadequately used lands in Tropical Oceania. I do not believe that, at present, any significant number of Japanese are thinking about territorial expansion; the military clique is in retirement, and even the Zaibatsu, the controlling business clique, is relatively quiet. But under increasing pressure to make a decent living, the people of Japan may be much more ready a few years hence to listen to those who will tell them that the only solution is to take some of the land still under the control of European peoples. The alternative would be to join China and the Soviet Union in the communization of Asia under Soviet leadership, in the hope that the resources of the communist countries would become a common pool from which Japan could draw what she needed.

CHAPTER VIII

INDIA:

POPULATION

INTRODUCTORY

India has an area of approximately 1,265,000 square miles, or 812 million acres.[1] In 1951 its population was almost 357 million. Among the nations of the world, only China has a larger population. For comparative purposes it may be noted that while the population of India in 1951 was over two and one-third times that of the United States, the area is only about 42 per cent as great. For each Indian, consequently, there were only two and one-fourth acres of land, while for each person in the United States there were approximately twelve and one-half acres.

The changes in the population of India from 1891 to date, and of prepartition India from the time census taking began (1872) to the present, are shown in Table 7. The reasons for the differences in the figures in columns 2 and 3 are explained in the notes to this table. Our discussion here will relate primarily to the data in columns 3 and 5 and to the percentages of change shown in columns 4 and 6. The most interesting facts are the high degree of variability in the rate of population change (growth) in prepartition India during the five decades preceding 1921 and in India from 1891 to 1921, and the relatively small variability in the fairly high rate of growth since 1921 in both areas. Around the year 1921, changes of the greatest importance took place in the conditions determining India's population growth.

It will be well to explain first the substantial differences in the rates

[1] Unless some qualifying term like "prepartition India" is used, the simple name India will be employed to designate the present Indian Union, which consists of all of prepartition India, except Pakistan and Kashmir-Jammu. The political status of Kashmir has not yet been finally settled, although India appears to be in process of absorbing it; Pakistan has become a sovereign state like the Indian Union and will be treated separately (chap. xiv). Burma was separated from India administratively in 1937 and is now a sovereign state; it is also treated separately here (chap. xv).

of growth shown in columns 4 and 6 for the decades 1931–41 and 1941–51. The higher rate of growth (15.0 per cent) in prepartition India during the decade 1931–41 (12.4 per cent in 1941–51) is due primarily to the fact that no allowance was made in the data in column 3 for overenumeration in the census of 1941. This overenumeration arose from the desire of both Hindus and Moslems to appear the dominant

TABLE 7

POPULATION (IN THOUSANDS) AND PER CENT CHANGE,
INDIA, 1872–1955

Year	Census Population*	Adjusted Population†	Per Cent Change in Column 3	Estimated Population Union of India‡	Per Cent Change in Column 5	Pakistan§	Per Cent Change in Column 7
(1)	(2)	(3)	(4)	(5)	(6)	(7)	(8)
1955....	464,100	464,100	6.2	381,700	....	82,400	....
1951....	437,200	437,200	12.4	{(361,400) / 356,900}	14.1	75,800	7.9
1941....	388,998	388,998	15.0	{(316,800) / 312,800}	13.5	70,300	18.8
1931....	338,119	338,171	10.6	275,500	11.0	59,100	8.8
1921....	305,693	305,679	0.9	248,100	−0.4	54,400	6.7
1911....	303,013	302,985	6.2	249,000	5.7	50,900	11.9
1901....	283,872	285,288	1.1	235,500	−0.2	45,500	....
1891....	279,446	282,134	9.6	235,900	....	....	....
1881....	253,896	257,380	0.8	....	....	....	....
1872....	206,162	255,166	....	....	....	....	....

* Prepartition India. Data for 1872 and 1881 are from 134, 1931, I, Part 1, 5; the 1872 figure was obtained by subtracting the total increase for 1872–81 from the 1881 enumeration; the 1891–1941 figures are from 134, 1941, I, Part 1, 62; the 1951 figure is combined from sources 134, 1951, I, Part 1-A, 122; 221, 1951, I, 25, and Table 3, p. 3-3 (Pakistan); plus an estimated 4.4 million for Kashmir-Jammu.

† These figures are also for prepartition India. Those for 1872–1921 are from Kingsley Davis (86, p. 27), and were adjusted to make them comparable from one census to the next; hence, the per cent change (col. 4) is based on them. The 1931–51 figures are from the sources referred to in the previous note. The 1955 estimate is from 293, 1956, pp. 157 and 159, and includes an estimate for Kashmir-Jammu of approximately 5 million.

‡ The data for 1891–1951 are taken from 134, 1951, I, Part 1-A, 122, and relate to that part of the Union of India within which the 1951 census was taken. The figure for 1941 makes allowance for overenumeration in 1941. Hence, the rate of increase for 1931–41 is reduced, and that for 1941–51 is raised (see text). The figures in parentheses for 1941 and 1951 include estimates for Kashmir; the population of Kashmir at the end of 1955 was probably about 4.8 million.

§ Source: 220, I, 25, and Table 3, pp. 3-2 and 3-3.

group in certain areas which would be claimed by both India and Pakistan if partition took place. The Punjab and West Bengal were the two areas in which India was especially interested. The estimates of the Indian census authorities in 1951 (col. 5) made an allowance of two million for this 1941 overenumeration, chiefly in these two areas. The subtraction of this number from the enumerated population of 1941 would reduce the 1931–41 rate of increase from 14.2 per cent for India to 13.5 per cent, the rate shown in Table 7, column 6, and would thereby raise the rate for 1941–51 to 14.1 per cent (134, 1951, Vol. I, Part 1-B).[2]

DISTRIBUTION OF INDIA'S POPULATION, 1951

Map 6 shows the distribution of India's population according to the census of 1951. The heavy concentrations of population are found in the areas of heavy rainfall and in the fertile alluvial valleys— the Ganges valley in the north, the delta region watered by the Ganges and Brahmaputra rivers on the east, and the eastern coast south of Calcutta, including the extreme south, which receives rain from both the summer monsoon (southwest) and the winter monsoon (northeast). The west coast south of Bombay is also densely settled, but its area is very small, since there is only a narrow belt of land between the Arabian Sea and the mountains (the Western Ghats). There are also some "islands" of relatively dense population in areas, outside the regions just described, due to rather extensive irrigation works (see chap. ix). As will be shown, however, most of the other regions of India, except the western deserts where rainfall is almost negligible, are subject to wide variations in the annual rainfall (see Map 8) and do not have dense populations. These are the regions in which famine and hunger have played such a large role in determining population growth in the past. But it should be noted that even in these regions of uncertain rainfall and poor soils the population is quite dense by Western standards.

GROWTH BEFORE AND AFTER 1921

The striking variations in the rates of population growth in the Indian Union during the thirty years before 1921 and the variations during a like period since that time, as well as those in prepartition India between 1872–1921 and 1921–51, call for explanation. As was

[2] In chapter xiv the increase of population in Pakistan (area of 1951) between 1931 and 1941 is given by the census of 1951 as 11,200,000, or 18.8 per cent, and the increase for 1941–51 is given as 5,500,000, or 7.9 per cent (221, 1951, Vol. I, Table 3, Variation). It is recognized that there was probably a significant overenumeration in the 1941 census in East Bengal and in that part of the Punjab now included in Pakistan (*ibid.*, pp. 25–28), but there are no estimates of this overenumeration in the Pakistan census referred to above. However, in the reference given above, the Indian census states that the Pakistan authorities have assessed the 1941 overenumeration in the Punjab at 900,000 to 1,000,000, and in East Bengal at 3,700,000. If a total of 4.5 million is used as the amount of this overenumeration, then the rate of increase in Pakistan between 1931 and 1941 is reduced to 11.3 per cent, and the increase between 1941 and 1951 is raised to 15.2 per cent. On this basis, prepartition India shows (col. 3) the same growth trend as India does.

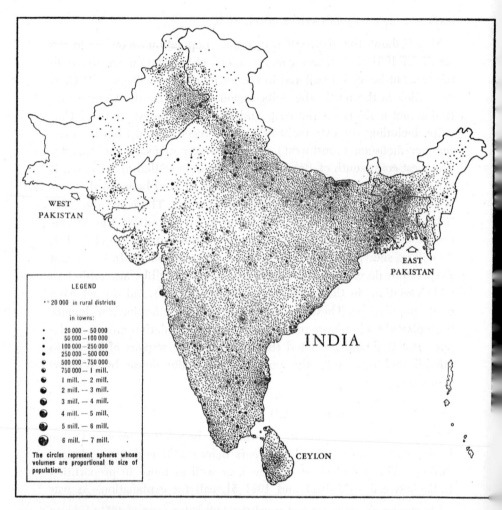

MAP 6.—Population distribution in India, Pakistan, and Ceylon. (Adapted by permission of Dr. Friedrich Burgdörfer and the Heidelberger Akade mie der Wissenschaften from *The World Atlas of Population* [Hamburg: Falk-Verlag], copyright 1 957 by Heidelberger Akademie der Wissenschaften, Heidelberg, Germany.)

pointed out in chapter ii, substantial variations in rates of population change have probably taken place over short periods of time, among all peoples, throughout most of human history. It was also shown that until quite recently these changes have been due predominantly to wide fluctuations in the death rate rather than in the birth rate. India provides clear evidence of very wide fluctuations in the death rate over relatively short periods of time during the several decades since census taking began; but there is no evidence of any significant fluctuations in the birth rate.

The evidence regarding the fluctuations in the death rate consists chiefly of the census figures given above considered in relation to the reports of famine or scarcities of food, and in relation to the varying intensity of epidemics (cholera, plague, malaria, typhoid, dysentery, influenza, and other acute contagious and infectious diseases). The registration of births and deaths is still so incomplete that no firm conclusions can be derived from the use of registration data (see below).

Column 3 shows that in prepartition India the growth of population was only 0.8 per cent in the period 1872–81. Since the 1872 figures probably have a higher proportion of omissions than the 1881 figures, even this very small rate of increase is more likely to be too high than too low. The 1891 census showed an increase of 9.6 per cent over 1881. A part of this increase may be attributed to a more accurate enumeration in 1891 than in 1881, but most of it was undoubtedly an actual increase.

Famines and scarcities, 1872–81.–The 1951 census of India gives a list of famines and scarcities which occurred between the first census (actually, this census was taken over a period of more than five years, 1867–72) and the second census; it shows seven famines, some of which affected many millions of people, and five scarcities of wide extent (134, 1951, I, Part 1-B, 265–70). The effect of the famine of 1876–78 on the population was summed up by the Indian Famine Commission of 1880 as follows: "No deficiency at once so serious and so widespread in its effects as that which from 1876 to 1878 was experienced in various parts of the country had previously occurred in the century" (*ibid.*, p. 271). "It has been estimated, and in our opinion on substantial grounds, that the mortality that occurred in the provinces under British Administration during the period of famine and drought extending over the years 1877 and 1878 amounted, on a population of 190 millions, to five and one quarter millions in excess of the deaths that would have occurred had the seasons been ordinarily healthy; and the statistical returns have made certain, what has long been suspected, that starvation and distress greatly check the fecundity of the population. It is probable that from this cause the number of births during the same period has been lessened by two millions; the total reduction of the population would thus amount to about seven millions" (*ibid.*, p. 273). This applies only to British India. The native states then contained about one-fourth of the population of prepartition India.

The decade 1881–91.—There were only minor famines and scarcities during this decade, and the All-India Census Report of 1891 says, "Most fortunately, the 10 years under review have been almost free from this calamity [famine], and the one or two cases of serious failure of crops that did occur were purely local and restricted to very narrow limits, both territorially and with respect to the population affected" (*ibid.*, p. 274). During this decade, the population of prepartition India increased by 9.6 per cent, possibly by somewhat less for reasons stated above.

It is also very interesting that every account of severe shortage of food in India mentions the increase of pestilence and disease—cholera, smallpox, and fevers—during and immediately following the period of starvation. People weakened by prolonged undernourishment are, of course, highly susceptible to the contagious and infectious diseases which have always been present in India on a large scale. Moreover, because famine frequently causes great migrations of people in search of food, the spread of the contagious diseases over wide areas is almost inevitable.

The famines of 1891–1901.—In the decade 1891–1901 famine again occurred over rather wide areas, with a heavy incidence of disease; the 1901 census showed a population gain of only 1.1 per cent in prepartition India, and in the Indian Union (col. 6 of Table 14) there was a small decrease (−0.2 per cent) (*ibid.*, pp. 274–80, 282–83). On the whole, this was a *bad* decade.

The decade 1901–11.—This was a fairly *good* decade regarding both food shortages and the ravages of epidemics. The gain in population was 6.2 per cent in prepartition India, but only 5.7 per cent in the Union.

The influenza epidemic.—The following decade (1911–21) reverted to a very low rate of growth (0.9 per cent in prepartition India and −0.4 in the Union) quite similar to that of 1872–81 and 1891–1901.

A number of districts suffered from drought, and nine famines of considerable extent were listed between 1911 and 1921 (*ibid.*, pp. 267–68); but the great calamity of this decade was the influenza epidemic of 1918–19. Although lesser epidemics of plague and cholera claimed many lives, and deaths from the causes which had long kept India's death rate high continued as usual, the influenza epidemic of 1918–19 was the chief determinant of population change during this decade.

In the 1921 census report, the official estimates of deaths from influenza totaled about 8.5 million in the reporting areas; deaths in all India were estimated at 12 to 13 million. This estimate was derived from the reports of officials in different areas and is generally recognized as conservative. For one thing, the registration of deaths in many areas broke down completely during the height of the epidemic. Second, the expected population for 1921, the population derived from the difference between registered births and deaths (allowance being made for the estimated underregistration), was higher by 4 million than the actual count of 1921. Most of these 4 million should probably be added to the influenza losses.

In 1944 I wrote: "When these deficiencies in reporting influenza deaths are taken into account, we must assume that a minimum of 15 million persons died of this disease in India in 1918 and 1919, and it is quite possible that the number was several million more" (279, p. 221). In 1951 Davis calculated that the "grand total loss of life due to influenza epidemic" was 18.5 million; and he adds, "It thus appears that the total loss was in the neighborhood of 20 million lives, or about double the usual estimates" (86, p. 237). The census report also calls attention to the fact that the loss of 12 to 13 million in the space of three or four months exceeded by nearly 2 million the total deaths from plague extending over twenty years (1898–1918), and was more than double the deaths attributable to the famines of the period 1897–1901 (134, 1951, I, Part 1-B, 290). This discussion of the influenza epidemic relates to prepartition India.

A word should be added here about population growth in the area of the Indian Union, as enumerated in 1951, since growth in the Union was somewhat different from that in prepartition India from 1891 onward. The figures in column 5 are official, compiled from previous censuses (beginning with 1891) to make them comparable with the 1951 data, i.e., with the census taken after partition. These data show that during the two periods 1891–1901 and 1911–21 there was a slight decline in numbers in the Indian Union as compared with a very small growth in prepartition India. This further emphasizes the deadliness of the famines and epidemics and also indicates how different the incidence of such catastrophes in different parts of a large underdeveloped country may be. At the same time (1911–21) that the Indian Union probably suffered a loss amounting to about 1 million, the area that is now Pakistan showed an increase of about 3.5 million, or 6.7 per cent. This difference in population change is due partly, no doubt, to variations in the severity of famine and disease in these two areas, but it is also due partly to the opening of new irrigation districts, most of which lay in the area that is now Pakistan. Irrigation not only made crops more certain but also drew immigrants from other parts of the country, thus reducing the rate of growth for a time in the areas of emigration, which lay in India, and adding to it in the newly opened areas in Pakistan.

Famine and disease since 1921.—Since 1921 there has been only one famine of such severity that it caused great suffering—the Bengal famine of 1943. This famine is estimated to have been the direct cause of 1.5 million deaths. The poor harvests of 1943 could not be supplemented by even the normal imports of rice from Burma, which was then in the possession of the Japanese. Moreover, wartime conditions interfered in other ways with famine relief operations, which had been improving steadily for some years. However, public health work had also been making progress, so that cholera, plague, smallpox, and other diseases did not become rampant, as they had in many earlier famines. As a result, the Indian Union population has grown steadily since 1921, at a rate increasing from 11 per cent in 1921–31 to 14 per cent in 1941–51 (Table 7). The total increase during this thirty-year period was approximately 108.8 million, as compared with an increase of approximately 12.2 million in the preceding thirty years; all of the increase in this earlier period took place during the relatively *good* decade 1901–11. The increase since 1921 has been about 8.5 times as great as that between 1891 and 1921.

DEATH RATES AND BIRTH RATES

In spite of the very incomplete registration of births and deaths in India, such evidence as registration data do supply supports the view that the difference in rates of population growth between the periods 1891–1921 and 1921–51 was caused chiefly by the decline in the death rates.

The official death rates, from registered deaths, show a steady decline by five-year periods, from 30.2 in 1911–15 to 22.3 in 1936–40, except for the quinquennium 1916–20, when the death rate was 38.2 because of the influenza epidemic. Although there are large omissions in the recording of deaths, it is likely that there was some slight improvement in the registration of deaths between 1911 and 1940, except at times when, and in localities where, famine and pestilence were especially bad. However, there is reason to believe that between 1941 and 1951 registration became rather badly disorganized and less reliable than it had been during the two preceding decades. This disorganization was caused in part by the great migratory movements associated with partition, which took place in the latter part of the

TABLE 8

BIRTH AND DEATH RATES, INDIA, 1881–1950*

YEARS	BIRTH RATES		DEATH RATES ESTIMATED
	Estimated	Registered	
1941–50..........	39.9	27.5	27.4
1931–41..........	45	34	31.2
1921–31..........	46	33	36.3
1911–21..........	49	37	48.6
1901–11..........	48	37	42.6
1891–1901.......	46	34	44.4
1881–91..........	49	....	41.3

* For the period 1881–1941 the rates are those of Davis (86, pp. 36, 69) and are for prepartition India. The rates for 1941–50 were calculated by S. P. Jain (134, 1951, I, Part 1-B, 136–37) and apply only to present India.

decade. To arrive at either death rates or birth rates for India which are at all reasonable, students have found it necessary to resort to indirect methods of calculation. Kingsley Davis calculated the average annual death rates and birth rates by decades from 1881 to 1941 for prepartition India, as shown in Table 8, and S. P. Jain calculated those for the Indian Union for 1941–51. The rates calculated by Jain are not, in my opinion, directly comparable with those of Davis for preceding decades. The rates calculated by Jain yield an average annual natural increase in India for the decade 1941–51 of 12.5 per 1,000, whereas, when allowance is made for an overenumeration of two million in 1941, the census increase during the decade 1941–51 is 14.1 per cent, or an annual average increase of approximately 14 per 1,000.

The severe but localized famine of 1943 did not have much influence on India's population growth, since the area chiefly affected now belongs to Pakistan (see chap. xiv), with which it was enumerated in 1951. However, the total population of India in 1951 was probably somewhat increased by a *net* immigration following partition, while the natural increase as calculated by Jain took no account of "displaced persons." Hence, the total increase in India between 1941 and 1951 may very well have been somewhat larger than the natural increase. However, it cannot be assumed without further evidence that the decline in the birth rate and the death rate between 1931–41 and 1941–51 was as large as the differences between Davis' rates for the earlier decade and Jain's rates for 1941–51.

About all that can be said positively concerning India's birth and death rates is that the censuses prove there has been an increasing difference between the birth rate and the death rate in recent decades, most of which took place between 1921 and 1931. On general grounds (see chap. ii) we are justified in assuming that much the larger proportion of this difference is attributable to the decline in the death rate. Jain says: "In the light of the estimates of birth and death rates for the previous decades it is possible to hold the view that the figures for 1941–50 may be underestimated. A critical examination of the data on which the earlier estimates have been obtained does not rule out the possibility that they [these earlier estimates] are overestimated" (*ibid.*, p. 145). It is certainly not improbable that the decline in the birth rate shown above, from 45 (Davis) in 1931–41 to 39.9 (Jain) in 1941–50, is due in part to the different methods and data employed in making these estimates.

If the birth rate has declined significantly since the decade 1931–41, most of the decline should probably be attributed to particular temporary circumstances rather than to a secular downward trend. The very large mobilization of military forces during the war, the vast disturbances associated with partition (great numbers of both Hindus and Moslems were killed, and a total of probably more than fifteen million persons fled either from India to Pakistan or in the opposite direction), and the severe famine in Bengal were circumstances which might have reduced the birth rate temporarily; but it would not be reasonable to assume they would have a permanent effect.

There is one demographic change now taking place, however, which some people think may have a relatively permanent effect in reducing the birth rate: the decline in the proportion of women marrying under fifteen years of age. The law now forbids the marriage of females under fifteen years of age and of males under eighteen years of age. However, there are still a great number of such marriages. In 1941 married females under fifteen constituted 9.6 per cent of all females married; in 1951 they constituted only 7.4 per cent (*ibid.*, Part 1-A, p. 72). But such a decline in early marriages would have very little effect on the general birth rate. During the time when the proportion of child marriages was decreasing significantly, and before the women who were marrying a little later had had time to bear more than two or three children, this change would tend to decrease the crude birth rate, providing it took place fairly rapidly. But the data just given indicate that the decline in child marriages was taking place rather slowly and, up to the 1951 census, could not have exercised any significant effect on the crude birth rate.

Moreover, a small decline in the proportion of married females under fifteen years of age is not conclusive proof of a decline in child marriages, because if the death rate is declining through a general improvement in health services many married women over fifteen years of age who formerly would have died are now surviving. This fact alone would reduce the proportion of all married women who are under fifteen years of age, even if there were no decrease in child marriages. This is not to deny that there has been a reduction in child marriages, for there probably has been; it is merely to call attention to the possibility that these census figures might easily lead one to overestimate the reduction and its effect on the birth rate. Furthermore, the postponement of marriage, even from fifteen to eighteen years of age, may not reduce the average number of children born per woman, because there is reason to believe that the greater maturity of women marrying at eighteen years of age may enhance fertility in the later years of the child-bearing period.

Another factor which may raise the birth rate in India significantly within the next two or three decades is the remarriage of several million young widows. But since there does not seem to be any appreciable relaxation of the tabu against remarriage as yet, this is not of immediate importance. It will be discussed more fully in connection with the long-range outlook for population growth.

It will be recalled that the death rate for the decade 1941–51 as calculated by Jain was 27.4, or 3.8 points below that of prepartition India for 1931–41 as calculated by Davis. It was pointed out that these two rates probably are not strictly comparable; it should be realized, however, that if one accepts a decline of about 4 points in the average death rate during the decade 1941–51, as compared with 1931–41, one must also accept an almost equal decline in the birth rate, because the rates of natural increase must have been about the same in these two decades (making an allowance for some net in-migration into India) and they are the most dependable data available regarding the changes which have taken place in India's population. The chief reasons for doubting any such change in death rates from 1931–41 to 1941–51 are: (1) the deterioration of agriculture and the other hardships resulting from war (including the Bengal famine in 1943), (2) the great loss of life suffered by young children and old people during migration, as well as the direct slaughter of great numbers in riots and guerilla attacks, and (3) the great hardships suffered by many of the eight to ten million migrants after they arrived in India, where the new national government could not meet the impossible task of providing them with the necessities of life. I cannot accept a decline of 3 to 4 points in the birth rate until better evidence is available.

THE OUTLOOK FOR THE IMMEDIATE FUTURE

Chapter ii pointed out that advances in the control of infectious and contagious diseases during the past fifty years, and especially in the last twenty-five to thirty years, have now made it possible to reduce the death rate very quickly and cheaply where public health work is well organized, provided the economic *necessities* of life are available to the population. The recent declines in India's death rate are generally attributed to more effective public action in making available to all of the people, all of the time, a minimum food supply, and to the improvement in public health services. Since 1951 these services have been greatly improved, although much remains to be done. Somewhat more than Rs. 130 million were spent on health services during the first Five-Year Plan, which ended in 1956. The second Five-Year Plan makes provision for the further improvement of health services by allotting more than twice this sum to such work (140, p. 151). Personally, I have little doubt that the average annual death rate of 27.4 for the decade 1941–51 as calculated by Jain (see Table 8) had been attained by the end of the first plan and that it will be reduced still more in the near future—always assuming that the physical necessities of life are available (see chap. ii). Furthermore, there is little doubt that India's death rate can be reduced to the vicinity of 17 per 1,000 per year within the next ten to fifteen years.

On the other hand, there is no convincing evidence indicating a downward trend in the birth rate of the country as a whole. The accumulating evidence that women in the upper economic and social class have fewer births than those in the lower classes does not invalidate this statement, since the upper class is such a small proportion of the total population.

For the reasons already given, I do not expect a very significant decline in the birth rate in the next decade, and the decline in two decades will probably be only a small one. Consequently, I expect the rate of population growth to rise during this period about as fast as the death rate declines.

THE LONGER OUTLOOK

Projections of population growth.—In any program for raising the level of living of the people of India, the size of the population is naturally of basic importance. The account of changes in the size of the population since 1872 (prepartition India) and 1891 (India) showed how influential economic and health conditions have been in determining the rate of growth. When this information is related to the more general statement of patterns of population growth as outlined in chapter ii, it is possible to make projections concerning population growth for two or three decades which should be useful, even though no particular projection may be fulfilled exactly. A number of such calculations have been made, both by Indians and by others. The differences between these calculations arise primarily from differences in the expected birth rates, and only secondarily from differences in the expected death rates. Because it is generally recognized that changes in birth and death rates cannot be foreseen with much assurance, several sets of calculations have generally been made by the same persons or authorities to show how population growth will vary according to the degree to which the different assumptions are realized.

It is also generally recognized that changes in the death rate during the next two or three decades depend not only on the development of public health work but also upon the availability of *necessities*, the lack of which will render health work of little use. Naturally, all projections assume that these necessities will be available. A discussion of the conditions most likely to affect the provision of these necessities will be found in chapters ix and x.

Birth rates for projections.—It is clear from the considerations in chapter ii that the level of the birth rate in any society is a consequence of the culture of that society. In human societies there is no such thing as a birth rate determined solely by the physiological capacity to reproduce. The most uncertain factor India faces today, in connection with planning to improve the level of living, is the behavior of the birth rate after about 1965–70. Any projection of the birth rate must necessarily rest on the judgment of the person or persons making the projection. This does not mean, however, that the judgments of all persons are equally good.

Practically all projections of India's population assume that the death rate will continue to decline. This seems a reasonable assumption in view of our present extensive knowledge of how to control contagious and infectious diseases. The rate of decline cannot be foretold with great accuracy, however, chiefly because of uncertainty about the amount of funds which will be available for health work, and the varying efficiency with which the funds may be used, both in training people to carry on health work and in establishing the clinics and services needed to reach the people in the villages. Because of these uncertainties, alternative rates of decline in the death rate are generally used in calculating the future growth of India's population.

Changes in the birth rate during the next twenty-five to thirty years are far more uncertain than changes in the death rate. We know that the birth rate is high—probably in excess of 40 per 1,000 per year. It is also probable that it has declined only slightly, if at all, in the past thirty years. Several questions will indicate the nature of the difficulties involved in attempting to project the course of India's birth rate during the next twenty-five to thirty years. Can the period 1921–51 in India, during which the population grew 43.9 per cent, be considered the equivalent of the substantially longer period in most of the countries of the West during which the rate of growth slowly but steadily increased to a maximum chiefly because of the decline in the death rate? Will India's rate of growth continue to increase during the next two or three decades as the death rate declines fairly rapidly while the birth rate declines slowly or not at all? Or will the rate of growth remain at about the 1941–51 level for several decades because of parallel changes in birth and death rates? Will conclusive evidence that the birth rate is beginning to decline justify the assumption that it will decline far more rapidly than the birth rate did in most Western countries, because of the more rapid dissemination of contraceptive information and the more urgent need for reducing the rate of population growth?

None of these questions can be answered with any assurance. For this reason, most projections of future population growth in India have been made on the basis of clearly stated assumptions which were considered "reasonable" by their makers.

Census projections.—One such set of projections is found in the Census of India, 1951 (134, 1951, I, Part 1-A, 179). The assumptions are: ". . . first, let us suppose that during each of the three decades 1951–60, 1961–70, and 1971–80 the mean decennial rate of growth of population will be—(a) the same as that of the average of the three decades 1921–50; or (b) the same as that of the latest of the same three decades (when the growth rate was highest)." Calculations on

TABLE 9

POPULATION PROJECTIONS (IN MILLIONS), INDIA, 1951–81*

Year	Lower Limit	Upper Limit	Population of India Deduced from That Calculated for Uttar Pradesh, Madras, and Madhya Pradesh†
(1)	(2)	(3)	(4)
1951..............	361.3	361.3	361.3
1961..............	407.7	411.9	407.8
1971..............	458.5	469.7	452.7
1981..............	527.6	535.5	515.7
Per cent increase 1951–81........	46.0	48.2	42.7

* Includes Kashmir and Jammu.

† The assumptions used here are: (*a*) child marriages will disappear, but married women of all ages will give birth to the same number of children per 1,000 during 1951–80 as they did during 1921–50; (*b*) mortality at each age will also remain the same as during 1921–50. These calculations were first made for three states which have the better data and then were expanded to cover the whole of India, on the assumption that these three states were typical. Source: 134, 1951, I, Part 1-A, 179–82.

these assumptions are shown in Table 9. The calculations on assumption *a*, which is considered the lower limit, are given in column 2. Calculations for assumption *b*, which is considered the upper limit, are found in column 3. The calculations in column 4 are explained in the notes to this table.

Assumptions regarding specific changes in birth and death rates are avoided by making the general assumption that the net effect of any changes in these rates will issue in a rate of increase equal to the rate prevailing at the specified period in the past. Hence, the total percentage increase 1951–81 does not vary greatly (46.0 per cent to 48.2 per cent) from the increase for the period 1921–51 (43.9 per cent). In column 4 the age-specific birth and death rates in three large states are used as applicable to the whole of India. These rates are the average of the years 1921–50. It is recognized that these calculations are based on age-specific rates involving estimates and, hence, that the results are only approximate and that column 4 in particular shows minimal growth.

The Coale and Hoover projections.[3]—Coale and Hoover (80) start with a birth rate of 43.2 per 1,000 for the decade 1941–51 as more probable than 39.9 (Jain), and a death rate of 31.0 as more probable than 27.4 (Jain). The birth rate they use is only 2.0 points lower than the one Davis calculated for 1931–40, and the death rate is approximately the same. These more elaborate projections of India's population, i.e., more elaborate than those in the Indian census given above, squarely meet the problem of projecting specific birth and death rates. I personally believe that these initial rates (1941–51) represent more reasonable points of departure than Jain's rates. The results of these projections are given in Table 10.

Column 2. If there is no reduction in fertility (age-specific birth rates), but a reduction in age-specific death rates which will yield fairly rapid reduction in the crude death rate from 31.0 in 1951 to 15.2 in 1976 (the last year for which a change in death rate is used in calculating the 1981 population), the total population will rise to 682 million (about 690 million including Kashmir), or approximately 154 million above the "upper" limit in the census projections and about 162 million above the "lower" limit. This amounts to an increase of over 90 per cent in thirty years.

Column 3. With the same death rates (age-specific), but a decrease in fertility of 50 per cent between 1956 and 1981 which would gradually become effective by 1976, the total population would only amount to 562 million (about 569 million including Kashmir) by 1981. This is higher by 33 to 41 million than the calculations of the Indian census given above and yields an increase of about 57 per cent over 1951. The third calculation (column 4), using the same death rates as the other two projections, and using birth rates which only begin to decline in 1966 but which decline very rapidly to 1981 (50 per cent), yields a total population of 603 million (about 610 million including Kashmir), or 69 per cent above that of 1951.

---

[3] Table 10 and its notes were compiled from a "Preliminary Draft" of 80, which was published too recently to make use of before the page composition of our essay became necessary. However, this space was reserved for an explanatory note and, if possible, a definite reference to 80; pages 34–42 contain the materials relevant to our discussion of these projections.

Observations on projections.—It should be emphasized again that all these projections are based on certain assumptions which may or may not be realized. My basic criticism of these assumptions is that it seems quite reasonable to believe that significant progress has been made in health work during the first Five-Year Plan and that, consequently, the death rate has already fallen below the 1941–51 level. It further seems

TABLE 10

POPULATION PROJECTIONS (IN THOUSANDS), INDIA, 1951–81*

YEAR (1)	ESTIMATES		
	High† (2)	Low‡ (3)	Medium§ (4)
1951:			
Total..............	357,000	....	....
Male............	179,000	....	....
Female..........	177,000	....	....
1961:			
Total..............	424,000	420,000	....
Male............	213,000	211,000	....
Female..........	211,000	209,000	....
1971:			
Total..............	532,000	496,000	524,000
Male............	268,000	250,000	264,000
Female..........	264,000	246,000	260,000
1981:			
Total..............	682,000	562,000	603,000
Male............	343,000	283,000	304,000
Female..........	338,000	279,000	299,000
Per cent increase 1951–			
81................	91.0	57.0	69.0

* Source: 80, pp. 3, 4, 5, and 6; see also pp. 34–42. The population of Kashmir is not included. These figures would need to be increased by about 1.2 per cent to compare with the census projections.

† The assumptions here are: (*a*) no change in fertility; (*b*) crude death rate declining from 31.0 in 1951 to 25.6 in 1956, and by a steady decline to 15.2 in 1976 and to 14.6 in 1981.

‡ The assumptions here are: (*a*) fertility declining by 50 per cent, 1956–81; (*b*) death rates declining at the same rates as in column 2, but to somewhat different levels because of differences in age composition.

§ The assumptions here are: (*a*) fertility declining by 50 per cent, 1966–81; (*b*) death rates declining at the same rates as in column 2, but to different levels because of differences in age composition.

reasonable to assume that with the increased budget allotted to health work in the second Five-Year Plan, the actual accomplishment in reducing the death rate will be somewhat greater during this current plan. On the other hand, there appears to be no basis for assuming that there has been an equal decline in the birth rate up to 1956, nor that there will be a decline in the birth rate to parallel the probable decline in the death rate during the next two or three quinquennia.

In the Coale-Hoover high projections the death rate per 1,000 declines from 31.0 in 1951 to 25.6 in 1956 and then steadily, although not by equal amounts in each quinquennium, to 14.6 in 1981. If, in the meantime, the age-specific birth rates decline, as assumed in the medium and low projections, the crude death rates will decline even more because of differences in the age composition of the population favorable to lower death rates. Such a decline in the death rate is by no means impossible. However, it seems to me too precipitate for a large country like India, even in light of our present health knowledge and experience. I believe it will take somewhat longer to bring the death rate to these levels.

In the first place, I do not believe that the postwar achievements of Japan and Ceylon in reducing their death rates (see chaps. ii, iv, and xiv) provide a very useful guide for estimating the speed with which most underdeveloped countries can reduce their death rates, although such experiences in health work are highly suggestive and should be studied with care. Ceylon is a small country, and its health conditions are relatively homogeneous throughout its area, although there are, of course, differences in the problems of urban and rural areas and among the rural areas in which climatic factors and the past experiences of the people with health work vary. However, differences in health conditions in Ceylon are relatively small as compared with those existing in India.

Japan is not an underdeveloped country, of course, but has a culturally homogeneous population that is literate and is accustomed to co-operating with public authorities. Like Ceylon, Japan can have a single basic health program for the entire population, with minor modifications for urban and rural communities and for different types of rural communities. Language difficulties seldom arise and, when they do, are of minor significance.

India, on the other hand, is a subcontinent covering about 1.25 million square miles. In spite of the tropical character of most of the country, there are climatic differences among the various regions which significantly affect their health problems. This does not mean it is inherently more difficult to reduce the death rate in one region than in another, but it does mean that the same health program is not equally well suited to all regions. But the climatic variations are probably insignificant as compared with the cultural differences, which are to some extent related to differences in language. In India fourteen different languages are officially recognized, and many times that number are actually in use in different parts of the country—some of them spoken by several million people—to say nothing of the hundreds of dialects used among the hill tribes. In addition to the language barrier, there are many other reasons why different groups find it hard to co-operate actively with the modern health agencies. In a large country like India, where health services are set up on a state basis and thus vary considerably, progress in reducing the death rate will not be uniform. For example, in many areas the people oppose mass inocula-tion against smallpox, dysentery, typhoid, and other diseases; in many other areas the people simply do not believe that sanitation will help control disease, and the Western-trained health worker often finds that the people prefer the traditional methods and medicines to the modern ones.

Many of these same difficulties arose not too long ago in our own country, as any older reader can testify from his own recollections. (For a more extended discussion of some of these points see 278.) The fact is that illiterate peoples who have strong traditional attitudes re-garding methods of improving health often do not immediately accept *better* services; hence, improvements in health services take place slowly. But it must be emphasized that new health services are almost certain to be accepted much more rapidly than new practices which would change reproductive behavior.

THE PROSPECT FOR A DECLINE IN THE BIRTH RATE

The Coale-Hoover assumption that a significant decline in the birth rate will be postponed to 1966, their medium projection (Table 10, column 4), seems more reasonable to me than the assumption that such a decline will begin in 1956 (column 3); but that fertility can be halved between 1966 and 1981—in fifteen years—seems to me highly optimistic. The reasons for this view deserve some examination, since the rate of decline in the birth rate is the nub of the problem with respect to controlling population growth in all of Asia within the next twenty to forty years.

As has been said, there is still no convincing evidence of any sig-nificant decline in the birth rate in India. There is, however, increasing evidence of a differential birth rate between the higher castes and the upper socioeconomic classes in the cities, on the one hand, and the lower castes and social classes in the agricultural villages, on the other. There is also increasing evidence that a significant proportion of the upper classes in the cities do practice contraception (248, pp. 157–69).

I have talked personally with many educated Indians who had no hesitation in saying that they themselves practiced contraception and that they believed or knew that many of their friends also did. These differentials in birth rates are of the same general character as those found in the West two to five decades ago—the higher the social and economic status, the lower the birth rate. Within the strictly rural population there is some evidence that this differential is reversed (247*a*, pp. 44–53.)

For several decades the censuses have also shown a significant urban-rural differential (86, pp. 70–73). The latest data available to Davis when he made his study of urban-rural differentials, using the ratios of children to women, were from the 1931 census (the 1941 census was never completed) (86, pp. 70–82). I can find no reason at the present time, however, to modify his first and most important conclusion—that although there has long been a significant urban-rural differential, there is no evidence that this lower urban birth rate is spreading to the rural areas. His second conclusion is that the lower birth rates of the upper castes and economic groups are not due primarily to contraception but to the fact that failure to marry and widowhood are more common in these groups; this conclusion may need some modification now because, as noted, there is growing reason to believe that contraceptive practices are spreading slowly among the upper classes in the cities. However, it must be remembered that the upper social and economic groups living in the cities constitute only a small proportion of the total population, so even if they are having fewer births per family than the lower classes this change can have very little effect on the birth rate of India as a whole; and it may not have any effect as yet on the number of children living to the reproductive age, because of a lower death rate in the upper classes.

Among scholars who have studied India's economic and social problems during the past three or four decades, there has been much interest in the relation of population growth to the welfare of the people. Many writers in this field have been more or less Malthusian in their outlook. They have recognized that an improvement in welfare inevitably involved a reduction in the death rate and, consequently, a more rapid increase in population unless there were a parallel decline in the birth rate. They also agreed, in general, with Malthus that the birth rate would remain high unless it were deliberately (voluntarily) controlled. In India, however, at least in recent times, there has been almost no taboo against discussing the voluntary control of conception by methods other than continence, a taboo which prevailed in the West until quite recently. Malthus himself observed this taboo and considered postponement of marriage and continence as the only permissible forms of birth control. Gandhi took much the same attitude. But in India there has never been the organized opposition by religious groups to the use of the mechanical and chemical means of contraception that has been, and still is, encountered in the West. However, although the social atmosphere in India has been much more favorable to open discussion of the control of population growth by contraception, this discussion has never reached the masses of India's people.

Since independence there has been an even more widespread realization among India's leaders that improvement in economic conditions was closely connected with the increase in population and that the rate of population increase was being raised by the more effective health work being established. The population problem is now quite widely recognized among educated people. A number of individuals and private organizations are studying the attitudes of the people toward the control of the birth rate, and the central government is definitely committed to a program of encouraging family planning. The results of a few of the studies that have been made regarding attitudes toward family limitation will be summarized briefly.

Several surveys have been undertaken in particular communities to ascertain the size of family wanted and the attitudes of the people toward controlling the family size by contraception. The fact that most of these surveys were taken in villages indicates a wide recognition of the fact that the effectiveness of family planning in producing a substantial and rapid decline in the birth rate depends upon the attitudes of the villagers who constitute such a large proportion—about four-fifths—of the total population. In general, these surveys show that high percentages (two-thirds or more) of the persons interviewed, who were chiefly women, expressed a willingness—even a desire—to have fewer births and to learn how contraception might be practiced (61, p. 70; 85; 251; 250; 191). However, most of these studies were not organized to test the effectiveness of this desire by providing people with an opportunity to put contraception into practice. In one Poona study, less than 10 per cent of the 850 "city" fathers practiced any form of contraception, and less than 5 per cent practiced any form other than abstinence and withdrawal, while 509 of them said they knew nothing about contraception. Of the 236 who desired such information, 131 said that they would at once adopt it (85, pp. 141–43).

As yet, there appears to have been no follow-up study to determine how many of these 131 actually did adopt it.

Of the 855 "noncity" fathers interviewed in this study, only 13 reported that they used contraception, including 7 who practiced some abstinence. The great majority knew nothing about contraception, but 306 wanted information, and 198 said they would adopt it. Again, there is no information on actual adoption after the information was made available. It seems probable that very few adopted contraceptive practices, for reasons which will be given.

Of 511 "city" women questioned in this study, only 40 knew about and practiced contraception; only 295, however, said they knew nothing about it, and 102 of these (35 per cent) said they would welcome information about it (85, p. 169). The situation was much the same among the "noncity" women. There is no information from "follow-up" studies to show whether "willingness to learn" a method of contraception resulted in the consistent practice of an effective method by any appreciable proportion of the "willing."

The reasons these women gave for wanting smaller families were chiefly dissatisfaction with the care they could give their children, and poverty. But in this study, in which over one-half of the people were classed as "city," only 20 to 30 per cent of all the women said that they would welcome information on contraception, and there was a noticeable lack of interest among women who did not already have three living children. This study seems to show that the advantages of spacing conceptions farther apart were little understood or appreciated, and that there was little disposition to look ahead until urgent need was felt. Although it is not expressly stated that the women felt the size of the family to be principally the husband's concern, if one reads between the lines one cannot avoid feeling that the decisive factor in the wife's willingness or unwillingness to take any positive action is the husband's attitude. If this is the case, little progress can be made until the husband decides in favor of family limitation and until methods of contraception satisfactory to him are made available. The strongly traditional character of the marriage relation, and the high degree of subservience of wives to their husbands, undoubtedly present formidable obstacles to the rapid spread of contraception.

A study of "Attitudes of Males toward Family Planning in a Western Indian Village" throws some light on husbands' attitudes in another community (201). Briefly, the men in this village stated that they would have no interest in contraceptive practices until they had three living sons. This would amount to about six living children, and one seems justified in interpreting it to mean that the number of births wanted by these husbands was determined largely by the traditional number considered desirable under the conditions of high mortality to which these people have long been accustomed. (Under the conditions that have prevailed until quite recently, only about one-half of the children born would survive to reproductive age.) There seems to be little realization among these people that improved health conditions will assure a couple of as many surviving children as in the past even if the number of births is substantially smaller.

In a recent study in several rural communities in the state of Uttar Pradesh, it was found that there was almost no interest in the control or spacing of births until the women had four or more births or four living children. In these rural communities the interest in birth control was found to be much greater among the nonagricultural classes than among the farmers, and among those classes where the husband had had several years of formal education than among the poor and illiterate workers. The farmers and the illiterate workers constituted the great majority of the population (247a, pp. 61–83). In this connection it may be noted that, if every married woman had only four births and if the mortality of the children up to about five years of age was reduced to the approximate level of that now prevailing in Japan, the growth of India's population would be much more rapid than at present.

Space will not permit specific reference to other studies of a private character, but those which I have read point to the same general conclusions: (1) There is no opposition to talking about the voluntary control of family size; in fact, there is considerable interest in learning that its size can be voluntarily controlled. (2) There is occasionally enough interest, when the work is organized and outsiders are in charge, to induce a few families to adopt family planning; in one community the men who already had as many children as they wanted showed some interest in sterilization, as long as outsiders were in charge of the work and their neighbors did not know about their interest. (3) In the villages surveyed, there seems to be no local demand strong enough to lead any appreciable proportion of the couples to plan their families by the regular practice of contraception with the means now available to them.

The central government itself is responsible for two surveys, similar in character to those already described but more thorough, which are of much interest. Early in the period covered by the first Five-Year Plan, ending March 1, 1956, the World Health Organization was asked by the Minister of Health to make a study of the applicability of the *rhythm* method of conception control to Indian conditions.[4] This study was set up in two communities, one in Ramanagaram, a rural community in South India, and one in a suburb of New Delhi. In the study in Ramanagaram a considerable majority (75 per cent) of the couples covered by the attitude survey indicated a willingness to be taught how to practice this form of contraception. In the Lodi community near New Delhi, 70 per cent of the women—who were for the most part wives of government workers, some of whom already knew something about other methods of conception control—said they were willing to learn this method of control. However, in both communities only a small proportion carried through with the rhythm method alone to the point where they could use it effectively: 41 of the 811 "willing to learn" in Ramanagaram, and 27 of the 898 "willing to learn" in Lodi (37 and 59).

Because so few people carried through with the rhythm method, and because certain other factors were not adequately controlled, it is quite impossible to say anything about the effectiveness of this method in reducing the birth rate in either of these communities as a whole. However, it does appear that for the few couples that went through with the experiment, the length of time between the onset of the menses following a birth and the next conception was from two and one-half to five times as long as it was for couples that made no effort to follow any method. But it is clear that a method of conception control which is so far from acceptable that it is practiced regularly by only 3 to 5 per cent of those who have indicated a willingness to learn it can have little effect in reducing the birth rate in the country as a whole.

This official study points up very markedly the contrast between the readiness with which the people express an interest in planning the size of their families and their willingness to make any serious effort to do so. The unwillingness to learn and practice the rhythm method is undoubtedly due in large measure to the nature of the method itself in relation to the traditional patterns of marital relations and, hence, of reproduction. This study did answer, in the negative, the question,

[4] The Minister of Health at that time was a disciple of Gandhi, and Gandhi, like Malthus, believed that the size of the family should be controlled by continence or late marriage only.

Is the rhythm method of birth control suited for widespread use in India? It also confirmed other surveys in showing that there was no widespread opposition to learning about contraceptive methods. The results of this survey also make it reasonable to conclude that the people might be quite receptive to official propaganda intended to encourage fewer births per family. But its results do not seem to justify the expectation that the mass of the people will take any effective action to reduce the size of the family in the near future.

THE PLANNED-PARENTHOOD MOVEMENT

The planned-parenthood movement in India is well organized and quite vigorous, but its leaders would be the first to recognize that it does not reach many people and that it is having only a negligible effect on the birth rate at present. Handicapped by inadequate funds and by a lack of trained workers, it cannot carry on any large campaign for family planning or establish any considerable number of clinics. Most of the clinics now in operation are in the larger cities, and some of these are not yet being used to capacity, probably because of inadequate propaganda. To say the least, this situation is profoundly discouraging to those people who are the most deeply convinced of India's need for family planning and who are giving generously both of their time and their money. Two conditions of a very general character are involved in this problem, aside from the lack of funds, and will go far to explain why family planning is making comparatively slow progress. One of them has been alluded to several times and is all-pervasive: within India's cultural patterns it never occurs to the great mass of the people to do anything about the size of their families. Among the masses, reproduction is determined by the traditional patterns of family life, and these patterns are still too powerful to permit effective effort toward reducing the number of children born to a couple. Only a very small proportion of the women, or of the men, know that it is possible to control the size of the family, and only a few of these are sufficiently interested as yet in reducing the number of births in their own families to take any effective action (278).

The second condition affecting India's family-planning situation is that even when some of the people become interested in spacing their children and in controlling the total number of births, they find that the methods they must use are not suitable or are too costly. Thus the lack of contraceptive methods which are cheap, safe, effective, and suited to the living conditions of the masses is now a deterrent to effective contraception that may very well become more important as more people learn that contraception is possible. This lack of a suitable method is of very great importance. But it must be said that there is no clear indication as yet of a rapid weakening of the cultural patterns which would lead to its widespread use in the near future even if such a method were available.

In several countries work is now proceeding on the development of contraceptives that will be safer, simpler to use, more effective, and cheaper than those commonly employed in the West. Actual field trials of some of these new methods of contraception are now being made, and the preliminary results of some of the tests are encouraging. This is all to the good, but it does not seem to me that our knowledge of how basic cultural patterns can be changed to permit the operation of new values and practices justifies the hope that the development of even ideal contraceptives will assure the spread of their use in India within much less than a generation. The erosion of the cultural patterns controlling reproduction may take place much faster in India than it did in the West, but even so the process may require a generation rather than a decade. In any event, great cultural change is a *critical* "must," just as better contraceptives are a *critical* "must," if family planning is to spread fast enough to reduce the rate of population increase substantially within the next two to four decades. It must be remembered that even a fairly rapid decline in the birth rate may not be enough to prevent a rise in the rate of population growth for two or three decades if health work reduces the death rate as rapidly as is generally expected.

In the studies of attitudes toward the control of family size referred to above, the finding that considerable numbers and proportions of the men and women interviewed express a desire to learn about contraception is quite impressive. It is also important that organized religion does not oppose the spread of such knowledge. But the opposition inherent in the traditional attitudes of the people themselves is truly formidable, and it must be recognized that until this is overcome it is not reasonable to expect any rapid spread of even ideal contraceptive practices.

THE GOVERNMENT AND FAMILY PLANNING

The first Five-Year Plan provided Rs. 6.5 million to the Ministry of Health for a family-planning program. The second Five-Year Plan allotted it Rs. 40 million for the same purpose. "It is expected that about 300 urban and 2,000 rural clinics will be set up during the Second Plan" (140, p. 156). As late as the summer of 1957 very little seems to have been done to implement this part of the plan, and one-fourth of the five-year period had already passed. Propaganda, or education, explaining the need for family planning also appears to have received very little attention as yet, although it seems safe to predict that unless a well-planned propaganda campaign actually reaches into the villages before the clinics are established, comparatively little use will be made of their family-planning facilities even though their facilities for maternal health and child care are fully utilized. This judgment is based on personal observation of results in several private clinics of this kind, as well as on the belief that erosion of the traditional patterns of behavior which determine reproduction has scarcely begun outside the small educated upper class.

There are said to be 550,000 to 600,000 villages in India. Even if family-planning facilities were established by 1961 in the 2,000 rural clinics the plan has provided for, and if each clinic were able to serve 10, or even 20, villages, a total of only 20,000 to 40,000 villages would be reached, i.e., only 6 to 8 per cent of all villages. But it must be repeated that the facilities offered by these clinics for the improvement of health and the reduction of the infant death rate will probably be fully used for some years before those which explain family planning and teach the practice of contraception. The fact is that, in spite of the widespread recognition in official quarters of the urgent need to reduce the birth rate, very little seems to have been done to prepare the people for family planning. It is to be hoped that in the future the Ministry of Health will pursue a more vigorous policy of educating the mass of the people in the need for reducing the birth rate.

Improvident maternity: reduction targets.—What is needed to bring population growth to a practical standstill in India, and some of the means for accomplishing this, are discussed at some length in the 1951 Census Report (134, 1951, Vol. I, Part 1-A, chap. v). A few quotations from this report will be of interest here, although the conclusions seem to assume that most of the people will accept the rational attitudes of the educated Indians far more rapidly than seems reasonable to me.

"So then, we have reached two conclusions. *One is:* that we cannot grow as much food as we shall need, if we go on increasing in numbers as we do. *The other is:* that if we do not grow more food, we must eat less food. . . . It follows that we should make up our mind that we shall not go on increasing in numbers as we do" (*ibid.*, p. 210). "We must count it a fortunate circumstance that the religious faith of most of our people is not bound up with this taboo [the taboo being that contraception is sinful]. It is, therefore, easier for us—while affirming due respect for religion, morality and the integrity of family life—to insist that the question whether contraception is good or bad for the people shall be considered in the light of uninhibited reason" (*ibid.*, p. 211).

"*This movement of public opinion* [on the need for contraception] *has now acquired coherence, crystallisation and a sense of direction with the publication, by the Planning Commission, of its report on the First Five Year Plan*" (*ibid.*, p. 213).

"*Let us, therefore, define 'improvident maternity' as a child-birth occurring to a mother who has already given birth to three or more children, of whom at least one is alive*" (*ibid.*, p. 217). "Improvident maternity" as thus defined is calculated to amount to 40 to 45 per cent of all births, and "*if we can put an end to improvident maternity . . . the excess of births over deaths will be reduced to negligible numbers and a substantially stationary population achieved*" (*ibid.*).

"Out of the total of 15 years which are available to us for the attainment of the target [the elimination of improvident maternity], the first phase would need at least three years from the word 'Go.' It may take as long as five years" (*ibid.*, p. 219). Six or seven years have already passed since this was written and, as was noted above, little appears to have been done.

The work envisaged during the five years mentioned in the preceding quotation would consist of "the creation of organisation" and "the standardization of technique" (*ibid.*). Moreover, it should not be thought "that it is impossible to make any progress in limiting births until we have completed our development programme in other respects. . . . *But it is necessary to isolate that part of our health programme which relates to the provision of maternity and child welfare services; give it top priority (along with, say, irrigation and ahead of all other development) and undertake accelerated development of these services to the point at which the needed organisation is created*" (*ibid.*, pp. 219, 220).

The author of this section on "improvident maternity" believes that in five years' time an organization of clinics for maternal and child welfare, including family planning, could be developed. This service would utilize the local *dais* (midwives), would have available the information, the appliances, and the other materials needed, and would be ready to function "before a nation-wide campaign for reduction of improvident maternity can be launched" (*ibid.,* p. 220). "The Central Research and Information Unit should be required to recommend a few *acceptable, efficient, harmless and economic methods* which are suitable for being sponsored by the government" (*ibid.,* p. 221).

The *annual* cost of maintaining such a family-planning service, once it is organized and operating, is estimated at approximately Rs. 200 million, on the basis of a center for each 5,000 population costing Rs. 2,500 annually (*ibid.,* p. 411). This is nearly three-fourths of the *total* sum allotted to the Ministry of Health for the entire second Five-Year Plan and is twenty-five times the *annual* allotment to family planning in this period. There is as yet no sign that such a program will be given the high priority referred to above. In fact, it appears more probable that family planning will remain the stepchild in the general health program. Furthermore, even if adequate support were forthcoming, it does not seem at all probable that the program would succeed within twenty to twenty-five years in inducing practically the entire population to reduce family size by the 40 to 45 per cent needed to eliminate "improvident maternity."

In chapter ii it was pointed out that the birth rate of any group is an integral part of that group's culture, and that the cultural values involved in reducing the birth rate concern every individual in a very intimate manner. This means that each couple will have to accept new cultural values before the couple will change their observance of the customs and practices which determine the number of children they will have. In a society where traditionalism is still strong, individuals are very reluctant to break away from the patterns of conduct approved by their group. Moreover, efforts from above to force positive changes in cultural patterns arouse a great deal of antagonism, so that if such efforts are not undertaken with great circumspection they may very well delay the adoption of the new practices they are intended to foster. This fact is quite widely recognized. In India, for example, the educated classes believe that raising the age of marriage to eighteen is a much-needed reform. A law has been on the books for some years raising the legal marriage age of women to fifteen, but almost no effort has been made to enforce it. The authorities have undoubtedly been wise in not pushing this reform too hard. It is probable that marriage under fifteen years of age is declining slowly, but it is not at all certain that active efforts to enforce the law would hasten this decline. The rural communities still accept very early marriage as proper and desirable, as do the lower economic classes in the cities, and they will probably maintain this attitude until changes in the conditions of life lead them almost subconsciously to regard such early marriages as *not good*.

In India, as everywhere else, education, and the broad environmental changes involved in living in cities and participating in an economy in which children contribute almost nothing to their own upkeep until they are old enough to work at jobs away from home, are changing people's attitudes about the desirable age for marriage. They will also change the desirable number of births for a family. But these changes in environing conditions will take place rather slowly, although I have no doubt that the pace can be hastened as compared with past times in the West. The fact is that nobody knows how to effect in a few years changes in basic social values which have heretofore changed very slowly over relatively long periods of time. No one knows how to go about an intensive propaganda campaign for smaller families, nor how a population which is now largely illiterate in the adult ages will respond to a campaign for smaller families.

I am personally of the opinion that a generation—about twenty-five years—will be needed to reduce the rate of population growth substantially below its present level, and that in the meantime, for the most part, it will be higher. I say that this reduction will require a generation because I do not believe that most of the people who are now twenty-five years of age and over will be much influenced by the propaganda which is likely to reach them before they have completed their families under the influence of the prevailing traditional values.

In general, my own conclusions regarding the growth of India's population in the next twenty-five years run as follows, assuming that there will be no significant decline in the per capita food supply during that period. The death rate is declining, and will continue to decline; but, for reasons already given, I very much doubt that it will fall quite as fast as predicted by the Coale-Hoover medium projections, i.e., to 11.7 per 1,000 by 1981. I am especially doubtful about the decline in the death rate from 18.1 in 1966 to 11.7 in 1981. I refer to the medium projection here because I believe it unlikely that the birth rate will change appreciably before 1966, and I do not consider it at all likely that there will be a decline from 40.9 per 1,000 in 1966 to 22.6 per 1,000 in 1981. What I do believe, then, is that the population of 1981 is likely to lie somewhere between the Coale-Hoover medium projection of 603 million and their high projection of 682 million, which assumes that there will be no change in the age-specific birth rates up to 1981. Their low projection (562 million), which assumes a rapid decline in the birth rate beginning in 1956, seems to me highly improbable. Since the rate of population growth that seems most reasonable to me is considerably higher than that assumed in the five-year plans, I doubt that the expectation of improvement in the level of living aimed at in these plans will be achieved. Additional reasons for this doubt will be presented in the two succeeding chapters.

CHAPTER IX

INDIA:

AGRICULTURE

AREA AND CROP LAND

The area of India, including Kashmir-Jammu, is approximately 1,270,000 square miles, or 813 million acres. India, thus defined, is about 42 per cent as large as the United States.

In 1951 the net area sown to crops was about 287 million acres, and the area sown a second time (double-cropped) was about 38 million acres; thus the gross area sown was about 325 million acres (134, 1951, I, Part 1-B, 39). The land fallow in that year amounted to about 60 million acres, of which about one-half was current fallows (*ibid.*, pp. 29, 39); the Food and Agriculture Organization reports 370 million acres as arable land in 1953 (111, 1956, p. 5). This figure included net area sown, fallow land, and land in tree crops, and is about 23 million acres more than the figure given by the census report (1951) on net sown area plus all fallow land (about 347 million acres).

There are likely to be substantial variations from year to year in each of these three types of land: (1) net area sown; (2) gross area sown; and (3) fallow area. But net area sown plus fallow land equals "cultivated" or "arable" area, which does not vary much from year to year. It is possible, however, that the difficulties resulting from war conditions (1939–45) and from the displacement of many millions of people during the great migrations following partition had caused the "cultivated" area to decline appreciably and that it had not yet been rehabilitated in 1951. The fallow area is likely to increase in years of low rainfall, because when the rainfall is very light it is almost impossible to prepare some soils for crops. This is especially true for crops planted in the autumn and harvested in the spring. As fallow land increases, net area sown decreases, and, usually, gross area sown also decreases. In *good* years this process is reversed: fallow land decreases, and both net and gross areas sown increase. Under the cirumstances, about all that can be said with reasonable assurance is that the "cultivated" land in India probably amounted to somewhere between 350 and 370 million acres in the period 1951–53, i.e., in the early years of the first Five-Year Plan. The important changes in land use about which we can be reasonably certain will be considered in later sections.

Per capita sown area.—In 1951 the gross area sown was about 325 million acres. This meant that since the population, including Kashmir, was approximately 361 million, only 0.90 of an acre per capita was sown. There are no exactly comparable figures for the United States, but there are figures showing area harvested. There were 2.3 acres per capita harvested in the United States in 1949. Since the area harvested is almost certainly smaller than the area sown, it somewhat understates

TABLE 11

POPULATION, CULTIVATED LAND, AND CULTI-
VATED LAND PER CAPITA, THIRTEEN
DISTRICTS INDIA, 1891–1951*

Year	Population (Millions)	Cultivated Land (Millions of Acres)	Acres per Caput
(1)	(2)	(3)	(4)
1951.......	117.9	99.1	0.84
1941.......	101.7	95.8	0.94
1931.......	90.7	94.3	1.04
1921.......	83.3	92.7	1.11
1911.......	84.2	91.5	1.09
1901.......	81.8	84.0	1.03
1891.......	81.5	89.0	1.09

* Source: 134, 1951, I, Part I-B, 48–49; see also pp. 1–71.

the difference between the two countries to say that two and one-half times as much land per capita is harvested in the United States as in India.

In order to trace the change in per capita net area sown over the past sixty years, the census authorities of India made a special study in thirteen districts where the data were considered reasonably good for the period 1891–1951 (Table 11). Using five-year averages, they were able to avoid any error that might arise from annual fluctuations in the sown area due to this area "increasing when the rainfall is adequate and timely and decreasing when it is inadequate or untimely" (134, 1951, I, Part 1-A, 140). Certain other districts, which also had reasonably good agricultural data for 1891–1951, had undergone such boundary changes that it was impossible to include them in the sixty-year comparisons.

These thirteen districts contained 29 per cent of all the tilled land in

India in 1951, and 32.6 per cent of the population. In these districts in 1891 there were 1.09 acres of net sown land for each inhabitant. This amount dropped to 1.03 acres in 1901, rose to 1.11 acres in 1921, and declined thereafter to 0.84 of an acre in 1951. The decline has been steady since 1921, the approximate time when the population began to increase regularly.

For the period 1921–51, a similar trend was found in those districts and states for which good data were available only after 1921—with the exception of two states, Bihar and West Bengal, in the decade 1941–51, where there was a small increase in sown land per capita; but in both these states the net sown area per capita was significantly smaller in 1951 than it had been in 1921.

But even the comparable and reliable data on sown area since 1921 cover only about 62 per cent of the total sown area of 1951 (including the 29 per cent in the thirteen above-noted districts). However, the census officials are confident that the downward trend in sown land per capita as shown in these two areas holds for all of India in the period 1921–51 (*ibid.,* Part 1-B, pp. 46, 47).

Furthermore, this downward trend was accompanied by a similar trend both in double-cropped land and in irrigated land (*ibid.,* Part 1-A, pp. 144–50), although the trend was not so strongly marked for these latter two types of land. This means that irrigated and double-cropped land had been increasing (prior to 1951) slightly faster than net sown land (*ibid.,* p. 204). It appears probable that the gross sown area will increase during the next few years much more through additional water being made available for double-cropping than through the tillage of new land not previously cropped.

CHANGES IN YIELDS, IMPORTS, AND CONSUMPTION

Since it is practically certain that there has been a per capita decline in the net sown area, in the double-cropped area, and in the irrigated area during the thirty years 1921–51, it will be well to note briefly at this point three other changes which affect the per capita food supply: (1) change in the yield per acre, (2) change in the volume of food imports, and (3) change in the amount of food consumed per capita.

Yields.—Data showing the yields of the principal food grains in four large states for the years 1910–46 (*ibid.,* Part 1-B, pp. 61–71) do not indicate any significant increase. The lack of increase during this period is probably due in part to the fact that only a relatively small area (3.4 million acres) was brought under irrigation between 1921 and

1940, most of it before 1930 (*ibid.,* p. 354). Moreover, for all practical purposes it can be said that there was no increase in the irrigated area as of 1930 until after 1951. Thus the addition to the irrigated area in the intervening twenty years was not large enough to have any noticeable effect on average yield per acre, even though the yields on the small amount of newly irrigated land may have been well above the average.

Imports.—Data concerning the importation of foodstuffs are more adequate than the data on acreage and yields. From 1891 to 1921, prepartition India was still a net exporter of food grains, although her annual average exports varied considerably. In 1890–91 to 1894–95 the exports averaged 1.24 million tons and consisted chiefly of wheat; in 1905–6 to 1909–10 they averaged only 0.52 million tons; and in the five-year period 1915–16 to 1919–20 they amounted to only 400,000 tons a year (*ibid.,* Part 1-A, pp. 164–66). After 1921, imports regularly exceeded exports, and in succeeding five-year periods until 1940 the net average imports were 160,000, 760,000, 1,270,000, and 1,380,000 tons. (The net annual imports, including grain from the present Pakistan, into the Indian Union in 1936–40 were about 2,070,000 tons.) During the war, net imports averaged considerably lower. After the war they rose very rapidly, and after partition they rose again. According to the Planning Commission, net imports averaged 3,270,000 tons during 1947–52. A part of this postpartition rise was due to imports from Pakistan which, except in 1936–40, did not appear as imports but were merely a regular feature of prepartition India's internal trade. Thus, from about the time India's population began to grow rather steadily at a moderate rate (1921), and until the first Five-Year Plan began to function (1951), imports made up for part of the increasing shortage in the per capita production of food.

Consumption.—Because of India's growing shortage of domestically produced food and her inability to secure adequate imports, there was also a decrease in per capita consumption. The FAO gives the per capita intake of food in India and Pakistan in the years preceding the war (1934–38) as 1,970 calories, and in 1947–48 as 1,690 calories (111, 1956, Part 1, p. 224). The per capita intake of India in 1950–51 (not including Pakistan) was 1,640 calories. If the intake of calories per capita was approximately the same in India as in Pakistan in prewar years, then by 1950–51 India's intake had been reduced by about 16 per cent in a period of about twelve to fourteen years. This serious reduction in a diet which was already too meager will explain the great efforts made to increase India's food imports and to regulate the distribution of food in the five years following partition. It will also account for the great emphasis the first Five-Year Plan placed on improvement of agriculture, since a significant part of India's exports had to be used to pay for food imports, and this meant that she had less foreign exchange available for other kinds of goods, particularly for capital goods.

NATURAL CONDITIONS AFFECTING AGRICULTURE

Topography.—Like all large countries, India has many areas which are topographically unsuitable for cultivation. Table 12 shows the sur-

TABLE 12

LAND AREA (MILLIONS OF ACRES), BY TOPOGRAPHICAL FACTORS, FOR ZONES, INDIA, 1951*

ZONE	TOTAL LAND AREA	TOPOGRAPHICAL FACTORS				DEDUCT UNUSABLE AREA	TOPO- GRAPHI- CALLY USABLE AREA
		Moun- tains	Hills	Pla- teaus	Plains		
India (incl. Jammu and Kashmir)............	812.6	87.3	150.6	224.8	349.8	308.2	504.4
India (excl. Jammu and Kashmir)............	753.2	32.5	147.9	223.2	349.5	253.5	499.7
North India.........	72.6	7.9	4.1	3.4	57.2	14.3	58.3
East India..........	167.5	14.5	52.1	20.4	80.4	62.0	105.5
South India.........	107.5	0.4	27.8	28.6	50.6	31.0	76.5
West India..........	95.7	......	19.8	28.4	47.6	31.4	64.3
Central India........	185.2	......	33.3	112.5	39.5	55.0	130.2
Northwest India......	122.6	9.7	8.8	30.0	74.2	58.3	64.3

* Source: 134, 1951, I, Part 1-A, 8.

face of India divided into topographical categories. Without Kashmir, and when only altitude and surface configuration are taken into account, about two-thirds of the area of India might be considered tillable, while less than one-half of the total area is now sown and fallow. These physical features are shown graphically in Map 7.

Soils.—The soils of India, like those of other large countries, vary greatly in fertility from area to area. There seem to be no data classifying the topographically tillable land in terms of soil fertility. Unquestionably, the approximately 500 million acres of usable land would shrink a great deal, possibly by 15 to 20 per cent, if the soils which do not yield enough to keep the cultivator alive were eliminated. There are large areas of rocky, sandy, and thin soils which, quite apart from the adequacy of the rainfall, are unsuited to cultivation. Erosion has ruined other large areas.

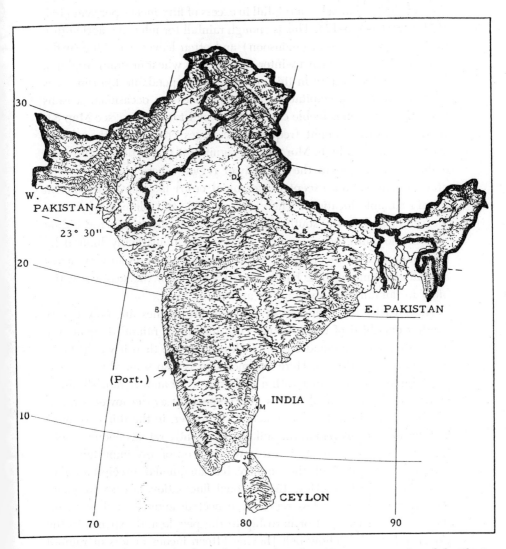

MAP 7.—Physiographic map of India, Pakistan, and Ceylon. (Base map a section of the Physiographic Diagram of Asia, © by A. K. Lobeck, reproduced with permission from the Geographical Press, a division of C. S. Hammond & Co.)

Rainfall.—A map of India outlining the areas which have different amounts of rainfall (see India on Map 2) shows that approximately one-third of the total area has a rainfall in excess of fifty inches per year (134, 1951, I, Part 1-A, 6–12). This is enough rainfall for intensive agriculture during the rainy season (monsoon) and often leaves a residue in the soil adequate to produce a winter crop such as wheat or grain sorghum. In addition, the rainfall in this area is more dependable than in areas of lower average precipitation—although there are occasional seasons when the monsoon is feeble even in these moister regions (see Map 8). In such seasons drought frequently damages crops even though the average rainfall is high. Moreover, a significant proportion of this area of heavy rainfall is in the Himalayan region where the topography prevents cultivation, except of perennial crops like tea and fruits in certain suitable locations. There are also hill and plateau regions in the center and in the south where the topography is less forbidding than in the north, but where the tillable area is markedly limited by the roughness of the terrain. These regions of heavy-to-very-heavy rainfall also contain some badly eroded areas. (For the seasonal variability in rainfall see also Maps 3*a* and 3*b*).

The area having a rainfall of thirty to fifty inches annually covers another one-third of the country. This amount of rainfall is generally adequate for fair-to-good crops, but less adequate than it would be in the temperate latitudes. Here the monsoon is also somewhat less dependable than in the area with a higher average annual rainfall. Short crops are not infrequent in this area, especially as the lower limit of rainfall (thirty inches) is approached. Moreover, in the thirty-to-forty-inch portion of this region the soil less frequently retains enough moisture from summer rains to insure a winter crop of any importance.

Another one-third of the country has an annual precipitation of thirty inches or less. "Here the seasonal fluctuations are so frequent, that they are more or less regularly expected; and when they occur, they cause a great deal of hardship to the people and expense to the Government. The yellow belt [having fifteen inches or less of rainfall and containing 7 per cent of the land area] has so little rain that a great many people do not live there. The brown belt [having fifteen to thirty inches of rainfall and containing 24 per cent of the land area] where one-fourth of our people live, is exposed to special hazards which are a permanent problem for the people and the Government" (*ibid.*, p. 11). It is clear that this area of light and highly variable rainfall, although much of it is topographically usable, must remain an area of

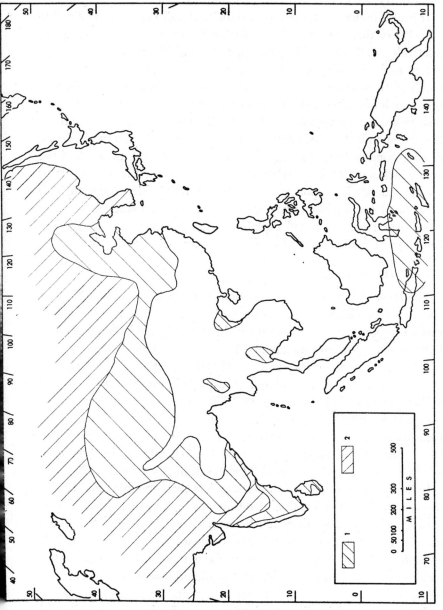

MAP 8.—Precipitation variability in Asia. Variability of precipitation: *1*, zones of moderate variability occasionally damaging to agriculture; *2*, zones of great variability often damaging to agriculture. Blank areas possess no dangerous variability during most years. (Reprinted with permission from Joseph E. Spencer, *Asia, East by South: A Cultural Geography*, © 1954 by John Wiley & Sons, Inc.)

relatively low productivity, except where it can be irrigated—and not a great deal more of it is irrigable (see Map 8).

It is also important to note that India's rainfall is largely confined to a period of three to four months during the summer, except in a few relatively small areas. This means that although the winter is very mild except in the Himalayan region, the area sown to winter crops, and the yields of these crops, are largely determined by the amount of moisture remaining in the soil after the summer rains are over and the summer crops are harvested. An increase in winter crops, therefore, is highly dependent on irrigation from water supplies stored in reservoirs, or on ground waters which can be pumped as needed. In much of the area which has twenty to thirty inches of rainfall, even summer crops are often dependent upon additional water supplied by irrigation. This great need for supplementary irrigation of both summer and winter crops over large areas will explain the great importance attached to irrigation in the five-year plans for agriculture discussed below.

PRESENT LEVEL OF PRODUCTION

The level of agricultural production in India is very low. It is low even for rice, which is by far the most important crop. In 1953, which was a very good year, the average yield of paddy (unhulled rice) was 1,204 pounds per acre, or about 746 pounds of hulled rice—approximately 12.4 bushels of 60 pounds (111, 1955, Part 1, p. 36). In Japan in the same year, which was not an especially good year there, 7.37 million acres yielded an average of 3,078 pounds of paddy per acre, or 2.6 times as much as India's yield. The yields in Thailand, Burma, and Pakistan are about the same as India's. South Korea, Taiwan, and China have considerably higher yields (see later chapters). In Asia as a whole, the yield of rice is about 30 per cent higher than in India.

India's yield of wheat is substantially less than one-third that of Europe as a whole; it is less than two-thirds as high as that of the United States, and only about three-fourths as high as the yield of the whole of Asia. The yield of barley in India is only a little more than one-half as high as that of Europe, and only about two-thirds as high as the yields of Canada and the United States. In addition to rice, wheat, and barley, other crops—corn, millet, sorghum grains, sugar cane, dry beans and dry peas, and lentils—are also important food crops in India. Of these additional crops, only the yield per acre of lentils, one of the less important crops, seems to be approximately as high as in Europe and America.

Although the reasons for India's low yields of crops are many, a few stand out rather prominently. Even the best soils—the alluvial soils—are deficient in nitrogen, phosphoric acid, and humus. Hence their productivity is reduced by the lack of plant nutrients, while the lack of humus makes the soil hard to till, reduces its ability to absorb and hold moisture, and hinders normal bacterial activity in the soil. This lack of humus results in large measure from the extensive use of cow dung for fuel instead of for manure, and from the inadequate use of composting and green manuring, which would serve the same purpose. It is very difficult to develop composting and green manuring on an adequate scale in a country like India, where every acre of tillable land is urgently needed for the growing of human food and where a very large cattle population keeps all fallow land stripped almost clean of vegetation the year around.

With only minor exceptions, the cattle in India are used only for their power, milk, hides, and bones. They are fed almost no grain, and subsist largely on the roughage from the grain crops and on the volunteer vegetation on fallow land. The grain, of all kinds, is used directly for human food.

The less fertile soils, which exceed the alluvial soils in area, lack not only nitrogen, phosphoric acid, and humus, but also potash and lime. They will require some years of very careful husbandry before they can be expected to produce substantially larger yields regularly.

The primitive agricultural practices prevalent in most areas are also responsible for low yields. Shallow plowing, poor preparation of seed beds, the sowing of grains like wheat and barley with little effort to cover the seed, and the inadequate cultivation and weeding of row crops are not favorable to good yields even under more favorable climatic conditions and on soils of better quality than those of India.

In addition, when no attention is paid to securing the seed of the better-yielding varieties of a crop, nor even to selecting the better seed from one's own crops, e.g., rice and wheat, there is apt to be a deterioration in the average yield of that crop. Even before scientific information regarding heredity was available, many farmers and landlords in a number of countries had been able to raise their yields considerably by selecting those seeds and animals which produced more or grew faster than most others. Such practical "rule of thumb" improvement, prior to the recent awareness of the possibilities of scientific agriculture, seems to have been less prevalent in India than in Japan and probably in China. It is not easy, of course, to introduce new farming

practices in any region where the practices have become strongly traditional over the centuries. It is especially difficult to change such practices in a country like India, where the farmer has long lived very close
to the subsistence level; he has not dared to risk any change in his agricultural practices, for fear it might reduce even his customary low returns. When some innovation failed in practice, it often meant actual
starvation. Under these circumstances, innovation was regarded with
suspicion until there was unmistakable proof that it could guarantee
equal or better yields. Besides, if there is no organized means of getting this proof to the farmer in a form he can readily understand, he
has no chance to make a choice between better- or poorer-yielding
crops and practices. It may also be noted that even after the farmer has
adopted a better-yielding strain of rice or wheat he may not find the
taste satisfactory, or the wheat may be too hard to grind by the methods available to his household, and these factors may cause him to
return to the poorer-yielding strains.

INCREASE IN THE FOOD SUPPLY

In broad terms, there are only two ways to increase agricultural production: (1) to extend the cropped area, and (2) to increase the yield
per acre of the cultivated land. The latter improvement may be
achieved by a large number of effective practices. Very few of these
proved practices are as yet widely known to the farmers of India.

Increase in cropped area.–The cropped area, or gross sown area
(counting double-cropped land twice), increased from 326 million
acres in 1951, at the beginning of the first Five-Year Plan, to 352 million acres in 1954–55 (139, p. 259). This is an increase of 7–8 per cent.
The increase was due in part to recovery from the disturbed conditions
which existed during the war and during the vast migration between
India and Pakistan following partition; but the major part was probably due to the increase of irrigated land between 1951 and 1955, which
amounted to 10–12 million acres. Such an increase in irrigated land
would also have made possible an increase in double-cropped land, so
additional irrigation might account for one-half or more of the increase
in the cropped area just noted. Finally, there was some actual reclamation of land by tractor cultivation, and some development by the farmers themselves of land not previously tilled; this may have meant that
5 million acres of land were usable by 1955 which had not been cultivated and had not been in current fallows in 1951.

The actual land surface used for the 352 million acres of cropped land existing in 1954–55 was about 317 million, since about 35 million acres were double-cropped. At the same time there were about 28 million acres in current fallow, about 29 million acres in "fallows other than current fallows," and about 95 million acres of other "uncultivated land" (139, p. 322). Any increase in cultivated land would have to come very largely from these last two categories—"fallows other than current fallows," and "uncultivated land"—which contained a total of 124 million acres. Thirumalai thinks that 15 million acres, or approximately 15 per cent, is a minimum estimate of the area that might be added to the cultivated area from "other uncultivated lands." On the basis of the 124 million acres just noted, 15 per cent would amount to 18–19 million acres which could be added to the cultivated area.

This unused land is to be found largely in the areas designated by the hatching (2) on Map 9. A comparison of this map with Maps 7 and 8 will aid the reader in understanding the "natural" reasons why this large area has such a high proportion of unused land. But in addition to these natural reasons (see above) there are many other reasons of a local and cultural character making it difficult to expand cultivation on this unused land. One important reason, no doubt, is that these lands, some of which have been used in the past, have become so eroded that they can no longer be used without extensive rehabilitation. Another reason is that some of them are swampy and so malarial that they cannot be used until drainage is installed and malaria is brought under control. Malaria can now be controlled rather quickly and cheaply, but drainage is often expensive, and for several years after drainage is completed the land will be hard to cultivate and crops will be poor. A third reason these lands have not been used is that some of them are infested with deep-rooted grasses and shrubs that can be eradicated only by deep tractor plowing, a process that takes several seasons of rather expensive work, during which no crop can be raised. Other parts of the unused land lie on the fringes of low-rainfall areas where, without irrigation, farming is highly hazardous. Finally, some of these lands, quite possibly the larger part of them, have thin infertile soils which cannot be farmed for grain, although they might be used for forests or grazing.

It is impossible to be precise about the new land that might be reclaimed from this uncultivated area of 124 million acres, but if we raise the probable proportion to 20 per cent it would amount to only 25 million acres, or a little over 7 per cent of the present cropped area. It will

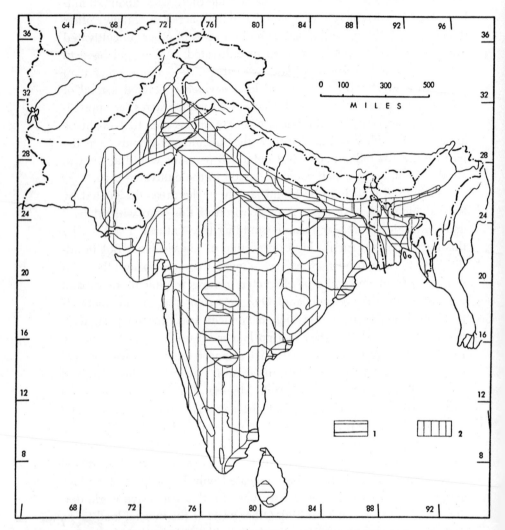

MAP 9.—Cultivated areas of India, Pakistan, and Ceylon. Land in cultivation: *1*, over 60 per cent of land in crops; *2*, between 20 and 60 per cent of land in crops. Blank areas have under 20 per cent of land in crops. (Reprinted with permission from Joseph E. Spencer, *Asia, East by South: A Cultural Geography*, © 1954 by John Wiley & Sons, Inc.)

take time and a great deal of money, even with the best technical means now available, to bring new land such as this into cultivation, and the yields are certain to be quite low for some time. If such an increase in new land took place in the next fifteen to twenty years, it would be surprising, and if this new land, which is now submarginal, were to be brought to the present average yield in the same time it would be still more surprising. At best, this increase would take care of the rise in India's population, at the present level of living, for only about four or five years.

Because of the difficulties involved in bringing new land into cultivation, the agricultural programs adopted in the first two five-year plans count very little on additional food from this source. Regarding new land, it is said that "though the gross cropped area has increased as a result of double cropping, little new area has come under cultivation during the past 40 years in spite of the growing pressure of population on the land. The fact that there has been little extension of cultivation to waste lands seems to indicate that the cultivable waste does not lend itself to reclamation by individual farmers and that its development requires an organized effort by the State" (137, p. 77). It was further expected "that the cropped and irrigated areas are likely to increase by 10 and 19 million acres respectively" during the first plan period (137, p. 101). This plan also envisaged the reclamation of 7.4 million acres. However, only a little more than one-third of this, or about 2.6 million acres, was to be developed through "an organized effort by the State"; the remainder was to be developed by the farmers themselves.

It has been announced that these goals have been approximately achieved (139, p. 259). But it must be recognized that this development by the farmers themselves probably consists chiefly in cultivating small adjacent tracts which had been lying fallow for some years. Clearly, the new land brought into use during the first plan, and which amounted to less than 2 per cent of the land already being cropped, could add but little to the total yield. Besides, the yield per acre on this new land is almost certain to be below average for the first few years.

In the second Five-Year Plan, "land reclamation and land development" is again assigned a very small role in the increase of the food supply. Only 8 *per cent of the increase* in food is expected to come from this source, and not even all of this 8 per cent is expected to come from land never previously tilled. The use of older fallows is included, as well as the reclamation of land previously irrigated but now useless because of water-logging or impregnation by alkali salts.

Irrigation.—The extension and improvement of irrigation is the chief means being relied upon to increase production in the first two plans. Under the first plan about 6.3 million acres, in major and medium-size projects, were added to the 18.0 million acres already irrigated by government canals and the 2.8 million acres irrigated by private canals. Through minor irrigation works, another 10 million acres were added to the 30.8 million acres already irrigated by such works, which consist chiefly of wells and tanks (ponds). These additions made a total of approximately 67 million acres, of which about 27 million acres were under major and medium-size works and about 40 million acres under minor works. Another 16 million acres were to be irrigated by major and medium works which were under construction at the end of the first plan. About three-fifths of the increase in agricultural production during the first plan was expected to come directly from this extension and improvement of irrigation. A considerable increase must also have been expected to come from the farmers' own improvements, the value of which, by their very nature, cannot be specified precisely. Such increase would consist largely in a general recovery from the low estate into which agriculture had fallen during the war and partition. Altogether, it may well be that irrigation improvements and extensions were expected to supply three-fourths of the entire increase in food production, aside from those "windfall" gains which might result from unusually good monsoons.

During the second plan 21 million acres were to be brought under irrigation, 12 million acres through large and medium projects and 9 million acres through minor projects. However, 9 million of the 12 million acres just noted are included in the 16 million acres to be added through the large and medium projects which were still under construction at the end of the first plan (139, pp. 321–23, 325–26). Presumably, the 7 million acres remaining from the projects begun but not completed in the first plan, and not otherwise accounted for, are included in the 9 million acres to be irrigated through minor projects during the second plan. On this basis about 88 million acres would be irrigated at the end of the second plan, of which 39 million acres would be under large and medium projects which, presumably, would provide adequate water at all times, even in drought years. About 49 million acres would be under minor projects such as wells and tanks; since the usefulness of this kind of irrigation depends largely on the current monsoon, such projects are not a secure source of water for irrigation in years when the monsoon fails. As yet, little is known about the dependability of the ground waters supplied by the wells. In the United States and in Australia these ground waters, which in the past were frequently described as "inexhaustible" and "unlimited," have generally been rather quickly exhausted when used heavily for irrigation and have sometimes proved to be so mineralized as to be unsuitable for agricultural use. In addition, as heavy use lowers the water table, the expense of pumping these ground waters increases greatly. In this second plan the development of irrigation was expected to supply 42 per cent of the increase in agricultural production.

The future development of irrigation in India is, of course, highly speculative. Rough estimates indicate that about 75 million acres can eventually be irrigated by large and medium projects, which presumably would be independent of the annual monsoons for a year or two at least, and that an approximately equal number of acres can be irrigated by minor projects (139, p. 224). As just noted, these minor projects depend in part directly on the current monsoon, and in part on wells whose permanent flow is highly uncertain.

Another very serious problem involved in irrigation is the waterlogging of lands lying below the canals that carry water from storage dams and diversion dams to lands farther downstream. In areas of light rainfall, this waterlogging is also often accompanied by the surfacing of alkali salts which destroy all useful vegetation. In the drier areas of north and west India, some tens of thousands of acres that have already been irrigated are being ruined annually by this seepage and by alkali infiltration.

From what has been said above, it is obvious that bringing land under irrigation in India does not usually signify cultivating new land, as it does in the United States. In much of that part of India where the monsoon is generally adequate for a summer crop, irrigation means primarily a better winter crop or insurance for a better summer crop when the monsoon is feeble. In the areas where the rainfall is likely to be inadequate for a summer crop, irrigation may insure a summer crop and, if the storage is adequate, also a winter crop. But irrigation is not expected to bring much entirely new land into use; it is expected, rather, to enable the farmer to raise larger crops and to avoid some of the failures due to variations in the adequacy of the monsoons.

It is quite impossible to estimate the ultimate increase in agricultural production that might come from irrigation. However, Coale and

Hoover have estimated that if 120 million acres are irrigated by 1981 there might be a 16 per cent increase in production (80, p. 99). This takes no account of the effects of other improvements in combination with irrigation.

Fertilizers.–In the first plan it was expected that the use of more manure and fertilizers would contribute but little (about 650,000 tons, or 10 per cent) to the increase aimed at in the production of food grains and pulses. The total amount of commercial fertilizers (ammonium sulphate and superphosphate) used during the first plan increased from about 300,000 tons of ammonium sulphate (1949–50) to about 600,000 tons (1955–56), which was as planned (139, p. 258). Since the second plan provides for an increase to about 1.5 million tons by 1961, or just a little less than three times the amount available in 1955–56 (139, p. 59), it seems reasonable to expect a significant gain in production from this source during the second plan. In the second plan about 25 per cent of the increase in production is expected to come from the greater use of all fertilizers and manures. This would amount to 3–4 per cent of the total production aimed at in this plan. Coale and Hoover have calculated that an application of 124 pounds of ammonium sulphate per acre on 180 million acres (probably in 1981) would add 20 million tons of food grains, or about 30 per cent of the 1955–56 production. The total amount of nitrogenous fertilizer needed to accomplish this would therefore be 10 million tons (80, p. 100).

Nitrogen is only one of the three important mineral constituents of most commercial fertilizers, although it is the only one used to any extent in India at present. The other two are phosphates and potash. About 600,000 tons of superphosphates are expected to be produced by the end of the second plan, which will constitute an important addition to the amount now available. And there is little doubt that more superphosphates will be provided in later plans, as well as an increasing amount of potash.

It should be noted, however, that most commercial fertilizers contain only negligible amounts of organic matter (manure and compost); these substances are often as important as, or even more important than, the minerals, especially under circumstances requiring that as large an amount of water as possible be retained in the top soil. This retention of water is a very important consideration for India's winter crops, since they receive practically no rainfall in most parts of the country (see Map 3a).

Cattle and manure.—India has the largest cattle population of any country in the world—about 200 million, including cows and buffaloes. With such a number of cattle, India might expected to have no lack of manure. The fact is, however, that most of this manure is dried and burned as household fuel for cooking and for heating water. Cattle are not used as meat by the Hindus; they are used for draft purposes and for milk while they are alive, and for hides and bones after death. Because of the scanty feed, their power as work animals is very low, and the milk production of the cows is almost negligible by Western standards. Until quite recently there has been almost no interest in the breeding of better cattle. The religious veneration which Hindus have for the cow prevents both the eating of the meat and rapid improvement by breeding. Better breeding is being introduced, but perhaps several decades will be required to make significant improvement in the stock. The provision of more and better feed for the cattle, in order to increase the milk supply and to make available more adequate power for farm use, involves problems which seem insoluble as far as the foreseeable future is concerned. Very little of the land that is now producing food grains can be spared for the production of fodder and the coarser grains for animal feed or for green manuring. Furthermore, India's most serious nutritional deficiency today is in animal proteins; until the eating of meat is more widely sanctioned, which no one expects to occur soon, these proteins must come chiefly from milk. This vicious circle is going to be extremely difficult to break as long as all the vegetable foods are so urgently needed by humans.

The prospect of any substantial increase in the use of manure and compost also appears rather remote, and, as a consequence, the restoration and maintenance of high fertility in the soil become extremely difficult. It must be recognized that high soil fertility depends on the presence of adequate organic matter and of many trace minerals, as well as the three minerals mentioned above. Furthermore, the use of commercial fertilizers adds steadily to the acid content of the soil if large amounts are applied regularly. This may adversely affect both the bacterial life in the soil and its ability to produce many useful and needed legumes unless lime is added regularly. The use of more and more commercial fertilizers, therefore, is by no means a wholly satisfactory answer to the problem of increasing yields and maintaining high productivity, although it will increase production substantially for the time being.

Better seeds.—India is also relying on the use of better strains of the more important crops to add to her agricultural production. It seems reasonable to expect that the use of better seeds will spread fairly rapidly. More seeds from improved and tested varieties of cereals and pulses are becoming available, and the farmers are gradually learning that the use of these seeds will increase their production. However, India is encountering many practical difficulties in her attempt to extend the use of better seeds. Three examples, briefly stated, will indicate the nature of some of these difficulties. A new variety of wheat, which was quite superior in yield, was rejected in some communities because it was too hard to grind into flour with the implements available to the village women. The people of certain other communities rejected a new variety of rice because it did not taste like the rice to which they were accustomed. Again, the better farmers in one area refused to try a new variety of wheat. After considerable investigation, which caused a delay of only two or three years in this particular community, it was found that in this area a good farmer believed it inconsistent with his self-respect to buy his seed. He felt that if he did so, it implied that he was too poor to save his own seed and had to eat all his crop before the next planting time came, and also that this farming practices were so shiftless that he could not raise good seed.

Since the widespread use of superior seed depends in large measure on inducing the better farmers to take the lead, such attitudes as those just noted constitute a real obstacle to rapid agricultural improvement. This fact is apparently recognized to a certain extent, since the proportion of the *increase* in production which was expected to come from this source during the first plan was only 9 per cent, and in the second plan only 10 per cent. It is highly significant that the scientific and economic difficulties being encountered today in the production and distribution of better seeds are often far less of an obstacle to better farming than the difficulties involved in persuading farmers to accept these improved seeds and practices, i.e., the cultural obstacles.

Community and extension work.—In its rural community programs, India is trying to show the farmers and their families the social and economic advantages they can gain by making certain changes in the traditional practices of farming and in the organization of village life. There is no doubt that the influence of such programs is already being felt and that the effectiveness of these community services will grow. But the task of organizing to carry useful information to the farmers of India, and of getting it put to practical use, is enormous. It involves securing the villagers' acceptance of new ideas in so many fields—farming, health, co-operative activity in credit, in marketing, in certain types of land reform, in road building, in minor irrigation projects, and in many other areas in which changes in organization are essential to a better village life. Many of India's leaders are aware of the tremendous job ahead of them and their people, but many of them also seem to underestimate the difficulties. A few facts may help the reader appreciate the size and nature of the task India faces in carrying information about better agriculture to the villagers, and in creating and activating the new forms of village organization necessary for the improvement of village life.

There are 550,000 to 600,000 villages in India, and they have a total population of 275 to 300 million. Fourteen major languages are recognized in India's constitution, and some hundreds of local dialects are spoken. Most of the villagers have never communicated with outside people, except those in neighboring villages not more than a few miles away. Not more than 12 to 15 per cent of the villagers can read, and the proportion of the older and more influential people in the villages who can read is far smaller than this. The cultural differences between some of the major language groups have great significance for the establishment of agricultural and community extension services. These differences mean that, for all practical purposes, India must establish many extension services to meet a great variety of needs and conditions. Local cultural differences are often critically important, since they act as barriers to the operation of broad general plans for extension work until such plans are adapted, through practical experience, to local conditions.

The village workers are being selected and trained as carefully as is possible in view of the great need for haste and the relatively small numbers of persons with suitable backgrounds from which trainees must be drawn. In spite of very careful selection, many of the trainees are not well fitted for the difficult job of unobtrusive leadership and counseling in village life. This is not surprising. It is much more surprising that so many of them do make good in such a delicate position, since most of the young men who have the equivalent of a high-school education (approximately the minimum of general education needed by such an extension worker) have been out of touch with village life for several years at least, and many of them have never lived in a village and know nothing about agriculture except what they learn from a book. Under present circumstances, most of these village workers cannot confine their efforts to agricultural improvement alone. They must be able to advise on health problems, to give the farmers information about their credit and marketing problems, to show the villagers how to take advantage of the other services being provided by the state and the central government, to help in the organization of schools, and to explain to the villagers how they can co-operate in many other enterprises to their mutual benefit. Thus, the village worker must be competent to deal with all the problems which are important to the villagers and, above all, he must be tactful and discreet if he is to be accepted as a counselor and friend in the village. His task is truly a difficult one; considerable time will be needed to find the right people for these jobs, to train them and to provide them with the needed experience.

The program for village improvement is going forward, but not too much should be expected of it in five years, or even in ten or fifteen years. As more and more of the villagers learn to read, and as electricity is carried to more and more villages so that radios can be used to disseminate information, the program for village improvement should gain momentum. But it does not seem reasonable to expect that progress in agricultural practices will be much more rapid than progress in the improvement of village life as a whole, since agricultural production is simply one aspect of the life of the village.

An example of what the preceding statement implies may help give it greater clarity. Many references have been made to the importance of health work in the villages, the implication being that the improvement of agriculture is closely bound up with the improvement of health. This is certainly the case. The diseases most markedly affecting the farmer's ability to work may be divided, for convenience, into two categories according to their somewhat different effects on agricultural production. There are the acute diseases which have had a relatively high incidence of mortality in the past, such as typhoid fever, cholera, smallpox, diphtheria, and typhus. Many victims of these diseases died within a short time. Those who recovered often had long periods of convalescence during which they were unable to work. These diseases are now in process of being eliminated, but are still quite deadly. However, another category of diseases is probably even more important from the standpoint of agricultural production. These diseases —malaria, dysentery or chronic diarrhea, and tuberculosis—do not have a high incidence of mortality immediately following infection, but they weaken the victim over a prolonged period and greatly reduce his vigor and efficiency. Most of these latter diseases are still extremely prevalent in India, although their incidence is also being reduced.

The economic significance of the prevalence of these debilitating diseases is generally recognized today. India's health authorities are taking all the measures within their power to reduce—both in the villages and in the cities—malaria, filariasis, tuberculosis, kala azar, etc., and to encourage sanitation in water supplies and in sewage handling. These measures will reduce the death rate, of course, but their effects on the vitality of the people may be even more important for the time being. It seems highly probable that increased vitality may contribute as much to increased agricultural production through better care of crops during the next decade or two as will the spread of knowledge regarding scientific agriculture, although both, of course, are indispensible to a highly efficient agriculture.[1]

AGRICULTURAL ACHIEVEMENTS OF THE FIRST
FIVE-YEAR PLAN

First, a few words must be said regarding the conditions under which the first Five-Year Plan was formulated. This plan, which ended in the spring of 1956, should be thought of largely as a practical effort to get the national economy of India on its feet and moving on the path of progress. Partition, which took place at the same time independence was achieved (1947), created serious economic problems for both India and Pakistan. It disrupted in many ways the integrated economy of the subcontinent which had developed under British rule. At the same time, partition left India with the problem of caring for a refugee population of about 7 to 8 million in 1947 and 1948, and perhaps nearly 2 million more in 1950–51. (About 8.5 million of the people in India in 1951 had been born in territory which, by partition, became part of Pakistan.) The food situation had been growing increasingly precarious for some years (see above) and became extremely serious during the war. By 1949 India's imports amounted to 3–4 million tons of food grains annually, which placed a very heavy burden on her foreign exchange. Such imports would soon exhaust India's credits abroad, and meant that little of the exchange earned by

[1] It is estimated, for example, that for each death attributable to malaria, there are probably between 100 and 200 persons suffering from the disease. The wiping-out of this one disease should have tremendous significance for agriculture, even more than for industry and commerce, since malaria is more prevalent in rural than in urban areas—as are filariasis and many of the intestinal ailments caused chiefly by unsanitary water supplies and sewage disposal.

her exports would be left to pay for the import of much-needed capital goods and certain indispensable consumption goods, such as medicines and educational equipment. These urgent problems, plus the preoccupation with establishing a new government staffed entirely by Indians, delayed until 1951 the effort to set up any definite plans and goals for economic development.

Under the existing circumstances it seemed clear to the people responsible for the country's economic development that little improvement in productivity could be expected in the economy as a whole until the country was made practically self-supporting with respect to food. Furthermore, partition had deprived India's cotton and jute mills of the raw materials which had previously been produced in what is now Pakistan. Pakistan had also sent some food into the area which later became India. This situation made it very urgent to increase the production of food and fibers within the Indian Union, and explains in large measure the relatively heavy emphasis the first Five-Year Plan placed upon improving agricultural production.[2]

The chief direct means the first Five-Year Plan depended upon to increase agricultural production have just been discussed, and their contributions to increased production should not be underrated. It remains highly uncertain, however, how much of the increase in crop production during this first plan, an increase amounting to about 20 per cent in the last year of the plan, resulted from the basic improvements achieved under the plan—improvements which could reasonably be expected to endure and to supply a foundation for further increase in coming years. The chief reason for this uncertainty is that three of the five years enjoyed *good* monsoons. In addition, it is hard to say how much of the gain was due to recovery from the harmful effects of the vast partition migration and of the war. The larger part of the increase in the irrigated area, amounting to 17 million acres, or about 5 per cent of the total cropped area, should be considered a permanent improvement, rendering production on perhaps two-thirds of that area more immune to annual fluctuations in the monsoons. Any new land brought into cultivation could be put in the same category, but the

---

[2] Lest this statement leave a wrong impression with the reader, it should be said that, although the improvement of agricultural production was often declared to be the chief goal of the first plan, not more than one-third of the capital expenditures for which it provided were allotted to agriculture, including all types of village improvement, irrigation, and multipurpose power projects. Of course, considerable proportions of the development expenditures allotted to transport and social services (education and health) would be of great benefit to the agricultural population and would have an effect on agricultural production in due time.

amount of this was small. The increase in the use of better seeds and the increase in the supply of commercial fertilizers may also be regarded as beginnings of new agricultural practices likely to spread year after year. But when all is said, three good monsoons in five years, one of them very good, must be regarded as a windfall of very great importance, whose recurrence is not to be *expected* in every succeeding five-year period, no matter how greatly it may be hoped for.

SOME FURTHER DIFFICULTIES

I do not want to dwell unduly upon additional difficulties which must be overcome in order to insure steady and rapid agricultural improvement, but I feel I must be realistic at least to the point of mentioning several such difficulties I regard as highly important.

Illiteracy.—As has already been noted, the task of getting the farmers to adopt better agricultural practices is greatly complicated by the fact that a high proportion of Indian villagers, perhaps more than 85 per cent, are illiterate. The proportion of illiteracy among the villagers (chiefly farmers) who are over forty years of age is, of course, even higher, and these are the men who are largely in control of most aspects of village life. Although much effort is being devoted to bringing elementary education to the villages, the funds available are so small that actual accomplishment lags far behind intent. Quite naturally, most of the schools being established are for children; adult education has scarcely more than begun. It will be some years before any significant proportion of the more influential farmers can read. Until then the written word cannot be used to any great extent to inform farmers about those developments in agriculture which would help them to be better farmers. Even the radio cannot be used to any great extent as yet, nor will it be for some years. About 99 per cent of the villages do not have electricity, and only an additional 1 per cent are expected to receive it during the second Five-Year Plan. At present the villagers cannot afford to buy both radios and batteries. Language differences further increase the cost of all types of communication in the country as a whole.

Suspicion of officials.—In India, as in all countries where a high proportion of the people are illiterate and where the villagers have had almost no contact with outsiders—except with government officials who were police or taxgatherers, and with landlords and their bailiffs— the people are highly suspicious of any and all officials, and of outsiders generally. Much of this suspicion will disappear as literacy increases and as the villagers realize that the government is trying to help them and that the landlords no longer possess the power they formerly had to appropriate most of the gains from increased production.

Land reform.—Two aspects of land reform are also of importance. (1) The relationship between the tenant and his landlord has been greatly improved in some of the states, but much still remains to be accomplished in this respect. Besides, comparatively little has been done as yet to provide the mass of farmers with adequate motives to improve their production. For example, it is said that about 30 per cent of the farmers, many of whom are owners but do not till all their land themselves, still get about 70 per cent of the national agricultural product. If this is true, a large proportion of the actual farmers must have little economic incentive to improve production, because so large a part of the increase would still go to the landlord. (2) The second important aspect of land reform concerns the excessive fragmentation of the holdings of many of the farmers who have average-size farms. A farm of three to five acres is frequently composed of several parcels of land scattered over different parts of the area surrounding a village. This makes it impossible for the farmer to use the land efficiently, besides wasting much land to provide paths between tiny fields. Very little has been done as yet to consolidate these small parcels into single units which could be farmed more efficiently.

Village credit facilities.—The village moneylender, present everywhere, usually charged excessively high rates of interest and kept many farmers constantly in his debt. In a number of states he is no longer allowed to operate, but his suppression did not automatically improve the farmer's credit facilities and thereby benefit him economically, because there was no credit agency to take the moneylender's place and to provide production loans at reasonable rates. This kind of service is gradually being set up on a just basis, but its establishment takes time, just as it takes time to overcome the villagers' reluctance to deal with the outsider who represents a state agency.

FAVORABLE FACTORS IN THE OUTLOOK

In India, as in the other underdeveloped countries of South and East Asia, the expansion of agricultural production should proceed faster today than seemed probable before World War II. The most up-to-date knowledge regarding the production of all kinds of crops and livestock products is being made available through many channels, particularly by means of technical aid, to every country which is organized, as India is, to make use of such information in agricultural schools and to give it field trials on experimental farms. India has a number of good agricultural schools staffed with well-trained men. These men are just as quick to appreciate the significance of scientific advances taking place in agriculture in any part of the world as are their colleagues who live in the West. But in agriculture, as in industry (see following chapter), India does not have enough trained personnel. In view of the vastness of her agricultural problems, she needs many more trained men, and they in turn need better equipment with which to work. Furthermore, the emphasis now being placed on industrial and engineering education and research means that there is great danger of agricultural education and research being relegated to a secondary position. In the second plan there is considerable evidence of complacency with the agricultural accomplishments of the first plan. In spite of the fact that the absolute amount of money allotted to agriculture and community development in the second plan is much larger (52 per cent) than it was in the first plan, proportionally it is only 12 per cent of the total development fund, whereas it was 16 per cent in the first plan. This slighting of agriculture may prove a very serious mistake, not only as regards agricultural development itself, but also with respect to industrial development; for, as has been shown in chapters iii, v, and vi, much of the capital for nonagricultural development in any underdeveloped country must come from agriculture. In India such capital can be secured through agricultural production only by means of a fairly rapid increase in agricultural efficiency, since India cannot rapidly expand her cultivated area.

CONCLUSIONS

This discussion of India's agricultural development since independence has attempted to arrive at as objective an answer as possible to the question, Can India provide her population with an increasingly adequate diet and, at the same time, produce an increasing supply of other essential agricultural products (cotton, jute, tea) for export while her population continues to increase at a fairly rapid rate at the present and at a still higher rate in the near future? I presume that it is impossible to be highly objective in answering such a question, because different people will give different weights to the relevant factors and, as a consequence, will come out with different answers, all of which will be in terms of probability. If the probabilities in this case are graded as *poor, fair,* and *good,* then I must rate the probability of India's providing enough agricultural products to make possible a rise of, say, 3 per cent a year in the level of living as only *fair* to *poor.*

I am driven to this conclusion chiefly by the weight I attach to two factors. In the first place, I am less hopeful than many Indians and foreigners that the birth rate will decline fast enough in the next twenty to twenty-five years to substantially reduce the rate of population growth, to say nothing of reducing it to zero, i.e., that the population will become virtually stationary in twenty to twenty-five years. In the second place, I am less hopeful than some people that the farmers of India will quickly adopt those improved practices and new forms of village organization which would add rapidly, say 4 to 5 per cent, to agricultural production year after year for the next generation. Basically, the grave doubts I have expressed concerning both of these points arise from my conviction that the age-old cultural patterns of the Indian people cannot be changed fast enough to permit a large and steady increase in production year by year, beginning immediately.

I have no doubt whatever that India's agricultural production can be increased greatly in the course of time, but I am not convinced that it can be increased rapidly enough to provide for the population increase likely to come in the next two or three decades, to provide for a substantial improvement in the level of living of the masses, to supply the agricultural raw materials and exports that increasing industrialization will demand, and to furnish a large part of the capital needed during the next two decades. My doubts arise from what seem to be the most reasonable answers to such questions as the following: Are enough of the funds which have been allotted to economic development in India being used for agricultural development to insure the most rapid possible increase in agricultural production? Is the relatively complacent attitude induced by the increase in agricultural production during the first plan justified? Or was this increase so largely of a windfall variety, due to good monsoons, that it constitutes a poor basis on which to estimate probable future increases? Is enough attention being given to modifying the cultural obstacles which prevent the more rapid adoption of better farming practices?

Since it seems to me that the problems implied in these questions cannot safely be ignored, I find myself seriously doubting whether Indian agriculture will meet the test to which it is being put; notice that I say *will* meet, not *can* meet. In India, as in many other countries, *possibilities* are too easily confused with *probabilities*. I very much fear that this is now happening with respect to India's future agricultural production. It is easy to assume that because a certain course of action—in this case, better farming—is rational it will rapidly become the modal action. It is easy to forget that what is rational to an illiterate farmer living in an environment where tradition still has great power differs markedly from what is considered rational by a more educated person relatively emancipated from tradition.

In a word, I seriously doubt whether India has more than well begun to work on her agricultural problems; I even regard the lack of vigorous efforts to acquaint the people with the need for a slower growth of population as a piece of indirect evidence that the difficulties confronting agricultural improvement are being underestimated.

CHAPTER X

INDIA:

INDUSTRIAL DEVELOPMENT

If the term industry is used broadly, to include all aspects of the economy except agriculture, there will be little question that industrial development is just as essential as agricultural development for improving the level of living in underdeveloped countries. The aim of this chapter is to examine India's industrial development in somewhat the same manner as the preceding chapter examined her agricultural development.

Implicit in the term *underdeveloped,* as applied to South and East Asia, is the assumption that the resources of these countries, both human and material, have not been and are not being used efficiently according to modern standards. The leaders of India fully realize that the resources of their country are not being well used, and they are now undertaking to remedy the situation in industry as well as in agriculture. A series of limited, but enlarging, industrial objectives are being set in the successive five-year plans.

THE INDUSTRIAL STATUS, 1951

Rural and urban populations.—The urban (nonagricultural) population of India has been growing at a much more rapid rate in recent decades than the rural (village) population, as Table 13 shows.

This relatively rapid growth of towns (cities) has been characteristic of countries in which industry, as contrasted with agriculture, has been developing rather quickly; such growth has usually been accompanied by a decrease in the proportion of the total population which depends directly on agriculture for its livelihood. As late as the census of 1951, such a decrease in the agricultural population does not seem to have taken place in India. A significant part of the very rapid increase in India's "town" population between 1941 and 1951 was stimulated by partition, not by the development of industry. It has already been noted that in 1951 there were about 8.5 million displaced persons from Pakistan living in India. Nearly two-thirds of them apparently settled in the cities (139, pp. 610, 611). The census data indicate that, in spite of this large increase in "town" population, there has been no appreciable decline in the proportion of India's population that is dependent on agriculture.

In 1931 "all earners and working dependents with agricultural occupations" constituted 67 per cent of "all earners plus working dependents," while in 1951 "all self-supporting persons in agricultural

TABLE 13

POPULATION (IN THOUSANDS) AND PER CENT CHANGE,
VILLAGES AND TOWNS, INDIA, 1921–51*

CENSUS YEAR	POPULATION		PER CENT CHANGE	
	Villages	Towns	Villages	Towns
1951.........	295,000	61,900	8.9	41.3
1941.........	271,000	43,800	12.0	31.1
1931.........	242,000	33,400	10.1	18.4
1921.........	219,900	28,200	....	....

* Source: 134, 1951, I, Part 1-A, 152.

classes and earning dependents with agricultural income" constituted 70 per cent of "all self-supporting persons plus earning dependents" (134, 1951, I, Part 1-B, 206). Although it must be recognized that these 1951 categories cannot be equated exactly with the categories of 1931, the statement of the census authorities that "the relative weight of dependence on agriculture for gainful employment has not declined in the country as a whole" during this twenty-year period, seems to be justified (*ibid.*, p. 225).[1]

Classes of industrial workers.—Both in 1931 and in 1951, almost one-third of India's workers were engaged in nonagricultural tasks. This proportion of nonagricultural workers is much higher than that of many other underdeveloped countries. It indicates that for some time India has had an economy which supported a relatively large number of workers engaged in commerce, manufactures, and the services.

The total number of persons employed in nonagricultural occupations in 1951 was 32.37 million. Of this number, 12.15 million (37.5 per cent) were engaged in production, 5.9 million (18.2 per cent) in trade, 3.29 million (10.2 per cent) in health, education, and public

[1] Comparable figures based on the 1941 census were never issued.

administration, 1.9 million in transport, storage, and communications, 1.59 million in construction and utilities, and 7.54 million in other services (*ibid,* Part 1-A, p. 98).

In 1951, 3.3 per cent of the persons earning a living through non-agricultural employment were classified as employers, 44.3 per cent as employees, 49.4 per cent as self-employed, and the remainder, 3 per cent, were not classified (*ibid.,* p. 96).

There are apparently no data showing the number of persons employed in factories and workshops classified by number of employees, e.g., 1–4, 5–9, etc. All references to nonagricultural production, however, assume that a large majority of the workers are either self-employed or are employed in very small workshops where handwork prevails, as contrasted with mechanized factories. This assumption is certainly confirmed by the number of persons employed in factories, 1947–52, as reported by the Census of Manufactures; this number remained practically stationary during this period at about 1.6 million, or at about 13 per cent of those reported engaged in nonagricultural production (330, p. 16). Further evidence that a great preponderance of the nonagricultural workers are found in small unmechanized workshops is contained in the "Report of the Village and Small Scale Industries Committee (Second Five Year Plan)." According to this report, the number of employees expected to be affected by the schemes proposed by this committee amounted to almost 5 million (138, p. 82). Since this report dealt only with a selected group (sixteen) of such industries—those which could be organized to contribute most advantageously to the aims of the second Five-Year Plan—it can be assumed that vast numbers of self-employed artisans in the villages, small cities, and even in larger cities were not included in this 5 million.

In light of the available facts, it seems probable that about 85 per cent of the persons engaged in nonagricultural production in 1951 were either self-employed or were working in very small and largely nonmechanized workshops. Even in the cotton textile industry, which is comparatively highly developed, only about 780,000 persons worked in factories and mills, while about 2.5 to 2.75 million worked in small shops which used only hand power. In metals and chemicals, where basic production requires large-scale mechanized enterprises to insure efficiency, only 110,000 persons out of a total of 1.24 million, or less than 10 per cent, were classed as employed in the basic manufacture of iron and steel. The great majority of the remainder engaged in these two heavy industries were employed in small workshops which fabricated various types of light metal products by hand, or in equally small chemical manufactures.

Although the data given above relate chiefly to the period just before the beginning of the first Five-Year Plan (1951), there appears to have been practically no change in employment "in the leading sections of the organized industries between 1947 (index 136.6) and 1954 (index 135.9)," with 100 representing the employment in 1939 (330, p. 16). Thus it seems very doubtful whether the highly organized and mechanized industries employed a larger proportion of the workers engaged in nonagricultural production when the first plan was one-half over than at its beginning. However, about 4 million more persons, or approximately one-half of the increase which took place in the labor force in 1951–56, seem to have found employment during the plan, although not in factories using power machinery.

At the present time, therefore, 80 to 85 per cent of the nonagricultural workers engaged in production must still be working for themselves or in small shops which very often employ only one or two workers. In these shops practically all of the work is done with hand tools. When machines are used at all, e.g., looms, they are operated by hand power, as they have been for generations. Fewer than 1 per cent of the villages, and very few of the small cities, have electricity, and even in many cities of 100,000 or more it is not available for power. Modern power-driven machinery is confined chiefly to a few of the larger cities and to certain industries where large-scale production is particularly advantageous, e.g., to cotton textile mills, shoe factories, jute mills, railway equipment shops, the iron and steel industry, and a few others. In many cases, such factories find it necessary to furnish their own power. This great preponderance of very small hand-production units goes far to explain the great interest India now takes in village and small-scale industry, although it is by no means the sole reason for this interest, as will be noted below.

Transportation.—India has more than 40,000 miles of railways and, although it is a large country, is better served by rail transportation than most underdeveloped countries (18, pp. 130–48). Much must be done, however, if rail transportation is to be made adequate to meet the needs of a modern industrial economy. This fact is recognized in both the first and the second five-year plans, as will be shown later. It is not so clear that the importance of roads and road transport is fully appreciated, although almost one-third as much of the developmental funds is being allotted to the improvement of roads as to railway services. In any event, it appears that India's transport services are being improved to meet the demands of a rapidly expanding industrial economy. But it should be noted that the heavy expenditures on railways do not return an immediate increase in production, although they are essential to industrial development.

Electric power.—In 1951, India's total generating capacity for electricity was 2.3 million kilowatts. This was only about one-fourth the capacity of Japan's power industry, although India's population was more than four times as large as Japan's. Power production was heavily concentrated in Calcutta and Bombay. It is little wonder that much emphasis is being placed on the expansion of electric generating capacity and, especially, on wider distribution of power to small cities and villages. The improvement of small-scale industrial production and of village life in general depends, in large measure, upon the rapid extension of electric service. Relatively large sums are now being devoted to this purpose.

The improvement of communications is also being pushed as a basic service which is needed not only by the economy in general but also for the extension of education and other cultural projects.

THE FIRST FIVE-YEAR PLAN FOR INDUSTRY

The conditions under which the first Five-Year Plan was inaugurated have been described briefly in the preceding chapter. It was also shown there that even on a very generous estimate of the allocation of developmental funds for agriculture under this plan, such funds did not exceed about one-third of the total.

Industrial expenditures.—In the public sector, only about one-half of the amount the first Five-Year Plan allocated to the expansion of large-scale industries (chiefly heavy industry) and to scientific research and development was actually spent—Rs. 750 million out of an allocation of Rs. 1,490 million (140, p. 23). In the private sector, however, about Rs. 3,400 million were spent on industrial development. This amounted to approximately 89 per cent of the Rs. 3,830 million originally allocated (140, p. 110). Transport and communications (practically all public) were given the largest developmental allotment in the first Five-Year Plan, Rs. 5,560 million (140, p. 35). The actual expenditure in this category fell only a little short of the planned goals, but a great deal still remained to be done to make the railways efficient, to extend transportation service into additional communities, and to improve and extend communications. The moneys spent apparently did not go nearly as far as expected. The increase in electric power capacity amounted to about 50 per cent during the first plan, raising the total capacity from 2.3 million to 3.4 million kilowatts, which was approximately as planned (140, p. 103).

As regards the attainment of material goals in the industrial sector of the first plan, the most serious failure was in an attempt to build additional steel mills and to carry on industrial research. These enterprises proved both more difficult and more costly than anticipated. But definite advances were made in these areas, and should begin to yield results toward the end of the second plan.

On the whole, the failure to attain certain production goals in the industrial sector was far less disturbing than the failure to increase employment as fast as the labor force increased. In broad terms, it appears that the additional jobs created by increased investment during the first plan provided for only about one-half of the additional entrants into the labor force: employment was found in nonagricultural work for an additional 4.5 million, whereas the number of workers needing employment increased again by nearly 10 million (140, pp. 40–47). This fact is widely recognized and is causing much concern. At the end of the first plan, the estimated backlog of unemployed persons amounted to 5.3 million. These presently unemployed persons cannot be absorbed into agriculture without creating much additional underemployment and thereby increasing the poverty of the villagers. Furthermore, many—perhaps most—of the industrial enterprises already begun require intensive use of capital rather than extensive use of labor. But even in the organized and mechanized industries referred to above, no increase in employment took place up to 1954, although there had been about a 50 per cent increase in production (330, p. 16). The outlook for an adequate increase in industrial employment is not good.

Social services.—The social services—education, health, rehabilitation of the 8–9 million refugees from Pakistan, and housing—were improved approximately according to plan, which called for the expenditure of Rs. 5,470 million (140, p. 35), practically all of which was, of course, in the public sector. But everyone realized that only a beginning had been made in the extension of education and in the application of health measures. Much has been done toward the rehabilitation of refugees, but this remains a pressing problem, as does the provision of adequate housing in those cities which are growing most rapidly.

The first Five-Year Plan, as already noted, was generally regarded more or less as an emergency measure, put together under great difficulties and intended chiefly to relieve the urgency of the food situation and to begin the laying of foundations for future industrial expansion. The first plan seems to have encountered relatively little criticism, and its accomplishments, especially in agriculture, seem to be regarded by the planners with considerable complacency.

THE SECOND FIVE-YEAR PLAN

When the outlines of the second plan were issued for discussion, they brought forth many suggestions and much criticism, as was to be expected. Not even the chief criticisms can be enumerated here, but two or three of the most fundamental should be mentioned.

Vakil and Brahmanand made several basic criticisms with which I find myself in substantial agreement (330). The chief of these are that: (1) the underlying assumptions of the second plan are derived from the study of more developed economies and of Soviet plans, and probably are not equally valid when applied to India's economy; (2) the emphasis on heavy industry is not likely to bring as great an increase in employment as would the use of a similar amount of funds for "wage goods" and construction, enterprises requiring a relatively small investment in proportion to the labor used; (3) the second plan starts from an assumption of a rate of increase in national income of 25 per cent in five years and then works out the amount of investment and the other details on the basis of what will be needed to secure this rate as an end result if the ratio of investment to increase in production is about 2.2 to 1—a ratio entirely too low for the type of investment planned; and that (4) the expected increase in employment (about 8.5 million) is only about 85 per cent or less of the expected increase in the labor force, and it makes no provision for the increase in the unemployed labor force which accumulated during the first plan. This increase amounted to about 5.5 million, which makes a total increase of about 7 million in unemployed probable by the end of the second plan (1961), as well as a substantial increase in the number of underemployed persons.

I would add on my own account that the rate of population increase (1.25 per cent per year) used in the second plan is too low—the rate may even be as much as one-half larger (1.7–1.8 per cent); also that the funds allotted to planned-parenthood clinics and propaganda are entirely inadequate to inaugurate any substantial decline in the birth rate, while those allocated to health work will almost certainly continue to reduce the death rate. Furthermore, it is altogether possible—in my opinion, probable—that greater effort to improve agriculture would yield more solid results economically than some of the heavy industrial investments which are planned. I do not find myself as much disturbed over the plans to improve village and small-scale industries as are the authors mentioned above. I am much more concerned about taxation policies which seem to assume that agriculture cannot be expected to contribute much more than it is now contributing to the investment fund and to the support of the social services. There is still much inequity in the distribution of the agricultural income which might be taxed for use in economic development.

The total outlay contemplated in the public sector by the second Five-Year Plan is just about double (Rs. 48,000 million) that scheduled in the first plan (Rs. 23,560 million) (139, p. 52), but its allocations to the several sectors of the economy are quite different, and these differences raise many important questions.

Because the planning authorities believed that the organization for improving agricultural production set up during the first Five-Year Plan had worked well, and because they believed that further expansion of agricultural production at a fairly rapid rate would require *relatively* less investment of new capital, they felt that a second Five-Year Plan could and should place more emphasis on the development of basic industry and the further expansion of the basic services needed by industry than had been practicable in the first Five-Year Plan. The six main categories set up for expenditure in the public sector of India's economy by the first and second plans, and the proportions of the expenditures in each, are given in Table 14.

In every main category the amounts allotted by the second plan are substantially increased, but the proportions assigned to agricultural and community development, to irrigation and power, and to social services have been considerably reduced as compared with the proportions assigned to these same categories in the first plan. The large proportional increases are found in the allotments to industries and minerals and to transport and communications. These two categories together are assigned 48 per cent of the total, and if electric power generation is added they account for between 57 and 58 per cent of the total.

Some concrete goals.—The generating capacity of electric plants is to be doubled during the second plan. Finished steel production—which increased from 1.1 million tons to 1.3 million tons during the first plan—is to be expanded to 4.3 million tons by 1960–61, while production of pig iron for foundries is to be increased from 380,000 tons to 750,000 tons. Coal production is to be increased from 36.8 million tons to 60.0 million tons (63 per cent), and iron ore production is to be tripled (from 4.3 million tons to 12.5 million tons). Aluminum production is to be increased even faster than iron production, but the total will remain quite small (25,000 tons). Cement production is to be doubled (10 million tons), while fertilizer production is to be quadrupled (2.2 million tons). Production of such consumer goods as bicycles, sewing machines, and automobiles is to be doubled, or more than doubled. The production of many specific items is to increase at even

TABLE 14

EXPENDITURES AND PER CENT DISTRIBUTION BY CATEGORY, SCHEDULED IN THE FIVE-YEAR PLANS, INDIA*

CATEGORY	FIRST FIVE-YEAR PLAN (ENDING MARCH 1, 1956)		SECOND FIVE-YEAR PLAN (ENDING MARCH 1, 1961)	
	Amount Provided (Millions of Rupees)	Per Cent Distribution	Amount Provided (Millions of Rupees)	Per Cent Distribution
Total....................	23,560	100	48,000	100
Agriculture and community development.................	3,720	16	5,650	12
Irrigation and power..........	6,610	28	8,980	18
Industries and minerals........	1,790	7	8,910	19
Transport and communications.	5,560	24	13,840	29
Social services, etc............	5,470	23	9,460	20
Miscellaneous...............	410	2	1,160	2

* Adapted from 140, p. 22. This includes only expenditures in the public sector.

more rapid rates, e.g., machine tools, 300 per cent; sugar machinery, 400 per cent; and textile machinery, 376 per cent (140, pp. 37–38). But even if these increases are achieved, the actual volume in many instances will remain quite small.

Education.—The urgent need for specialized education that will provide the scientists, engineers, and technicians on whom the development of the industrialization program depends is fully realized. Strong efforts are being made to establish new technical institutes and to improve the quality and increase the quantity of work in the existing research centers. There can be little doubt, however, that India will continue to need all the technical assistance she can get from abroad for some years to come. She will have urgent need for men who have had wide practical experience in the types of work India must undertake and who, at the same time, have had actual contacts with peoples of Eastern culture while working on modern industrial enterprises.

The great emphasis India is placing on technical training and industrial research has without doubt adversely affected the spread of conventional education at the primary, secondary, and even higher levels; for India, like all underdeveloped countries, is woefully short of the financial resources needed to build, equip, and staff elementary and secondary schools for her vast population.

The work which has been done in the villages to improve agriculture and other aspects of village life has emphasized the fact that elementary education is greatly needed if progress in agriculture is to be fairly rapid. Nothing will be more helpful in breaking down the traditional barriers to the adoption of new ideas and practices than an increase in literacy and an elementary knowledge of arithmetic. At the beginning of the first plan, primary school facilities were available to only 42 per cent of the children aged six to eleven, and the facilities in cities were more adequate than those in villages. Facilities were increased to care for 50 per cent of this age group during this plan, and are expected to be adequate for 60 per cent by the end of the second plan. Schools were available to only 14 per cent of the children aged eleven to fourteen in 1951; by 1956 schools had been provided for 17 per cent of this age group, and are expected to be adequate for 19 per cent of children aged eleven to fourteen years in 1961 (140, p. 39). This is good progress; but as long as a large majority of the people over thirty to thirty-five years of age remain illiterate, especially in the villages, we must expect a great deal of resistance to changes in those traditional values and patterns of thought which determine both social and economic behavior. This will be especially true in the villages, where the individual farmer must be "converted" to the new ideas and practices in order to increase his efficiency. The case is quite different in industry, although even there formidable obstacles stand in the way of ready adaptation to new tasks.

In chapter iii attention was called to the importance of breaking the power of tradition if rapid progress is to be made in the development of a modern economy. Are the Indian plans for expanding education adequate to supplant quickly the dominance of tradition in the behavior of the people, so that they can adjust themselves to the demands of the new economy both in agriculture and in industry? It seems to me highly doubtful whether this transition will take place as fast as appears to be assumed in the allocation of expenditures for these purposes.

THE NEED FOR TRAINED PERSONNEL

If it is assumed that the volume and rate of investment envisaged in the second plan are realized, and if it is further assumed that this investment is so distributed that it will not lead to a critical imbalance in the economy (although this second assumption, in particular, is open to question), there still remains the question of how effectively the concrete projects of the plan will be carried out, i.e., how efficiently the capital will be used. The answer to this question depends largely on the adequacy of the technical personnel, which, in turn, depends on the availability of funds for the building, equipping, and staffing of new scientific and research institutes and technical schools. These funds, of course, must come in large part from the annual national income (very little can be obtained from abroad for such purposes), thus reducing the funds available for capital goods.

But organized education, as well as training in schools, by no means insures the efficient operation of modern production and service enterprises in the early years of development. Actual experience is greatly needed by managers, by supervisors, by foremen, and by operatives. Such experience can only be acquired on the job. In the early stages of modern industrial development, this lack of experience will necessarily be reflected in a relatively high ratio of investment to increase in production. Efficiency in actual production, unlike technical knowledge, cannot be learned from a book. The individual can become proficient in his own job only through experience. In addition, the efficiency of an enterprise demands the right kind of organization; a large number of persons must be able to work together as an integrated group in which every person can be depended on to adjust his efforts to those of his fellows so that all processes move smoothly and the whole operation proceeds in balance. There is inevitably a time lag between the completion of formal training and education and the acquirement of technical skills on the one hand, and the achievement of a well-integrated plant organization on the other. When most of the personnel engaged in a new enterprise have had little experience, the volume and the quality of the product or the service will be relatively low for some time. This, no doubt, was one of the points Vakil and Brahmanand had in mind when they criticized the second Five-Year Plan for placing too much emphasis on heavy industry.

In India the development of an adequate supply of trained workers of all grades encounters many social, as well as economic, obstacles. Many of these social obstacles do not exist, at least to the same degree, in the West. For example, the Indian with a good education is quite likely to consider any kind of handwork beneath his dignity. A graduate engineer in India would be much less likely to help a workman or millwright install or repair a machine, or to do any other type of handwork, even in an emergency, than would an American engineer. Then, too, the traditions of caste are closely associated with specialization in occupation, which often hinders the effective organization of labor within an enterprise. Although caste regulations are no longer legally in effect, they still place many restrictions on the social mobility of individuals and, hence, will continue to retard the most efficient use of Indian labor for some time. There is no reason to doubt that these social limitations on the efficient training and use of workers of all grades will be overcome in time, but rigid caste distinctions and traditional attitudes toward occupational status cannot be expected to dissolve in a few years. Shortages of adequately trained workers, particularly of professional men with good scientific background and with adequate practical experience, of handworkers highly skilled in machine operation and maintenance, and of men experienced as foremen and supervisors are certain to persist for some years. Good education is a *critical* must, but so is practical experience.

THE NEED FOR CAPITAL

Obviously, the rapid expansion of the heavy and basic industries and the improvement and extension of such essential services as transportation and power will require relatively large amounts of capital per worker as compared with agriculture and the light industries. Expansion of these basic industries and services will also call for a large and rapid increase in trained and experienced personnel of many kinds, as has just been indicated.

No one knows precisely what annual capital investment is needed in India to insure a given amount of increase in the national income or to generate a given amount of new employment; nor does anyone know how the expediture of the limited amount of investment funds available should be distributed in order to insure a balanced production, i.e., enough production in each sector of the economy to keep the whole functioning effectively. But it seems safe to say that an underdeveloped country like India is not only going to be short of capital for some years, but is also going to make many mistakes in using such capital as is available, with the result that much of it will not be used efficiently, especially in the early years of industrial expansion.

If a national economy which is a going concern has a ratio of investment to increase in national income of 4 to 1, then, for each per cent of annual increase in population, that country will need an investment equal to 4 per cent of the national income to maintain the current level of living—to say nothing of improving this level. But this will be true only in a balanced economy where there is an established relation between the various sectors of production. India, with an annual increase in population of perhaps 1.5 per cent or more, would need, on this basis, an investment of 6 per cent or more of the national income merely to maintain the current level of living. But when investment is concentrated in basic and heavy industry producing capital goods, a larger investment ratio is needed to maintain customary living standards. This situation probably prevails in India today and may very well continue until the capital goods provided by the present investment in basic industry begin to yield larger returns in consumers' goods.

It was estimated in 1950–51 that India was then investing 5 per cent of the national income (137, pp. 14–15) and that the amount might be increased to 6.75 per cent by the end of the first plan (1956). This increase seems to have been accomplished (140, p. 25), and its achievement means that the annual average investment during the first plan was about 6 per cent. Such an investment would just about maintain the current level of living if production continued to maintain a balanced pattern. The Planning Commission has assumed that in India the ratio of investment to increase in national income is substantially lower than in more developed countries. It does not seem to me valid to assume that this is the case until more evidence is available, and the Planning Commission has not provided such evidence. The average annual increase in national income which it assumes took place during the first plan, an increase of about 3.6 per cent (140, p. 20), cannot properly be regarded as having been produced by the investment made during the plan. There was too large an element of "windfall" gains from good monsoons and from the full use of factory capacity already in existence. Good monsoons may recur in 1956–61, but factory capacity which was unused in 1951 and fully used at the end of the first plan (1956) cannot be used for additional production during the second plan, which will end in 1961.

India's second Five-Year Plan envisages a total expenditure, including both public and private sectors, of about Rs. 71 billion, or close to $15 billion (140, pp. 22–25). Of this amount, about Rs. 10 billion are regarded as current expenditures of a developmental character rather than as entirely new investments. Hence, about Rs. 61 billion, or an average of Rs. 12 billion annually, are considered as new investment. This would amount to a total of about $12.8 billion and an annual average of about $2.5 billion. Such a figure may not seem large to Americans, but for India it is truly prodigious and amounts to almost 12 per cent of the national income in 1956. However, if the *average* annual national income during the second plan rises to Rs. 121.4 billion (by 5 per cent a year), which is the goal set, the proportion of new investment to average national income for 1956–61 will amount to 10 per cent. This is total investment; the proportion coming from domestic investments is expected to increase from about 7 per cent of the national income in 1956 to 10 per cent in 1961, in view of "external assistance" of all kinds (140, pp. 24–26).

It does not seem unreasonable to assume that India could save and invest 10 per cent of her national income by 1961. Japan had probably done somewhat better than this (possibly 12–14 per cent of her national income) by 1900, or shortly thereafter, when her industrial development was at much the same stage as India's is today (see chaps. vi and vii). Japan's agricultural development at that time, however, was ahead of India's present development. Moreover, Japan's population was not then increasing as fast as India's is now. It seems highly probable that India would need to invest more than 10 per cent of her national income today in order to make any substantial improvement in the level of living among the masses.

SMALL-SCALE INDUSTRIES

The masses of the people in India still depend on village and small-scale industry for most of their nonagricultural goods except cotton textiles. They also depend largely on village industry for such services as rice cleaning and polishing, sugar making, and the pressing of oil from seeds.

It will not be possible here to examine in any detail the reasons which have led India's planning authorities to place great emphasis on preserving and encouraging village and small-scale producers in the consumption industries, while they are at the same time pressing hard to develop large-scale, fully mechanized enterprises in the basic and capital goods industries. It must suffice to mention only a few of the chief reasons. The most important of these seem to be that (1) there is a large body of men who can carry on such small-scale work without any additional training; (2) comparatively little capital is needed to continue and even to improve production in most of these small-scale industries, which are engaged almost entirely in producing consumers' goods; (3) it seems probable that considerably more employment can be generated by these industries during the next few years than by the mechanized factories that will, in time, replace them; (4) these small-scale industries are decentralized and will remain so, and therefore their continuance will help prevent the concentration of industry in a few large cities; and that (5) a large amount of small-scale enterprise, in which the workers are accustomed to co-operate in many ways, will make the establishment of a socialist economy easier.

There certainly is no agreement among the Indians about the validity of these reasons, nor about how well the schemes to increase production in small-scale workshops will succeed. Under the conditions prevailing in India today, it seems worthwhile to continue production in a number of types of small-scale industries, even though they may not yield as large an increase in goods as expected. This kind of production might help ease the hardships of unemployment and of underemployment inevitable in a period of transition from hand-operated industry to machine industry. The Indians would do well to study more carefully the development of small-scale industry in Japan.

MINERAL RESOURCES FOR INDUSTRY

There can be no reasonable doubt that India possesses the basic mineral resources essential to rapid industrial development during the next several decades. In this respect India is much more fortunate than Japan.

Fuel.—India's workable reserves of coal are estimated at about 20,000 million tons. (Some estimates run considerably higher.) About 5,000 million tons are of high quality, but only 1,000–2,000 million tons are classed as good coking coal suitable for metallurgical use (137, p. 165). Further exploration may very well lead to new discoveries, but the possibility of a shortage of coking coal within five to six decades is not being ignored. Plans are being made to reserve coking coal for metallurgical use, to economize on its use by mixing it with lower-quality coals, and to develop coking processes which will make possible the use, for metallurgical purposes, of some of the coals that cannot now be so used. For other uses, India's coal supplies should be ample for a century or more, since practically no coal is used for household purposes. India's industrial development during the next fifty or seventy-five years should not be hampered by a lack of coal. In addition, India has substantial supplies of lignite in the south. These are estimated at 2,000 to 3,000 million tons, and can probably be used for power production. As yet, only a small amount of petroleum has been discovered, chiefly in Assam. More widespread prospecting is now being undertaken, and hopes are rising that India may become less dependent on imported crude oil in the near future.

India's hydroelectric resources are quite large, the estimates varying from about 27 million horsepower to 39 million horsepower (102, 1942, p. 71). Comparatively little of this has been developed as yet, but a considerable proportion of the increase in generating capacity, in both the first and second plans, comes from hydroelectric sources.

Iron ore.—India possesses relatively large quantities of high-grade iron ore. The estimates vary considerably. In its official statement, the first Five-Year Plan says that "The reserves of good quality iron ore (containing over 60 per cent iron) are estimated to be over 10,000 million tons" (137, p. 167). The United Nations gives "measured and indicated" reserves as 6,420 tons, and "inferred" reserves as 21,300 million tons (296, pp. 295, 296). In any event, India's reserves of high-quality iron ore are adequate for her needs for some time to come, even if steel production should grow faster than now planned. Moreover, much of India's best iron ore is located within a relatively short distance of her best coking coal. Thus, the transportation costs of raw materials to the steel mills should be low.

Manganese.—India has large amounts of high-grade manganese, estimated at 18 million tons, and much larger amounts of lower-grade ores (44, p. 21). India's manganese deposits may very well be the largest in the world.

Bauxite.—It is estimated that India's bauxite, of a quality which contains 50 per cent or more of aluminum, exceeds 25 million tons, and that she has several times this amount of lower-grade ores.

Copper, lead, zinc, and tin.—India now imports most of her copper, 40,000 tons, as compared with about 6,000 tons of domestic production (44, pp. 146–54). At present it would not seem to pay her to make the effort needed to increase this production significantly. Lead and zinc are quite scarce, and tin seems to be lacking entirely.

Magnesite, mica, and titanium appear to be relatively abundant, but most of the nonferrous metals not already mentioned have not yet been found in workable amounts. India is a large country, however, and more thorough exploration may very well add significantly to the known reserves of many other useful minerals.

Building materials, pigment materials, abrasives, and refractory materials are abundant. Rather strict secrecy is being maintained regarding the raw materials needed for atomic power.

On the whole, it can safely be said that India possesses ample reserves of the minerals she needs for basic industry, and that what she lacks can be imported without putting a severe strain on her economy, once her steel industry develops a significant export capacity. Even her lack of phosphates and of sources of high-grade sulphur are not serious.

THE OUTLOOK FOR THE INDIAN ECONOMY

Some favorable factors.—There is no doubt that India's industrial development will be rapid, compared with that of most Western countries in the nineteenth century. It will also probably be rapid as compared with Japan's industrial development until about 1905–10.

1. *Understanding of economic development.* Today there is a much fuller understanding of what is needed for economic development, and of the processes involved in it, than there was in the past; this knowledge is being used in the making of plans, and in the organizing of national efforts, toward both agricultural and industrial development. However, there is still a great deal to be learned and many mistakes are bound to be made.

2. *The role of the state.* It is increasingly realized that the state can perform many useful functions in organizing the resources of the community for more efficient production. In the West, under the laissez-faire regime of the eighteenth and nineteenth centuries, the state performed comparatively few economic functions. This difference is probably inevitable, in view of the differences in cultural values and historical development between the East and the West. It is true, of course, that centralized governmental control of economic development raises many problems in the field of social and political values. These matters cannot be discussed here. However, the experiences of Japan and of the Soviet Union have shown beyond doubt that the state can do a great deal to hasten certain aspects of economic development. For the immediate future India and most of the other underdeveloped countries of Asia have chosen to use the state as the directive agency in such development. However, the present intention of the Indian government is to do this within the framework of democratic institutions.

3. *Rapid spread of knowledge.* Technical knowledge of how produc-

tion has been and can be improved is disseminated much more easily and more efficiently today than it has ever been in the past. India can secure, for less than it would have cost Japan when she began to industrialize, the most advanced scientific and technical knowledge. This would be true even if free, or almost free, technical assistance were not available from the outside. Until quite recently, much of the technical knowledge concerning more efficient processes of production was considered private property and was not freely imparted to others.

4. *Patriotism.* In India today there is a strong and widespread feeling which, for want of a better term, may be called patriotism. This provides many thousands of people with a stronger motive for devoted service to the nation than was possible under colonialism. For a time, at least, this patriotic motive is leading many men to exertions which we are accustomed to believe can be induced only by the profit motive or by a national emergency. In fact, a large number of Indians regard the need for rapid economic development as a national emergency comparable to war.

5. *Reception of new ideas.* Today the leaders and the educated people are generally highly receptive to new ideas, and this augurs well for India's speedy economic development. However, among the poorer classes in the cities, and especially among those in the villages, tradition puts heavy brakes on agricultural progress.

Some unfavorable factors.—Certain factors are distinctly unfavorable to India's rapid economic development and present unusually formidable difficulties. Two of the most important have already been discussed above at some length: (1) the scarcity of capital, and (2) the lack of an adequate supply of well-trained and experienced technical and managerial personnel and of skilled workmen.

3. *Traditionalism.* An additional word is needed here regarding traditionalism as an unfavorable factor for economic development. It can scarcely be insisted upon too strongly that the great mass of the people in the villages is still illiterate and that their behavior is still guided largely by custom. They cannot be forced, in the same way as industrial workers can, to accept new practices. But it is not possible to foretell how fast the agricultural extension work and the community services being established in the villages will break down the farmer's reluctance to put new ideas into practice and to develop new forms of community co-operation. Many examples could be cited which show quite rapid success in particular villages and areas. On the other hand, even more examples can be cited to show that many villages are highly

indifferent to improvement or even actively opposed to the new ideas which would lead to higher production and hasten the establishment of co-operative enterprises in the community. How obstructive traditionalism is, and will be, is necessarily largely a matter of opinion. Personally, I am convinced that both Indians and foreigners tend to underrate the retarding effect of tradition when they are calculating the probable speed with which agricultural production will increase in the villages.

There is no doubt that the degree of resistance to new ideas is also closely related to the degree of illiteracy; perhaps these two factors should be thought of as aspects of the same phenomenon. This matter of the retarding effect of illiteracy has been discussed above and need not be repeated here.

4. *Health.* In spite of considerable progress in health work, India still suffers heavily from many preventable diseases such as tuberculosis, smallpox, malaria, and many types of intestinal ailments. Some of these repeatedly incapacitate vast numbers of workers for long periods of time. It will certainly be some years before the amount of time lost from work through absence and impaired ability caused by illness will fall to the level prevailing in most Western countries today.

5. *Centralization and the states.* The centralized control of the Indian economy has been mentioned several times. To correct any wrong impression that may have arisen, it should be said that direct implementation of many of the public projects, and control over many economic matters, remain in the hands of the individual states rather than with the national government. This may or may not be a factor favorable to economic development. It undoubtedly tends to reduce the likelihood of highly centralized authoritarian control and makes it easier to adapt plans to local conditions, but it may also lead to significant differences in the efficiency of economic efforts in different parts of the country. This latter situation is probably inevitable in a large country like India, where many languages are spoken and where the real attachment of the masses is often to their own language group and its distinctive cultural patterns rather than to the nation as a whole—although, compared with other nations, the patriotism of the Indian masses probably leaves nothing to be desired. Furthermore, preservation of the integrity of the state or province within the nation may help to maintain personal and political freedom, whereas the tendency of a monolithic central government is to require a rather rigid conformity in all aspects of life.

SUMMARY AND CONCLUSIONS

In the preceding discussion an effort has been made (1) to describe the growth of India's population in recent decades and to evaluate the factors now operating to produce changes in its growth during the next two or three decades; (2) to indicate the status of agriculture at the beginning (1951) of India's five-year plans and to look ahead to what improvement seems probable within the next two or three decades; (3) to examine the nonagricultural aspects of the economy with the same objectives in view. In the very nature of the case, except for the factual descriptive material (which has been greatly condensed and is often inadequate), it is obvious that we are dealing here with probabilities interpreted personally from rather unsatisfactory materials.

Population.—The population of India in the spring of 1958, seven years after the census of 1951, is probably about 390 to 395 million if Kashmir-Jammu is not included, and about 395 to 400 million if it is included. The higher limit seems to me the more probable, considering the progress in health work and the lack of any evidence showing a decline in the birth rate. Twenty-five years from now, in 1983, the population is likely to be not less than 580 million; it may very well exceed that figure by 20 million or more, provided (*a*) health work continues to improve, (*b*) the per capita food supply is equal to that of the period of the first Five-Year Plan (1951–56), and (*c*) the birth rate does not begin to decline significantly for about ten or fifteen years. Proviso (*a*) seems highly probable to me, proviso (*b*) does not appear so probable as (*a*), and proviso (*c*) seems about as probable as (*a*).

It is generally recognized by India's leaders that the population is increasing fairly rapidly, although the rate of growth accepted as the basis for the official plans—about 1.2 per cent per year—seems substantially too low in light of the progress being made in improving the health services. However, as shown in chapter viii, it is not reasonable to expect a large country with great variations in climate and with important cultural differences from region to region to achieve as rapid a decline in the death rate as Japan and Ceylon. But it does not seem unreasonable to hold that India's death rate had fallen enough below the average prevailing in the period 1941–50 to have raised the rate of natural increase from 1.3 or 1.4 per cent to 1.5 or 1.7 per cent per year by the time the second plan began in the spring of 1956.

Production.—This probable underestimate of the rate of population growth makes it likely that even the fulfilment of the second plan would not improve the living conditions of the people as much as is officially expected. In addition, there is good reason to think that the increases in production aimed at in the second plan are calculated on the basis of achievements in the first plan which involved rather large "windfall" gains—due, in agriculture, to unusually favorable weather and, in industry, to the use of capacity which was already in existence but was not being used in 1951. Such achievements cannot properly be considered the result of fundamental improvements in production.

Partly because of the failure to recognize the "windfall" character of these increases in production, there seems to be inadequate appreciation of the role of food and fiber production as a source of capital for construction and, therefore, as the basis for increased employment using native products almost entirely. India already had much "open" unemployment, and this unemployment increased by several million during the first plan. Much underemployment also exists, especially in agriculture, and it too seems to be increasing. Hence, India has a relatively large unused labor supply. These people could work on many kinds of capital construction (roads, railroads, communication lines, electric transmission lines, flood control and irrigation works, schoolhouses and other public buildings, food storage warehouses, housing, etc.) at little more than the customary subsistence wages— chiefly food and clothing—or for only a little more than the public dole they receive or the amount they obtain as underemployed workers on their families' farms. Too great a preoccupation on the part of Indian planners with the pattern of economic development provided by the Soviet Union—such as vast amounts of capital spent on heavy industry—is undoubtedly also responsible for their relative neglect of agriculture. If Japan's economic development had been studied more carefully, there would probably have been more appreciation of the overwhelming predominance of agricultural improvement as a decisive factor in the early days of economic revolution in the crowded countries of Asia.

It should also be pointed out that the emphasis on heavy industry in the second plan means that even if the plan is fulfilled so that the expansion of production is as great as expected, this production will be used almost exclusively for further production for several years at least and will, therefore, contribute very little toward providing incentive goods to the great mass of farm workers, goods which would make them strive toward more productive labor. The more distant goals which motivate the educated people and the leaders will have little power to arouse the masses of the people to greater efforts. They must be offered immediate and tangible rewards in return for more efficient production.

On the whole, it seems to me that India's prospect for increasing production enough to raise the level of living is less bright than it is generally assumed to be by her leaders. As a consequence, it seems highly probable that the expectations of many educated people concerning a rapid improvement in living conditions will be realized less rapidly than anticipated. Moreover, the extension of education is arousing in an increasing number of young people desires and expectations of improvement that are not likely to be satisfied in the near future. Under a democratic system, this disappointment will almost certainly lead to vigorous demands that something be done quickly to improve living conditions—especially if unemployment among certain segments of the educated class, and in some labor groups, increases as it seems to be doing now. It is by no means impossible that these discontented groups, prodded along by the Communists, will demand an authoritarian government in the hope that such a government can force the pace of economic development and find good jobs for everyone.

Thus, increased population pressure in India in the near future seems less likely to support aggressive action against other countries for the purpose of gaining more land and resources than it does to open the way for establishing an authoritarian government, probably a communist government. There can be little doubt that if an authoritarian government were to supplant the present democratic one, India would soon be looking for more land and resources for her crowded population. Thus, although it does not appear probable that India will take aggressive action to secure larger resources in the near future because of population pressure, it cannot be taken for granted that the great difficulties she is encountering in speeding up her economic development will not put severe pressures even on a democratic government to search for additional means of improving living conditions. A totalitarian government could find many economic reasons ready and waiting to justify expansion into Burma, into Madagascar, and perhaps into the continent of Africa, in addition to the ideological reasons for expansion accepted by every totalitarian power.

CHAPTER XI

CHINA:

INTRODUCTORY AND POPULATION

INTRODUCTORY

The area of the Chinese Empire before World War II, including Manchoukuo, was probably about 4.5 million square miles. Of this area, the eighteen provinces of China Proper constituted a little less than one-third—about 1.4 million square miles. Manchoukuo contained 500,000 square miles. Most of the Empire outside of China Proper and Manchoukuo consisted of semidesert and desert lands in Mongolia and Central Asia, and of great areas in the high plateaus and mountainous regions stretching from Burma on the southwest, past India, and on westward to Afghanistan. For vast distances the western and northern borders were contiguous with the U.S.S.R. At present, due to the splitting-off of several "autonomous peoples' republics," the area of People's China is generally considered to be within the range of about 3.75 million square miles (293, 1955, p. 107) and 3.9 million square miles (98, 1957, p. 170). Mainland, or Communist, China is, therefore, somewhat more than one-fourth larger than the United States (see Map 11 in following chapter).

Naturally, in this vast area which stretches from about the Tropic of Cancer on the south to about 350 miles north of the northern boundary of the United States, there are great regional differences in climate. The southern part of the country, from about north latitude 32°–33° to the Tropic of Cancer, is subtropical to tropical (the latitude of New Orleans is about 30° north). Even in these low latitudes rainfall is confined largely to the summer months (monsoon), but along the coast and several hundred miles inland the rainfall is usually sufficient for good crops. In all southern Asia, however, the monsoon is less dependable than the rainfall of central and western Europe and of the United States east of the Mississippi River (see Maps 2, 3a, and 3b).

In the southern part of China two crops are often raised on the same land each year. In the summer—the rainy season—rice occupies a large proportion of the land that is level enough to be flooded either by the rains or by irrigation, and in the winter, wheat is the principal crop. In some parts of the country two rice crops can be raised on the same land in one year; the area on which this is possible is small, however, because during the winter months frequent cold winds from the deserts of central Asia make the double-cropping of rice quite precarious even in the far southern areas.

North of about 35°–37° the growing season is not long enough to permit double-cropping, nor is the summer rainfall suitable for the growing of rice. The principal crops here are wheat, the sorghum grains, the millets, soybeans, and some corn (maize). These same crops are the staples in Manchuria. As the distance from the Equator and from the Pacific Coast increases in this northern area, the rainfall diminishes, and its seasonal variability increases (see Maps 2 and 8). Many of China's worst famines have been due to drought in the northwestern areas which are far from the coast. Moreover, not only is the monsoon feeble at times, but it also comes in great excess at other times; hence, China has always been plagued by great floods as well as by severe droughts. Cressey says that, from 1644 to 1908, more than 8,500 localities suffered from floods, while more than 4,600 regions suffered from droughts (83, pp. 93, 97). He cites A. Lius' treatise on the climate of China as showing that, since the time of Christ, 1,392 serious droughts have been recorded. Mallory describes famine as being so frequent in China that it constitutes a regular factor in Chinese life (186, p. 1). What is now being done to control this situation will be noted in the following chapter.

The conditions briefly noted above have resulted in a high concentration of China's rural population, which constitutes over five-sixths of the total, in the relatively few valleys and more level areas where the rainfall is generally sufficient to support a fairly intensive agriculture. Consequently, the improvement of agriculture and the development of an increasing amount of industry might be expected to raise many difficult problems of migration similar to those we have experienced in the West. In general these problems have been associated with the migration of the growing surplus in the agricultural population to the cities and with the concentration of a rapidly increasing proportion of the total population in a relatively few metropolitan areas. Insofar as internal migration follows the same pattern in China, it needs little discussion in this essay. However, there are aspects of the redistribution of population arising as a consequence of the planned economic development of China which may give it a character quite different from that which has long been going on in the West. The more important of these will be noted and briefly commented on in this and the two succeeding chapters.

POPULATION

The size of China's population has long been a matter of much dispute. Until the census of 1953, which will be discussed in some detail below, there had been no real census in China in the sense in which this term is generally understood today. Throughout the centuries, there had been many attempts to ascertain the number of China's inhabitants, but not even the more recent of these commanded much respect—either in China or abroad—from the people most interested in the matter. It will suffice to say here that the figure most commonly used in recent years was in the range of 450 to 500 million.

In view of the following discussion of the census of 1953 of People's China, I should confess that I have been among those who believed that the size of China's population during the past century has generally been much exaggerated and that, in particular, I have regarded the very common assumption of a large increase in the population of China Proper (the eighteen provinces) during this period as quite unreasonable. The vast amount of political instability in China since the early 1800's and the many natural calamities known to have occurred during this period seem to me to have been highly unfavorable to any large increase in numbers, and the influence of these factors seems to have persisted until the past few years. On the other hand, it has seemed quite reasonable to believe that a relatively large growth of population took place in Manchuria after about 1900. Table 15 shows a number of estimates for the years 1926–53 and for several dates in the more distant past.

RESULTS OF THE 1953 CENSUS

On November 1, 1954, the State Statistical Bureau of the People's Republic of China released a communique concerning the results of the census taken as of midnight, June 30, 1953.[1] Only a few of the data which would be of much interest for our study have yet been

---

[1] Actually, the enumeration took some months, but it is claimed that successful efforts were made to adjust the population in each district and area so that the results are valid as of June 30 (62, p. 2).

released.[2] This census is often referred to in Chinese publications as "our first scientific census." This "census and registration of the population" was linked with the general elections which were to be held shortly afterward. It is said that more than 2.5 million persons participated in taking this census. The published results can be summarized quite briefly. The total number of Chinese citizens was 601,938,035. Of these, 574,205,940 (another source, 62, p. 4, gives 574,205,095) in Mainland China were "counted directly and registered" (for the

TABLE 15

ESTIMATES OF THE POPULATION (IN MILLIONS) OF
THE CHINESE EMPIRE, 1578–1953

Authority for Estimates	Year	Population
Census*	1953	583
Directorate of Statistics†	1946	449
Ministry of Interior‡	1940	450
Willcox§	1937	350
Ministry of Interior‖	1931	474
D. K. Lieu‖	1930	470–80
M. T. Z. Tyau‖	1930	463
Warren H. Chen‖	1930	445
Maritime Customs‖	1930	444#
Chang-heng Chen**	1930	480
Post Office††	1926	486
Ching Dynasty‡‡	1812	362
Ching Dynasty‡‡	1740	140
Ming Dynasty‡‡	1578	61

* Source: 293, 1956, p. 143.
† Source: 83, p. 7.
‡ Source: 69, 1937–43, p. 2.
§ Source: 343, p. 528.
‖ Source: 81, p. 19.
\# Eighteen provinces and Manchuria.
** Source: 64, October, 1933, p. 326.
†† Source: 71, 1931–32, p. 2. Does not include Mongolia and Tibet.
‡‡ Sources: 83, p. 5.

distribution of this population see Map 10). The other 27,732,095, who were surveyed indirectly, consisted of 8,397,477 in remote and border areas "where basic-level elections did not take place," of 11,743,320 Chinese overseas who are considered Chinese citizens, and of 7,591,298 who were living in Taiwan, "which remains to be liberated." Of the "population directly surveyed and registered," males constituted 51.82 per cent or 297,553,518, and females 48.18 per cent or 276,652,422. These figures result in a ratio of about 108 males to each 100 females, as compared with a ratio of slightly less than 100

[2] If they have been released, they have not been made available to foreign scholars, except possibly to the Russians.

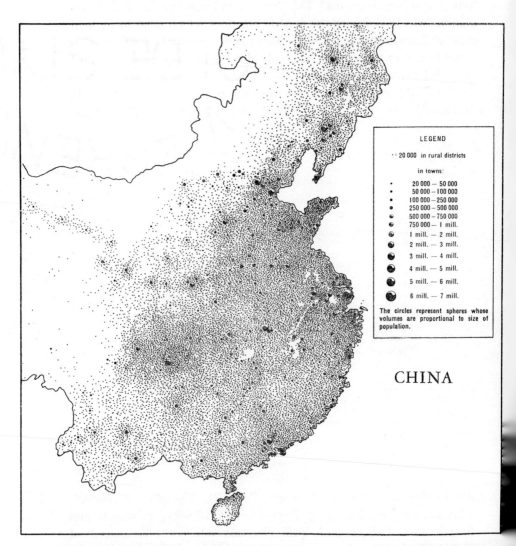

LEGEND

·= 20 000 in rural districts

in towns:

·	20 000 — 50 000
·	50 000 — 100 000
·	100 000 — 250 000
·	250 000 — 500 000
·	500 000 — 750 000
·	750 000 — 1 mill.
·	1 mill. — 2 mill.
·	2 mill. — 3 mill.
·	3 mill. — 4 mill.
·	4 mill. — 5 mill.
·	5 mill. — 6 mill.
·	6 mill. — 7 mill.

The circles represent spheres whose volumes are proportional to size of population.

CHINA

MAP 10.—Population distribution in China. (Adapted by permission of Dr. Friedrich Burgdörfer and the Heidelberger Akademie der Wissenschaften from *The World Atlas of Population* [Hamburg: Falk-Verlag], copyright 1957 by Heidelberger Akademie der Wissenschaften, Heidelberg, Germany.)

males to each 100 females in the United States. (Source 62, Table 2, p. 21, gives a sex ratio of 107.7.)

The age data available for the "surveyed and registered population" showed that 58.92 per cent (338,339,892) were 18 years old and over, which leaves 41.08 per cent under 18 years of age (66, January, 1955). This younger group is further divided into those aged 0–4 (15.6 per cent) and those aged 5–9 (11.0 per cent), leaving the 10–17 age group (inclusive) with 14.48 per cent of the total (67, April, 1955).

Table 16 contains all the age data from the 1953 census of China that seem to have been published and which may be considered official; that is, each percentage and/or each definite figure used has been published, or a percentage has been derived directly from published data by simple subtraction. In most cases only percentages have been published, and the number of persons shown in the table has been calculated on the basis of the total population. Columns 3 and 4 are based on population "surveyed and registered" and on "total mainland population," respectively.

In 1957 the United States Bureau of the Census made a study of the age distribution of China's population before source 62 became available. The results by five-year age groups are shown in Table 17, columns 2 and 3. In order to facilitate comparisons, columns 4 and 5, derived from Table 16, have been added. The numbers refer to total mainland population. In addition to the definite references cited here (except 62), the Bureau found statements about certain other age groups for which no specific references could be cited (probably because the statements came from radio broadcasts) but which seemed definite enough to be used in its calculations of age, especially for ages of 25 and over.

Among the statements considered useful by the Bureau were those to the effect that 76 million persons were aged 9 to 15 (inclusive), and those making "frequent references . . . to 120 million 'youths,'" the latter of which was considered equivalent to saying that the population aged 14 to 24 amounted to 120 million. In addition, a statement that "nearly 80 million young men and women are enabled 'to take part in and manage state affairs'" was regarded by the Bureau as equivalent to a statement that these are "young" persons under 24 who are eligible to vote and, therefore, over 18 years of age: hence, that these 80 million were aged 18 to 23, inclusive (312, P-91, No. 3, p. 3). This interpretation appears to have been in error, since the use of official percentages that were published later, in calculating the age group 18–24, would result in a total of only 70.6 million (see Table 16). As regards the 120 million "youths" assumed to be aged 14–24, the age group 15–24 constituted 17.3 per cent of the total population according to official data published later and, therefore, contained only 100.8 million. On the basis of the age-adjusted groups in India

TABLE 16

POPULATION (IN THOUSANDS) AND PER CENT
DISTRIBUTION, BY AGE, CHINA, 1953

Age (1)	Per Cent Distri- bution* (2)	Surveyed and Registered† (3)	Total in Mainland† (4)
Total.......	100.0	574,206	582,603
0–1...........	3.3	18,949	19,226
1–4...........	12.3	70,627	71,660
5–14..........	20.3	116,564	118,269
15–24.........	17.3	99,338	100,790
25–34.........	14.6	83,834	85,060
35–44.........	12.0	68,905	69,912
45–54.........	9.3	53,401	54,182
55–64.........	6.5	37,323	37,869
65–74.........	3.4	19,523	19,809
75 and over.....	1.0	5,742	5,826
5–9‡..........	11.0	63,163	64,087
10–14§.........	9.3	53,401	54,182
10–17‡.........	14.48	83,145	84,361
15–17‖.........	5.18	29,744	30,179
0–18#.........	41.08	235,884	239,334
18–24**........	12.12	69,594	70,611

* Source: 62, p. 23, except n. ‡ below.
† Based on percentages in col. 2.
‡ Source: 71, April, 1955.
§ Per cent derived from: population aged 5–14 (20.3 per cent) minus population aged 5–9 (as given in n. ‡, 11.0 per cent) equals 9.3 per cent aged 10–14.
‖ Derived by subtraction of per cent aged 10–14 from per cent aged 10–17.
Source: 66, January, 1955.
** Col. 2 above shows 53.2 per cent aged 0–24; n. # refers to published per cent of 41.08 aged 0–18; 53.2 per cent minus 41.08 per cent equals 12.12 per cent aged 18–24.

in 1951, the 14-year olds in China would constitute 19.05 per cent of the age group 10–14, which would amount to 10.3 million. Thus the age group 14–24 (inclusive) would amount to 111.1 million instead of 120 million.[3]

Excluding the Taiwanese and the overseas Chinese, 93.94 per cent

[3] The United States Bureau of the Census recognized from the outset the probability that rather large errors would be involved in calculating age groups on the basis of the data then available.

of the population were Han Chinese and 6.06 per cent were minority nationals (66, January, 1955; and 62, p. 7). Of this mainland population, 86.74 per cent lived in rural communities and 13.26 per cent lived in cities (no definition of cities is given). It will be noted that the above data relate to the whole of Mainland China. They constitute all the age data available for China as a whole, as far as the author can ascertain.[4]

TABLE 17

POPULATION (IN MILLIONS) AND PER CENT DISTRIBUTION, BY AGE, CHINA, 1953

Age (1)	Total in Mainland* (2)	Per Cent Distribu- tion[†] (3)	Total in Mainland[‡] (4)	Per Cent Distri- bution[‡] (5)
Total....	582.6	100.0	582.6	100.0
Under 5....	90.9	15.6	90.9	15.6
5-9.......	64.1	11.0⎫	118.3	20.3
10-14......	54.1	9.3⎭		
15-19......	52.1	8.9⎫	100.8	17.3
20-24......	57.2	9.8⎭		
25-29......	55.5	9.5⎫	85.1	14.6
30-34......	46.6	8.0⎭		
35-39......	39.0	6.7⎫	69.9	12.0
40-44......	32.3	5.6⎭		
45-49......	26.2	4.5⎫	54.2	9.3
50-54......	20.6	3.5⎭		
55-59......	15.5	2.7⎫	37.9	6.5
60-64......	11.2	1.9⎭		
65-69......	7.6	1.3⎫	25.6	4.4
70 and over.	9.7	1.7⎭		

* Source: 312, p. 2.
† Calculated from col. 2.
‡ From Table 16.

Apparently, at about the time of the census a need was also felt for data which could be used in the calculation of birth rates and death rates. This resulted in a "survey of 29 large and medium-sized cities, counties, district towns and villages in the Ningsia Province and some

[4] More detailed data concerning Manchuria have been published since the above was written, but they are not of direct interest for our discussion (316). The total population of the provinces also appears to have been published recently (163, pp. 152, 153).

other provinces, containing 30,180,000 people, [which] revealed an average birth rate of 37, death rate of 17 and natural increase of 20" (67, April 1, 1955, p. 23). These figures appear to have been used quite widely in Communist China for a year or two, as applicable to the entire country. However, in recent months there have been frequent references to a natural increase of 22 per 1,000, or even more. The author can find no specific data supporting any of these statements regarding vital rates.

Concerning the accuracy of this census, it is said: "After the preliminary national survey was completed a sample check was made in 343 counties in 23 provinces, 5 municipalities and one autonomous region, covering altogether 9 per cent of the total population—52,953,400. It was found that duplications amounted to 1.39 persons per 1,000 and omissions to 2.55 persons per 1,000. These errors were corrected during the rechecking" (66, December, 1955, p. 11; 62, p. 8). This is a higher degree of accuracy in enumeration than is claimed by any other I know of.

The data which have been officially issued seem to be generally accepted by the communist government and are constantly referred to in discussions of plans for economic development (see chap. xiii). If taken at face value, this census shows that the population of Mainland China in 1953 was approximately 100 million larger than Premier Chou En-lai himself believed it to be in 1950 when he spoke to the People's Political Consultative Conference on June 16, 1950. He said at that time, "according to the most trustworthy investigation, the population of Liberated China totals 487,690,000" (163, pp. 37–42).

The figure of a 2 per cent natural increase annually does not appear to have been arrived at until shortly after the publication of the results of the 1953 census, and it is said to be twice that of 1937 (66, January, 1955). Even if this 2 per cent rate of increase is used to calculate the growth in population between the time of the Premier's 1950 statement quoted above (488 million) and the census of 1953, the population would have been only about 517 million in Mainland China instead of the 583 million reported by the 1953 census—a difference of 66 million. It is clear that if the 1953 census figure is correct, there must have been a vast underestimation of China's population for a long time in the past. This is not impossible, but its implications need some examination. However, before this examination is undertaken it will be well to give a brief critique of some of the figures in this census.

A CRITIQUE OF THE 1953 CENSUS

In 1949 the Communists completed the "liberation" of the mainland of China and soon established firm control over the whole country. One of the first and most important tasks undertaken was the redistribution of the land. This was completed by about the end of 1951. There can be no doubt that by 1953 the communist administrative organization was well established throughout the country. The statement that two and one-half million persons participated in taking the census, not including "activists" who served voluntarily, would seem to indicate that a large proportion of the local communist officials were involved in this operation (62, p. 8). The actual technique used in taking the census seems to have been about as follows: the officials in the smallest governmental administrative areas notified all heads of families to report at the depot of registration in the area where they lived to give the information required by the census (62, pp. 3 and 4). Since this office presumably already had a record of landowners and their families—data necessary for redistributing the land—and since they almost certainly had a record of the "enemies of the people" and probably some information regarding all occupied dwellings in the villages, it would appear that the local officials were in a position to know whether all the heads of households had reported, and to put pressure on those who had not done so. If a report was missing, because of illness or for some other reason, an official from the local office was supposed to visit the family to secure the information. This would appear to be an adequate setup for taking a good census in the rural areas, if the local officials were alert and energetic, and if they were sufficiently encouraged and supervised by higher officials.

In the cities there were officials in charge of every small block of dwelling units and of all factories and offices, and they were in a position to see that every head of a household made a report. Thus, although the problems of securing reports from all households were somewhat more complicated in the cities than in the rural villages, the administrative machinery would seem adequate to the task. Besides, it is likely that by the time the census was taken most heads of families had learned that it was not wise to overtly disobey the local officers. The higher officials, especially those in the central government offices, were very much interested in a good census, considering it essential to economic planning, and it seems probable that their attitude regarding the importance of the census was well understood by the local officials.

Adequate political power, a reasonably good local organization, and a strong motive to secure schedules from all households do not, of course, insure an accurate census. The schedule was quite simple, containing only questions on age and sex. For most heads of families it was necessarily filled in by the officials, since the vast majority of the people could neither read nor write. Ignorance alone may have been responsible for many errors, e.g., in the reporting of age, but this kind of error should not have affected the total count to any appreciable degree. Several other types of errors might have affected the total count, however, in spite of the best efforts. In most Western countries there is generally an undercount of children aged 0–4. In the United States, until the last two censuses, this undercount amounted to as much as 5 to 8 per cent of the children of these ages. The possibility of double counting should not have been too much of a problem in China's census, since the people were reported at place of residence, although the term *residence* may have been misunderstood by some people—in China it would not be surprising to find the head of a family counting sons who lived elsewhere as members of his household while, at the same time, the sons reported themselves as residents of the place where they were then domiciled. The local registrars could have caught most such errors if they had tried; there is no basis for judging whether or not they did. Again, in the redistribution of the land, the size of the family had been taken into account—the larger the family, the more land it received. Whether this had led to any considerable amount of padding of family size and, if it had, whether such additions carried over to the census, there is no way of knowing. Furthermore, exemption from the agricultural tax is increased as the size of the family increases, which might have provided a fairly strong motive for exaggerating the number of children in the family. There is no evidence on this point.

On the basis of these rather general considerations, I am personally disposed to believe that the total count in the census may have been reasonably accurate according to Western standards.

On the other hand, Chinese officials have always been characterized by a strong inclination to tell their superiors what they think these superiors want to be told. If there had been any widespread feeling that a large population was wanted by the higher authorities, local census schedules could very easily have been padded. There is no information available on this point. However, it has been suggested that the top government officials were anxious to have China appear far and away the largest nation in the world, particularly compared with the Soviet Union. On the other hand, the fact that the first shots in the official birth control campaign were fired only a few weeks before the results of the census were made public suggests that the top officials may have been frightened by the economic task confronting them. With a population of nearly 600 million growing at a rapid rate, they may have taken advantage of the interest the census results would arouse to launch this campaign, realizing that the high figures would give the campaign strong support.

But while there is no evidence of either an undercount or an overcount in this census, there is much evidence that the leaders of Communist China accept the figures as given. They are using the figure of 600 million, increasing it by 2 to 2.5 per cent a year in the framing of their five-year plans. They have suddenly become greatly concerned over the consequences of this high rate of increase in such a huge population. They also appear to believe that this rate is now rising. Their concern is shown by their almost frantic efforts to introduce birth control on a wide scale, and by the recurring discussions of unemployment. For example, the *New York Times* of September 15, 1957, reports that people needing jobs each year are said to be three times as numerous (about 4 million) as those able to find jobs (about 1.3 million). The authority for these figure is *Study* (130), the chief ideological publication of the Communist party. The leaders of Communist China are obviously coming to realize the seriousness of their population problem, and their growing concern about it arises, in part at least, from their acceptance of these 1953 census figures and the accumulating evidence of a decline in the death rate.

Certain more specific criticisms of this census will be considered in the sections discussing birth rates, death rates, and natural increase.

CONDITIONS AFFECTING GROWTH SINCE 1800

As early as 1800 there were evidences of internal disorder in some of the western provinces of China Proper. The central government even then had begun to lose its power to maintain the internal tranquillity that had been preserved for about a century and a half after the Manchu rulers were firmly seated. The so-called Opium War of 1839–42 proved further that the central government of that day was unable to defend China against a small, well-disciplined army equipped with European arms. The Taiping Rebellion, which began about 1848 and continued to 1864, proved that the power of the central government was waning over a large part of southeast China. This rebellion resulted in the devastation of great areas in south and central China reaching as far north as the Yangtze Valley. The great loss of life in this uprising—sometimes estimated as high as 50 million—was undoubtedly caused more by the disruption of the regular production of the farmers over wide areas and by the disease which inevitably accompanied the movements of a rabble military force than by the actual slaughter in battle. The Taipings were more like a plague of locusts on the land than like an organized fighting force. The weakness of the central government increasingly provided happy hunting grounds in the provinces for opportunistic adventurers, and opportunity for a constant succession of "war lords" and "bandit chiefs."

The loss of the war with Japan (1894–95) only emphasized again how feeble the central government had become. The adventurers in the provinces no longer needed to fear Peking. The Boxer Uprising soon followed. Within a few years, especially after 1911, the "war lords" had become even more rampant; they were in the ascendancy over much of the country for some years and were often in conflict with each other. The forces organized under Sun Yat-sen and commanded by Chiang Kai-shek after the death of Sun in 1924 established themselves in Nanking in 1927 and kept order in certain parts of the country for several years. However, the communist faction led by Mao Tse-tung had already split off, and controlled a considerable area in central China. Between the Communists and the war lords, Chiang Kai-shek and the Kuomintang party never had firm control over much of China.

During and after World War I, and especially after 1931, the Japanese interfered increasingly in Chinese affairs. They sent several expeditionary forces into the country to keep things stirred up and took complete control of Manchoukuo in 1931. The great invasion of China occurred in 1937. Tens of millions of Chinese fled before the Japanese invaders. The lives lost because of the disruption of agriculture over vast areas and the diseases which always accompany such vast migratory movements must have numbered many millions.

Because of this almost constant turmoil in many areas of China for more than a century, it seems unlikely that there was any consistent population growth in the country after about 1825–40, except that connected with the resettlement of Manchuria after 1900 and whatever growth may have taken place since "liberation" in 1949. Political instability and local warfare have always and everywhere been highly unfavorable to the increase of population. They have always led to a deterioration of agriculture through the abuse of the farmers—who in China constituted 80 per cent or more of the total population—by the military adventurers or the provincial officials. Civil strife multiplies the uncertainties of life and makes property insecure, leaving the farmer little incentive to increase his production. Commerce and industry, as well as agriculture, are greatly limited by such political uncertainties.

Widespread internal disorder was not the only obstacle to China's economic development between 1825 and 1950; it seems clear, however, that without civil order the forces which might have encouraged a gradual increase in agricultural production and the slow but steady adoption of more efficient production processes in other sectors of the economy had little chance to operate, except in the treaty ports after about 1875. The same political conditions which made for a stagnant economy also contributed to high death rates, both because no health work was carried on until quite recently and because the frequent natural calamities—famines, epidemics, and floods—were not mitigated to any appreciable extent by public action. Moreover, the regular processes by which people made a living, chiefly agriculture, were interfered with continuously, decade after decade, over vast areas containing great populations.

If it is assumed that by 1825 a population which had numbered 100 million in 1650 grew not to 570 million (1 per cent a year) but to around 540 million, and that the population in the area of Manchoukuo and Inner Mongolia increased by about 20 million after about 1900 when migration from the northern provinces became important, the population might well have been 570 to 580 million around 1953 when the census was taken, even if there had been only small and sporadic increases between 1825 and 1950. It should be understood that there is no proof of this pattern of growth; but it seems more reasonable to accept such a pattern than one assuming a very substantial growth since 1825, perhaps a doubling of the population in 125 years—a growth, say, from 275–80 million in 1825 to 550–60 million in 1950. It must be recognized, of course, that the census of 1953 may be so greatly in error that there is no need to attempt a rational explanation of the unexpectedly large population at that time. This point will be discussed below.

It was not until 1949, after the Communists had come into full control, that China again had a central government capable of maintaining peace over the whole country. Even then, for several years there was so much resistance to communist measures that in 1951 Lo Jui-ching, Minister of Public Security, claimed that his office had "liquidated 15 million counter-revolutionaries" (163, p. 38). Even the most lenient interpretation of the term "liquidated"—that most of the victims were sent to forced-labor camps—implies a situation unfavorable to the increase of population. The death rates of "counter-revolutionaries" in labor camps are extremely high; and millions of families were broken when the husbands were sent to these camps, a situation bound to have had some effect on the birth rate. Moreover, in the years 1950–53, the Korean war must have taken a heavy toll of births through the mobilization of millions of young men. Actual casualties, and the heavy losses from disease and infected wounds, must also have helped to keep the death rate high in the military forces. In addition, the Communists admit that there have been very severe floods and droughts in some of the years since their accession to power. These may not have resulted in actual starvation, but they would almost certainly raise the death rates in the stricken areas to somewhat above normal. Hence, it seems unlikely that a 2 per cent increase per year, which was derived from the birth rate of 37 and the death rate of 17 as explained above, could have prevailed even during the three years between mid-1950 and mid-1953.

BIRTH AND DEATH RATES

It is now necessary to give closer attention to the vital rates—birth rate (37) and death rate (17)—which appear to have been officially adopted shortly after the census of 1953.

The birth rate.—The above birth rate, for which no definite date is given (probably 1954) seems much too low in light of the other data available; moreover, the areas surveyed are only vaguely defined.

The data relating to the birth rate in Taiwan are probably the most reliable available for any considerable number of Chinese (about 5.2 million in 1935). The rates reported for Taiwan in the prewar years when it was still a Japanese colony were: 1920–24, 41.8; 1925–29, 44.0; 1930–34, 45.5; and for 1950–54 the rate is reported as 45.8 by the Nationalist Government (293, 1955, p. 615). This postwar birth rate may have been increased by the migration of young adult Nationalists to Taiwan, but the increase from this source would not appear to be of much consequence.

Several studies made in small areas in prewar China found birth rates substantially above 37 (281, p. 70; 63, pp. 28–30; 48, p. 361). My own experience in organizing and directing one small study convinced me that a significant number of the births were not registered, in spite of unusual care and effort. In most studies it has not been possible to spend as much time ferreting out unrecorded births as in this particular one, which recorded an average annual rate for the 4 years from September, 1931, to August, 1935 (inclusive), of 45.1 per 1,000 (281, p. 41).

Regarding the character of the survey which showed a birth rate of 37, the brief official statement seems to indicate that the sample was drawn chiefly from cities and from the northeastern provinces (67, April 1, 1955). In these cities there was almost certainly a large preponderance of young males, and many of the mothers-to-be may also have returned to the family home of the husband for confinement. Hence, a birth rate of 37 could be reasonably accurate for these particular areas and still be well below the average for the country.

Since the above was written, data on birth rates, obtained by sample surveys in sixteen rural communities (minor administrative areas) since "liberation," have become available. These data relate to periods of differing lengths between June, 1951, and February, 1954, but all have been converted to yearly rates. The total population of these areas was 1,811,000. The birth rates varied considerably from one area to another, as might have been expected. The average rate for the sixteen areas combined was 41.6 per 1,000, but the lowest was only 26.1, while the highest was 52.8. However, only six of these areas had birth rates of 37 or under, while ten had rates above 37 (62, Table 6, p. 25). The absence of any knowledge regarding the age and sex composition in these different areas makes it impossible to explain these wide variations. Furthermore, my personal experience, referred to above, leads me to believe that a reported birth rate averaging 41.6 would be too low, because a number of births would be unregistered, especially when the baby had died within the first week or two after birth.

But the most convincing evidence that a birth rate of 37 is substantially too low is found in the census itself. According to the 1953 census there were 90.9 million children aged 0–4, and they constituted 15.6 per cent of the total population. If the death rate of infants and young children from birth to 5 years of age (0–4 inclusive) had been the same in the five years preceding this census as was the comparable rate in Massachusetts in the five years preceding the 1890 census, these 90.9 million children aged 0–4 would have been the survivors of approximately 113.6 million births. A calculation of the average population in that five years (1948–52)—accepting the 1953 census figure (583 million), assuming a 2 per cent annual increase for the year preceding the census, and reducing the rate gradually to 1.25 per cent in the fifth year (1948–49) preceding it—results in a figure of approximately 560 million. A birth rate of 37 in this average population for five years would give a total of 103.6 million births. This is 10 million fewer than would be needed to account for the children 0–4 reported in the census, unless the survival rate was as high as it was in the United States in 1920. To assume a birth rate of 40–42, rather than one of 37, is the simplest way to explain the presence of 90.9 million children aged 0–4 in 1953. A substantial underenumeration of children 0–4, which is by no means unusual even in countries with long experience in census taking, would necessitate the assumption of a still higher birth rate, possibly even 43 or 44. Until more is known about these recent surveys and about the age and sex composition of the populations surveyed, it is not reasonable to assume that the crude birth rate is less than 41 or 42, and it may very well be higher.

The death rate.—The possibility of reducing the death rate in China fairly rapidly cannot be doubted, but one may reasonably doubt whether it has yet been reduced to the 17 per 1,000 reported by the first of the surveys made under the Communists, as noted above. It is possible that in a few communities with both an unusually favorable age composition, i.e., a high proportion of young adults, and a superior organization of public health work, the death rate has fallen to this level. As an average, however, this rate is inconceivable to anyone moderately familiar with the health conditions which have prevailed in China. Lowering the average death rate to 17 per 1,000 in twenty years would be a great achievement; that it has been accomplished in five or six troubled years surpasses belief.

In Taiwan, where health conditions in prewar years were far better than in Mainland China, and probably better by 1930–34 than on the mainland today, the crude death rates recorded in prewar years were: 1920–24, 25.8 per 1,000; 1925–29, 22.8; 1930–34, 20.6. It is also probable that there was still some nonregistration of deaths in this last period. The rates recorded in prewar years by the few special studies on the mainland referred to above are far higher: 38.7 for 1931–35 in Hsiao Chi, Kiangyin (281, p. 70), and 24.6 for February, 1940, to June, 1944, in Cheng Kung, Yunnan (63, pp. 32, 96, 97). Dr. Ta Chen believed that the national death rate in 1934 was about 33.0 per 1,000 (63, p. 32). It seems incredible that this could have been cut in half by 1953 or 1954, when the Communists had been in power only four or five years, although there is good reason to believe that real health progress was made in many areas during this short period.

The sample survey of births in rural administrative areas also included the registration of deaths. The average death rate for these sixteen areas was 21.0 per 1,000. The lowest death rate, 13.4, was found in the same area that had the lowest birth rate. (This suggests that the survey was particularly defective in this area.) The highest death rate was 24.0, and was found in the area having the highest birth rate; this is not surprising, because a high infant mortality generally accompanies a high birth rate in most countries which have poor health services. Only four of the sixteen areas had death rates of 17 or under, the rate that is being most widely used as the average in Mainland China today. In most Western countries a lower proportion of births than of deaths are generally registered during the early years of registration. In many Chinese communities there is a belief that to speak of the dead brings bad luck. It is probable, therefore, that if a survey inquired about births and deaths which had occurred in a family during the several months or the year preceding the survey, more deaths than birth would remain unmentioned. As a consequence, the recorded death rate of 21.0 is likely to be more deficient than the birth rate of 41.6; both may very well be deficient by several points. Besides, as was the case regarding birth rates, the lack of knowledge about the composition (age and sex) of the population in the areas where the survey was taken make an accurate comparison of their death rates impossible. It would seem more reasonable to assume that the average death rate is somewhere between 21 and 25 than that it is 17.

Thus, although all the data on births and deaths coming out of Mainland China now point to a natural increase of around 20 per 1,000, or 2 per cent a year, there is much reason to believe that the death rates reported are more deficient than the birth rates and that the natural increase is, therefore, significantly smaller than is claimed at present. There can be no doubt, however, that health services are improving and that the death rate is falling. A few figures will help us appreciate the type of progress being made in health services.

It was reported that in the first six months of 1950 the following vaccinations and inoculations were made: 36.5 million against small-

pox, 0.2 million BCG. (against tuberculosis), 6.8 million against cholera, 5.0 million against cholera and typhoid combined, and 4.7 million
against plague (67, October 1, 1950). On January 16, 1952, health
centers were reported to be operating in 85 per cent of the 2,000
counties and in 1,498 districts (smaller administrative areas within
the counties). By that time more than 200 million vaccinations had
been made against smallpox, as well as many inoculations against
cholera (67, January 16, 1952). On December 16, 1953, it was reported
that no less than 214 million injections against cholera, typhoid, plague,
and diphtheria had been made, and 511.6 million vaccinations against
smallpox (67, December 16, 1953).

In addition, by the end of 1952 a network of 186 anti-epidemic
teams had been established and many mother- and child-care centers
and clinics were in operation; also, 27,400 modern maternity stations
had been set up, and over 260,000 modern and old-style midwives had
been trained or re-educated. Medical education and nurses' training
were said to have been greatly expanded. Similar references to the
spread of such health services appear regularly, but little is said about
the control of malaria; there is also a definite lack of information
about sanitation in the villages, which is extremely important for reducing infant and child mortality.

One need not assume that all these claims are accurate, nor that
all the health services are highly efficient, in order to believe that substantial progress is being made in reducing the death rate. But it may
be pointed out that the services listed above, except for the vaccinations against smallpox, could have been rendered largely to people
living in the cities, although some of these services are known to be
reaching the villagers. It is not at all certain, however, whether there
has been much progress in general sanitation in the villages. The
training of enough health workers to staff the hundreds of thousands
of rural health centers that would be needed to bring even very
modest health service to the villagers cannot possibly have been accomplished as yet. This is why it does not seem reasonable to assume
that the survival rate of infants and young children born in China in
the five years preceding the 1953 census was as high as that of those
born in Massachusetts in 1920; it seems more reasonable to assume that
it was more like the survival rate which prevailed there in 1890.

This doubt concerning an extremely rapid decline in the death rate
of young children is reinforced by the fact that the children 5–9 years
of age in the census numbered only 64.1 million. If the average pop-

ulation during the five years in which they were born (1943–47), all years of great hardship when the death rate was probably very high, was about 550 million—which is about what it would have had to be to account for 583 million in 1953—and if the birth rate was 37, the total number of births would have been about 100 million. Assuming that about 80 per cent of the children born survived to ages 0–4 (see preceding section), about 73 per cent should have survived to ages 5–9. Instead, only about 64 per cent survived, according to this calculation. Such a low survival rate might seem fairly reasonable in view of the harsh conditions in those years. However, as has already been shown, the birth rate of 37 is almost certainly too low. A birth rate of 42 would have meant 115 million births, and the survival rate from birth to ages 5–9 would have been only about 55 per cent. Even with a birth rate of 40, the survival rate of the children who were 5–9 in 1953 would have been only about 58 per cent. Thus the rather scanty age data in the 1953 census tend to increase one's skepticism regarding the birth and death rates in common use. However, there can be no reasonable doubt that the death rate is falling, and will continue to fall for some time unless famine intervenes; nor is it unreasonable to believe that the rate of increase is rising.

Recent pronouncements on natural increase.—In March of 1957 the Minister of Health, in a speech before the Chinese People's Political Consultative Conference, said that, "taking the rate of our population growth as 2.5 per cent, there will be an increase of 15 million people every year" (176, March 7, 1957). She also said, "Our birth rate is really very high" (*ibid.*). Another speaker, Chung Hui-lan, told the same conference that, "According to the incomplete and preliminary statistics of the different places, the rate of birth in recent years has amounted to as high as 35 to 55 per 1000 per year." Although he appears to accept an increase from 600 million to 630 million in two years (2.5 per cent), he still speaks of an average birth rate of 37 and a death rate of 17, but is afraid that the rate of increase is more than 20 per 1,000 per year (77, March 17, 1957). Again, "Over the years, the population of our country has been increasing at an annual rate of 2.2 per cent, exceeding any of the other countries in the world" (77, March 5, 1957). In any event, it appears that a rate of population growth in excess of 2 per cent per year is in process of being officially accepted, in spite of the frequent claims that the birth rate is declining rapidly in some places where birth control is spreading under the stimulus of official prodding (67, April, 1957).

THE BIRTH CONTROL CAMPAIGN

The rather remarkable growth of propaganda favoring contraception is hard to explain except on the assumption that the leaders themselves now believe China has about a hundred million more people than they thought she did, and that they also believe the rate of increase is higher than had been anticipated and is growing. The acceptance of these beliefs might very well convince hardheaded realists, even though they are good Marxian Communists, that their plans for improving the life of the people are imperiled by this vast increase (12 million a year, until the past few months when 15 million has frequently been mentioned).

Much of this sudden propaganda for birth control comes from very high sources. The *New York Times*, June 13, 1957, p. 8-c, reports that Mao Tse-tung, Chairman of the Communist party, recently expressed himself as follows: "Mr. Mao said that the number of births, now 30 million a year, was a 'sign of great progress made in medical service and the general rise in living standards, especially in the countryside, and of the faith the people have in the future.' "[5] Mr. Mao also said that China's population was growing by 13 to 15 million a year. I quote further: "But this figure [i.e., 13–15 million increase] must be of great concern to us all." He added that grain had increased by 10 million tons in the last two years (i.e., in the two years preceding February, 1957). He went on to say that this 10 million tons is barely sufficient to cover the needs of China's growing population. "Steps must therefore be taken to keep our population for a long time at a stable level, say, of 600 million. A wide campaign of explanation and proper help must be undertaken to achieve this aim." All this would seem to indicate that the propaganda for birth control was approved in the highest quarters, and largely on economic grounds.

Chou En-lai, Premier and Foreign Minister, in an interview with the Indian Delegation to China on Agricultural Planning and Techniques, July and August, 1956, opened his remarks by stating that China and India, as poor and overpopulated countries, had many common interests, and that they could not afford to be complacent just because, for the moment, food production was increasing at a faster rate (in China, 4 to 5 per cent a year) than population (2 per cent a year) (136, pp.

[5] Thirty million births annually would mean a birth rate of 50 per 1,000 per year, instead of 37 per 1,000, in a population of 600 million. It is, of course, the decline in deaths which is a "sign of great progress," etc., rather than the rise in the number of births. No claim is made that the birth rate has risen.

22, 23). This "situation did not mean that population could increase without any limit." He stated that he was "personally strongly in favor of family planning but he emphasized that his reason was very different from that of, say, the French people. His reason for wanting family planning was to space the number of children suitably with a view to improving the health of the mothers and the education of the children." He went on to say that there was a growing demand for family planning, and that he himself had received many letters from women pressing for a campaign for family planning; he added that there was a strong group in the National People's Congress in favor of such planning.

At the third session of the First National People's Congress, Shao Li-tsu, a deputy to the Congress, quoted from a speech of Li Teh-chuan, Minister of Health, as follows: "In regard to the problem of birth control which has been put into practice for the health of women and babies, for the education of children, and for the growth of our people, our propaganda has not been sufficient. Henceforth, we should under the leadership of the Party and the Government, further develop the work of propaganda and education and strengthen the work of technical guidance in cooperation with the units concerned" (70, June 26, 1956). Regarding his own position a year earlier, Shao Li-tsu said further, "In my proposal (1955) for 'strengthening propaganda on contraception,' the emphasis was on propaganda in the villages." He thinks the women in the villages are ready for birth control and that information about it should be made available to them. In regard to sterilization by operative techniques, he says that "in relaxing its legal use so that couples with four children can take advantage of this method if they so desire the Ministry of Health has not gone far enough." It retained certain restrictions such as that "the woman must be in poor health, over 30 years of age, busy with her studies and in financial difficulties," which should be dispensed with. This same deputy (Shao Li-tsu) has been talking and writing frequently on the subject of birth control, at least since December of 1954 (176). His speeches and statements are given much space in official publications.

The Minister and the Vice-Minister of Health have both concurred in these views in statements before the National People's Congress and in interviews with the press. Many articles are also appearing in the press discussing various aspects of the need for contraception, e.g., an editorial in *China Youth* (72, September 6, 1956) says that early marriage is not advisable and gives many reasons for this view, and an article in the *Tientsin Ta King Pao* on "Economic Work" (August 6, 1956) states that the supply of contraceptive materials is inadequate and should be improved. In *New China's Women* (74, Nos. 4 and 5, 1955), family planning and contraception are discussed as essential to better living and the improvement of the health of the nation. It is further stated that this does not mean a reduction of population, and that the adoption of scientific methods of contraception is not to be construed as a reversion to bourgeois and decadent habits of thought.

It is of interest that although many articles in official publications go to considerable pains to deny any relation between the growth of poverty and population growth, the campaign for birth control waxes stronger. One example may be worth citing: "the root of poverty lies neither in the diminished production of foodstuffs, nor in the rapid increase of population, but mainly in the irrational distribution of foodstuffs, in the fact that the development of productive forces is hampered by artificial handicaps" (67, May 16, 1956, p. 5). The author goes on to explain that in Communist China these "artificial handicaps" have now been removed—landlords have been stripped of their land, agricultural co-operation has been instituted, and even nature (floods and drought) has been thwarted by flood prevention works and irrigation projects. Better agriculture has also been taught to the farmers, so that the production of food grains has increased "from 113,120,000 tons in 1949 to 184 million tons in 1955. This means an increase of 62.6 per cent in 6 years" (*ibid.*, p. 8). The writer of this article concludes that "our country will never improve the well-being of her inhabitants by seeking to reduce their number, but only by striving for a constant growth of production. It is just because we are such a vast population that our nation can make such progress" (*ibid.*, p. 10). He appears to equate propaganda for family planning with "seeking to reduce their numbers," but this is quite a minor flaw in thinking compared with much of the anti-Malthusian reasoning.

The views of Marx, Engels, and Lenin are frequently cited and are explained in the usual terms. Thus, once and for all, the idea that there need be any concern regarding the effect of the increase of population on the level of living is refuted. China has again proved that there is no need to worry about the further increase of population. On the other hand, it is quite proper to be concerned over the health of the mother and her children and to look ahead to the upbringing and education of the children, and, hence, to practice contraception for these practical reasons. It is pointed out that this attitude is not to be confused with, or in any way associated with, the ideas of Malthus. The strange nature of this argument is brought out clearly in the following brief quotation: "In view of the above, in order to lessen the difficulties currently facing us, to protect the health of maternity womanhood and finally to ensure that the next generation may be brought up better, we are not at all opposed to birth control. At the same time the publicity given by certain newspapers and magazines to the methods of birth control is also necessary as well as proper. This has no point in common with Malthus' theory at all" (130, October 2, 1955, pp. 1–6). Several other passages in this article are just as confused and confusing.[6]

It seems to me that if the propaganda for birth control is continued and expanded, and if the people are made to feel that the duty of a good Chinese Communist is to have fewer births—i.e., if a smaller family is made a mark of party orthodoxy—the practice of birth control might spread rapidly among Communists and among those anxious to cultivate their good will. But it should be noted that virtually all the practical obstacles to the spread of contraceptive practices among a poor, ignorant, and largely peasant people still remain. Cultural patterns must be drastically modified before contraception will be widely practiced; this modification will take some time, certainly more than the ten years allotted for it by some writers (62, p. 17). Besides, a cheaper, simpler, and more effective method of contraception is needed before contraception can be expected to spread rapidly among a largely illiterate people, most of whom live in one- or two-room houses. An authoritarian government like China's can probably get the idea of contraception before the masses of the people more quickly than can a more democratic government like India's, but we cannot be sure how soon and how effectively until after the event.

Dr. Kirby wonders whether the type of article which attempts to divorce birth control from the doctrine of Malthus is not a build-up in preparation for abandoning the campaign for voluntary control over conception (165), but there is no evidence of a slackening in this campaign up to late 1957. In fact, the most important statements by Chairman Mao Tse-tung and Premier Chou En-lai on this subject have appeared since the publication of some of the theoretical articles just noted.

[6] For a detailed discussion of the Chinese population policy and for more examples of the weird logic involved in the efforts to divorce birth control from Malthus' doctrine, see Dr. Taeuber's article on this subject (264).

It is highly unlikely that any significant number of people in the countries where birth control is now widely practiced have ever kept their families small because they believed the population of the nation was growing too fast; rather, birth control became widespread in many Western countries because it helped parents achieve a better way of life for themselves and their children. There is no reason to suppose that it will not be the immediate practical reasons for controlling the size of the family—better health and education, better everyday living conditions, and more freedom from pressing want—that will lead to the increasing practice of birth control in China, just as in the West.

THE "FORWARD LEAP," 1958

Since the above was written, what may become a highly significant change in the social organization of Communist China is being vigorously pressed by China's leaders. This "forward leap" of 1958 appears to be basically an effort to organize *all* the population into military-like communes, ostensibly for the purpose of making the labor of all adults available to the government at *all* times, so that it may be employed more efficiently for communist purposes. The economic aspects of this new movement are most emphasized in *China Reconstructs* (66), with most space being given to agriculture, public reclamation works, and the steel industry. Most of the references here to the forward leap and to the organization of the communes through which it is to be achieved are based on propaganda materials such as are to be found in *China Reconstructs* and on newspaper articles which are now (February, 1959) becoming quite numerous. However, this new form of social organization also has implications which may be of great significance for the control of population growth; hence, this aspect deserves brief mention at this point. It appears that in some of the new communes, which are the basic units in this new organization of Chinese society, there is already some measure of enforced segregation of the sexes and that still stricter segregation on a wider scale is contemplated. Furthermore, these communes are expected to assume many of the functions of the family in the rearing of children and in providing for the needs of the household. The children are being cared for in public crèches and children's homes operated by the commune. The degree of segregation of the sexes enforced in this communal organization cannot be of much significance yet, for only a few are fully organized. But it is obvious that if this segregation of the sexes is carried to the point where it results in a great reduction of normal marital relations, or if organized prostitution takes the place of customary marital relations, it may well have a profound effect on the birth rate in the not distant future. Even if marital relations are rather freely allowed on the condition that effective contraceptive practice will be employed after a woman has had two or three live births, the rate of population growth might be reduced substantially in a few years.

Thus although, as noted above, the chief reason given for this rapid and forced organization of communes is that it will be the quickest method of increasing production of all kinds, one can but wonder whether the primary but unexpressed hope is not to reduce the birth rate quickly and thus prevent the rise in demand for the essentials of subsistence. This would indeed be something new in the modern world—governmental effort to determine the conditions under which marital relations will be permitted. Because of the great uncertainty regarding the effects of the organization of these communes on the birth rate, the following summary section attempts no evaluation of their effect on population growth within the next generation. However, the possibility that they may have a great influence on the birth rate in the near future should be kept in mind.

It may also be noted here that if these communes, of which, according to plans, there will ultimately be between twenty and thirty thousand, are successful in becoming practically self-sufficing economic units within a few years, as the leaders hope, the magnitude of the problems of internal migration will be greatly reduced. The expectation of the leaders apparently is that each commune will be able to expand its own industrial enterprises fast enough to give employment to most of its own natural increase in population as well as to the displaced agricultural population, and that there will, therefore, be no such vast movement of population from the rural areas to a few great industrial, commercial, and governmental centers as has taken place in the West. There can be no worthwhile prognosis of the reasonableness of these hopes at the present time.

The economic effects of this forward leap are fully as unpredictable today as are its effects on the birth rate and on internal migration, but some of the possibilities of economic change will be noted briefly in the two succeeding chapters.

SUMMARY AND OUTLOOK

Even if, as has been stated above, the birth rate in China is significantly higher than 37 and the death rate is not yet 20 points below the birth rate, the prospect for population growth during the next generation (about twenty-five years) is no less alarming than it would be if these rates now prevailed. If anything, the prospect is more serious if the birth rate in China is now about the same as in Taiwan, perhaps 43 or 44, and if the death rate is now 24–26 with a natural increase of 17–19 per 1,000. There can be no reasonable doubt that if the per capita food supply becomes even a little more plentiful and if the health program, which is already well launched, is carried forward steadily, the death rate will decline quite rapidly within the next ten to fifteen years. But China is a vast country where, even more than in India, there are large regional differences in the health problems that must be solved before the death rate will fall to the low level prevailing in Japan or in some of the smaller Asian countries.

Under the circumstances, a substantial increase in the rate of growth is reasonably certain to take place, but the rate may rise more slowly than China's leaders seem to expect, and a high rate of growth may continue longer than the ardent birth control advocates anticipate. Even with active propaganda for birth control, it would not be in the least surprising to see the rate of natural increase rise within ten or fifteen years to the 2.5 per cent per year already being used by some officials.

The voluntary reduction of the number of births per family is a difficult task in a country like China even when it is approved by the leaders. In the first place, from time immemorial China's birth rate has been high. No doubt this has been a largely unconscious response to the need for births to replace the infants and young children, a very large proportion of whom have always died before reaching the age of reproduction. Moreover, in China unusual emphasis has long been placed on the importance of family survival and particularly on the need for sons who will carry on the family. A high birth rate has been a basic value in Chinese culture for ages. The taking of concubines was sanctioned, in part at least, because it further insured the survival of the family. But even a high birth rate and concubinage did not always assure the biological survival of the family; hence, the adoption of sons also became a recognized institution, through which the social survival of the family could be assured when actual biological survival failed, and adoption often also insured biological survival through the female line by the marriage of an adopted son to a blood daughter. Thus Chinese culture, even more than most cultures, encouraged the biological survival of the family and put great social pressure on most married couples to produce many children. Can the "forward leap" change all this quickly?

In the second place, even under favorable circumstances most basic cultural patterns change slowly, and beliefs and practices relating to the family, e.g., those concerning marriage, reproduction, and the position of women, are among the most basic of all cultural patterns.

In the third place, in China, as in most other underdeveloped countries, the conditions of daily life are very hard for the vast majority of the people. The houses are small and crowded. There is a great lack of privacy and of the simplest facilities for cleanliness. Under these circumstances, the methods of birth control commonly used in countries where living conditions are better cannot be practiced effectively, if at all. Again it must be said that cheaper, more effective, simpler, and safer methods of birth control must be found before its practice can become general in China and in other underdeveloped countries.

In the fourth place, although modern means of communication can place ideas before vast numbers of people more quickly than ever before, and although China has an authoritarian government, this does not mean that basic cultural patterns can be changed in a few years— only that they can be changed more quickly than they could in the past. Hence, even though the interval of time between the beginning of a steady and fairly regular decline of the death rate and a similar decline of the birth rate may prove to be substantially shorter in China today than it was in most Western countries in the eighteenth and nineteenth centuries, this does not mean that the birth rate will decline proportionally faster than the death rate within a few years, e.g., in the ten years considered adequate by Dr. Chen (67, p. 17).

Furthermore, it may be noted that the belief that the death rate will continue to decline fairly rapidly during the next two decades is justified only on the assumption that production of the necessities of life will increase fast enough to provide at least the present per capita amounts to the growing population during this period. If the necessities should fail to increase fast enough to provide such an amount to the increased population, the privation factor would retard the decline in the death rate in spite of a growing control over the infectious and contagious diseases

Hence, although I am personally very doubtful whether China's rate of population increase is now 2 per cent per year, I am quite certain that it will be that high soon if the assumption just stated regarding the adequacy of the food supply is realized, and that it will be still higher for a decade or two before it begins to decline substantially. This might easily lead to a population in excess of one billion by 1983.

Although the "forward leap" of 1958 may introduce new factors into the population situation in China, and although these new factors may result in a more rapid decline in the birth rate than it is now reasonable to expect, I cannot believe, on the basis of present information, that they will substantially alleviate the pressure of the population on the necessities of life within the next decade or two.

CHAPTER XII

CHINA:

AGRICULTURE

It was noted above that the mountainous character of China, together with its climatic conditions—chiefly rainfall, temperature, and length of growing season—greatly limits the area on which crops can be grown. Since there has never been a thorough survey of China's land, the area suitable for agriculture cannot be estimated with any pretense of precision. The land reforms of the communist government should not only have provided the data for the land actually in use, the cultivated area, but should also have yielded reasonable estimates of the new land available in different parts of the country and its suitability for different crops, as well as reliable estimates of the double-cropped area and the irrigated area. Data on the cultivated area, the annual crop area, and the irrigated area are now being published, but there appears to be no reliable estimate of new land that might be brought into use. Instead, there are numerous statements, couched in vague terms, to the effect that many millions of acres can be added to the existing crop area. All such statements must be viewed with a large measure of skepticism until they are made more precise or until the data on which they are based are made available—data on rainfall, length of growing season, character of soil, type of terrain, etc. Until this is done, the most reasonable presumption is that such data do not exist.

THE PREWAR TILLED AREA

As of about 1936 Buck estimated the tilled area in China Proper (eighteen provinces), plus some small parts of three of the contiguous provinces on the north and east, at about one-fourth the total area, or approximately 232 million acres (48, pp. 165, 166). He also estimated that about 35 million acres might be added to this area if adequate reclamation works, including irrigation, were undertaken. In 1940 the Japanese reported about 41 million acres under cultivation in Manchoukuo, which included a considerably larger area than that com-

Map 11.—Physiographic map of China (east of the 90th meridian). (Base map a section of the Physiographic Diagram of Asia, © by A. K. Lobeck, reproduced with permission from the Geographical Press, a division of C. S. Hammond & Co.)

monly known as Manchuria (155, 1940, p. 710). Very little of this
area, if any, would have duplicated the area included in Buck's estimate. At the same time, the Japanese estimated that about 60 million
additional acres in this region could be tilled. Since there are some
fairly large cultivable plains there, and since this 100 million acres of
tillable land only amounted to about two-sevenths of the entire area
of Manchoukuo, the estimate does not seem unreasonable. If the Japanese estimate of tilled land (41 million acres) is added to Buck's estimate (232 million acres), the total of tilled land in prewar days would
have amounted to about 270 to 275 million acres.

It would also seem reasonable to assume that in an area (Manchoukuo) where there had been a large pioneering movement onto
new land in the twenty-five to thirty years before 1937, and where
the population had undoubtedly been growing faster than in any other
part of China, some land had been added to the tilled area between
1938 and the time the present government gained complete control
(1948–49). There is no direct evidence for this assumption, but a
pioneering people whose private lives were little affected by the war,
who lived close to new land which could easily be brought under
cultivation, and who were almost certainly increasing in numbers,
were not likely to remain confined to their prewar territory for ten
or twelve years. It would appear that the prewar tilled area (270–75
million acres), plus another 3–5 million acres occupied during the
war years—a total in the range of 275–80 million acres—is a reasonable
estimate for the land tilled before and during the war.

There can be little doubt, however, that several million acres of this
area had fallen into disuse during the war and that even more of it
had deteriorated in the period between 1937 and 1949. Armies had
moved back and forth over large areas, destroying irrigation works
and making impossible the maintenance of flood control works in
some areas. The farmers had at times abandoned their homes and
fled westward as enemy armies approached, leaving the land unused
for a time. Farm tools had fallen into disrepair or had been stolen,
and the draft cattle had been stolen or slaughtered by invaders who
lived off the country. Most of this land would lie in China Proper
south of latitude about 35° north. In this area there had always been
a great deal of double-cropping.[1] The significance of these estimates

[1] Buck's studies had led him to believe that approximately one-half of the tilled
land in China Proper was double-cropped before the war (45, pp. 167, 191). Thus
there may have been about 115 million acres of double-cropped land before the war.

of the amount of land tilled during the prewar and wartime periods will become apparent when the progress of agriculture in the postwar period is under discussion.

The diet.—The diet of the great mass of the Chinese people has long consisted preponderantly of the "food grains"—rice, wheat, barley, the sorghums, the millets, and some corn. The proteins in their diet have come largely from the pulses, chiefly peas, beans (including soybeans), and other leguminous plant seeds. They have obtained only a small proportion of their proteins from meat, fish, or eggs, although they eat more of such foods than the Indians do because they have no religious taboo about eating meat. However, the Chinese use even less milk than the Indians. They are vegetarians by force of necessity. Practically no grain that can be eaten by man, and this includes even the sorghums and the millets, is fed to cattle or other livestock. Some hogs are raised, but they are used chiefly as scavengers.

Crop yields.—It has long been assumed by many people in the West that the intensive agriculture practiced in China returned large yields per acre. However, those more familiar with Asian agriculture knew that while yields of rice were substantially higher in China than in most parts of Asia, they were much lower than those of Japan in recent decades. Buck's farm management surveys confirmed this view (46, p. 207). The yields of wheat, the sorghums, and the millets—the staple crops north of latitude about 35° north—are quite low, in general lower than those in Europe and North America.

POSTWAR AGRICULTURE

The quality of the data.—In the summer of 1956 India sent a delegation to China to study Chinese agriculture, to see what they could learn that might be useful in India. The report made by this delegation (136) will be drawn upon quite heavily in the brief account of developments in China since 1949. In this report the reliability of the statistics given to the Indian delegation is discussed at some length. Only the conclusions can be presented here. First, it was considered doubtful whether any comparisons should be made between the data for the years 1952 and earlier and the data for 1953–55. The chief reason for this conclusion was that the land reforms referred to below were not completed until about the end of 1951, and the governmental machinery for securing fairly adequate reports on agriculture was quite inadequate before 1953. One might also add, as another rea-

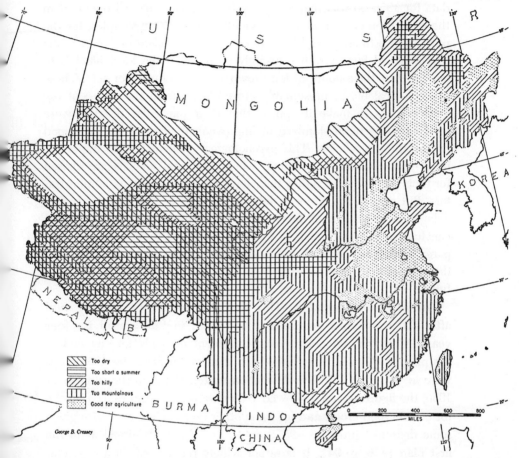

Too dry
Too short a summer
Too hilly
Too mountainous
Good for agriculture

George B. Cressey

MAP 12.—Land usability in China. Large areas receive less than fifteen inches of rain, have less than three ⌐hs free from frost, or have slopes which are too steep for cultivation. The best agricultural land ⌐ole) is found along the valleys of the Sungari, Liao, Hai, Hwang, Hwai, Yangtze, and Si rivers. (Re-⌐ed by permission from *Land of the 500 Million: A Geography of China*, by George B. Cressey, © 1955 ⌐cGraw-Hill Book Co.)

son, that the government itself did not feel in a position to start a five-year plan until 1953. More of this later.

Second, the conclusion regarding the reliability of the agricultural data for 1953–55 was that a large subjective element still operated in the estimation of both areas and yields. Crop-cutting samples, for the purpose of estimating yields, were not yet being taken in China, while psychological factors rather strongly encouraged the local officials to overestimate the amount of land sown and the returns per acre. These psychological biases presumably arose chiefly from the desire of the local officials to make it appear that their particular districts were meeting the general standard of improvement planned for, or hoped for, by the top officials. This psychological element is very important in an authoritarian government, where the local officials are chosen for their party loyalty rather than for their competence as administrators. But even if the Chinese data for 1953–55 as given to the Indian delegation are taken at face value, some interesting and important conclusions can be drawn, as we shall see when these data are compared with many official and semiofficial pronouncements regarding the agricultural progress now being made and expected in the near future.

The first Five-Year Plan.—This plan was not begun officially until after the communist government had been in full control for four years. Moreover, no definite announcement of goals for the end of the plan (1957) seems to have been made until after the 1955 crops were in.[2] When the Indian delegation visited China in the summer of 1956, the figures given it showed 1955 data for agriculture as a whole, for certain food crops, and for some other crops. They were also given some definite figures for 1957 targets, i.e., the goals aimed at in the first plan (136, p. 94). It is rather widely recognized, however, that before 1953 the increases in tilled area, in sown area, and in irrigated area were due largely to recovery from the effects of the turmoil of the preceding fifteen years. In spite of this, most of the statements measuring progress are based on production in 1949 and 1950, or even on prewar production. As noted, the Indian delegation thought that such comparisons were of little value.

On the basis of the data for 1953 to 1955 found in the report of the Indian delegation, the tilled or cultivated area increased from 268

[2] If there were definite targets at an earlier date, the writer has been unable to find them.

million acres in 1953 to 272 million acres in 1955 (136, p. 92). Thus even in 1955 it was no larger than the best estimates available for prewar years. It seems rather probable, therefore, that the frequent statement that 6 million acres had been newly reclaimed by 1955 (66, October, 1955) refers to land which had been rehabilitated, rather than to new land, although some new land may have been cultivated in the state farms set up in Manchuria. However, there were only a few such farms in 1957.

In the same period (1953–55) an increase of about 17 million acres in the sown area was reported, from 356 million to 373 million acres (136, p. 94), and an increase in the irrigated area from 59.4 to 64.5 million acres (136, p. 92). Subtracting the cultivated land from the sown land in 1953 (356 − 268 = 88 million acres) and in 1955 (373 − 272 = 101 million acres) indicates an increase of about 13 million acres in double-cropped land (from 88 million to 101 million acres) between 1953 and 1955 and a rise in the proportion of cultivated land that was double-cropped from about 32.5 per cent to 37 per cent. The reported increase in irrigated land was about 5 million acres. These increases do not appear improbable if one assumes that they consisted largely of land rehabilitated by the repair of irrigation facilities that had been damaged during the war and the land reform period, and by the resumption of regular maintenance operations that had been interrupted by the same disturbances. Since much of the irrigated land is also double-cropped, the rehabilitation of irrigation works might account for a substantial proportion of the increase in the sown area between these two dates.

The Indian delegation was given no target figure for total area to be sown in 1957. However, it was given a target figure for food crops as a whole and for the two most important crops—rice and wheat. According to these figures, the area already sown to food crops in 1955 exceeded the 1957 target by about 8 million acres, or nearly 3 per cent, while rice sowing had not quite reached its target and wheat sowing had barely exceeded its target. Since precise acreage targets do not appear to have been set until about the time of the visit of the Indian delegation, it is not improbable that they were set for the purpose of showing the delegation that the plan was being overfulfilled. If this is borne in mind, these data relating to acreage increases strongly suggest that there had been very little increase over prewar acreages in any of these three categories—cultivated land, land sown, and land irrigated—in spite of many vague official statements regarding the large amounts of newly cultivated land and of newly irrigated land.

New land.—It was noted above that no reliable survey had ever been made indicating how much additional land might be brought into cultivation. However, Buck had estimated that probably 35 million acres in China Proper could be added to the tilled area through reclamation and irrigation works, and the Japanese had estimated that about 60 million acres could be added in Manchoukuo—a total of about 100 million acres. The Indian delegation was given a figure of approximately 247 million acres, or almost 10 per cent of the total area of China, "which . . . can be reclaimed" (136, p. 92). It is not at all clear what this means. It almost certainly does not mean that this is the total area that can be used for agriculture, since more than that amount was already in use. If it means that this much more can be reclaimed for agriculture, it seems a rather fantastic claim in view of the desert and mountainous character of most of the country outside China Proper and the northeastern provinces (see Maps 11 and 12).

Until much more is known about reclaimable land, it appears unreasonable to assume that much more than the 100 million acres mentioned above can be tilled in the foreseeable future. Moreover, much of the 35 million acres of new land in China Proper (Buck's estimate) will require heavy expenditures for reclamation, especially for irrigation, and must await the completion of great developments on several of the larger rivers in China. The 60 million acres in the northeast, as well as some of the land in the northern areas of China Proper, can probably be brought into use rather quickly and cheaply, since much of it is suitable for tractor farming on a large scale. The chief crops on this land would be wheat, soybeans, sorghums, and millets. This area has a climate quite similar to that of large portions of our "wheat belt." Much of this land is rich, but its yields will certainly be rather low and will vary considerably from year to year because of a low and variable rainfall. This is the case in our own wheat belt (see Maps 2, 3a, and 3b).

Yields.—The figures given in the Indian delegation report show that the yields per acre of all food crops combined increased by about 7.5 per cent in weight between 1953 and 1955, from 1,225 pounds to 1,318 pounds (136, p. 101). However, since 1955 was a "good" year, and since practically all the increase had come in this year, it seems probable that this increase was due to the weather rather than to any basic improvement in agricultural practices. Later statements say that

1956, like 1954, was a "bad" year (66, May, 1957). However, at the same time, the index for grain harvest in 1956 is given as 175 (1949 = 100 [*sic*]), in comparison with 162.5 in 1955 (*ibid.*). In another publication wheat production for 1956 is given as 107 (1936 = 100) and rice production as 146 (67, February, 1957). The most reasonable conclusions to be drawn from the unsatisfactory data now available are: (*a*) that up to 1955 China had experienced only a fairly complete recovery from the effects of the war with Japan and the civil war which followed; (*b*) that little increase in tilled land had taken place; (*c*) that yields per acre had also changed very little, except as affected by seasonal variations; (*d*) that although the area of double-cropped land may have increased rather substantially between 1953 and 1955, it was still below Buck's estimate that about one-half of the tilled land in China Proper was double-cropped in prewar days (46, pp. 167, 191).

The increase in the total yield of the food crops reported was about 2 per cent greater in 1954 than in 1953, in spite of the "bad" year in 1954; in 1955, however, there was an increase of 9 per cent over 1954, which would not be unreasonable for a "good" year. In view of the absence of any definite statement regarding the size of the 1956 crop, and in view of the statements giving the yields of certain crops in indexes based on those of earlier years, there is little firm ground for believing there was substantial progress in crop yields up to and including 1956 as compared with prewar years. Even a substantial increase in total production over prewar days is open to serious question.

That there should have been very little improvement in agriculture up to 1956 is not at all surprising. In the first place, China suffered a dozen years of turmoil, from 1937 to 1949, of unusual severity even considering the unsettled conditions of the preceding century. The difficulties of rehabilitation were very great. In the second place, the redistribution of the land, which was completed only in 1951, dispossessed not only the noncultivating landlords but the so-called *rich* peasants, most of whom were deprived of one-half or more of their land. These rich peasants, according to the farm management surveys in prewar China, were much the best farmers in China. Hence, however expedient this land reform may have been politically, it almost certainly led to an increase in the number of small farms. It also gave many good party members double portions of land, which they were then allowed to rent. Since the rich peasants were in a better position than the smaller farmers to make improvements in their land, to buy better seeds and fertilizer if, and when, they became available, to repair and improve their implements, and to make other capital investments likely to increase agricultural production quickly, this redistribution of land was almost certainly a backward step in agricultural production. This happened in Soviet agriculture under somewhat similar conditions. Moreover, there can be little doubt that many of these rich peasants were among the 15 million "enemies of the people" whom the Minister of Internal Security claimed to have liquidated by 1952 (see preceding chapter) and who ended up in forced-labor camps building railroads, flood control works, harbors, highways, and other public projects.

However, there seems to be no reasonable doubt that many of the Chinese leaders take it for granted that there has already been a great increase in agricultural production, not only in total amount, which is generally said to be increasing at about 5 per cent per year (136, p. 22), but also in yields per acre. They also seem to believe that these increases in production are due to basic improvements, among which the collectivization of farming is always given first place. In fact, the many specific references to greatly increased crop yields nearly always give the name of the co-operative group or state farm which has achieved this increase. Even Mao Tse-tung says that yields per acre will be doubled or tripled by 1967 and attributes this to the enthusiasm of the people on the co-operative (collective) farms (67, February, 1956).

On the other hand, there are many reports to the effect that some millions of young people who had crowded into the cities are being sent back to the farms to help increase production. In view of the vast amount of underemployment already existing in the rural areas, it is hard to understand the reason for this forced "back to the land" movement; if a steadily increasing amount of food per capita is available, it might be used to employ these young people on the public works so badly needed if China's agricultural area is to be rapidly enlarged. The "forward leap" referred to in the preceding chapter was no doubt partly undertaken to provide employment for these young people being sent back to the rural areas.

Methods of progress.—What one should look for if one is to judge intelligently the progress being made in China's agricultural production is some evidence of the actual adoption of the practices that have been proved to result in higher production everywhere. In brief, these changes may be listed as (*a*) better tillage, (*b*) a more efficient use of manures and an increase in the use of commercial fertilizers, (c) the use of better varieties of seeds, particularly of the leading grain and industrial crops, and (d) an extension of irrigation, which is of very great importance in increasing both the rice area and the yield per acre and in mitigating the effects of drought. There is no convincing evidence that these better practices are widely used as yet.

On the other hand, there is evidence that flood prevention works along the Yellow and Yangtze rivers and their larger tributaries are under construction and are already helping. Judging from 1957 reports of floods in these areas, however, these works are still far from complete or are not adequate to the purposes for which they were designed. Moreover, the mechanization of agriculture in those areas of northern China where this is feasible seems to be proceeding very slowly.

The Chinese leaders are apparently relying chiefly on the organization of co-operative farms to generate the drive toward a more productive agriculture that will provide not only more and better food for a rapidly increasing population but also larger and larger industrial crops—cotton, tobacco, oil seeds, jute, etc.—for the factories. There are many enthusiastic statements about the number of farmers rushing to join producers' co-operatives, over 60 per cent by February of 1956 (67, February, 1956) and over 96 per cent by the end of 1956 (67, April, 1957). These statements, and others, also imply a great increase in production per acre and picture a glowing future for *socialist agriculture.* One is reminded of the similar wishful thinking about agricultural production in the Soviet Union in the early 1930's, which has not yet been translated into reality. Also, one cannot overlook the significance of such a statement as the one saying that the free market in vegetables that was introduced in 1957 resulted very quickly in a doubling of the 1956 supply (66, June, 1957).

Since the adoption of the "forward leap" the most fantastic statements of increased agricultural yields are appearing month after month (66). Some statements speak of yields of 800–900 bushels of cleaned rice per acre (two crops) and of wheat yields three or more times as great as the best in Europe. Even when these most extravagant claims are somewhat qualified, they are calculated to leave the impression with the general reader that there has suddenly been a tremendous increase in average yields. It is quite impossible for anyone at all familiar with agricultural development to give any credence to most of these statements.

Since one of the greatest drawbacks to the improvement of Chinese agriculture is the small size of the average holding, which very often consists of several tiny pieces of land scattered in different parts of the village area, there is little doubt that consolidation of these small fragments into larger units would have a beneficial effect on production. Co-operation in several other respects—credit, use of implements, use of draft animals, etc.—would also have beneficial effects. The evidence that such co-operation is taking place, however, consists almost entirely of assertions on the part of leaders that fully co-operative farming is spreading like wildfire, and thus must be regarded with considerable skepticism.

From whatever angle one looks at the agricultural situation in China today, the most reasonable conclusion seems to be that very little progress has yet been made in effecting basic improvements in China's traditional agriculture. It appears that only 7 to 11 per cent of the expenditures under the first Five-Year Plan (different statements give such varying proportions) has been allotted to agriculture, including the large flood control works being undertaken in several parts of the country. The tried and proved methods of increasing crop yields seem to be receiving comparatively little attention and support, and agricultural education is seldom mentioned in the accounts of what is being done to train men for the new economy. The "surging tide of socialism," which is to lead shortly to a complete collectivization of farming, seems to be relied upon to furnish a motive for the rapid adoption of all those practices upon which the improvement of agricultural production actually depends.

Lest such skepticism regarding basic improvement in agricultural production up to 1957 be misunderstood, I wish to say that I accept without hesitation the view of Buck that the wide adoption of better farm practices, of improved varieties of crops, of an increased use of manures and commercial fertilizers, and of the extension of irrigation, etc., could lead to a 50 per cent increase in production (46, 47, 48). But this does not mean that such an increase can be achieved in a few years by "enthusiasm for collective farming" and the adoption of the "forward leap." There are many reasons why one should be skeptical not only regarding the accomplishments claimed to date but also with respect to rapid future improvement. The doubts regarding this latter point will be summed briefly, even though this involves some repetition.

REASONS FOR DOUBTING RAPID FUTURE PROGRESS

Collectivization.—There is no good reason to doubt that collectivization can be forced at a rapid pace, nor that it will be accompanied by a relatively rapid modernization of agricultural practices in those parts of the country where the topography will permit mechanized production of wheat, the sorghums, and the millets. There is very good reason to doubt, however, whether rice growing can be collectivized in the near future with advantage to the yields. Even in the U.S.S.R., where natural conditions are much more favorable for organizing mechanized large-scale farming than they are in China, agriculture still remains, after thirty years, the weakest link in the economy, and as this is written it appears that collective farming and state farming are being reorganized completely because they have failed to improve production as fast as the leaders desire.

Traditionalism.—It does not seem reasonable to expect that new practices and revolutionary forms of organization will be readily adopted and followed wholeheartedly by farmers who have long lived on the edge of starvation, where the failure of a crop means great hardship and possible death. Under such conditions, farmers will prefer crops and farm practices that have proved capable of yielding a living, even a meager one. They may be forced to accept a new organization of agriculture, but they cannot be forced to pursue improvement simply through enthusiasm for reform.

The size of the job.—It is a staggering job to reach 110 million farm households distributed over a vast area almost twice as large as the United States, in a million or more small villages. Most of these households—perhaps over 80 per cent—contain no member who can read and write, and they have almost no outside contacts except with a few neighboring villages. Even with the best intentions and the most vigorous efforts, a great deal of money and years of hard work will be required to carry agricultural demonstrations and knowledge to these people and to gain their *positive* co-operation in a new form of agricultural organization. The success of such a program will probably have to await the rising of a new generation, educated to accept the new forms of organization because they know no other form or because they are convinced that such practices are *good* and are fraught with real advantage to the farmer.

The Chinese family.—The entire program for agricultural improvements, as well as the program for industrial expansion, is based on the expectation that the traditional Chinese family as a factor in social control can be quickly abolished. It seems highly unlikely that the control of the family over farming practices and farm organization can be changed so rapidly in rural China that collectivism will be enthusiastically and generally accepted in a few years by the present generation of farmers, in spite of all the claims being made to this effect. It does not seem reasonable to expect that explaining the rational advantages of collective farming will in five to ten years miraculously eliminate the family as a highly effective institution controlling the thinking of the adult population. I cannot believe that even the "forward leap" will work miracles in this respect.

The motivation of farmers.—The whole problem of motivation in agricultural work is very complex and differs in many respects from the problem of providing incentives to workers in other sectors of the economy. Even in the Soviet Union, where it has operated for nearly thirty years, there is certainly no conclusive evidence that collectivized farming has evoked the enthusiasm needed to make farmers work long and hard for extra production. It is almost certain to be even more difficult to secure efficient production on collective farms in China.

Smothering the love of a particular piece of land and the satisfaction of seeing one's own livestock thrive will very likely work to the detriment of agricultural production, both currently and in the long run. Land cannot be treated like industrial capital, as something to be used to the best immediate advantage of production and then discarded for something better. And it certainly remains to be proved that livestock farming can be successfully carried on with an eight-hour day and with changing shifts of workers who have no personal interest in the animals they care for.

Furthermore, even though the present government may be more efficient than the one that existed for the preceding century or more, it is almost certain that the social services it is providing have not yet reached very far into the lives of the village people (the mass of the population) and are not yet highly valued. On the other hand, new taxes have reached the villages, and the local officials are interfering with the use of the land, with the use of livestock and tools, with cropping practices, and with many other aspects of village life involving cherished "rights." If the Chinese farmers are to be stimulated to unusual efforts, it must be by more earthy means than an ideological conviction that they are helping to build a new and better social system. China's agriculture, like that of all underdeveloped areas, must necessarily bear a heavy burden in the early years of her modern economic development if this development is to progress fairly rapidly. Agriculture must provide the means to sustain the increasing proportion of the population working in the nonagricultural sectors of the economy, especially in those concerned chiefly with increasing the production of capital goods. This makes heavy taxation of the agricultural population inevitable for some years and thus leaves very little to be invested in agriculture beyond the work the farmer puts into his own improvements. But these improvements are vital to increasing yields and to maintaining them at a high level.

Will the farmer who is forced into a collective, where he has no control over a definite piece of land, put much effort into improving the land of the collective? If the livestock is not *his* livestock, will he give it the care it must have if it is to thrive? Will he give just that extra care to crops which insures better yields, if at least a part of the results of such care does not accrue to him and his family? It does not seem reasonable to me to expect that the rather abstract ideological motives of the convinced Communist will have much effect on the productivity of the agricultural population of China in this generation. The incentives offered the farmers for their hard work must be simple, direct, and easily computable in terms of needed goods.

National granaries.—In China, as in India, all agriculture is greatly dependent on the monsoon (summer rain). This rainfall is highly variable from season to season. Provision against *bad* years is more important in monsoon areas than in regions of more regular rainfall and is especially urgent, of course, where the population is dense and where it lives almost exclusively upon grain. In such areas there is almost nothing to fall back on in the way of food from animals or the human consumption of animal feeds when the annual crops of grain and pulses are short. Moreover, in tropical and subtropical areas the storage of food grains is very difficult and costly and is quite beyond the means of most farmers. Collective farms might arrange such storage if they were operated by the government or were guaranteed against loss by the government. But, however they may be achieved, reserve grain supplies of great volume are needed, and adequate transportation must be provided for their distribution when shortages occur. Comparatively little such storage appears to have been built up as yet.

Unemployment in agriculture.—If any substantial improvement takes place in Chinese agriculture in the near future, it is almost certain to be accompanied by an increasing amount of underemployment and unemployment, for the very idea of improvement means greater per capita output. The agricultural program in China aims to achieve not only greater total production—this is of first importance in all the densely populated areas of Asia—but also to decrease the proportion of workers engaged in agriculture while increasing the consumption of food per capita. Unless the per capita production increases, there is almost no hope for raising the level of living of the farmer and providing for the rapid increase of nonagricultural workers.

Buck's studies (46) have shown that labor efficiency in Chinese agriculture is lower on small farms than on larger farms and that there is more underemployment on these smaller farms.[3] These studies led him to estimate that if the more efficient size of farm became the average size, at least one-third of all the labor then employed on farms would become superfluous. In the areas now under cultivation where only the small grains, except rice, are grown, i.e., the areas where large-scale mechanized tillage is generally feasible, the displacement ratio would be much greater. Although some of these displaced farmers could be transferred to new mechanized farms as fast as the new land was brought into tillage, not many could be provided for in this way. A very rapid collectivization of Chinese farms, if it were accompanied by the increased production per worker that is expected, would create an unemployment problem the like of which the world has never visualized. Even a slow improvement in Chinese agriculture, with the operation of collective farms continuing much as at present but with an increase in size, will mean that a considerable population can be spared year after year for nonagricultural work. It is impossible to believe that an additional mass movement from farms could be absorbed into urban life in the near future or that the "forward leap" in communes will provide them with nonagricultural work.

Already the communist government is facing a situation in which about three times as many new workers (persons arriving at about sixteen years of age) are being added to the labor force each year as can find nonagricultural work (see preceding chapter). Here is the Malthusian dilemma in an acute form. The more efficient the agricultural workers become, the fewer are needed; with a slowly improving

[3] In the rice area, a larger farm may consist of only 4–7 acres, and a smaller farm of 2–3 acres.

diet, due to more efficient agriculture, the death rate tends to decline more rapidly; the spending of even relatively small amounts on health work accelerates this decline, thus adding greatly to the number of persons who will need jobs a few years hence. In the meantime, efforts to create jobs in nonagricultural industries and services are greatly impeded by the low rate at which capital can be accumulated, since most of it must be provided—for the time being, at least—by the surplus of agricultural production above that which must be consumed by the agricultural workers and their families, plus small loans from the Soviet Union for capital goods in specific enterprises. It should be noted, however, that claims are now being made to the effect that in 1956 almost 23 per cent of the national income was invested as capital (66, July, 1957). This seems incredible, and it is quite likely that the *investment* claimed here is something different from *new investment* as we think of it.

CONCLUSIONS

It is by no means certain that the sustained increase in food and other crops will equal the increase in population during the next three decades. China's prospect for keeping her food and fiber supply ahead of population growth seems little, if any, better than India's. China is already supporting about one-half more people than India on a tilled area that is about the same as India's. Other things equal, it will be more difficult to increase the rice yield in China than in India, because it is already nearly twice as high. There does not appear to be much difference between the yields of the other grains in the two countries. The amount of new land available appears to be rather small in both countries, but in proportion to population it is probably somewhat larger in India. In both, however, most of the new land appears to lie in regions where yields of grain will always be rather small.

On the other hand, there is some reason to believe that India's approach to the problems involved in providing her farmers with incentives to increase agricultural production is more realistic than that of Communist China. If this turns out to be the case, India may improve the diet of her people faster than China. But in the case of both countries serious doubts must remain about whether there will be significant improvement in the per capita supply of agricultural products unless birth rates decline much more rapidly than now appears probable.

CHAPTER XIII

CHINA:

INDUSTRIAL DEVELOPMENT

MINERAL RESOURCES

Some time ago, in the latter part of the nineteenth century, it was assumed that China had "unlimited" mineral resources. This judgment resulted largely from the observations of untrained people who found many small iron furnaces operating, saw many small coal mines being worked, and saw, or were told about, numerous oil seepages. It was also known that tin was being mined in some parts of southern China and that antimony and tungsten were being produced in relatively large quantities. Under these circumstances it was not unnatural for many laymen to assume that China was a country of vast mineral resources, and that these resources only awaited exploitation by modern techniques to make China one of the great industrial centers of the world.

The prewar situation.—As geological exploration proceeded, and as the techniques of exploration improved, it was found that many of the earlier observations had been misleading. The outcroppings of iron ore and the oil seepages, in particular, were often disappointing when more carefully investigated (25). The quantity and the quality of the iron ore which was found made unlikely the development of steel production on a large scale, except in three or four areas. In addition, the low iron content of much of the ore, and the composition of some of the ores, made their preparation for blast furnace use relatively expensive. Thus, the cost of steel production seemed likely to remain rather high.

Although these explorations tended to disprove the idea that China's coal was "unlimited" in quantity, they did indicate the presence of very large amounts—so large that no shortage of solid fuel need be feared for some generations (25, pp. 49, 51). Moreover, the varieties of coal needed for different purposes—metallurgy, power production, domestic use, and even for the manufacture of liquid fuel—were all present in

246

large amounts, although the best coking coal, except in Manchuria, was not always found as close to iron ore as could be desired.

By the early 1940's further exploration for oil, especially in the north-west (outside the area commonly known as China Proper) began to uncover more oil than had been discovered previously. The *China Handbook* (69, 1943) and the *Austral-Asiatic Bulletin* (22, suppl., December–January, 1940–41) reported large reserves in the northwest, and the actual operation of a few wells.

After Japan had taken over Manchuria and established Manchoukuo (1931), more intensive exploration for minerals was undertaken there. The results, on the whole, were very encouraging. Table 18 shows how

TABLE 18

MINERAL RESOURCES (IN MILLIONS OF TONS),
MANCHURIA, 1930 AND 1938

Mineral	1938*	1930†
Coal....................	20,000‡	4,800‡
Iron ore................	1,669 (2,500)§	1,000
Oil shale...............	8,408	5,300
Magnesite..............	5,512	....
Fire clay...............	110	....
Aluminum shale........	2,756	....
Gold ore (troy ounces)....	193	129‖
Manganese.............	10#	....

    * Source: 155, 1940, p. 751.
    † Or nearest to 1930 possible. Source: 12, November, 1930, pp. 300, 332.
    ‡ Source: 102, 1942, p. 185.
    § Source: 242, p. 404.
    ‖ Source: 155, 1934, p. 643.
    # Source: 321, 1940, p. 583 (1940 estimate).

the Japanese explorations between 1930 and 1938 changed the estimated amounts of the reserves of some of the more important minerals in Manchoukuo. The Japanese also believed that further and more thorough exploration would lead to the discovery of larger reserves of iron and coal as well as additional deposits of many other useful minerals. But what they had already found justified the investment of large sums to improve transportation, to build and enlarge steel mills, and to open many new mines. On the whole, the northeast was proving quite rich in the minerals most needed in a modern economy. However, before the war (1937), the riches of Manchuria were bringing almost no profit to China.

Even in 1940—when little oil was actually being produced and little was known about the size of oil reserves—the fuel outlook of China (including Manchoukuo) was quite favorable, since the liquefaction of coal was rapidly becoming cheaper. As regards steel production, the outlook for the next two or three decades was quite favorable. The Japanese had proved that it was feasible to use the lower-grade ores, had discovered new deposits—some of them of better-quality ore—and had probably raised pig iron production to 1.5–2 million tons by 1941. Steel production was probably close to 1 million tons. The Japanese also had definite plans to triple the production of pig iron in the following few years and to increase steel production even more. In spite of these developments, the lack of really large amounts of high-quality iron ore seemed likely to make China's iron and steel production fairly expensive even if Manchoukuo were restored. But the development in this region under Japanese control proved that the quality of the ore was not a critical obstacle to substantial progress in the steel industry. Japan's experience and accomplishments in Manchoukuo are now proving of very great value to China, since they supplied a sound basis for the rapid growth of heavy industry which is taking place in Communist China today. The outlook for the steel industry and other heavy industry in China today is more favorable than appeared probable before 1940.

Before 1937 China produced a considerable part of the world's antimony, and it was believed that the reserves, estimated at from 1.5 million tons (25, p. 184) to 2.7 million tons (69, p. 490) of metal, were sufficient to enable her to retain this export market for many years, although Mexico and Bolivia were already displacing China in the American market (236, p. 271). But since the world was using only about 30,000 to 40,000 tons annually before the war, of which China supplied about half (321, 1940, p. 721), her future exports of antimony would not go far in providing her with foreign exchange.

China also supplied a large part of the world's tungsten and, with reserves of perhaps a million tons of high-grade ore, seemed likely to continue exporting tungsten for some time (196, p. 115). But here again the total amount used in the world is small, so China's 10,000–12,000 tons of exports in normal times—almost 20,000 in 1937—would not go far in helping her to pay for needed imports, in spite of the fact that tungsten is several times as valuable as antimony.

There appeared to be enough bauxite or alunite in the northeastern part of China (Shantung and Manchuria) to supply her needs for many years at a rate of use that would have been considered normal before World War II. How adequate it will prove under present conditions is much more doubtful. The *China Handbook* (69, 1943, p. 491) indicates that large new reserves of bauxite had recently been found in both the northwest (Kansu) and the southwest (Yunnan), but these have not yet been proved, as far as can be ascertained.

Several discoveries of copper had also been reported in western and southwestern China shortly before the war. The *China Handbook* (*ibid.*, p. 488) gave estimates of reserves amounting to about 2.6 million tons of pure copper, or a little over one year's supply for the world. Up to the war, China's copper production had been almost negligible, perhaps 1,000 tons (105, p. 5). About all that could be said at that time was that China's copper would probably not go far in the development of an important electrical industry. In the United States we use from three-fourths of a million to a million tons of copper in a normal year.

Before the war, China did not seem to have a significant amount of sulphur or pyrites. Development of the chemical industries would require the importation of large amounts of sulphur.

Even before the war, China (including Manchoukuo) seemed to have a fairly adequate supply of magnesite, but she was not well supplied with a number of other important minerals—manganese, mercury, lead, zinc, silver, nickel, molybdenum, gold, etc. China appeared to have most of them, but in such small amounts that she would have to rely largely on imports, except possibly in the case of manganese. This seems to have been true also of phosphates, potash, and nitrates for fertilizers, although here again it seemed possible that her abundant coal supply might enable her to provide synthetic nitrates at a fairly low cost.

The present situation.—Just how the mineral supply situation of China has changed as a result of the relatively intensive geological exploration carried out since the Communists came into control cannot be determined with any precision.

People's China says that "all former estimates of China's resources in coal, iron and a number of nonferrous metals have been proved to be too low" (67, February 16, 1953). Iron ore is singled out for special mention as being more abundant and of better quality than formerly supposed, but no specific discoveries are listed describing location, amount, or quality. This same publication also reports, "There are ten large geological teams and 52 oil prospecting teams now in Shensi, Kansu, Ningsia and Sinkiang Provinces [all in the northwest] looking for minerals and petroleum" (67, August 1, 1953); and that "petroleum, coal, iron and salt have been discovered in abundance; nonferrous metals such as manganese, tungsten, bismuth, beryllium and zinc have also been found." It adds copper and a great deal of oil as other new finds, stating that the oil deposits surpass those of Iran and that the iron deposits constitute a big share of the world's supply. It further states that China is now self-sufficient in manganese, nickel, tungsten, vanadium, and chrome, and claims new discoveries of molybdenum, copper, magnesium, aluminum, antimony, and tin. No specific details of location or amounts are given, beyond the mention of some provinces and the Gobi Desert, and no estimates of actual reserves are available (67, August 16, 1953). The same article says that China possesses water power capable of driving generators producing 150 million kilowatts. This is far above prewar estimates.

China Reconstructs also notes large oil and copper deposits in Sinkiang Province (northwest) and says that this province is rich in other minerals, adding sulphur, asbestos, and alkali to those already mentioned above (66, April, 1955).

The tone of the articles which describe the discovery of new mineral resources reminds one of the Soviet press in the early 1930's. The information is vague; it seems intended to arouse national pride and to spur on efforts to exploit the new resources. Many of the Soviet Union's early claims have since been substantiated by the actual establishment of basic industries in many of the places named and by the rapidly and steadily increased production. Although many of these Chinese statements of the discovery of *vast* mineral reserves must be regarded with some skepticism, the experience of the Japanese in Manchoukuo, the accomplishments of geological exploration in the Soviet Union, and our own discoveries of new oil fields, copper ranges, uranium mines, etc., should lead us to expect that a country as large as China (which has not yet been very adequately prospected) might very well find great mineral resources in addition to those already known. Hence, even discounting many of the vague claims regarding new discoveries, it seems probable that China does possess the minerals essential to industrial development during the next several decades and that she will continue to find new reserves of important minerals for some years. In view of such a probability, it would appear that the limitations on China's industrial development in the foreseeable future are more likely to be those cultural, political, and organizational factors which affect the economy than any lack of mineral resources. In this respect the picture appears considerably more encouraging today than it did fifteen to twenty years ago.

As is generally known, the development of a modern economy in China in the prewar years was slow as compared with such growth in Japan and even in India. The consumption goods which the masses used consisted largely of the bare necessities of life—food, clothing, housing, and the utensils and furnishings absolutely essential to a poverty-stricken existence. Most of the nonagricultural goods they used were produced in the villages or in the small cities and market towns scattered over the country. The well-known cities such as Peking, Tientsin, Shanghai, Canton, and a number of others were primarily commercial cities or centers of government, rather than industrial cities. For several decades before the 1937 invasion by Japan, however, most of the larger cities had been developing certain types of modernized industry. Cotton textiles may be cited as an example of the slow but substantial development of machine industry in one important field. Although this was the best developed of all the branches of industry, it is estimated that 80 per cent of the cloth used shortly before 1937 was woven by hand in the home (131, p. 96). Much yarn was still spun by hand, but this proportion was declining rapidly. Next to cloth manufacture, it is probable that the making of household utensils and farm tools were the most important industries. These items were practically all made by hand in local shops or at home.

THE PREWAR DEVELOPMENT OF SELECTED INDUSTRIES

Textiles.—In China, as in most other countries in recent times, the first important development in machine industry was in textiles. But since Chinese textiles had to compete not only with those from the well-organized industry of Western countries but also with those of Japan, and since, until 1929, China could impose only a nominal tariff on such imports, even the textile industry did not expand as rapidly as might have been expected. Although China had a practically unlimited and very cheap labor supply and grew her own cotton, the development of cotton mills was slow during the period from the establishment of the first mill in 1890 to World War I (131, p. 188).

In 1913 there were only twenty-eight mills, with 1,210,000 spindles and a few thousand looms. During this period the mills were largely engaged in spinning, the yarn being sold chiefly to local hand weavers. Between 1913 and 1925 the number of spindles increased about threefold, the number of mills almost fourfold, and the number of looms at an even faster rate. This was the heyday of the modern Chinese cotton industry, for the European nations were entirely out of the market for several years during World War I, and Japan could not keep up with the demand.

After 1925 the rate of growth was much slower, and an increasing proportion of the production of cotton cloth seems to have taken place in the mills passing into Japanese hands, especially after 1930. It appears that the Chinese-owned mills could not compete in efficiency with those owned by the Japanese in the same localities and were progressively going out of business or selling out to the Japanese, particularly in the larger treaty ports. As a result, most new Chinese-owned mills were being built in smaller places where they depended largely on nearness to raw material and a local market for their product to offset the greater efficiency of the workers in Japanese-owned mills (39, p. 63).

With the growth of the cotton industry in China after 1913, the imports of yarn began to decline, and after 1920 the exports mounted rapidly (131, p. 191). At the same time, the imports of cotton cloth began to decline and the exports to increase. By 1934 the exports of cloth were almost equal to the imports. But, as noted, although the manufacture of cotton cloth by machinery had made rapid progress after 1913, it had by no means displaced hand-woven fabrics.

Steel.—The steel industry had encountered even more difficulties than the textile industry. Bain gives the annual capacity in 1920 of relatively modern blast furnaces in China as about 900,000 tons (25, pp. 104–5). However, it appears that in 1922 actual production was not in excess of 180,000–200,000 tons. This included the production of Manchuria as well as of China Proper. In 1928 the total production (including Manchuria) was about 434,000 tons, of which 244,000 tons were produced in Manchuria under Japanese management, 179,000 in the small native furnaces in China Proper, and only a little over 10,000 in the larger furnaces. The *China Yearbook* gives the production of pig iron in 1934 in the more modern furnaces of China Proper as only 21,000 tons, with 135,000 tons coming from the small native furnaces and about 445,000 in Manchuria (71, 1936, p. 335).

After 1934 the government definitely undertook to encourage the establishment of basic industries and the development of power, but it accomplished little before the invasion by Japan (1937). In describing the progress after the removal of the government to Chungking, the *China Handbook* refers to thirty-ton blast furnaces as "large" and to ten-ton Bessemer furnaces as though they were the largest in operation (69, 1943, p. 443). It gives no figures for production, merely saying that private ironworks produced about 2.3 times as much in 1941 as in 1940, and 5.5 times as much in 1942.

Production in Manchoukuo.—The situation was quite different in Manchuria, where the Japanese were in control. The production of pig iron in Manchuria in 1930–31 averaged about 380,000 tons (155, 1940, p. 756). This rose to about 700,000 tons in 1936 (242, p. 388) and to 935,000 tons in 1939 (102, 1942, p. 184). Even after 1939, several new blast furnaces were completed, and additional equipment was installed for concentrating low-grade ores. It is not possible to say with any assurance what the production of pig iron in Manchuria was at the end of 1941, but it may have been as much as 2 million tons (*ibid.*, p. 184). Steel ingots are not listed as being produced in Manchuria before 1935. In 1937 production amounted to 470,000 tons, and in 1939 to 638,000 tons (*ibid.*). In 1941 it is believed to have been about 1 million tons. In Manchoukuo a beginning had also been made in the production of magnesium and aluminum, and the generation of electric power had gone forward rapidly.

Small hand-operated industries.—There were, of course, a number of other industries in operation in China. Many of these were luxury industries which had a long history and were still hand-operated, as they always had been—silks, tapestries, rugs, porcelain, jewelry. In some of the larger cities a few small factories used power machines to make various articles of clothing and light steel goods, but they did not employ many workers as compared with the handicraft shops, and the market for their products was quite limited. It can be said quite accurately that modern industry in China had only begun to develop before 1937, except in Manchoukuo under Japanese control.

THE CONDITION OF PREWAR TRANSPORTATION
AND COMMUNICATION

Prewar China was almost as backward in the development of modern transportation as in the development of machine industry. Undoubtedly this was one of the causes of her slow industrial development.

Railways.—At the time Japan took control of Manchuria (1931), the total mileage of railways in China was said to be about 9,300 miles (69, 1937–45, p. 213). It appears that about 3,500 miles were located in Manchuria. This would leave only about 5,800 miles in the rest of China. The Japanese apparently built about 2,700 miles in Manchoukuo between 1931 and 1939, because in the latter year they reported

6,200 miles in operation (102, 1942, p. 182). This provided Manchoukuo with fairly satisfactory railway service.

In the meantime, very little new construction of railways had taken place elsewhere in China. It is very doubtful whether at the time of the Japanese attack in 1937 the total operating mileage in this great area exceeded that of 1931 by more than 200–300 miles. However, some connections were completed between lines already built, which made them more useful.

Canals and rivers.—There are said to have been about 40,000 miles of canals and navigable rivers in prewar China. Most of this mileage consisted of shallow canals located in the Yangtze basin and used only for local transport. However, the Yangtze River was navigable for vessels of 10,000 tons for about 600 miles, and cities like Tientsin and Canton were served by ocean-going ships even though they were located some 30 to 40 miles from the coast on smaller rivers. As already noted, most transport was purely local and depended almost entirely on manpower.

Highways.—Before 1937 there were very few highways in China on which motor transport could be used, and these few were located chiefly near the larger cities. They brought better local transport to a few areas but were unimportant in the economy of the country. In Manchoukuo, on the other hand, the Japanese undertook a vigorous program of road building and claimed to have built 6,000 miles of roads over which bus lines were operated by the end of 1937 (155, 1940, pp. 685–88).

Communication.—Communication was also in a primitive condition in 1937. The postal service was quite limited, and only a few of the larger cities enjoyed telegraph and telephone service. Most of the people of China—those living in the farm villages—had no postal service at all (nor did they need it, since very few of them could read and write).

Electricity.—Electric service, which has become all-important in the rapid development of modern industry, existed in only a few places, chiefly the larger cities. Even in these cities it was not generally available for industrial purposes and was not used at all by most of the inhabitants.

REASONS FOR SLOW PREWAR DEVELOPMENT OF
TRANSPORTATION AND COMMUNICATION

Naturally, one wonders why economic development took place so much more slowly in China than in Japan. Considered solely from the standpoint of available natural resources and the skills of the people, China seems to have possessed some rather definite advantages over Japan in resources, and probably was not behind Japan in the possession of skilled workers. Only a few of the more obvious factors which retarded China's economic development can be mentioned here. Some of these have already been stated or implied in the discussion of the important factors in Japan's economic growth (see chaps. vi and vii).

Lack of central government.—In the first place, for a century or more China had had no strong central government which, like that of Japan, could take the lead in industrial development as entrepreneur, as supplier of capital, and as guarantor of peace and order within the country. The risk in industry and trade becomes very great when every local authority or war lord can levy taxes as he pleases but is not able to insure protection in return. A strong, stable central government with a definite fiscal and industrial policy is the first prerequisite for developing modern industry on any significant scale, whether that industry be state or private. Extraterritoriality in the treaty ports guaranteed order, and the services needed by modern industry, in limited areas only.

Colonial status.—In the second place, China's semicolonial status deprived her of tariff autonomy until 1929. Thus she had only a few years in which to foster "infant" industry by the use of tariffs, even if the Nanking government (Kuomintang) had had an industrial policy and the power, the will, and the money to embark on the industrial development of the country. The Western powers and Japan were far more interested in keeping China in a colonial status—as a supplier of raw materials and a market for manufactures—than in seeing her develop her industry. They did not want her to become more self-sufficient because this would almost certainly result in the development of industries that would cut into the markets for foreign goods and would also, in time, give her the strength to throw off external control. Witness the importance of Japan's industrial strength in keeping her from becoming a colonial appendage of Europe.

Lack of capital.—In the third place, comparatively little native capital was available for developing large-scale enterprise—for building rail transportation and ports, for example, or for establishing factories using expensive machinery. Besides, such capital as there was in the country could not be readily mobilized because the structure of Chinese society was not conducive to the organization of joint-stock enterprises managed solely in the interest of economic efficiency. Large blocks of capital probably could not have been assembled except under government leadership. In addition, foreign capital was afraid to venture outside the treaty ports, and when it did, it made such demands regarding both returns and supervision of the enterprise that the Chinese Nationalists did not care to yield the political control involved.

Lack of trained personnel.—In the fourth place, few Chinese were trained in the management of modern business, in the organization of complex industrial processes, in engineering, and in the operation and care of machines. Again, the lack of a strong central government which could undertake large-scale training both at home and abroad, as the Japanese government had done, was a serious handicap.

Cultural factors.—Finally, there were many social handicaps to be overcome. The stigma attached to working with one's hands prevented educated men, even engineers, from making good use of their training in showing laboring men how to operate and care for machines. The great dominance of the family in Chinese society made it almost necessary for anyone in business to give jobs to members of his family regardless of their fitness for the work. This will explain in part the inefficiency, referred to above, of Chinese-owned textile mills. Many other cultural characteristics also hindered the development of industry in prewar China. They will not be discussed here, as most of them are closely related to the factors treated in chapter iii.

INDUSTRIAL DEVELOPMENT IN COMMUNIST CHINA
BEFORE THE FIRST PLAN

In the years 1949–52, immediately following the "liberation" of China by the Communists, the government of People's China was occupied chiefly in consolidating its power and in bringing the level of production, both in agriculture and in the nonagricultural industries, closer to what it had been at an earlier period—presumably, back to what it had been about 1936. The heavy industries, the mines, and certain other industries and services had been nationalized by 1952, and land reform had been accomplished. However, many private enterprises producing consumers' goods were allowed to continue operating under the same management during this period of recovery, so that the government might make use of the technical knowledge and the profits of the private owners and managers. But nationalization was being steadily extended, and control over the remaining industries was also being strengthened by the requirement that they buy their raw materials from the government and use them to fill government orders.

On the whole, it appears probable that by the end of 1952, and in spite of the Korean war, most nonagricultural industry had attained a level of production approximating that of 1936. Furthermore, because Manchoukuo had again become an integral part of China, the heavy industries which the Japanese had established there—especially the steelworks, which could be rehabilitated rather quickly with Soviet aid—gave Communist China a substantial amount of steel of her own making. This enabled her to produce certain steel products and to undertake certain construction works at an earlier date than would otherwise have been possible.

In connection with the increase in industrial production during this recovery period (1949–52), it should not be forgotten that for about three years (from June, 1950, to September, 1953) Communist China was rather heavily involved in the Korean war, in spite of the fact that the Soviet Union supplied practically all of the military equipment used by the Chinese armies. This was undoubtedly an important reason, possibly the most important, why no five-year plan was proposed until July of 1953—about two months before the Korean armistice. Dr. Wu thinks that this timing may have been more than a coincidence (348, p. 261).

Regarding this period prior to July of 1953, Hsia says that planning activity had been confined to (*a*) setting up planning machinery, (*b*) holding planning conferences, (*c*) drafting plans for particular economic activities from year to year, and (*d*) fixing targets for certain basic commodities (127, p. 5). "There were, it is true, plans, but there was no Plan" (*ibid.*). Thus goals for 1952 were set for certain types of production, based on the production of the best year preceding 1952 (the year is not the same for all industries, nor is the particular year always specified). Because of this vagueness it is quite impossible to say whether an index of 100 for any particular commodity equals the highest production since the Communists attained complete control, or the highest in the pre-1937 period (probably 1936), or even later in the case of the industries which were centered in Manchoukuo and were under the control of the Japanese until after the war.

Indexes and quantities of actual production in 1952 for some of the more important industries are given in Table 19.

Two examples will serve to show the difficulty of arriving at any reliable conclusion about the precise meaning of some of these figures.

These examples are typical of the difficulties encountered in using most of the published data.[1] An official journal (66, May–June, 1952, pp. 4–9) gives an index for food production in 1951 of 92.8 (1936 = 100). It is very unlikely that the index of 109 for grain given in Table 19 is also based on 1936, for an increase approximating 17 per cent in one year is very questionable, except as the result of windfall gains due to highly favorable weather. Secondly, there is some reason to think that the production of pig iron in Manchuria in 1941 (Japanese) may have approached 2 million tons (102, 1942, p. 184) and that it may have in-

TABLE 19

INDEX AND QUANTITY OF ACTUAL PRODUCTION, CHINA, 1952*

Product	Index (100 = Best Preceding Year)	Actual Quantity	Units of Measure (Tons Are Metric)	Goal 1952
Pig iron.........	83	1,438	000's of tons	1,801
Steel ingots.....	135	1,620	000's of tons	1,860
Coal...........	90	47,382	000's of tons	47,382
Electric power...	114	6,968	millions kw-h.	7,029
Petroleum......	118	389	000's of tons	441
Cement.........	153	3,000	000's of tons	2,900
Cotton yarn.....	144	2,453	000's of bales	2,453
Cotton cloth....	168	68,785	000's of bolts	65,919
Cotton (raw)....	155	1,290	000's of tons	1,290
Grain..........	109	164	millions of tons	164

* Source: 127. The figures given here and in most of the following description of the first Five-Year Plan cannot be considered exact. Different writers and publications often give different figures for what appear to be the same periods, and for the same goals, commodities, amounts of production, expenditures, etc. These contradictions cannot be resolved. A reasonably accurate but general picture of what has been happening in Chinese industry up to about 1956 will have to suffice.

creased somewhat in 1942. The index of 83 for 1952 was probably calculated from a prewar base (1936) or from some other base, including Japanese production in Manchuria, since there was almost no production of iron or steel in China Proper at that time. The fact is that with the data available it is impossible to say with any precision how industrial production as a whole, or the production of any particular type of goods, in 1952 compared with that of the best prewar year in the territory now comprising Communist China.

[1] Whether the uncertainties and contradictions so often found in the statistics of Communist China are deliberate, no one can say. Since very little effort is made to eliminate inconsistencies, it seems more probable that the data supplied to the several ministries of the central government come from different sources, and that the officials in charge of their collection and use are often ill-prepared and make little or no effort to remove inconsistencies, or even glaring mistakes.

INDUSTRIAL DEVELOPMENT UNDER THE
FIRST FIVE-YEAR PLAN

When the first plan was launched in July, 1953, very little information was published about it. What is said here will be based largely on the more detailed information given by Li Fu-ch'un, the head of the planning authority in July, 1955 (348, pp. 261–63; 66, October, 1955; 67, December 16, 1953). The total outlay for "economic construction and cultural and educational development" during the plan (1953–57) was to be 76,640 million yuan (new currency), which at the official exchange rate (U.S. $1.00 = Y 2.5) would come to $30,656 million. Of this amount 55.8 per cent, or $17,096 million, was to be allocated to

TABLE 20

EXPECTED DISTRIBUTION OF INVESTMENT,
FIRST FIVE-YEAR PLAN, CHINA, 1953–57

	Per Cent
Industry	58.2
Transportation, post, and telecommunications	19.2
Agriculture, forestry, and water conservancy	7.6
Trade, banking, and stockpiling	3.0
Municipal public utilities	3.7
Cultural, educational, and public health institutions	7.2
Miscellaneous	1.1
Total	100.0

capital investment, including depreciation. This would be an annual average of $3,400 million. This capital investment was to be distributed as indicated in Table 20 (348, p. 262). Since this investment includes depreciation as well as new investment, Dr. Wu estimates that the net increase in capital stock would amount to somewhat less than $12,000 million during the life of the plan.

Allocation of investment.—The most striking feature of this plan is the great emphasis on investment in industry (58.2 per cent) and transportation (19.2 per cent) as contrasted with agriculture, forestry, and water conservancy (7.6 per cent). After the large-scale water conservancy works—which probably include flood prevention, since it does not appear in any other category—are cared for, there is almost certain to be very little left for agriculture. This seems all the more significant in view of the fact that land reform was completed about two years before the first plan was begun in 1953. This land reform program should have yielded a vast amount of information regarding the need of investment in agriculture. Because most farmers at that time were still cultivating their own land and could be expected to improve it to the best of their ability with their own labor, it may have been assumed that there was no need to provide much public investment for agriculture, or even to provide much assistance to the farmers in the form of extension work and education in better farming practices. It was further assumed by the Chinese leaders that the stimulus of increasing collectivization of farming would provide adequate incentive for the rapid improvement of production.[2]

The point of interest to us here is that it is doubtful whether the first plan provided an annual investment in agriculture of more than $75–100 million, since the total for five years, including "forestry and water conservancy," came to only about $800 million, or $175 million per year. (See preceding chapter for discussion of *incentives* to better farming.)

The first plan was to provide capital for a total of 1,600 major projects, 1,271 of which were to be completed by 1957. Of these major projects 694 were in industry, and 455 of these were to be completed by 1957. These projects were to absorb almost three-fifths of all capital investment. Only 252 major projects were in the field of agriculture, forestry, and water conservancy, and they must have been relatively small, since the capital investment contemplated for all of them combined was so small (348, pp. 261–64).

In transportation 10,000 kilometers of railways were to be built, of which 4,000 kilometers were to be trunk lines; 10,000 kilometers of highways were also to be built, and 400,000 tons of shipping were to be constructed. These projects, together with communications, would absorb almost one-fifth (19.2 per cent) of the capital expenditures. Many other important construction works, public utilities, educational and health institutions were to be undertaken. Most of these would be able to make large use of relatively unskilled labor, which could be hired on a subsistence basis (348, pp. 261–65).

Production goals.—In general terms, industrial production as a whole was to be increased by 98.3 per cent by 1957, and modern industrial

[2] In early 1956 Mao Tse-tung said, "Over 60 per cent of her [China's] 111 million peasant households—more than 70 million households—have answered the call of the Central Committee of the Communist Party of China and joined semi-socialist agricultural producers' cooperatives" (67, February, 1956). He goes on to say that by 1960 all agricultural co-operation will be fully socialist.

production (probably meaning that involving the use of power-driven machines) was to increase by 104.1 per cent (Table 21). This would mean annual increases of 14.7 per cent and 15.3 per cent in the above two categories. In contrast, agricultural production was expected to increase by only 23.3 per cent, or between 4 per cent and 5 per cent annually (348, pp. 261–65). Population was expected to grow 2 per cent annually. The production of industrial (nonfood) crops was expected to increase much faster than that of food crops.

TABLE 21

PRODUCTION GOALS FOR 1957, FIRST FIVE-YEAR PLAN, CHINA*

Product	Index (1952 = 100)	Amount	Units of Measure (Tons Are Metric)
Coal	178	113,000	000's of tons
Steel	306	4,120	000's of tons
Pig iron†			
Cement	210	6,000	000's of tons
Paper (machine-made)	176	650	000's of tons
Sugar (machine-processed)	276	686	000's of tons
Electricity	219	15,900	millions kw.-h.
Electric motors	164	1,050	000's kw.-h.
Electric generators	765	227	000's kw.-h.
Motor lorries		4,000	units

* Source: 66, October 1955, p. 10. Several other sources might have been used, and all would have given different figures at certain points. Some of these differences are probably due to revision of goals from time to time, but one cannot always be certain of the date of different revisions. Some, perhaps most, of the differences found cannot possibly be accounted for with the data available. In this connection see 348, pp. 255–61.

† Not given in preceding source; however, Table 19 gives actual production in 1952 as 1,438,000 tons, and Dr. Wu, 348, p. 264, gives annual capacity to be added for 1953–57 as 2,800,000 tons. This would make a total annual capacity of 4,238,000 tons as a goal for 1957 and an index of approximately 300, about the same as for steel. These figures must be regarded as conjectural.

Achievements.—Almost no satisfactory information is now available regarding what was accomplished during the first plan. The references to production are vague and rather general. In some cases they are quite contradictory. In addition, it appears that the goals for particular goods were so frequently changed, and the base year so often shifted, that it is quite impossible to tell how far data which appear comparable are actually so. This does not mean that there are no statements regarding the increase in production and the progress toward goals. In fact, such statements are so numerous that they are confusing, but they are couched in terms that seem intended either to serve political purposes at home or to impress other Asian peoples with the great achievements of Communist China rather than to provide reliable information.

For the most part, these statements describe specific achievements in particular factories, in particular farming communities, and by particular teams of workers; all of these tales may be true, but such stories add up to little that is helpful in forming a reasonable judgment about the success of the efforts being made to improve the economy as a whole.

Despite the very unsatisfactory character of most of the information, certain facts and probabilities deserve careful consideration by anyone trying to arrive at conclusions regarding industrial improvements that may be preparing the way for better living conditions.

1. From Dr. Wu's analysis of investment in China in 1936 (the one prewar year of the 1930's which may be regarded as fairly normal) it appears that nonagricultural investment may have amounted to $500–600 million (348, p. 241). The first plan contemplated an investment averaging about $2,400 million annually, if depreciation is excluded from investment. Of this about $2,200 million or a little more was allotted to nonagricultural projects. It seems reasonable to assume that if this amount were actually invested, production should begin to show some effect before the end of the plan. This should hold in spite of the fact that it is quite impossible to tell what the Chinese are paying for capital goods under the barter terms of their agreements with the Soviet Union.[3]

2. The Japanese had invested 1,400 million yen (about $700 million) in Manchuria between 1932 and 1939, and their total investment by that time was somewhat more than 3,000 million yen ($1,500 million). The total Japanese investment by 1942 may very well have been close to 4,000 million yen ($2,000 million). Most of the later investments in industrial construction probably did not come into production during Japanese control, and the Soviet armies dismantled most Manchurian factories and mills by removing the machinery so that it would not fall into the hands of the Nationalists. It is altogether probable that the return of this machinery, and the assistance of the Soviet Union both in technical personnel and in loans, made it possible to get much Manchurian industry back into production rather

---

[3] It is reported, for example, that 1 ton of tea buys 10 tons of steel plates, that 1 ton of pork buys 5 tons of plates, that it takes 10 tons of pork to buy one tractor (as of Sept. 1957, about 7 tons of hogs on the hoof, or about 5 tons of pork using our methods of dressing, would buy a tractor of the size most generally used by the farmers of the United States), that 19,000 tons of shelled peanuts buys one electric plant (capacity not specified), and that one ton of raw silk buys one kilometer of steel rails (weight not specified) (82, p. 2).

quickly. The Japanese had also trained a considerable number of Chinese as workers in the heavy industries they had established.[4]

3. The Chinese had already had considerable experience in textiles. Since the capital needed to expand such production was not great, and since there was little opportunity for private owners to use profits except by reinvesting in their businesses, production in textile factories may have expanded rather rapidly after 1949. It is possible that for several years before 1949 the cotton mills of China had not made full use of their equipment, so that larger output could be quickly attained with a relatively small additional investment, as was the case in India (see chap. x). Most other private enterprises of a modern character may also have been able to increase production soon after the Communists came into control. However, the fact should not be overlooked that many private enterprises were removed from Mainland China to Taiwan and Hong Kong as the threat of the Communists increased. The tremendous growth in small industry in these areas is witness to the size of this movement.

4. In the early days of economic development in any large underdeveloped country like China, there is great need for many types of construction: railways, highways, communications lines, dams for flood control, water power and irrigation, electric transmission lines, public buildings and factories, housing, and many other types of preparatory construction such as surface works in opening mines, preparing streets in the cities for increased and heavier traffic, etc.

A great deal of such construction work can be done by manpower with comparatively little machinery and without expensive materials requiring elaborate production processes and highly skilled operatives. It is surprising to a Westerner to see how the roadbed for a railway can be built by human labor, if there is enough of it, and how fast the work proceeds. It is difficult to believe how many thousands of cubic yards of earth can be moved in a day by chain belts of laborers, each carrying two small baskets on the ends of a pole or yoke across his shoulders, each basket holding fifteen to twenty pounds of earth

---

[4] I have found no specific statement that the Soviet Union returned, free of charge, the machinery it removed from the factories of Manchuria. Since there are numerous fulsome statements showing appreciation of the loans made to China by the Soviet Union, but unaccompanied by acknowledgment of the free return of this machinery, it is probably being charged for under the loan agreement. It is also probable that the leaders of China want to make the rehabilitation of Manchurian industry appear to their own people not as rehabilitation but as an entirely new creation of the People's Government.

or stone. It is hard to imagine how quickly coal can be put aboard a ship by a line of workers passing along baskets containing perhaps twenty pounds of coal each. Human conveyor belts, human stone crushers, human elevators for bricks and mortar on the ramps of a new building, human horses on carts, and human ditchers with shovels can accomplish a great deal in many types of construction if they are well organized and are supplied with enough food, clothing, and shelter to keep them in working vigor. For some years there will be an abundance of such workers in China, and they will be reasonably content with a meager subsistence. It is highly probable that a great majority of the 15 million persons "liquidated" between 1949 and 1952 were sent to forced-labor camps for such work. The availability of so much manpower helps to make credible the claims that certain railway lines were completed in record time, that certain dams —particularly earth dams badly needed for flood control—were quickly thrown up, that certain highways have been built in a few months, and that many factory and office buildings have been erected within a short time.

5. Notice should also be taken of the claims of a rapid expansion of educational facilities. The increase in the proportion of children in primary schools was very rapid even during the civil war, 1945–49, following the evacuation of the Japanese. According to an article published in *Peoples' China,* dated September 17, 1952, the total number in such schools was somewhat over 43 million (67), an increase of 82.2 per cent over 1945. All children aged 7–14, inclusive, numbered in the neighborhood of 110–12 million, according to the 1953 census. On this basis it would appear that about 40 per cent of the children of primary-school age were attending school by the summer of 1952 and that this proportion was increasing rapidly. At about the same time, 1,568,000 were attending secondary schools, while at the census of 1953 about 20 million were aged 15–18. Thus it would appear that about 8 per cent of these children were in school. This was said to be only a 4 per cent increase over 1946. Even though the number of children in school and the increase in number may be considerably exaggerated, there appears to be no reasonable doubt that primary and secondary education are now spreading fast, as compared with the preceding two or three decades.

Much of China's educational effort, however, seems to be concentrated on higher education and especially on engineering and technical training. By the end of 1957, i.e., at the completion of the first

Five-Year Plan, it is said (66, October, 1955) that 283,000 students will have graduated from universities and colleges, of whom 94,000 would have completed work in technological and engineering institutions. By the end of the plan it was expected that 434,000 students would be attending 208 universities and colleges and that 177,000 of these would be enrolled in technical and engineering courses.

As has already been noted above and as is happening in India, there appears to be a considerable amount of unemployment among those students who have had the conventional training provided in the secondary schools and in the colleges and universities. The great need at present is for men with technical training and training in industrial organization and management. Although there is little doubt that Communist China's efforts to increase the supply of such men are meeting with considerable success, there can also be no doubt that the shortage of such personnel will remain a critical factor in the economic development of the country for some years.

I would again call attention to the fact that adequate technical training, while a prerequisite of rapid industrial development, by no means insures an early and adequate supply of men with the experience essential to the successful operation of modern economic enterprises. Only actual experience for some years in the operation of such enterprises by men with good technical training can produce managers who can steadily increase efficiency.

Another important aspect of training for greater economic efficiency, not generally included in the propagandistic accounts of educational achievement but of great significance, is the sending of experienced teams of workers from the more efficient plants to other plants where production is lagging, to teach the more efficient methods. For example, teams consisting of experienced workmen, supervisors, foremen, and minor officials from the Anshan steel works (Manchuria) are often sent to other steel mills to show the less experienced workers how to raise per capita production. This would seem to be a very important method of spreading rather rapidly the benefits of the experience of the trained workmen in the better-established enterprises to those in new or less efficient enterprises. This practice has proved useful in the Soviet Union, and there is no reason to doubt it will also prove equally useful in China.

6. The Chinese accounts of increased efficiency in industrial production remind one again and again of the official accounts which began to come out of the Soviet Union about thirty years ago. They often

repeat in almost the same words the information given the visitor to Soviet factories in those days. Many of those early claims of efficiency, and even of actual production, were based on the capacity of the plant, assuming it was operating at capacity under conditions prevailing in western Europe or the United States. Besides, achievements which seemed very low to us appeared relatively great to Russians at that time and were heralded as quite remarkable.

The situation in Communist China today is undoubtedly similar. One example will have to suffice. The opening of a new open-pit coal mine at Fushin (about 100 miles west of Mukden in Manchuria) is hailed as a great advance in mining, and its production is treated as a marvelous feat which could have been achieved only under the unparalleled drive of communism. It so happens that in 1930 I visited a great open-pit coal mine at Fushun (about 20–30 miles southeast of Mukden). It was then fully mechanized. The heavy layer of oil shale on top of the coal was being removed by power shovels and conveyed by rail to nearby retorts where the distillation of the oil took place. The coal was also being handled by power shovels, which loaded it directly onto the cars on the several different levels of tracks built along the sides of the pit. The installation as a whole compared favorably with open-pit mining operations for coal and iron ore in the United States at that time, and production also compared favorably with the best elsewhere. The journalists who describe this newest mine in Chinese periodicals certainly leave the impression in the minds of their Chinese readers that here is something new, marvelous, and of exclusively Chinese Communist construction.

Such descriptions probably make a profound impression not only on most of the Chinese Communists and other Chinese who ardently desire the economic development of their country but also on many other peoples in Asia who likewise lack the experience and the knowledge needed for an accurate appraisal of these achievements.

ASSESSMENT OF ECONOMIC PROGRESS AND GROWTH OF
POPULATION PRESSURE

Mainland China's greatest economic achievements since "liberation" (1949), or at least those most talked about, have been in the field of heavy industry and especially in the production of iron and steel. It is quite impossible to evaluate the gains in production because they are largely based on the rehabilitation of the heavy industry developed in Manchoukuo and on the expansion that may have taken place there during the first plan (1953–57). The latest figures from which calculations of steel production in 1957 could be made indicate that about 5.3 million tons were turned out (66, May, 1958). If this is correct, it indicates that even the Japanese potential at the end of the war was expanded by at least 2 million tons by 1957, and possibly by even more. The data on production of coal, cement, fertilizer, and a few other products of heavy industry indicate large increases by 1957 (*ibid.*). However, it is impossible to arrive at any clear idea about actual increases during the first plan as compared with the highest previous production, since the items most talked about are just those items (iron, steel, coal) on which the Japanese had concentrated capital in Manchoukuo before and during the early years of the war, and the potential production of the plants actually well along to completion by 1941 is not known. Moreover, it should be pointed out that practically all the steel made in China is being used as capital goods in expanding heavy industry and transportation, and that it will be several years, probably two to three five-year plans, before enough of it reaches the average consumer to improve his standard of living. This is the same pattern as in the Soviet Union.

It is highly uncertain whether the per capita production of non-agricultural consumers' goods increased substantially by 1957 over 1936. If it did, it was probably due to the more complete use of the factories and equipment already in existence rather than to new construction and added equipment. The evidence I have been able to find does not seem adequate to justify the claims of a substantial improvement in the level of living of the masses, except as compared with that of the very lean years from 1938 to about 1952. The data available on agricultural production have already been discussed.

It is reasonably certain that the firm establishment of the communist government has mitigated the evils arising from the shortages of food in particular areas because of drought and floods. The government did organize famine relief on a large scale and acted quickly to prevent the hoarding of grain and the vicious exploitation of famine sufferers, which had been common in China from time immemorial. This better distribution of the food supply could easily be made to appear to great numbers of people as a large increase in production, because, in a vast country like China, even a great drought or a great flood seldom covers more than a small proportion of the total agricultural area. Even though millions are suffering from hunger in one region, there may be a glut of food in other areas. When there is an organization capable of assembling this surplus and of moving it to the stricken areas, it may appear that this relief is made possible by increased production. Therefore, although there is good reason to believe that since about 1952 or 1953 the population of China as a whole has suffered less from food shortages than for a number of decades, it remains questionable whether the per capita production of food has increased.

Good progress also appears to have been made in establishing and expanding a number of important services—civil order, rehabilitation of the existing railways, new road and railroad building, the generation and distribution of electricity, flood control, health services, and the extension of educational facilities, particularly in science and engineering. Some of these services touch the lives of many people directly and certainly tend to make life a little better, e.g., civil order and health work; others act less directly or only after a considerable period of time. Thus flood control and irrigation may or may not effect a large number of people directly and immediately, while the increase in the generation of electricity or the improvement of education or the increase in steel production will, for a time, perhaps for a decade or longer, make almost no difference in the living conditions of the masses. It takes several years to educate engineers and several more years for them to acquire the experience necessary to make them *effective* engineers; it takes several years to develop the secondary steel-using industries that provide consumption goods on an expanding scale; and it takes even longer to get the economy into balance so that each part performs its function effectively.

The point I would make is not that China is not making economic progress but that this progress is considerably slower than is generally claimed, that it is not a balanced development that will enable all sectors of the economy to operate in a highly effective manner, and that it therefore will not yield much improvement in the level of living during the next two or three decades, especially in view of the rapid growth of population.

Although since the above was written a vast amount has been said about the miraculous expansion of industry under the "forward leap," I am not convinced that the views expressed here need significant modification. Claims that the production of steel in 1958 is more than twice as great as in 1957 and that in ten years China may be producing "several hundred million tons" (66, December, 1958, pp. 12–15) do not seem to me to deserve serious consideration. Likewise, most other claims of increased industrial efficiency during 1958 seem so fantastic that they do not add to the knowledge we need in order to arrive at a sound judgment regarding China's economic progress. In fact, such a mass of extravagant claims has the effect of making one skeptical even of lesser claims which otherwise seem quite reasonable. Finally one wonders what effect these fantastic claims will have on their own people when a better life fails to materialize within the next few years.

Because I believe the available facts indicate that improvement in living conditions in China has been little and will be very slow, I believe that the feeling of population pressure will grow rapidly in the near future. Large segments of the population will feel increasing deprivation because the concept of *necessities* will be steadily expanding. Indeed, the whole basis on which the Communist party in China rested its case for revolution was that only by wiping out the existing social and economic order could the people improve their living conditions. There is abundant evidence that the desire for a better living is already spreading slowly, especially among the younger people in the cities. That these ideas are beginning to penetrate into the villages admits of no doubt. Every health center set up, every school established, and every new contact with the outside world by radio, newspapers, etc., contributes its mite to make the villager dissatisfied with his poverty, his constant illnesses, and more conscious of the social and economic discriminations he suffers.

In this connection I am reminded of a visit I made to a village in South India. In the section of this village where the harigans, "Children of God" (Gandhi's term for the "untouchables" of Indian society), lived, a woman came up to our group and complained bitterly that the improvements being carried on were confined entirely to the section where the caste groups lived, that the harigans were being neglected. She said specifically that the wells of the harigans were not being improved as were the wells of the caste groups. Everywhere in the underdeveloped countries new bases for comparison are being created, and hardships which were accepted without question in the past are coming to be felt and resented. China is no exception. Indeed, in China the people are officially given information (propaganda) intended to create resentment toward the former colonial masters and all other "capitalists and exploiters." It is inevitable, under the circumstances, that masses of the people will develop new desires and wants long before they can be satisfied and that many of them will come to believe, from constant official repetition, that the chief reason they cannot live better is to be found in the machinations of the capitalist peoples.

What will be the consequence of this increasing feeling of population pressure on China's relationship with other peoples? How will the slow and small improvement in living conditions be interpreted to the masses by the communist leaders? It is not too difficult to imagine answers to these questions. There are many specific incidents, as well as the ideology of communism, to guide our thinking on this matter. Every dissatisfaction of the people will be laid at the door of the "capitalist exploiters"—even the failures of communist leaders to increase quickly the goods the people want, as well as the obvious mistakes made by the planners.

On China's southern borders lie the countries of the Indo-Chinese peninsula, with considerable areas of unused but tillable land and relatively sparse populations. Whether they have important mineral resources near the Chinese borders is not known. What China may be expected to do in these border areas is shown in what she has already done in North Korea and North Vietnam (Viet-Minh)—fifth-column infiltration, encouragement of insurrection, and constant incitement of troubles which will prevent economic improvement in these countries. When the preparation is deemed sufficient, communist governments will be proclaimed, and they will be incited to attack the established governments.

It should also be noted that there are still large areas in Tropical Oceania (perhaps as much as 400,000 square miles), most of which are now under the control of Australia and the Netherlands. These areas are thinly populated, and Asiatics are not allowed to settle there. What better opportunity could possibly be offered to the leaders of China to explain that the "European capitalistic peoples" are responsible for the poverty of the Chinese people? That the need of the Chinese for larger resources itself constitutes a denial of some of the fundamental tenets of Marxism will not for a moment deter the use of the feeling of population pressure as a reason for making all the trouble possible for "capitalist imperialists."

In addition, it is inconceivable that the growing feeling of personal hardship among the Chinese people will not be used by their leaders to create envy and hatred of the peoples who have attained a higher level of living, and thus to build up personal motives for the popular support of conquest. In fact, if the leaders develop a great hunger for power, it would serve their purposes best to keep the level of living low so that they could play on the personal wants of the people. However, I do not believe there will be any need to plan deliberately for a slow improvement in living conditions during the next few decades. The difficulties already operating, plus the rapid growth of population and the increased opportunities for comparing their standard of living with that of other peoples, will assure a growing feeling of deprivation for some time to come.

EMPLOYMENT

Another matter of the greatest importance, already noted in chapter xi but deserving further discussion, is the increase of unemployment during the first plan. In China, as in India, there has long been a great deal of underemployment in the agricultural population; there have been periods during the year when no work existed for a significant proportion of the labor force in the villages. Most of these underemployed persons would be available for nonagricultural employment if the plans for such employment were adequate and if there were a surplus in agricultural production so controlled that it was made available to these workers when engaged in nonagricultural tasks. (It is claimed that such a surplus has now been achieved.) Although these workers are unskilled, they can be used in many types of construction—roads, railways, flood control works, etc.

There is some evidence of serious unemployment in the official statements showing the increase in the number of workers in industry during the first plan. In 1955 there were 13,740,000 workers engaged in China's industry, and this was said to be an increase of 15 per cent over 1952 (66, June, 1955). If this rate, averaging 5 per cent per year, had continued during the last two years of the plan, the number engaged in industry would have increased from about 11.9 million in 1952 to 15.1 million by 1957, a total increase of approximately 3.2 million industrial workers during this five-year plan. Since the total number of workers added to the labor force during this plan (persons coming to working age minus persons retiring or dying) could not have been less than about 13.3 million, it would appear that about 10 million of them did not get jobs in industry. No definition is given of industrial workers, but even when a large allowance is made for new workers going into other types of jobs—all kinds of services plus those needed for the new land added to the tilled areas—it still seems reasonably certain that unemployment and underemployment increased greatly during the first plan. There are a number of facts indicating that this was the case. Some have already been cited in chapter xi, but more may be added.

"Because China is very thickly settled in some places and very sparsely in others, the government plans to help two to three million people to move to Kansu [an area in northwest China similar to our "dust bowl"] from the heavily populated North China provinces and crowded cities like Peping" (66, October, 1956). On December 1, 1957, the Associated Press reported that millions of city dwellers were being sent back to the farms to help produce more food, and it specifically mentioned white-collar workers (3 million) and communist cadres (millions) as being dislodged from the cities and sent to the farms. The reasons for this action are that "farms . . . were starving for manpower" (*Cincinnati Enquirer*, December 2, 1957, p. 24).

Thus, to the many millions of underemployed workers already on the farms, a few million more are to be added because no work can be found in the cities. In spite of the great expansion claimed in transportation, in flood control, and above all in heavy industry and in such services as government administration, health, and education, vast numbers are joining the ranks of the unemployed and underemployed each year. The number added to these groups during the first plan may very well amount to 6–7 million. The situation is much the same as in India, and it further emphasizes the great difficulties encountered in finding more productive work for all the young people entering the labor force each year in a country already overpopulated, where little new land is available, and where most of the new industries and basic services are being patterned after the most efficient models in operation elsewhere. If even a small part of the claimed progress in agriculture has actually taken place, the farmers are already more efficient, and agriculture needs less labor rather than more. At the same time, vast amounts of capital are needed to employ a comparatively small proportion of the increasing labor force, perhaps one-third to one-half, in the factories and in the ancillary services. Clearly, the faster the labor force increases in the early years of modern economic development the more difficult it is to find more productive work for all.

No doubt further great claims for the "forward leap" of 1958 will be made in the Chinese press before this book appears. All that I can say from my analysis of the statements now available to me is that I believe the leaders of China have been greatly disillusioned about the ability of their industrial program to provide employment for additional workers. As a result, they are encouraging some *revival* of small local industries as a source both of additional employment and consumption goods and are trying to make it appear that something new and wonderful is happening. There have long been many thousands of such small-scale enterprises, and their continuance and expansion may very well prove beneficial over the next decade or two, but to regard such a revival as a new feature of Chinese economy, as a great forward leap, gives a totally false impression of the probable increase in consumption goods likely to come from this officially encouraged interest in small-scale local industries.

CHAPTER XIV

PAKISTAN

AND CEYLON

PAKISTAN

Pakistan consists of two rather large areas carved out of the territory of India as it was under British control. The basis for allocating these two areas to Pakistan was their predominantly Moslem populations.[1] These two areas, now called West Pakistan and East Pakistan, are separated from one another by about a thousand miles of Indian territory. West Pakistan is relatively large (310,236 square miles, excluding Kashmir-Jammu), but according to the census of 1951 it contained only 44.5 per cent of the population (33,779,000), while East Pakistan, with only a little over one-seventh of the total area (54,501 square miles), contained 55.5 per cent of the population (42,063,000).

Climatically and topographically the two parts of Pakistan are very different. West Pakistan lies between 24° and 36° north latitude, and its agriculture, while tropical in the south, becomes more like that of the temperate zone in the north, although rice is the main summer crop everywhere (see Map 7).

On the whole, West Pakistan is an area of low rainfall. The eastern part, which is watered by the Indus River and its tributaries, contains much irrigable land of good quality, especially in the north—the Punjab. Toward the south the Indus valley becomes increasingly dry, and agriculture is entirely dependent on irrigation. Much of this area is desert, and seems likely to remain so. The headwaters of the Indus River rise in India and in Kashmir-Jammu, which is now controlled by India, and the division of these waters between the two countries is governed by treaty arrangements which appear to be rather am-

---

[1] Both Hindus and Moslems recognized the political inexpediency of allocating relatively small areas that were predominantly Moslem to Pakistan, or, similarly, small areas that were predominantly Hindu to India, because there were a great many such areas scattered over the entire subcontinent.

biguous, since dispute over the use of the waters causes a great deal of hard feeling between India and Pakistan. Almost all of the agriculture of West Pakistan is found in the area watered by the Indus.

The western portion of West Pakistan is mountainous and contains little usable agricultural land. For the most part it is sparsely settled. It contains most of the mineral resources of the country, but, as will be shown below, these are rather meager and of generally poor quality.

Kashmir-Jammu (with an area of 82,258 square miles and a population of 4,022,000 in 1941) contains a considerable majority of Moslems (2.8 million), but was not allocated to either country at the time of partition and has been a source of bitterness ever since. At present (1958) India appears to have gained fairly complete political and economic control over Kashmir and to be in the process of annexing this region. Climatically and topographically Kashmir is much like the northwest frontier province of West Pakistan. It is thinly settled and contains little good agricultural land. But since the western tributaries of the Indus River arise in Kashmir and are now controlled by India it bids fair to remain a source of friction between Pakistan and India.

East Pakistan forms a part of the delta of the Ganges and Brahmaputra rivers. It is a rich agricultural area with one of the densest populations in the world—over 770 persons per square mile. It lies between about 22° and 27° north latitude, and its agriculture is entirely tropical. It has a heavy rainfall due to two monsoons. The one in the summer months brings most of the rain and is the more important. The other comes in the winter months from the Bay of Bengal, so that much of East Pakistan is adequately supplied with rain for the growing of two crops each year (see Maps 7 and 8).

POPULATION

In connection with the 1951 census, the Pakistan census officials calculated the population which had been living in the same area at the five preceding censuses. In Table 7 (India) two columns (7 and 8) have been added which show Pakistan's population and its rate of growth since 1901. During the fifty years 1901–51 the population of Pakistan grew by 66.7 per cent (221, p. 25), or by an average of 1.03 per cent per year, while that of India grew by only 50 per cent during this time, or about 0.7 per cent per year. This difference in rate of growth can be explained in large part by three facts: (1) The Moslems have long had a higher birth rate and, apparently, a higher rate of natural increase, than the Hindus (86, p. 193). In 1881 the Indian census reported that Moslems constituted 19.97 per cent of the total population. By 1941 their proportion had increased to 24.28 per cent. (2) Some of this increase may have come from conversion of Hindus to Mohammedanism, and some may have come from the overenumeration of Moslems in the 1941 census; however, the ratios of children 0–4 to women 15–39 in the Indian censuses from 1891 to 1941 were consistently higher for Moslem women than for Hindu women. This difference could scarcely be due to lower infant death rates among the Moslems because they were, on the whole, worse off economically than the Hindus and would be expected to have higher infant mortality rates. A part of the higher birth rate, as well as of the higher ratio of children to women, is due no doubt to the fact that a larger proportion of young Moslem widows remarried. (3) It is also important to note that most of the great irrigation schemes in the Indus River valley between 1901 and World War II were located in what is now Pakistan, and that these lands were settled largely by immigrants, many of whom came from the territory now included in India. What effect this may have had on Pakistan's population in 1951, after partition, is impossible to say, but it may have raised it somewhat.

Several details of the differentials in growth of population may be noted. In the decade 1901–11 the population of Pakistan grew somewhat more than twice as fast as that of India. The chief explanation of this difference appears to be the fact that the famines and epidemics of this decade were much more severe in Indian territory than in that of Pakistan (134, 1951, Vol. I, Part 1-B, Appendix IV). In the following decade (1911–21) the influenza epidemic was the most important single factor in reducing the rate of growth in both Pakistan and India. However, accounts of other epidemics and famines indicate that India suffered more of these checks on population growth than did Pakistan (*ibid.*). The accounts of irrigation developments also show that the increase in irrigated land in Pakistan during this decade was much greater than in India (*ibid.*, Appendix VI). This latter fact may very well have been chiefly responsible for the substantial growth of population that took place in the territory of Pakistan (6.7 per cent) during the decade 1911–21, whereas, according to the calculations of the Indian census of 1951 (*ibid.*, Part 1-A, p. 122), that period saw a slight decrease (900,000) in the population of the territory now constituting India (see Table 7).

In the decade 1921–31 the rate of growth of India's population was somewhat higher (11.0 per cent) than that of Pakistan's (8.8 per cent). There is no satisfactory explanation for this difference. It has been suggested, however, that the nonco-operation movement which was active in 1931 may have resulted in some undercount. But there seems to be no satisfactory explanation of why this undercount should have been greater in Pakistan than in India, and the census authorities are disposed to think that the undercount was of little significance in any part of prepartition India.

In the decade 1931–41 Pakistan territory showed a substantially faster rate of population growth (18.8 per cent) than did Indian territory (13.5 per cent), although both had rates of increase above those of any preceding decade. Three factors will probably explain this situation. (1) There were no severe famines or epidemics in any part of the subcontinent during this decade. (2)There was a substantial extension of irrigated land in Pakistan as compared with India, resulting in some emigration from India to Pakistan. (3) The rising tensions between Hindus and Moslems led to an inflation of the census returns of both Hindus and Moslems in those areas where the outcome of partition remained doubtful. If this inflation were numerically about the same for Moslems in the areas which later became Pakistan as for Hindus in the areas which later became India, as may well have been the case, this would naturally raise the proportional increase of a population of 59.1 million (the total population in 1931 of the territory now constituting Pakistan) far more than it would raise that of a population of 275.5 million (the population at that time of the territory now constituting India). In calculating the increase for 1931–41 and 1941–51 (see chap. viii and Table 7) the Indian census authorities have allowed for an inflation of about 2 million in 1941 in the areas contiguous to the territory which is now in Pakistan. The Pakistan census authorities have made no such specific allowance for inflation in the data in Table 7 (221, p. 25, pp. 3-2 and 3-3). (For the distribution of Pakistan's population see Map 6.)

The failure to make such an allowance will explain, in part, the relatively low rate of increase (7.0 per cent) in Pakistan between 1941 and 1951. Much of the remainder of the difference can be explained by (*a*) the very large emigration of Hindus from East Pakistan (East Bengal) following partition and (*b*) the Bengal famine of 1943, which probably caused 1.5 million deaths above normal (134, 1951, Vol. I, Part 1-B, Appendix IV, Part F). Many of these deaths were in the portion of Bengal which later became East Pakistan. In this portion of Pakistan there was practically no growth (0.1 per cent) between 1941–51, while in West Pakistan the growth was about 5.5 million, or almost 20 per cent. West Pakistan not only suffered no famine in this decade, but it seems highly probable that it received greater numbers of Moslems who fled from India after the partition than it lost through the flight of Hindus to India. In sum, it is reasonably certain that the rate of growth of Pakistan's population in 1931–41 as shown here is several points too high, thus rendering its rate of growth for 1941–51 too low. Thus it is probable that Pakistan's real rate of growth for 1931–41 was about 3.0–4.0 points below the rate shown in Table 7, and for 1941–51 was 3.0–3.5 points higher. That it was not much above 11 or 12 per cent in 1941–51 is probably due chiefly to the Bengal famine and to the somewhat smaller total movement of Moslems from India into Pakistan than of Hindus from Pakistan into India following partition.[2] If the period since 1921 is considered as a whole, in order to avoid the inaccuracies which political conditions may have introduced into the 1931 and 1941 censuses, the increase in Pakistan's population amounted to 39.5 per cent in thirty years, while the increase in India's population was 43.8 per cent.

Birth rates and death rates.—Pakistan's registration area is said to contain about 90 per cent of the total population. The birth rates reported for the years 1947–51 averaged 19.5 per 1,000, and the death rates for the same years averaged 12.4 per 1,000 (293, 1956, pp. 617, 641). These rates would yield a natural increase of only 7 per 1,000. Clearly, the registration of births and deaths is so incomplete as to be of no value whatever. In very few nations even in the West has the birth rate fallen below 20, and then chiefly during the depression of the 1930's. Also, not until quite recently, and even then only under exceptionally good economic conditions aided by highly effective modern health services, have any Western countries maintained a death rate of 12 or below.

The most reasonable assumption regarding Pakistan's birth rate is that it is somewhat higher than India's chiefly because a larger proportion of young Moslem widows remarry and, to a minor degree, because a smaller proportion of Moslems than of Hindus are in the

[2] The census of Pakistan, 1951, gives the total number of displaced persons enumerated as 7,227,000 (221, p. 31), and the second Five-Year Plan of India (140, p. 610) refers to the 8,550,000 displaced persons for whom rehabilitation was undertaken. For a number of reasons these data may not be as accurate as could be wished, but it seems rather probable that Pakistan sustained a net loss of somewhere around 1 million, or a little more, in this interchange, and that East Pakistan suffered a large net loss while West Pakistan had a large net gain.

upper economic classes, where there is already some birth control. It is improbable, however, that the difference between lower-class and upper-class birth rates is of much significance. The birth rate in Pakistan is probably in the neighborhood of 40–42 per 1,000.

As regards Pakistan's death rate (Moslem), there is no satisfactory evidence that it varies much from that of India (Hindu). If there is a difference, the death rate of the Moslems may be slightly higher than that of the Hindus. There is considerable reason to suppose that this was so in the decade 1941–51, since Pakistan encountered even more difficult problems than India in setting up services to care for partition refugees. Moreover, Pakistan's health service was probably less efficient than India's. Displaced persons constituted about 10 per cent of the total population of Pakistan, whereas in India they were larger in numbers but constituted only about 2.2 per cent of the population. Since a very large majority—over 90 per cent—of Pakistan's displaced persons went to West Pakistan, they constituted over one-fifth of the total population in this area. Under these unfavorable conditions, it would not be at all surprising if the death rate in West Pakistan in the period 1947–51 was significantly above the normally high death rate. A death rate of 30 or 31 would appear to be about the minimum rate one could reasonably assume for Pakistan during the period of independence preceding the 1951 census, and it may very well have been somewhat higher.

Future of population growth.—Partition so greatly disrupted Pakistan's health service that, even with the assistance of WHO, UNICEF, and the United States, it probably did not attain prepartition efficiency until 1954 or 1955. The chief health campaigns now being waged are against malaria and tuberculosis. Work needed in the villages to improve sanitary conditions and thus reduce the incidence of intestinal diseases (typhoid fever, dysentery, cholera, enteritis, etc.) has hardly more than begun. There is still a great lack of trained personnel, as well as a lack of the materials and medicines needed for equipping health centers. The lack of transportation (railways and roads) and communications also retards the spread of health services to areas outside the larger cities. It will certainly be several years before such services become as effective in reducing the death rate as they are now in India.

There is as yet no birth control movement of practical significance in Pakistan. The women in Pakistan are much less free than those in India to organize movements for improving their status. This is due not to legal restriction on such activities but to the traditions and customs of a Moslem society, which are strongly opposed to the "emancipation" of women. Changes are taking place in this respect, but more slowly than in India. In 1956 there were said to be only ten planned-parenthood clinics in Pakistan, only one of which was in East Pakistan, where about 55 per cent of the people live. The movement had started, but was reaching only 1,000 to 1,500 women per year. It has now secured more funds and may grow somewhat faster in the near future (225, pp. 308, 309). Certainly there is no likelihood of government support for a birth control movement in the immediate future.

Under existing circumstances, therefore, the growth of population in Pakistan during the next three or four decades will likely be de-

TABLE 22

PROBABLE VITAL RATES, PAKISTAN, 1951–83

Years	Birth Rate	Death Rate	Natural Increase
1951–58 (7.5 years)......	42	30	12
1959–63 (5 years)........	42	28	14
1964–68 (5 years)........	41	26	15
1969–73 (5 years)........	40	24	16
1974–78 (5 years)........	38	20	18
1979–83 (5 years)........	38	18	20

termined largely by the degree of success attained by the health services—the birth rate will decline very slowly within the next two or three decades, if at all, while the death rate may drop fairly rapidly after another five or ten years; thus the rate of population growth will probably rise rapidly for some time. There are many Pakistanis who recognize this probability and who are aware of its implications for economic betterment, but they do not seem to have much influence on broad national policies. At present the interest of the people in charge of Pakistan's government seems to be directed primarily toward the development of industry to provide the higher level of living so much desired, and only secondarily toward the improvement of agriculture.

If, as seems quite probable, the birth rate is now around 42 and the death rate around 30, a natural increase of about 12, it is reasonably certain that this increase will rise for the next two or three decades, provided the necessities of life are available at even their present low level and no great catastrophe occurs. The figures in Table 22 give a general idea of what I consider the probable growth of population in Pakistan during the next twenty-five years. It is not a *prediction* but rather what I perfer to call an informed *guess*.

AGRICULTURE

Pakistan is even more predominantly agricultural than India. About 75 per cent of the population is engaged in farming, perhaps 5 to 7 per cent more than in India. Climatic conditions in East and West Pakistan are quite different. East Pakistan has a relatively abundant rainfall, and a secondary monsoon which comes in the winter months. The rainfall averages above seventy-five inches per year in most of its area. The soil is largely alluvial, built up in the deltas of the Ganges and Brahmaputra rivers, and much of the land is subject to occasional inundation and floods. On the whole, East Pakistan is a richer agricultural area than most of the Indian subcontinent. At present, irrigation from storage reservoirs is of relatively small importance in this region, but there is some talk of storing water for power and irrigation. The need for power is probably greater than that for irrigation, although occasionally the monsoon partially fails (see Maps 2, 3*a*, and 3*b*).

In contrast with East Pakistan, West Pakistan contains very little tillable land with enough rainfall to insure reasonably good crops; a large proportion of the land is either mountainous or irreclaimable desert. The northeastern region (Punjab) has much good soil and some rainfall. At other points along the Indus the soil is quite fertile, but irrigation is necessary everywhere to insure good and regular yields of both summer and winter crops (see Map 9).

Poor farming practices are almost universal, and the yields per acre are very low. The data available do not distinguish between the yields in East and West Pakistan, but for the country as a whole rice yields (presumably hulled rice) amounted to only thirteen bushels (sixty pounds) per acre. Wheat yields are only about eleven bushels per acre. It is reasonable to assume that rice yields were somewhat higher than this in East Pakistan, but even there they could not have been one-half as high as those of Japan, and West Pakistan's rice yields were probably not one-third as high as Japan's. The yields of other food grains, chiefly sorghums and millets, are also very low, as are those of the pulses—beans, peas, and other legumes. The nonfood crops consist chiefly of cotton and jute, with tea and tobacco as quite minor crops. In Pakistan cattle are valued for their meat as well as for their draft services, their milk, and their hides. Sheep are also used for meat. The improvement of livestock in Pakistan, therefore, would add more directly to the food supply than it would in India.

The need to improve agricultural production is widely recognized as extremely urgent, and efforts are being made to raise the yields per acre and per worker and to increase the area of tilled land, but as yet these efforts are rather feeble and reach only a small proportion of the farmers. The projects to increase yields are of the same general character as those in India and China and all the other countries in South and East Asia. They may be summed briefly: (1) The increased use of commercial fertilizers and the encouragement of green manuring and the more efficient use of farm manure are among the principal means advocated. The use of cattle manure as fertilizer instead of as fuel is being urged, but there will almost certainly be little change as long as no other cheap fuel is available for household use. The use of manure for fertilizer encounters many of the same basic difficulties as in India. (2) Better seeds are being distributed, particular attention being devoted to securing better varieties of cotton. On the whole, the better-seeds program seems to receive considerably less attention in Pakistan than in India. (3) The prevention of crop losses through the control of plant diseases and pests is being undertaken. (4) Better farm practices regarding the preparation of seed beds and the cultivation of crops are being brought to the attention of the farmers in many areas. (5) As would be expected, West Pakistan is giving most attention to making use of the water available for irrigation. The projected irrigation schemes are expected to provide better water supplies on about 4.6 million acres in West Pakistan and on about 1.4 million acres in East Pakistan. The irrigation program also includes bringing an additional 6.2 million acres under irigation. Presumably much of this newly irrigated land can be double-cropped, although definite information on this point does not appear to be available. Altogether, the 6.2 million acres of new land to be irrigated and the 6 million acres which are to receive more water might easily add 15 million acres of cropped land, or more, to the 50 million acres already cropped each year—an increase of between one-fourth and one-third. It is not possible to say just what this would mean in terms of additional production. I was told by a high official in the agricultural service that he had just learned that the amount of water used per acre on irrigated land in Pakistan was only about one-third that used in the United States. He was wondering, therefore, whether it would not be wise for the time being to reduce the area of new land being prepared for irrigation and to use the available water on fewer acres of superior land. In view of the serious shortage of capital in agriculture this would seem a reasonable procedure.

Pakistan, like India, faces the serious problem of having a considerable amount of irrigated land rendered unproductive each year because it becomes waterlogged through seepage from high-level canals. Rehabilitation of this land requires extensive and expensive underdrainage to prevent waterlogging and also, in many cases, to leach out the alkali salts brought to the surface by capillarity and rapidly deposited there because of the high surface evaporation that takes place in the hot, dry climate.

In East Pakistan irrigation from stored water is much less important than in West Pakistan, and the most practical means of securing larger agricultural production would be to encourage more efficient agricultural practices. Such work is being undertaken along with other community services, but it does not seem to be receiving very ardent moral or material support from the higher authorities, at least not enough to insure rapid improvement. Moreover, as he reads the available reports, it appears to the outsider that East Pakistan is being somewhat neglected in the country's planning for agricultural development, probably because it is a long way from the capital and because at present most of the national leaders come from West Pakistan.

Many of the serious and difficult problems Pakistan faces in increasing agricultural production rapidly enough to care for the growing population and to raise the level of living are made more difficult by the fact that she has comparatively few men trained in agriculture and in community organization, even fewer proportionally than India. This shortage of trained personnel is relieved only to a limited extent by technical assistance from the outside. As a result, the extension of knowledge of better farm practices to the villages and the demonstration of how these better practices can be adapted to the conditions actually existing on the farms proceed rather slowly. Furthermore, as has been pointed out (chap. ix), many cultural obstacles must be overcome before better farming practices will be readily adopted by ignorant and tradition-bound farmers. To hasten this process many experienced workers are needed; but even if many more were available, the adoption of better practices would still be slow.

INDUSTRY

The leaders of Pakistan, like those in other underdeveloped countries in South and East Asia, are very anxious to develop modern industries and services. Because of the even greater lack of modern manufacturing in the territory which became Pakistan at the time of partition, they probably feel the need for industrial development even more strongly than do the leaders of India. Although the area which is now Pakistan produced large amounts of cotton and jute, most of the mills which manufactured these products were located in Calcutta, Bombay, and a few other Indian cities. Most of the other more important modern manufactures in the subcontinent, as well as most of the more important banking enterprises, were also located in the area which became part of India. Because Pakistan consisted of the east and west fringes of prepartition India, even its transportation lines were less adequate for developing a national economy.

Finally, most of the men immediately beneath the British in important governmental positions and in British-controlled economic enterprises, as well as the men who controlled the most important native enterprises of the subcontinent, were not Moslems. Besides, many important Moslems elected to stay in India, as did more than 40 million Moslems living in smaller enclaves all over India. Thus, as serious as partition was for India from an economic standpoint, it was far more serious for Pakistan. Not only was Pakistan deprived at once of many economic and social services to which the people in her territory had been accustomed, but she was also deprived of the help of most of the more experienced and better-trained men both in civil administration and in economic enterprise.

Some Pakistanis have been inclined to regard the economic hardships the new nation suffered as having been more or less deliberately created by India. But to the outsider it would seem that the general backwardness of the area which became Pakistan, and the great poverty of the people, have been largely a consequence of conditions for which no group can be blamed. The whole of the Indian subcontinent was developing as an economic unit, and it so happened that the economic problems involved in partition received little attention beforehand, except on the part of the few well-informed people who could visualize the consequences of breaking this economic unit into two parts, each of which was in many respects dependent on the other.

That partition should have borne more heavily on Pakistan was inevitable, but only a few facts bearing on this matter can be noted here.

Resources.—The mineral resources of Pakistan are, in general, small in amount and poor in quality.

Fuel. Pakistan's coal reserves appear to be quite meager, and none of them seem suitable for metallurgical work. In 1955 only 567,000 tons of coal were mined. Lignite deposits of some size have recently been reported in East Pakistan. At best it seems that Pakistan will be hard put to produce the needed electric power in thermal plants using her own coal.

Fortunately, a large gas field has been found at Sui in Baluchistan (West Pakistan). A pipeline has already been laid to Karachi, where a number of new factories have been established and where more are being built. Other pipelines will soon be constructed to two or three more cities, where gas will be used for the generation of electric power as well as for other industrial purposes. Up to now there have been no important discoveries of oil, and oil production in 1955 amounted to only about 1.5 million barrels. At present, it appears probable that Pakistan's industrial development will suffer substantially from the scarcity of adequate fuels, and the cost of transporting those found in the mountain areas to the cities where they are needed will be heavy.

Iron. A Pakistan source (220, 1955–56, p. 138) reports discoveries of ore in several places, but gives estimated reserves (20 million tons) for only one deposit. A United Nations report (296, 1955, pp. 269–70) says that little is known about Pakistan's iron ore reserves and that those known are not easily accessible, making transportation costs high. This United Nations report gives an estimate of 60 million tons of ore, much of it of low quality. In spite of all this, an official report says: "In the meanwhile, steps are being taken to increase Pakistan's production of coal and iron ore to meet the anticipated requirements of the iron and steel plant" (220, 1955–56, p. 131).

Of the important nonferrous metals none appears to be abundant, and only a few seem to be adequate for domestic needs. The supply of chromite appears sufficient for home use in the future; at present, most of that mined is exported to help pay for imports of machinery. There seem to be laterite deposits which may yield aluminum. There also appears to be some manganese, lead, copper, and antimony, but none of these have yet been found in important quantities; no mention is made of tin. Most other minerals important in industry seem to be lacking, except for salt, which is relatively abundant. Although sulphur deposits of the better sort appear scarce, gypsum seems to be abundant and may help to remedy this deficiency. Building materials and materials needed for the manufacture of cement are abundant, but transportation expenses and the scarcity of fuel may make the cost of cement rather high in most parts of the country.

On the whole, Pakistan does not seem to have the mineral resources essential to cheap and rapid industrial development. More intensive exploration in the mountainous regions of West Pakistan may change this situation; intensive exploration, however, as well as the services—particularly the transportation—needed to make the resources of the mountainous regions available, will take time and will be quite costly.

Present status of industry.—Because of the difficulties involved in establishing basic and heavy industry, Pakistan so far has confined her industrial development largely to expanding the textile industry so that she can make use of her two principal agricultural products which are used as industrial raw materials—cotton and jute. By March of 1956 the number of spindles for cotton spinning had been increased from the 177,000 installed at the time of partition to 1,692,000, and the number of looms from 4,824 to 26,104 (*ibid.*, p. 127). Production had not increased in quite the same proportion, but such good progress was made that Pakistan now supplies her own needs for cotton cloth, besides exporting large amounts of raw cotton. An effort is being made to improve the quality of the cotton cloth, so that Pakistan's cotton goods can compete in world markets.

There were no jute mills in Pakistan territory at the time of partition. Thirteen such mills have now been established in East Pakistan, where practically all the jute is grown. These mills now have 6,000 looms, and during the year ending in March, 1956, they produced 121,000 tons of jute goods (burlap) worth Rs. 144 million, of which Rs. 100 million was exported. However, most of the jute exports still consist of raw jute. It is expected that when present plans have been carried out (1961) there will be 15,000 looms in operation and that much of the raw jute now being exported will be processed at home and sold in the form of burlap (*ibid.*, p. 120).

At the time of partition, Pakistan's iron and steel industry consisted entirely of a number of small mills which rerolled imported shapes to fill local needs. These mills handled 60,000 to 70,000 tons per year. Since partition these mills have been reconstructed and expanded, and they can now handle about 150,000 tons per year.

In 1956 Pakistan's generating capacity for electrical power was over three times what it was at partition, and this capacity is being expanded rapidly. Nevertheless, there is at present a serious power shortage, which will continue for several years even under the most favorable conditions that can be foreseen. Lack of adequate coal supplies is an important factor in this situation, and the use of gas from the Sui field can compensate only in part for this scarcity of coal. Water power is also being developed, but Pakistan possesses only small hydroelectric resources (*ibid.*, pp. 135–37).

Pakistan has found it necessary to spend large sums in order to restore her railways to prepartition condition. But even this rehabilitation will by no means provide adequate transportation for a country aiming to develop a modern industrial system. In transportation, as in so many other sectors of her economy, Pakistan found herself at a distinct disadvantage after partition. Most of the shops for the maintenance of railway equipment were inaccessible to Pakistan, and many Pakistanis felt, rightly or wrongly, that the division of rolling stock between Pakistan and India was manipulated to Pakistan's disadvantage. In any event, Pakistan has much to do before her railways will be adequate to her needs, and her highway system is still embryonic.

Other industrial enterprises to which much time and money are being devoted are fertilizer factories, cement plants, paper mills, shipbuilding and repairs, mines, and many light industries producing consumers' goods. Many of these enterprises were not started until after partition. There were few banking and credit facilities at the time of partition; those which did exist were quite inadequate to the needs of the country's agricultural economy, to say nothing of the needs induced by industrial development. A strong effort is being made to establish a financial organization which will not only manage money and credit intelligently, but will encourage the habit of investment among those few people who receive a little more income than they are forced to spend on the absolute necessities of life.

In order to further her plans for economic development, Pakistan welcomes private domestic enterprise; private investment by foreigners is also invited, provided it has "a purely industrial and economic objective" and is "not claiming any special privileges" (*ibid.*, p. 117). But all industrial investment, native or foreign, must operate in terms of two primary considerations: "(1) whether the industry will earn foreign exchange more than it spends on the import of equipment, raw material and replacements, and (2) whether the new industry will reduce imports and thus save foreign exchange" (*ibid.*). These conditions emphasize one of the important problems facing any underdeveloped country: the absolute necessity of finding sources of relatively large amounts of foreign exchange. Without this exchange, an underdeveloped country cannot buy the machinery to equip factories and powerhouses, it cannot keep the railways and the communication system efficient, and so on almost without end. However, many types of construction work which demand only native materials, and which can use unemployed or underemployed native labor at a near-subsistence wage, can go forward without the use of much foreign exchange. Thus the building of roads, railway roadbeds, many factories and public buildings, houses, can progress rather rapidly if subsistence can be found for those who do the labor. How much of this kind of work is possible depends largely upon the amount of agricultural surplus being produced above the subsistence needs of the people engaged in agriculture, since much of this surplus can be taken by taxation and its use diverted to the nonagricultural sector of economic development—though it must always be remembered that practically all the foreign exchange available to a country like Pakistan also comes from the sale abroad of agricultural products such as food and industrial raw materials.

Pakistan, like most of the other underdeveloped countries of South and East Asia, feels that she cannot wait for her resources to be developed through private enterprise. A corporation owned by the state—Pakistan Industrial Development Corporation (P.I.D.C.)—has been organized, and most of the projects concerned with the development of nonagricultural enterprises have been intrusted to it. This corporation undertakes many projects entirely on its own, using state funds, but it also collaborates with private enterprise in projects which fulfil the conditions relating to foreign exchange. Thus it insures the establishment of industries considered important for the development of the country. Up to September 30, 1955, industries sponsored by the P.I.D.C. had invested Rs. 580 million (about $115–20 million), of which Rs. 189 million (about one-third) were contributed by private investors (*ibid.*, pp. 119, 120). Thus, although private domestic and foreign investment is welcomed, all nonagricultural development is rather closely controlled by the government.

Needless to say, many of the industrial enterprises already in operation, and many of those now being established, are not yet self-supporting. As a consequence, many forms of subsidy and tax rebate are being used to sustain them until they are better established. Insofar as these devices result in higher prices of goods to domestic consumers they constitute an additional tax, which falls largely on the agricultural population and tends to reduce its buying power. If these subsidies are paid to any extent by the issue of new currency, inflation results and may very seriously interfere with the foreign trade essential to the continuation of industrial development. Up to the present the growth of the nonagricultural sector of Pakistan's economy has been forced at a pace, and in a manner, which is quite likely to cause damaging inflation.

Thus it cannot be taken for granted, as the official attitude seems to assume, that Pakistan's industrial development rests on a sound basis and will proceed rapidly and smoothly. Perhaps the rather easily obtained and generous aid—technical assistance, loans, gifts, and military aid—which Pakistan has received has encouraged the unduly rapid establishment of questionable industrial enterprises, managed by relatively inexperienced personnel. Such a situation could result in a severe setback to Pakistan's economy in the near future.

Outlook.—In Pakistan, as elsewhere, the vital question is: Can economic development, both agricultural and nonagricultural, proceed fast enough to absorb the expected increase in number of workers until such time as the rate of population increase diminishes significantly? I find myself even more doubtful regarding Pakistan's economic future during the next two or three decades than about that of India or China. I am not predicting famine accompanied by epidemics which will greatly raise the death rate; but I am saying that the outlook for any substantial improvement in the living conditions of the mass of the people is far from good as long as population increases even at the present rate of 12–14 per cent in a decade, and that the possibility of critical food shortages from time to time cannot be ruled out. If such a situation should arise, what will be its effect on relations between Pakistan and India, which are already embittered by what now appears to be the virtual annexation of Kashmir by India and by the dispute over the headwaters of the river Indus? What use will the U.S.S.R. and China try to make of hardships and crises in Pakistan? How will serious economic difficulties in Pakistan affect the willingness of the people to support efforts of the government to find outlets for surplus population in Africa or to the east in Burma? Such questions cannot be answered wih any assurance. But it certainly cannot be taken for granted that the people of Pakistan will quietly accept starvation if any other course appears likely to improve their condition.

Recently some of the processes of democratic government have been abolished in Pakistan, with effective power passing into the hands of army men. This concentration of power in a few hands may or may not have a significant effect on the economic development of the country in the next few years. One reason given by the military for the assumption of power is that Pakistan was not yet ready for a government elected by the people. There is probably much truth in this position. Another reason given is that there was much corruption in the "democratic" government which could only be eliminated quickly by an executive possessing sufficient power to deal drastically with corruption and, one may add, with incompetence and inefficiency. There can be little doubt that economic conditions might be improved somewhat faster by a benevolent dictator with a good staff of advisers; but it remains to be seen whether the dictator is benevolent and whether his advisers are able and honest. In the meantime we would do well to keep in mind Lord Acton's dictum that all power tends to corrupt and that absolute power corrupts absolutely.

CEYLON

After almost three centuries of Portuguese and Dutch rule, Ceylon became a British colony in 1796; it remained under British control until 1947, when it acquired full dominion status as an independent nation in the British Commonwealth.

"Ceylon is a pear shaped island lying in the Indian Ocean, north of the equator, between five degrees 55 minutes and nine degrees 50 minutes north latitude, and forms an appendage of the Indian sub-continent to the southeast" (54, 1952–53, p. 9). It contains 25,332 square miles, nearly twice the size of Taiwan. Because of its low latitude Ceylon's climate is wholly tropical, modified in a few areas by the altitude of the higher plateaus and a few mountains which rise above 6,000 feet. Roughly, there are three belts which show some climatic differences by reason of their varying altitudes: the coastal plain which is near sea level, the approach area to the hill country, and the hill country itself. Ceylon receives rainfall from both the southwest (Arabian Sea) and the northeast (Bay of Bengal) monsoons, which last from May to September, and November to March. The southwest monsoon is much the more important of the two. Between the monsoon periods there is also rain from "the alternating relative warmth of land and sea breezes respectively which account for the early morning showers near the coast and the afternoon showers toward the interior" (*ibid.*, p. 17).

Largely because of the favorable rainfall, the agriculture of Ceylon is concentrated on the fairly narrow coastal plain and in the lower portions of the hilly region. At present a relatively large proportion of the island in the hilly area is not used for agriculture. (For the topography and rainfall of Ceylon see Maps 2, 3a, 3b, 7, and 8.)

POPULATION

The growth of population in Ceylon as shown by the censuses taken since 1871, and the contributions which natural increase and immigration have made to this growth, are given in Table 23. Until 1911 immigration accounted for a very substantial proportion of Ceylon's total population growth, and in the decades 1871–81 and 1891–1901 for the greater part of the growth. The immigrants were largely from India and were brought in to work on the tea, rubber, and coconut planta-

TABLE 23

POPULATION, INCREASE, AND PROPORTION OF INCREASE DUE TO
NATURAL INCREASE AND IMMIGRATION, CEYLON, 1871–1953*

YEAR	POPULATION	POPULATION INCREASE		Natural Increase		Migration Increase	
		Number	Per Cent	Number	Per Cent of Total Increase	Number	Per Cent of Total Increase
1953......	8,098,637	1,441,298	21.6	1,364,661	94.7	76,637	5.3
1946......	6,657,339	1,350,468	25.4	1,280,916	94.8	69,552	5.2
1931......	5,306,871	808,266	18.0	656,990	81.3	151,276	18.7
1921......	4,498,605	392,255	9.6	319,410	81.4	72,845	18.6
1911......	4,106,350	540,396	15.2	356,147	65.9	184,249	34.1
1901......	3,565,954	558,165	18.6	225,406	40.4	332,759	59.6
1891......	3,007,789	248,051	9.0	144,260	58.2	103,791	41.8
1881......	2,759,738	359,358	15.0	119,792	33.3	239,566	66.7
1871......	2,403,380	....	......	....	......	....	......

* Source: 293, 1956, p. 143; 53, 1946, I, Part 1, 57, 59. The contribution of immigration to the growth of Ceylon's population in 1946–53 was calculated as a residual quantity based on the average rate of natural increase (birth rate minus death rate) for these seven years, viz., 27 per 1,000, which would raise the population to approximately 8,022,000 in 1953, leaving only about 77,000 of the increase to come from immigration. This calculation can only be regarded as approximate, but it seems highly probable that the natural increase in these seven years accounted for approximately 95 per cent of the total growth.

tions. Since 1911 immigrants have never accounted for as much as one-fifth of the total growth in any census period, and since 1931 they have supplied only 5 to 6 per cent. (For the distribution of Ceylon's population see Map 6.)

The registration of births and deaths has long been more accurate in Ceylon than in other areas of South and East Asia, with the exception of Japan. For the decade 1921–30 the birth rate averaged 39.8 and the death rate 26.5. For the next fifteen years (1931–45) the birth rate averaged 36.8 and the death rate 22.2. From 1946 through 1953 the birth rate averaged about 39.7 and the death rate 13.6. For 1954–55 the birth rate was about 37.0 and the death rate 10.7.

The above data are of great interest. For about thirty-five years, since 1921, Ceylon's death rate has been well below that of the other underdeveloped countries of South and East Asia,[3] and it has been falling during all this time (five-year averages). The decline was very precipitate between 1946 (20.3) and 1947 (14.3), when the antimalaria campaign, together with other types of intensified health work, became highly effective.

On the other hand, there is no clear evidence of any significant decline in the birth rate. The decline from an average of 39.8 in 1921–30 to 36.8 in 1931–45 might at first appear significant, but there is a rise to 39.7 in 1946–53. The average of 37 for the last two years for which official data are available at the end of 1957 may indicate the beginning of a decline, but an unofficial report of a substantial rise in 1956 makes any firm conclusion regarding a decline impossible. In any event, a birth rate of 37.0 and a death rate of 10.7 (1954 and 1955) leaves Ceylon with a natural increase of 26.3, which will double the population in 26–27 years.

It should be said in this connection that a postenumeration survey by the Department of Census and Statistics (Ceylon) in 1953 showed an underregistration of births at that time of 11.9 per cent and of deaths amounting to 11.4 per cent (91). Since the registered birth rate was 39.4 for that year, the real birth rate would have been 44.7; in the same manner, a registered death rate of 10.9 would become 12.3, leaving a natural increase of 32.4 instead of the registered increase of 28.5. It is highly probable that the registration of births and deaths, especially the registration of deaths, has become increasingly complete in recent years with the intensified postwar health program. It may be, therefore, that the latest official reports on births are now relatively more deficient than those on deaths. If so, the rate of natural increase would be somewhat more than the four points above the recorded rate indicated by the 1953 check on underregistration.

Even though we cannot know positively within three or four points just what Ceylon's rate of natural increase is, we do know that it is extremely high—high enough to double Ceylon's population in twenty-five years or less. Countries like India or China, whose health problems are much more complicated than Ceylon's, cannot be expected to reduce their death rates nearly as fast in the next few years as Ceylon has done since the war; nor can smaller countries like Burma and Thailand build up as efficient a health service in a few years as Ceylon now

[3] Japan is not classed as underdeveloped.

has. Ceylon's experience with health work has been relatively long, dating back almost a century (1859). Ceylon had eliminated cholera as an important cause of death as early as the 1880's and had reduced smallpox deaths to a relatively low level by 1911 (310, I, 411–38).

This experience placed Ceylon in a relatively good position to make use of the latest advances in health work within a very short period following World War II. The experience of Ceylon in controlling the death rate shows beyond question that underdeveloped tropical countries in which the necessities of life are reasonably adequate, and in which even modest means for the support of modern health services are forthcoming, can reduce their death rates much more quickly than any of the Western countries ever did. It is then only reasonable to expect a more rapid natural increase in these countries than took place in the Western countries, except for a few which, like the United States, were practically empty in 1700 and in which an abundance of new land of excellent quality encouraged early marriages and large families. In these newer areas, many of the contagious and infectious diseases rampant in the older and more densely settled countries of Asia were never of great importance as causes of death.

The views of informed Ceylonese regarding probable population growth there during the next two or three decades will help us appreciate the significance of the decline in the death rate that has already taken place, a decline that has raised the average expectation of life at birth (males and females combined) from 31.49 years in 1910–12 (241, p. 443) to 58.15 years in 1953 (91, p. 17). Dr. de Silva gives data showing that the rate of natural increase more than doubled between 1918–22 (6.8) and 1928–32 (14.7) and then practically doubled again by 1952–53 (28.0) (91, p. 19). These rates are the reported rates and may very well be too low by 2–4 points. Dr. de Silva notes the work of the Family Planning Association of Ceylon, but he believes "that the population control methods are not likely to reduce fertility drastically in the near future" (91, p. 20). He considers the chief reason to be the fact that Ceylon's population is approximately 85 per cent rural and that economic development being undertaken is chiefly agricultural. The farmers believe that children are an asset, and thus are not likely to be much interested in reducing the number of births per family until they come to appreciate more fully how the control of the death rate is affecting the size of their families—and such realization will not come soon. Dr. de Silva mentions projections of population made by the Registrar General's Department up to 1985, showing 21 million as a "high" and 17 million as a "low." He seems to consider both of these projections within reason. It should be noted that even the "low" projection gives more than twice the 1953 population by 1985.

A report on "Population Problems" prepared for the Central Bank of Ceylon (230, p. 1) also seems to accept the projection of 21 million in 1985 as within reason, because of further decline in the death rate and a growth in the proportion of the population at ages when fertility is greatest. Infant and child mortality are already at low levels and are still falling.

It seems to me quite reasonable to believe that the rate of natural increase will not decline significantly within the next fifteen to twenty years. The work of the Family Planning Association is as yet largely confined to a few clinics in urban communities. It does not seem to be actively opposed by the government, but neither is it actively encouraged, and the means at the disposal of the association are small. The great mass of the people do not yet appear to realize the close relation between the saving of their babies and young children from early death and the economic problems of the family. Furthermore, only a few of them know that it is possible to prevent conception, and when they do learn this fact they find that the methods available are not practical under the conditions in which they live. Finally, all the cultural patterns of marriage, of family life, and of reproduction assume that an almost unrestricted birth rate is desirable and is to be expected. The age at marriage is rising and may temporarily reduce the birth rate, but this is by no means certain, since greater maturity of women at marriage up to about eighteen years of age may tend to increase fertility in the latter years of the child-bearing period (see chap. ii). In the cities and among the better-educated people there is already some family planning, but only a small part of the population is found in this group. Family planning cannot be expected to spread rapidly. Dr. de Silva's view, quoted above, seems to be entirely justified.

AGRICULTURE

The economy of Ceylon centers largely around the export of three crops—tea, rubber, and coconuts. They constitute 95 per cent of her exports and provide the funds for practically all her imports. Rice is the chief import, in spite of the fact that 1.27 million acres were planted to paddy in 1954. The acreages of the four main crops in 1954 are given in Table 24 (55, pp. 2, 4, 6, 7).

From the standpoint of agriculture Ceylon is divided, in general, into a wet zone of about 4 million acres and a dry zone of about 12 million acres. The wet zone lies in the southwest portion of the island and benefits from both the southwest and the northeast monsoons. It has an average annual rainfall of about 135 inches. The dry zone, *dry* only by comparison, has an average rainfall of about one-half this amount; it comprises about three-fourths of the island and lies north and east of the wet zone (55, pp. 161–62). Tea and rubber are grown largely on the hilly slopes of the wet zone, with many coconut groves along the coast. Most of the rice is grown in the same zone on the more level land, because it can be flooded by the heavy rainfall. In 1951 when the total caloric intake per capita per day was 2,079, the grain imports supplied 1,222 of these calories, or about 59 per cent (54, pp. 188–89). This was well above that of India.

TABLE 24

ACREAGE OF PRINCIPAL CROPS,
CEYLON, 1954

Tea...................	575,569
Rubber...............	659,209
Coconut.............	1,070,942
Paddy (rice)........	1,269,892
Total.............	3,575,812

Ceylon's most urgent economic problem is to increase the domestic production of food and of agricultural exports fast enough to keep ahead of her population growth. It cannot be assumed that the exports of tea, rubber, and coconut products can be increased sufficiently year after year to provide the exchange needed for ever-increasing food imports. In the wet zone, agriculture already occupies nearly all of the available area. Measures requiring *estates* of over 35 acres to plant certain proportions of their land to paddy (rice) have been chiefly responsible for the increase in paddy fields from about 900,000 acres at the close of the war to 1,269,892 acres in 1954 (55, pp. 6, 7). The total domestic production of paddy increased from 22 million bushels in 1950 to 31.5 million bushels in 1954 (*ibid.*). This latter amount was estimated to be about one-half the domestic consumption after allowance was made for the seed, which meant that about 400,000 long tons had to be imported. This domestic shortage continued in spite of the increase of about one-third in acreage just noted, and in spite of efforts to increase the yields by "improved agricultural practices, such as transplanting, harrowing, weeding, the use of high-yielding paddy seeds, and also by ensuring to the producer a stable price for his product" (55, p. 7). These methods succeeded in increasing the yield per acre between 1950 and 1954 by about 25 per cent. This was a very gratifying increase, but it cannot reasonably be expected to continue at such a rate for several reasons: (1) Much of the increase in paddy acreage took place on the estates, which for a long time had been producing their particular specialties with a relatively high degree of efficiency. We can presume that when the estate owners were required to plant a certain number of acres to rice they went at it scientifically and with reasonably adequate capital. Hence, their yields should have been well above the average. (2) The first returns from better agricultural practices, better seeds, better tillage, use of fertilizers, etc., are relatively easy to obtain; further gains become increasingly difficult. (3) Perhaps most important of all, 1954 was a *good* season. (4) There was an improvement in "the system of enumeration of paddy acreages" between 1951 and 1954, which may account for part of the reported increase in acreage.

Food crops other than rice show no very significant change in their combined acreage, although there has been some shifting from one crop to another. It is impossible to say just what changes, if any, have taken place in the yields of the minor food crops. They were not enumerated separately before 1949. The acres planted to some of the spice and condiment crops appear to have been increasing, but these crops are chiefly for export and, as was noted above, are of quite minor importance economically.

Any increase in food production substantial enough to enable Ceylon to provide a better living for her rapidly increasing population must come from the irrigation of new lands in the dry zone, which occupies about three-fourths of the total area of the island (about 42.25 million acres). In this dry zone about 3.5 million acres are rocky and steep or lie in altitudes above 5,000 feet, and thus are of little use agriculturally. "The land available for further agricultural development is about 3,025,000 acres" (55, p. 2).[4]

From 1948 to 1953 irrigation was brought to over 165,000 acres of new land, and improved irrigation facilities were provided for 125,000 acres of paddy land already in use. Only a little over one-third of this new irrigable land was actually developed during this period. During the Six-Year Plan (1954–55 to 1959–60) somewhat more than 125,000 acres are expected to be added to the irrigated area, most of which will

[4] Another source (57, p. 158) gives the new land tillable as 3.25 million acres, of which 2 million acres can be irrigated.

be suitable for paddy. It is estimated, however, that the surface water available for irrigation in the dry zone is sufficient to provide for one crop per year on 3.6 million acres if it is efficiently used. Since plans call for the irrigation of only about 2 million acres, there should be enough water for two crops on one-half or more of these 2 million acres. It cannot be assumed, however, that double-cropping will be possible on as large a proportion of these 2 million acres as on the rice land already in use, nor can it be assumed that this new land is of as good quality as that now being tilled. Indeed, it would seem highly optimistic to expect this new land to add as much to the nonexport crops as is already being produced—to add enough, let us say, to replace the present imports of foodstuffs and make it possible for all the food for the *present* population to be produced at home. In the meantime the population of 8.1 million (1953) is increasing by about 3 per cent a year, and was estimated at 8.9 million in 1956 (227, January, 1958). It would now (1958) be about 9.4 million.

An increase of 12–15 per cent in food production from land to be newly irrigated during the current Six-Year Plan would seem to be an optimistic expectation, while in this six years the population will have increased by 18 per cent or more. It seems clear that even if the Six-Year Plan is fulfilled, there must be another substantial increase in production per acre just to keep food imports at their present absolute level. For the next few years such an increase may not be too difficult, but many problems will have to be solved if it is to be continued for two or three decades.

Acreage yields can probably be improved faster in Ceylon than in most of the other countries of South and East Asia, chiefly for two reasons: (1) The Ceylonese, on the whole, are more literate than most of the peoples in this region. In 1953 only about 42 per cent of the Ceylonese (including children under five) had had no schooling; seven years earlier (1946) 57.8 per cent of all persons aged five and over were literate—males 70.1 per cent, females 43.8 per cent (91, unpublished paper, pp. 6–7). It will be easier to communicate new ideas to the people in Ceylon and to make them understand the demonstrations of new agricultural practices than it will be in most other Asian countries. (2) Because of the greater homogeneity of culture and language in Ceylon than in most of the larger countries, it will be easier to devise plans for extension work in agriculture which will be suitable for the entire population, and which can be administered from a central source. The extension of agricultural knowledge and the encouragement of better farm practices, like the extension of health work, should be more easily accomplished than in larger countries with many local diversities in crops and in agricultural traditions and practices. But it should be made clear that Ceylon needs this rapid increase in agricultural production more urgently than most other Asian countries because her population is already increasing much faster than theirs and because she relies so heavily on exports to pay for such a large proportion of her food.

It appears highly unlikely that the agricultural development of Ceylon during the next two or three decades will enable the island to supply its people with a larger proportion of their total food needs than it is now supplying (about one-half), although this proportion may rise somewhat for a few years. With an increase of 3 per cent per year, Ceylon's population would number about 18 million in 1975, and close to 21 million by the end of 1980; even if she more than doubled her own food production, she would still need twice the current volume of food imports. The guess that Ceylon can somewhat more than double her domestic food production by 1975 assumes that there will be almost no increase in the acreage devoted to export crops. Where, then, can Ceylon find the exports with which to finance the necessary increase in food imports? Will she be able to export enough industrial products to make up for the increasing deficit?

INDUSTRY

Unfortunately, Ceylon has no mineral resources which can be of substantial aid in her economic development. For several decades Ceylon has been the principal source of the world's graphite (plumbago). The deposits are relatively large and of good quality. However, the world demand for graphite is small and uncertain, and the price fluctuates widely. The exchange earned by the export of graphite is, therefore, both small and uncertain from year to year and does not seem likely to become more important. The amount exported for several years past has been 12,000–13,000 tons, and the value has varied from $1.3–1.7 million.

The only known iron ore deposits are estimated to contain about 6 million tons, with an iron content of about 50 per cent (54, 1952–53, p. 203); a United Nations report gives only one-third of this amount (296, p. 296). Even 6 million tons is entirely too little to justify the construction of a basic steel plant. Such a plant would use 6 million tons of 50 per cent ore in about ten years, and the supply should be sufficient for twenty-five years or more to insure a reasonable rate of amortization of investment. Besides, the coal or coke to operate a steel plant would have to be imported, and this would add significantly to the cost of production. Ceylon possesses no coal or other fuel—lignite, petroleum, gas—of any industrial importance. It would appear that the only justifiable type of steel mill would be a small rolling mill using imported bars to make special shapes needed locally.

There are said to be rather substantial reserves of ilemite (titanium) in Ceylon, but these have little value now. Like almost all countries, even small ones, Ceylon has the materials needed for building and cement making and possesses some of the rare earth minerals. Except for these, however, Ceylon has little mineral wealth to which the labor of her people could be applied economically.

This lack of mineral resources means that the industry of Ceylon must be limited to the more intensive processing of her own agricultural products, e.g., coconut fiber (coir), rubber shoes and (possibly) tires, and to a few types of manufacturing where investment is small and power costs are low—e.g., cotton textiles, for which the cost of imported raw materials is low compared with the price of the imported finished product. Some of the industries already established, or to be undertaken during the second Six-Year Plan (1954–55 to 1959–60), are: a cement factory which was set up in 1950, producing about 75,000 tons annually at the inception of the second plan and to be expanded to a capacity of 170,000–200,000 tons; a leather factory to use native hides for shoes and other leather goods; a plywood factory using native timber to make the plywood chests in which Ceylon exports her tea; a vegetable-oil factory to intensify the processing of oil from seeds and coconuts; a paper factory using local straws and grasses; ceramic and glass factories; a chemical factory using chiefly salt produced in Ceylon; a tire factory to supply Ceylon's needs from her own rubber; a textile factory, operating largely on imported cotton, to supply yarn to the hand-loom cottage industry and to factories engaged in weaving; a sugar factory to supply part of the domestic needs from home-grown cane; a fertilizer factory and an ore-dressing plant to refine some of the rare earth minerals. Whether some of these factories—the tire factory, other rubber goods factories, and factories using vegetable oils—could produce for export would depend upon the cost of fuel and power and upon the efficiency of Ceylonese labor and production management.

Most of these industries should succeed eventually in reducing imports. Practically all the factories or processing plants are to be financed in whole or in part by the government, and in most cases subsidies, tariff protection, tax exemption, or some combination of these, is to be provided until the locally made product is established in the market.

On the whole it would seem to be to Ceylon's advantage to produce as much of her manufactured consumption goods as is possible; however, too much protection of home industry, whatever form it takes, may easily interfere with her present export trade and seriously affect the entire economy. But there seems to be no way in which Ceylon can avoid these risks. She is a small country with quite limited possibilities for economic development; she will have to depend, for some time to come, on the export of her agricultural products to provide the exchange with which to buy many of her essential needs. Indeed, these limited possibilities for industrial development make it unlikely that Ceylon can ever attain any considerable degree of self-sufficiency in manufactured goods and thus reduce the proportion of her land now devoted to tea, rubber, and coconuts.

The rapid growth of population, which is likely to continue for about a generation, greatly increases the difficulties of raising the level of living. At present (1958) Ceylon has to provide for an annual increase of 275,000–300,000 per year, and within five years the great number of babies and young children whose lives have been saved since World War II will add very rapidly to the number of young people marrying and needing jobs. It is difficult to see how jobs can be provided for these large annual additions to the labor force.

CHAPTER XV

SOUTHEAST ASIA:

MAINLAND

The group of countries which will be discussed under this heading occupies the area in Southeast Asia lying between India and the Bay of Bengal on the west and the Pacific Ocean on the east, and is bounded on the north by India and China. The areas of Burma, Thailand, and Malaya have not been significantly affected by the war or by the troubles that followed it. On the other hand, prewar French Indochina has been split into four parts, each of which is now independent—Cambodia, Laos, Vietnam, and Viet-Minh (communist).

This entire area is tropical. There are no *seasons* in the sense in which that term is used in the temperate zones. However, rainfall and temperature vary considerably at different times in the year and in different topographic regions, and these variations have a decisive influence on agriculture. Except for a few small areas, the agriculture of the region depends on the southeast monsoon for its entire water supply, and crops grown during the dry season are dependent on irrigation from reservoirs and rivers which are in turn fed by the monsoon. The time of arrival of the monsoon varies somewhat from country to country and from year to year. In general, the hottest and driest months are March, April, and May. The monsoon generally "breaks" in the latter part of May or early June, and most of the heavy annual rainfall comes in June, July, and August; there is still considerable rain in September, however, and in some areas showers may continue through October. During the monsoon season the maximum temperature averages about ten degrees lower than during the hot season. October through January are the cool months. In February the temperature begins to rise, and the hot season soon follows. Beginning with October and continuing through May, very little rain falls. (See Maps 2, 3*a,* and 3*b* for rainfall in these countries and Map 14 for the physiographic features, except Malaya, on Map 18.)

BURMA

POPULATION

The area of Burma (262,000 square miles) is about equal to that of Texas. In 1901, when it may be assumed that the census within this area was fairly complete, the population was 10.5 million. By 1931 it had grown to 14.7 million, and by 1941 to 16.8 million (293, 1948, p. 91). The estimated population in 1954 was 19.2 million (293, 1955, p. 121), and at that time it was growing by about 200,000 per year. In this 53-year period Burma's population increased by about 83 per cent. However, the density of population per square mile remains rather low—about 73 in 1954. (15, pp. 24, 25). In 1941 density varied from as low as 28 per square mile in the more mountainous districts to 215 in the more densely settled delta areas. Proportionally, these variations are probably much the same today. The population in 1931 was predominantly agricultural (66.5 per cent), with only 10.7 per cent engaged in industry, 9.0 per cent in trade, and 3.6 per cent in transport (15, p. 39).[1] Only about 10 per cent were engaged in all other types of work. These proportions may have changed somewhat since 1931, but the war and the insurrections following it greatly disrupted Burma's economy, and it is not improbable that as late as 1954 she was even more agricultural than in 1931 (see Map 13 for distribution of the population).

In 1931 over 1 million persons in Burma spoke Indian languages, about 178,000 spoke Chinese, and about 28,000 spoke English. The presence of these Indians and Chinese was beginning to create friction with the Burmese, in spite of the fact that these foreigners had no political power. The Indians worked on the large rice plantations of the deltas and became shopkeepers and moneylenders in the villages. Thus the Burmese came to feel that they were taking the jobs of natives on the plantations and exploiting the Burmese farmers in the villages. Most of the Indians have returned to India since the war. The Chinese at first furnished most of the labor in the mines, but, like many of the Indians on the rice farms, they graduated into shopkeeping and moneylending as they became better established economically and thus also earned the dislike of the Burmese. Since the war they have not been such an important economic group, because mining activity has not yet regained its prewar importance.

[1] The 1941 data were apparently destroyed in the war, and there has been no postwar census.

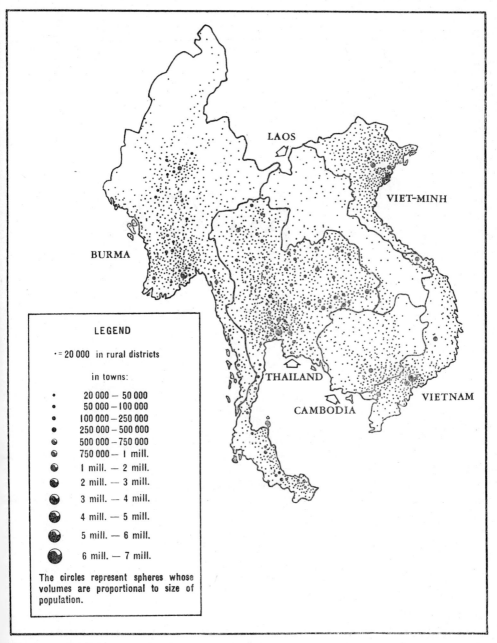

MAP 13.—Population distribution in the Indochinese peninsula. (Adapted by permission of Dr. Friedrich Burgdörfer and the Heidelberger Akademie der Wissenschaften from *The World Atlas of Population* [Hamburg: Falk-Verlag], copyright 1957 by Heidelberger Akademie der Wissenschaften, Heidelberg, Germany.)

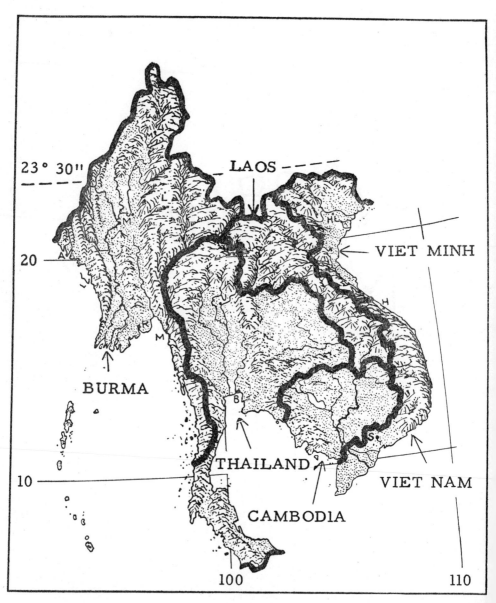

MAP 14.—Physiographic map of the Indochinese peninsula (except Malaya). (Base map a section of the Physiographic Diagram of Asia, © by A. K. Lobeck, reproduced with permission from the Geographical Press, a division of C. S. Hammond & Co.)

The registration of births and deaths in Burma has never been complete, and since the war there are no data except for some sixty towns and cities containing only 6 to 7 per cent of the population. These very fragmentary data show an average birth rate of 47.5 for the three years 1951–53 and a death rate of 35.7 for the same years (293, 1955, pp. 615, 655). These rates indicate a natural increase of about 12 per 1,000. The only conclusion justified by these data is that both the birth rate and the death rate are very high. Clearly, the kind of widespread and efficient health service which has reduced Ceylon's death rate to 9 or 10 per 1,000 does not exist in Burma. However, there is no reason to suppose that a vigorous health movement would not produce a rapid decline in the death rate, although it would probably take about a generation to bring it to the level of Ceylon. The immediate effect of such a decline would be a rapid rise in the rate of natural increase, since there is as yet no evidence of any decline in the birth rate. Moreover, there is no organization, official or private, that appears interested in bringing about a reduction in the birth rate. In fact, the leaders of Burma seem to feel at present that there is no economic reason why the population should not continue to grow at a fairly rapid rate for some time to come. They probably do not realize how fast a population with a birth rate of perhaps 45 per 1,000 can grow when health services become efficient. Even if they did, they might very well conclude that the time is still distant, perhaps three to five decades away, when the population will put any significant pressure on the land.

In 1931 the proportion of the population which was literate in Burma was quite large as compared with India, China, Indonesia, and several other of these countries. The census of 1931 reported that 56 per cent of the males over the age of five were literate and that 16.5 per cent of the females were also literate.[2] If the tribal peoples are left out of the calculations, the percentage of literacy among Burmese males over the age of five was 71.7 per cent, and among females 21 per cent (15, pp. 36–37). These proportions are about four times as high as those found in India at that time and are even higher than in Ceylon. There has probably been some rise in literacy in Burma since 1931.

[2] It would appear that the predominantly Buddhist countries—Burma, Thailand, Ceylon—and the Philippines, which are Christian, have the most literate populations of these underdeveloped countries.

AGRICULTURE

The total acreage planted in the crop year 1940–41 is given as 18.8 million (counting twice the 1.3 million acres of double-cropped land). Of this total acreage two-thirds, or 12.5 million acres, was in rice. Rice growing was rather highly concentrated in the delta area of Lower Burma (about 80 per cent), but since rice is by far the principal food in Burma it is grown in all parts of the country, although in the drier and rougher areas the amounts grown are not generally sufficient to meet local needs (15, p. 43). In 1940–41 the irrigated area amounted to 1.6 million acres; a great deal of this land was double-cropped, although two crops of rice were seldom grown on the same land in the same year. Before the war Burma usually exported one-half or more of the total rice crop.

Other important crops were oil seeds (about 2 million acres), beans (over 1 million acres), millet (about 700,000 acres), and cotton (300,000–500,000 acres). There were also many minor crops, which occupied only a few tens of thousands of acres. The cropped area had been expanding rather steadily, mainly in the rich delta areas where rice was grown as a commercial crop. For some years before the war Burma had been the world's largest exporter of rice (about 3 million tons annually); at the same time the Burmese were probably the best fed people of Asia—although the Japanese may have had a somewhat better-balanced diet.

The war led to a serious breakdown of Burma's agricultural economy. Production fell to such a low point that there have been serious food shortages in some parts of the country almost every year since the war, although no widespread famine. Immediately after the war it was estimated that rice production was only 38–40 per cent as large as it had been in normal prewar years (15, p. 44). Even as late as the crop year 1956–57 the United States Foreign Agricultural Service estimated the total area in the eight leading crops at only 16.1 million acres, perhaps 2 million acres less than prewar, with rice acreage still at only about 90 per cent of the prewar level (318, No. 35-56, October 25, 1956). In 1955 Burma was still importing considerable amounts of food (wheat, flour, vegetable oils, sugar, and dairy products) and was exporting only about one-half as much rice as she had been before the war.

The relatively good food situation which has prevailed in Burma accounts for the fairly rapid and steady growth of population since 1901. Had it not been for the severe influenza epidemic of 1918 and the deterioration of agriculture caused by World War II and the civil turmoil which followed, Burma's total growth during this period would certainly have been larger.

No very reliable survey seems to have been made of the probable future additions to tilled land in Burma. Andrus cites the *Season and Crop Report,* 1940–41, as listing somewhat more than 19 million acres of "culturable waste," much of it in the Irrawaddy delta where rice would be the principal crop (15, p. 44). He does not venture any estimate himself, but he does say, "It is doubtful, in fact, if there is any comparable area in Asia with as much potentially excellent rice land not yet under cultivation." Since only 10–11 per cent of the total area of Burma was under tillage in 1941, it seems not unlikely that the 19 million acres of "culturable waste" was a conservative estimate of the land that might be added to the cultivated area. However, Andrus also says, "Some serious students of Burmese rural economy doubt if there are large areas which can be brought under cultivation without heavy expenditure" (*ibid.*). These heavy expenditures would probably be used chiefly for flood-control in the delta areas of Lower Burma and for irrigation works in the drier zones of Upper Burma. In contrast to these rather conservative estimates, Stamp says, "There is room for considerable agricultural expansion in Burma, and official returns class 60,000,000 acres as cultivatable waste" (255, p. 352).

If it is assumed that the amount which can possibly be added to the tilled area is somewhere between 19 and 60 million acres, it would appear that merely by extending her cultivated area Burma can reasonably hope to care for two or three times as many people at as high a level of living as now prevails, or even at a higher level. This is not to say that the new land can be brought into cultivation with the same expenditure of labor per acre as was involved in preparing the land already in use. Furthermore, it is probable that the new land, acre for acre, will be somewhat less fertile than the land now in use was when it was new. On the other hand, it is highly probable that yields per acre on the new land can be improved in ten to twenty years until they exceed the present yields, and that these latter yields can also be much improved in that period.

In the five crop years 1935–40 the yield of cleaned rice in Burma averaged 14.23 bushels per acre (calculated from 340, pp. 318–19). In Japan the comparable figure was 40.18 bushels, and in Taiwan and Korea it was 28.10 and 26.09 bushels, respectively. It certainly seems probable that yields in Burma could be raised to the level of those in Taiwan and Korea, especially in view of the fact that in the five years 1911–15 Burma's yield averaged 15.3, Japan's 33.8, Taiwan's 18.2, and Korea's 17.5. Thus while the yields of rice in Japan, Taiwan, and Korea increased substantially between 1911–15 and 1935–40, the yield in Burma declined slightly. The difference seems to have resulted largely from the lower efficiency of the Burmese cultivator, and there certainly is no good reason to assume that this efficiency cannot be raised significantly in the course of the next fifteen to twenty years. Since Burma has enough unused land, at an ultra-conservative estimate, to double her crop area, it does not seem unreasonable to assume that the total crop can be doubled or even tripled within three decades; nor does it seem unreasonable to expect that this can be accomplished by a smaller proportion of the labor force than is now engaged in agriculture, which is probably not much different from that of 1931— about two-thirds.

The methods Burma must use to make agricultural labor more efficient and to increase yields are the same as those being used elsewhere in Asia and need not be described again. But it should be easier to induce Burmese farmers to use better seeds and to adopt better farm practices than it was to persuade the Korean and Taiwanese farmers to do so thirty years ago. The methods of effective agricultural extension work are better understood, the means of communication are far superior, and the organization of demonstration farms is now comparatively easy. Nevertheless, many social and cultural difficulties must be overcome before the tradition-bound mind of the Burmese farmer can be opened to these new ideas and practices. Because of these cultural difficulties, we must think in terms of two or three decades rather than of a few years in judging the period needed for decided improvement in agriculture.[3] Perhaps the most important factor in Burma's favor is her possession of a considerable area of potentially tillable land, which gives her more time than most Asian countries in which to improve agriculture; besides, Burma's population is probably not yet growing as fast as the populations of most Asian countries.

INDUSTRY

How much coal Burma possesses and whether any of it is suitable for metallurgical work are moot points at present. Brown and Dey (44, pp. 67–68) think there is considerable coal in Upper Chindwin

---

[3] For a more detailed discussion of some of these difficulties, see chapter ix, "India: Agriculture."

(they estimate 200 million tons or more) and fairly large amounts of lignite both in the north and in the south. Since Burma appears to have little, if any, usable iron ore, the question whether this coal is suitable for coking is not pressing at the moment. Both the coal and the lignite can be used for generating electric power, but whether they can compete with oil (petroleum) and gas at present seems doubtful.

Before the war Burma was producing about 1 million tons of oil annually, and it was generally assumed that her petroleum reserves were quite large (15, pp. 116–22). The export of oil constituted an important part of Burma's foreign trade. Because of the destruction of the wells by the Japanese, production of petroleum has remained quite low since the war; in the year 1954–55 it was only 191,000 tons (303, 1955, p. 58). Postwar production is barely sufficient to supply domestic needs. How soon the export of oil will again begin to provide the exchange Burma so badly needs, no one can tell; but if her plans for increasing oil production have been successfully carried out, Burma should now (1958) be exporting small amounts of oil. It is believed that the country also has large deposits of oil-bearing shale, which may be used later but are too costly to exploit at present.

In addition, Burma appears to have large reserves of natural gas (44, pp. 117–19). It seems, therefore, that Burma will not lack fuel in the near future.

No over-all estimate of potential hydroelectric power has been found, but several specific projects of considerable size are now under construction, and those destroyed during the war are being rehabilitated. These hydroelectric plants, in the aggregate, should be important in Burma's economic development.

For a relatively small country, Burma is also rich in a number of other minerals; lead, silver, copper, zinc, antimony, nickel, cobalt, tin, and tungsten were produced in considerable quantities before the war. The mine which was the chief producer of several of these minerals was destroyed during the war, and there is some question whether its remaining reserves justify its rehabilitation. Present mineral production is only a small fraction of prewar production, and it is not possible to say at this time just what Burma's mineral resources are likely to contribute to her industrial development during the next two or three decades.

Like all the countries in South and East Asia, Burma is very anxious to establish industrial enterprises; industrial progress will help raise the level of living and, at the same time, make her less dependent on the vicissitudes of her trade in rice, which at present supplies such a large proportion of her foreign exchange. Accordingly, the government has made strenuous efforts to provide the services essential to all sectors of economic development, e.g., better transportation and communication and more electricity, and to establish new industry as well as expand some of the industries already in operation. Plans for economic development were to be drawn up by a National Planning Board established in 1947. Although the course Burma has taken suggests that no over-all plan is yet in effect, it is clear that the government is investing in economic development to the extent of its ability and is keeping control of the enterprises essential to a planned economy.

It is important to note that before the war Burma had an even smaller proportion of her workers in factories which used power than did several of the other Asian countries (not including Japan). In other words, the industry of Burma was largely hand industry; it used very little machinery of any kind, and what it did use was generally operated by manpower in the home of the operator. As of 1940 Andrus (15, p. 142) lists 40 types of factories, numbering 1,027 and employing 89,383 workers—an average of 87 workers per factory. Most of these factories did not manufacture goods but processed agricultural products; these processing factories (768 in number) employed over 49,000 of the 88,000 workers. In 91 other factories, which provided services, more than 13,700 workers were employed. Thus not more than about 26,000 workers, employed in 168 factories, were manufacturing consumption goods with the aid of power machinery.

Up to the present, unfortunately, little has been accomplished in the rehabilitation of industry and in the establishment of new enterprises. The chief reasons for this slow recovery and development are: (1) Much of Burma's mining and industrial capacity was destroyed during the war. (2) Recovery had barely begun when insurrections redestroyed much industrial, mining, and transportation equipment. The troubles continued through 1950 and still break out sporadically. Moreover, these insurrections forced the government to spend large sums to maintain civil order which might otherwise have been used for economic rehabilitation and expansion. In addition, private investors have been reluctant to assume the risks involved in new enterprises, even if they have not been discouraged by the decided socialistic bent of the government. However, it should be said that joint government-private enterprises are permitted. (3) Much land went out of cultivation when the export market for rice vanished during the war.

Burma has also encountered all the usual difficulties involved in the economic development of a predominantly agricultural land: the lack of capital and of institutions which can assemble such capital as does exist; the lack of trained managers and engineers; the lack of skilled workmen; the lack of enterprise in agricultural extension work; the poor health of a large proportion of all workers, which seriously interferes with efficient work; the inadequacy of all basic economic services—transportation, power, etc.—and finally, but by no means the least of Burma's problems, the traditional cultural values, which attach little importance to economic efficiency (see discussion in chap. ii, and in chaps. ix and x relating to India).

In spite of all these ordinary and extraordinary difficulties, Burma is making some headway in modern economic development. During the four fiscal years 1952–53 to 1955–56 the government made capital expenditures amounting to K. 1,813.1 million (about $370 million at the official exchange rate). This investment has been rather heavily concentrated in rehabilitating transportation and communications, in restoring and expanding the generation of electricity (power), in rehabilitating and establishing a few new industries, and in constructing buildings. Comparatively little has been spent on agriculture, aside from loans to farmers, or on mining, in which there have been some joint ventures of private parties with the government (303, 1955, pp. 61, 62).

The shortage of exchange earnings, now derived almost entirely from a reduced export of rice, interferes seriously with the import of capital goods and, hence, adversely affects the rehabilitation of the economy as well as the establishment of new enterprises. Although foreign loans have eased the situation somewhat, they have been rather small. Moreover, Burma has been chary of accepting loans that might have political strings attached. However, several new factories have been established, some of them already in production, and some coal mines are being opened. Mineral production is improving only slowly. The principal factories established are a cement factory with an annual capacity of about 120,000 tons; a government spinning and weaving mill, intended primarily to supply yarn to the handlooms in the cottages; two small sugar mills which will just about meet domestic consumption; and a cigarette factory. The industrial program also calls for a small steel-rolling mill, a jute mill, a tile and brick factory, and a few other small factories. The general plan calls for reducing foreign exchange requirements for consumption goods as much as possible, in order to increase the import of capital goods.

The economic development of Burma is undoubtedly getting started, but it will probably still be several years before the prewar level of living is restored, even if there are no further political disturbances. However, since the increase in population can be cared for with comparatively little difficulty for at least two or three decades through expansion of the cultivated area, the outlook for improvement in Burma's level of living during this period is distinctly better than in those countries where little new land is available—even though these latter countries may make more rapid progress in the nonagricultural sectors of their economies. The very fact that health services remain somewhat less efficient in Burma than in some of these other countries may also mean a faster improvement in Burma's level of living, i.e., in her per capita income, since she will not have to provide for such a rapid increase in numbers as that which is now taking place in Ceylon and in several other of the smaller countries in this region. From the standpoint of Burma's own needs the pressure of her population will not be an important factor in determining relations with her neighbors in the next two or three decades. However, from the standpoint of the need for more land by some of her neighbors—particularly by China—it may be quite a different story (see end of chap xiv).

Much the same shift in the locus of power—by shelving democratic forms of government and concentrating control in military hands—has taken place in Burma as in Pakistan. The reasons given for this change by the men assuming leadership are also much the same as in Pakistan, although they place much more emphasis on the need of a strong government to combat communism.

THAILAND

What was said above about the climate of the Indochinese peninsula as a whole applies to Thailand. There is rich delta country in the south and center, where most of the population lives and where most of the rice is grown, both for home use and for export. This delta area resembles Lower Burma in that the rainfall is high in the monsoon season, but double-cropping depends entirely upon how adequately the land can be irrigated during the long dry season (October to May, inclusive). At present comparatively little land is irrigated during this season. This delta area extends well into central Thailand and contains much good land which has not yet been developed. It is said that a substantial proportion of this land can be irrigated. One project, which is now well under way, will provide water to about 2.3 million acres. Other projects will add considerably to the tilled area in the drier parts of the country, although much of northern and eastern Thailand, which constitute about three-fifths of the total area (200,000 square miles) of the country, cannot be used to any considerable extent for agriculture because of the mountainous character of the terrain. In eastern Thailand, in particular, the relatively scanty rainfall and the mountainous character of the country limit the agricultural area rather rigidly to small valleys which can be irrigated from reservoirs in the mountains. (See Maps 2, 3*a*, 3*b*, 8, and 14.)

POPULATION

The population of Thailand more than doubled between 1911 (8.3 million) and 1947 (17.4 million). In 1955 it was estimated at 20.3 million (293, 1955, pp. 123, 140)—an increase of almost 150 per cent in forty-four years. This increase may be somewhat exaggerated, due to the fact that later censuses have probably been more complete. (See Map 13.)

The birth rate.—For the years 1951–53 the average birth rate was recorded as 29.8 and the death rate as 9.8 (293, pp. 615, 667). These rates yield a natural increase of 2 per cent per year. There is good reason to be skeptical of these rates: in the years 1930–34 the birth rate was reported as 34.6; it fell to approximately 24 in the years 1946–48 and rose to 31.0 in 1953. Such changes could take place, but it seems far more likely that they resulted from fluctuation in the efficiency of birth registration. Furthermore, even the average birth rate of 34.6 in 1930–34 is so low for a Southeast Asian country in which agriculture is far and away the most important economic activity, and in which four-fifths or more of the people live in villages, that a student of population at once suspects very strongly that registration has always been far from complete.

The death rate.—The recorded death rates of 9.8 in 1951–53 and of 16.3 in 1930–34 also rouse suspicions of incomplete registration. Such changes in death rates during a twenty-year period have been found in Ceylon, where they are based on reliable data, although even there a substantial nonregistration was found as late as 1953 (see chap. xiv). But there is good reason to believe that the death rate is higher in

Thailand than in Ceylon because of less adequate health services; also that registration of deaths is less complete in Thailand. A death rate of 12–15 would appear to me a very low rate for Thailand today.

Natural increase.—In view of Thailand's past rate of growth as indicated by the censuses, her recorded natural increase of 2 per cent per year should be regarded as a minimum for recent years; it would not be in the least surprising if the natural increase were actually somewhat higher, possibly approaching 2.5 per cent per year. There is no doubt that the health services in Thailand have been much improved since the war; hence a proportional decline of over one-third in the death rate in the past twenty years as shown by the registration data is not improbable, even though these data may be quite incomplete. There is no satisfactory proof of any downward trend in the birth rate.

The planned-parenthood movement has only begun, and because it lacks money both for propaganda and for clinical services it cannot possibly be assumed to have had any significant influence on the birth rate as yet. "The Government, although not antagonistic, does not appear to be in agreement with family planning, because the view is taken that the country is not yet overpopulated" (225, pp. 314–15). The chief difficulties involved in the adoption of family limitation by Thailand's rural population are much the same as those elsewhere in this region, though different in some details: (1) complete ignorance of the possibility of birth control on the part of the mass of the people, (2) cultural patterns which encourage a high birth rate, (3) the lack of contraceptives suited to the living conditions of the people, and (4) the absence of severe hardship because of Thailand's relative abundance of land. Since the death rate is reasonably certain to continue its decline, though probably at a significantly slower rate than in the recent past, the rate of population growth during the next twenty to thirty years is quite likely to rise a little, so that the population will double in about a generation.

The native population of Thailand is related racially to the people in the central and northern areas of Burma and to some of the southern Chinese. This native population constitutes 80–90 per cent of the total. The remainder of the population consists chiefly of Chinese and of their children by mixed marriages. Many of the Chinese migrated to Thailand as laborers in the tin mines and on the plantations, but, as in Malaya and Burma, many of them soon became traders, merchants, and moneylenders. In these middleman enterprises they often took advantage of the farmers and made themselves thoroughly disliked, so there is considerable bad feeling between the Thais and the Chinese. At present there is also some fear that the Chinese in Thailand may act as a fifth column in the future expansion of Mainland China. Partly as a consequence of this situation, and partly because of mere contiguity to China, Thailand's military expenditures are rather large, even in view of the fact that she gets much military aid from the United States. In Thailand, as in most of the countries throughout this region, military and police expenditures seriously deplete the resources available for economic development.

AGRICULTURE

The land area of Thailand is about 103 million acres; including the area of lakes, marshes, etc., the total area is about 126 million acres. The "total agricultural area" is given as 19.3 million acres, or less than one-fifth of the land area. Most of the nonagricultural land is classed as forested, and no estimate seems to be available regarding unused land which might be brought into cultivation (111, 1956, Part 1, p. 6). Another source (303, 1955, p. 180) gives the "cultivated area" as 23.2 million acres. In any event, the area cultivated is not far from one-fifth of the total. The area planted each year does not appear to exceed 15 million acres at the present time, probably because much lies fallow (318, FATP 4-56, February 9, 1956, p. 7). Of the cropped land, 90 per cent or more seems to be in rice; however, failure to report many minor crops, especially in the mountainous areas, may unduly swell this percentage in the reports. The fact that rubber plantations seem to be included in the forested area may also give undue prominence to rice. Because of the lack of irrigation, and also because of the relative abundance of land, very little of Thailand's cropped area is double-cropped. Most of this relatively small area is found in the delta area where water can be raised from the rivers onto the fields. The completion of large irrigation works now under construction will add to the double-cropped area in the central region and will increase the area which can be devoted to legumes and vegetables during the dry season.

There has been an increase in the cultivated area during the past twenty years. Rice acreage increased from 8.3 million acres in 1934–38 to 12.3 million acres in 1954–55, or about 50 per cent, and yields per acre increased about 10–11 per cent (111, 1956, p. 47). Acreages in corn (maize), soy beans, sesame, sugar cane, cotton, and tobacco appear to have increased proportionally; data concerning these crops are less satisfactory, however, and some of the apparent increase is probably due to an improvement in the crop-reporting service.

The diet of the people seems to be improving, aided by the greater production of the pulses and of vegetable fats (oils) as well as by the increased production of rice. During the twenty years preceding 1955, Thailand's rice production rose about 75 per cent, while her population grew about 48 per cent. However, the production of rice in any given year, e.g., 1955, is not a good basis on which to calculate increase over a period of time, since that year may be "good" or "bad." The FAO has not calculated a per capita index for Thailand showing the calories now available as compared with an earlier date. It does, however, give an index of 158 for total food production in 1955 on the basis that the prewar index = 100. The 1955 index for all agricultural production on the same basis was 176 (*ibid.*, p. 26). Thailand's food production appears to be increasingly adequate.

Rubber is the only nonfood crop of much importance; production is 120–40 thousand tons annually, practically all of which is exported. The raising of jute is now being encouraged, since large numbers of burlap sacks are needed in the handling of export rice, and present production of jute is far below domestic needs. Cotton production is also being encouraged, but as yet amounts to only a few thousand tons of fiber. Teak timber for export is produced in considerable quantities.

The available data seem to indicate that Thailand has been able to keep agricultural production substantially ahead of population growth up to the present. The chief reason for this relatively rapid increase in per capita production is that many of the farmers in Thailand possessed some tillable land which was not actually in use but which they could bring into cultivation as fast as they felt the need to do so. Thus, agricultural expansion could proceed without waiting for the completion by the government of large irrigation projects or for the large-scale clearing of the jungle with expensive machinery. The average size of a farm in Thailand is about six acres (318, FATP 4-56, February 9, 1956, p. 1), about twice as large as the average farm in China and Japan and perhaps one-third to one-half larger than in India. Hence, many farmers in Thailand have not needed to till every acre every year in order to provide for their families. Many of them could prepare a little new land year by year by their own labor as the need for it arose. In this respect Thailand has probably been no more fortunate than Burma; unlike Burma, however, Thailand has been able to maintain internal order quite easily since the war and, in addition, did not have to build up her governmental administration from scratch, since she had never been a colony with political control in foreign hands. It should be noted here, however, that Thailand has also recently succumbed to a military dictatorship.

The agricultural outlook.—During the next two or three decades there will probably be a continued expansion of the tilled area through the enterprise of farmers who will till more of the land they already own, through the migration of young farmers to readily tillable new land, and through the public reclamation of considerable areas by irrigation. Irrigation will also make double-cropping possible on an enlarged area, and should add appreciably to the stability of production from year to year and to the adequacy of the diet during the dry months. It seems altogether reasonable, therefore, to expect a fairly steady and rapid increase in Thailand's food supply during the next fifteen to twenty years.

Perhaps the most important aspect of the availability of new land is the time it will give Thailand to organize an efficient agricultural extension service to carry agricultural knowledge to the farmers. Before Thailand has put all of her new land into cultivation, the farmers should have begun to add substantially to the acre yields of all the important crops. Demonstration farms are being set up, a considerable amount of research work is being done, and the organization of extension work is proceeding quite satisfactorily. In the course of the next two decades these efforts to improve agriculture should begin to produce substantial results. As yet there is no evidence of any significant improvement in the yields of the principal crops as the result of this educational work among the farmers. But, again, I would repeat that it takes time to break through age-old traditions of farming and to introduce the new ideas and values favorable to the adoption of new methods. Fortunately, Thailand can afford this time. However, if Thailand's population continues to grow by 2–2.5 per cent per year, the outlook will be quite different in three or four decades, when the population will reach twice, or perhaps more than twice, its present size.

INDUSTRY

On the whole, Thailand has shown less interest in the development of industry than most of the other countries of this area. Recently, however, her interest in industrial production seems to be increasing. In undertaking even a modest program of industrialization, in addition to making agricultural improvements, Thailand faces the same difficulties which plague all underdeveloped countries. She has a very poor system of transportation and communication. Very few communities outside of Bangkok and its environs have any electric service, and even in Bangkok electric service is inadequate for industrial development. There is a great shortage of capital for all purposes, and an even greater shortage of experienced business managers, trained engineers, and technicians. Almost no skilled workmen are available who can maintain and operate modern machinery. Furthermore, the experienced businessmen, technicians, and workmen are mostly Chinese, and the Thais do not want them to get in positions from which they can expand their economic power. As in most small countries, some of the mineral resources needed for modern industry are in meager supply or are lacking altogether.

Fuel.–Thailand has no known deposits of good coal. Although she has a considerable amount of lignite which can probably be used in the production of electricity, it is very unlikely that her lignite can be used for metallurgical purposes. As far as is now known, Thailand has no petroleum or gas. Although the country possesses a substantial amount of water power (303, 1955, p. 181), little of it has been developed, and it does not seem probable that when developed it will be adequate for even a modest industrial expansion. The necessary electricity will have to come largely from thermal plants using lignite or imported coal.

Iron ore.–Some recent discoveries of iron ore (317, Part 1, No. 57-22, p. 4) may contribute a supply adequate enough for a small steel plant, although the lack of coking coal makes such a development very uncertain. Some of this newly discovered ore is located close to the coast, and the Japanese are said to be interested in the possibility of obtaining regular exports from Thailand. Such an arrangement might be of mutual advantage.

For some years Thailand has produced considerable amounts of tin, 13–14 thousand tons of ore, all of which has been exported. About 1,000 tons of wolfram (tungsten) ore are also produced annually. The demand for these minerals, and the prices paid for them, fluctuate considerably, and the amounts mined fluctuate accordingly. Reserves of these minerals do not appear to be large.

Thailand seems to have comparatively small reserves of other important minerals except those needed for construction, which are relatively abundant in all countries.

Up to the present time, Thailand's nonagricultural economic development has been confined largely to improving transportation (harbors and railways), establishing cement mills, building small factories for the manufacture of burlap sacks and paper, building two or three small sugar refineries, and manufacturing cigarettes. Most kinds of manufactured consumers' goods are imported. The traditional goods used by the masses, except textiles, are made in small shops (cottage industry) where all the work is done by hand and the products are used locally.

Thailand's government, in contrast with Burma's, not only allows but encourages private investment in industry, and is trying to make conditions attractive to foreign investors. However, it does reserve utilities, mining and quarrying, banking and insurance, and some industries (e.g., cigarettes) for operation by the government or by the National Economic Development Corporation, which is the public agency for establishing and/or operating economic enterprises.

Up to the present time, industrial establishments using power machinery have not been able to employ more than a few thousand persons. Moreover, it is not likely that modern manufacturing will expand rapidly enough in the near future to absorb any considerable proportion of the increasing number of young workers entering the labor market. It would seem that these new workers, most of whom will be children of farmers, must look primarily to the expansion of agriculture for their livelihood.

As industry develops and as the efficiency of agriculture grows, more and more workers will find their way into ancillary types of work—transportation, communication, public utilities, and all types of service activities and government work. But the number and proportion of the workers in any country who can be supported at a modest level of living by such activities depends on the efficiency of the basic productive enterprises. At present agriculture is quite inefficient, and not more than about one-fourth of the population can be supported in nonagricultural activities; if no food were exported, however, the proportion available for nonagricultural tasks might be increased considerably even now. It is reasonably certain that this proportion can be further increased as agriculture becomes more efficient and more land is tilled. The chief obstacles to such a transition are the difficulties of accumulating capital and of training the personnel needed to operate a more complex economy with reasonable efficiency. As in all underdeveloped countries, the major portion of the capital must come, for the time being, from taxes on agricultural products. Even the education and training of technical personnel must be paid for largely from such taxes.

Still, there seems to be no good reason why Thailand should not make the transition, slowly and rather easily, to a more productive economy in which only one-half, or even less, of her people will be engaged in agriculture. The per capita production of Thailand's farmers is already higher than that of farmers in a number of other underdeveloped countries in Asia.

Thus, Thailand's situation today is relatively favorable. However, if she postpones for three decades, let us say, any effort to reduce the birth rate to conform to the decline in the death rate, her situation may well become as critical as that faced by the more densely settled countries of Asia. If, instead, Thailand can reduce her birth rate so that the rate of increase is only one-half or one-third of what it is now, her prospects for a continued improvement in the level of living will remain quite good—always provided that rising population pressures elsewhere and the ideologies of her neighbors do not lead to aggressive actions against her.

MALAYA

Although Singapore is not politically an integral part of the Federation of Malaya, the two areas will be treated here as *Malaya* except where it is made clear that the data apply specifically to one or the other. Malaya, thus defined, has an area of about 51,000 square miles and extends from approximately the Equator on the south to 6°30' north latitude. Both the Federation and Singapore are now self-governing dominions within the British Commonwealth (see Map 18).

POPULATION

As a consequence of the rapid development of export agriculture, the expansion of tin mining, and the large entrepôt trade of Singapore, Malaya's population has increased very rapidly in the past four decades. It has grown from about 2.7 million in 1911 (195, p. 25) to an estimated 7.52 million in 1955 (293, 1956, p. 159), thus increasing by about 180 per cent in forty-five years. Unlike the population increases of most of the other countries in this region, a substantial proportion of Malaya's increase has come from a large immigration, although the excess of births over deaths in the native population has no doubt been fairly large. The Malay population, which constituted about 51 per cent of the total in 1911 (195, p. 25) and numbered about 1,360,000, was estimated as only 43 per cent in 1953. At that time it numbered about 2.94 million (146, p. 9), showing an increase of about 116 per cent in forty-two years, a fairly rapid gain. The Chinese now outnumber the Malays, constituting 44 per cent of the total; the Indians, who were about one-third as numerous as the Malays and constituted about 14 per cent of the total in 1939, now constitute only 11 per cent, since many of them returned to India during and after the war (see Map 17).

The death rate.—If the data on Malaya's death rate for the years 1932–34 are reasonably complete (a death rate of 21.6), the health service even then must have been quite efficient. A death rate even two to three points higher (24–25) would have been considered low at that time. Since it is highly probable that the registration of deaths is now more complete than it was at this earlier period, the present death rate in the Malay Federation (1951–54, 13.4) is proof of a very greatly improved health service. The data for Singapore show an even more marked improvement—from 23.8 in 1932–34 to 10.7 in 1951–54 (293, 1955, pp. 615, 657).

The birth rate.—In 1932–34 the recorded birth rate for Malaya as a whole was 37.0, and in 1951–54 it was 43.9. For Singapore alone the rates were 38.5 and 47.8 in the same years. There was probably a substantially larger nonregistration of births in 1932–34 than of deaths, which would account for a considerable proportion of the rise in the birth rate between 1932–34 and 1951–54. In the case of Malaya, however, another factor—immigration—is very important in determining both birth rates and death rates. At a time of large immigration the migrants are largely young people, who have low death rates; since women constitute considerably less than one-half of the migrants into an area like Malaya, the crude birth rate of an immigrant group is relatively low even though the number of births per woman may be very high. Thus at the census of 1931, in what was then British Malaya, there were 146 males to each 100 females. The ratio of males was undoubtedly even higher in most parts of the country in 1911 and 1921. At the census of 1947, there were only 113.7 males per 100 females in the country as a whole, and there can be little doubt that the excess of males is less today.

The natural increase.—The prime significance of these death and birth rates for our study lies in the fact that the natural increase in Malaya rose from 15.4 (37 − 21.6) in 1932–34 to 30.5 (43.9 − 13.4) in 1951–54, and in Singapore from 14.7 (38.5 — 23.8) to 37.1 (47.8 — 10.7) during this later period (*ibid.*, pp. 192, 615, 657). Because the data for 1951–54 are probably more accurate than those for 1932–34, the increase may not have been as large as these figures indicate. However, there can be no doubt that there was a very large rise in the rate of natural increase. The 1951–54 data for Malaya as a whole indicate that, at the present rate of natural increase, the population will double in twenty-two to twenty-three years. Like Ceylon, Malaya has already attained a very high rate of population growth which seems likely to continue for some time, provided even the present rather low level of living of most of the people can be maintained.

Although it does not bear directly upon our primary interest here, the fact should be emphasized that the Chinese are now the dominant group in Malaya—in numbers and, probably, in economic power. They have not yet become as powerful politically, but with self-government now assured to Malaya, it is not unlikely that they will soon achieve a dominant political position also. The Chinese in Malaya gained their economic power under a relatively free economy which rewarded individual initiative and effort. The long struggle of the Communists for power in Malaya since the war could scarcely have been maintained, however, without a considerable measure of internal support from the Chinese laborers on the plantations, in the tin mines and smelters, in transportation, and in the processing industries of Singapore. Although the possibility that Malaya's political future may be controlled by China can only be mentioned here, it should be kept in mind.

There is an active family-planning movement in Singapore, and it is supported mildly by the government. "The total of clinic attendance during 1954 was nearly 10,000," which was twice as much as it had been in 1953 (225, pp. 311, 312). Both clinical work and propaganda are being carried on, but work is confined largely to Singapore, which contains only one-sixth to one-fifth of Malaya's population; even there the movement is only well begun. This is not said to disparage what is being done, but merely to indicate that even an active planned-parenthood association with some governmental support does not appear likely to produce much change in the birth rate during the next two or three decades unless it receives much more support than now seems probable and unless more suitable methods of birth control become available soon. Besides, such a movement always catches on much more slowly in rural areas than in large cities. There is no reason to believe it will be otherwise in Malaya.

AGRICULTURE

It appears that about 6 million acres are under cultivation at present in Malaya, or somewhat less than 10,000 square miles out of a total area approaching 51,000 square miles. The areas planted to the principal crops are about as follows: rubber, 3.7 million acres; rice, 850,000 acres; coconuts, 485,000 acres; oil palms, 100,000 acres; other crops (pineapples, sugar cane, fruits, etc.), about 350,000 acres (146, pp. 14–15). Practically all of the rubber, coconut products, palm kernels, and pineapples are exported. Rubber alone accounts for about 60 per cent of all domestic exports. Since tin accounts for 18–20 per cent, all other exports of domestic products constitute only about one-fifth of the total domestic export. Malaya's total exports are about twice as large as her domestic exports, since Singapore serves as a collecting point for vast quantities of products from the entire region. Many of these products are further processed there before they are re-exported.

Because Malayan agriculture concentrates so heavily on the production of export crops, chiefly rubber and coconuts, the food crops are much neglected on the plantations, and even on small holdings. Further, Malaya has a relatively high proportion of workers engaged in nonagricultural occupations—tin mining and smelting, the processing of rubber on the plantations, the preparation of imports from other parts of the region for re-export, the local manufactures and services needed by an entrepôt center, and the commercial operations incident to vast trade activities. Altogether, slightly over 35 per cent of all "economically active" persons are engaged in mining, manufacturing, commerce, transport, and services (293, 1955, pp. 538–40).

The Malays, as contrasted with the other racial groups in the country—Chinese, Indians, Europeans, etc.—live an almost self-sufficing existence, and the workers on the plantations which grow export products resemble factory workers in small industries more than they do the self-sufficing Malayan agriculturists. It is not surprising, therefore, to find that Malaya imports very large amounts of food. About one-fifth, sometimes less, of the rice which Malaya consumes is home-grown, though the proportion varies with the season. In addition, other foodstuffs are imported in very large quantities, their value being about twice that of the imported rice. Imports of foodstuffs in 1953 accounted for over 40 per cent of all imports for domestic consumption (146, pp. 15, 25).

Satisfactory estimates of how much new land might be brought into cultivation do not seem available. The Mission for the International

Bank regards as guesswork the estimate of a possible increase of 50 per cent over the present tilled area, but says, "there seems little doubt that to anticipate a 50 percent increase in total agricultural output would in the long run be very conservative" (146, p. 47). At present the agriculture of the Malays is very inefficient, and plantation agriculture, especially the growing of rubber, could also be much improved. The yield of cleaned rice per acre was only about 16.0 bushels in 1935–40 (340, p. 319; see also 111, 1956, p. 47). This yield had been raised by only about 11 per cent (to 18.0 bushels per acre) by 1955. Since there was an increase of about one-sixth in the area planted to rice during this interval, the increase in total rice production (about 30 per cent) seems to have been due chiefly to the increase in acreage. During this interval of about seventeen years the population grew by approximately 45 per cent, so that the demand for imported rice has been increasing rapidly.

Although actual production on the rubber plantations has increased by about one-half since the depression years 1934–38 and would undoubtedly have been held at an even higher level if prices had been better, plantation production is quite inefficient by modern standards. Varieties of rubber trees which give a much larger yield are available but have not yet been widely planted, and little new land has been planted to rubber in recent years in spite of the fact that "on the basis of present information . . . rubber is the only crop which is suitable for extensive cultivation in much of the large unoccupied area" (146, pp. 48–58).

Both the yields and the acreage of other important crops seem to have remained practically stationary in recent years. This lack of agricultural expansion undoubtedly is due in part to the guerrilla activities —the "emergency"—which the Communists have been carrying on in much of Malaya almost continually since the war. But this stagnation in agriculture must also be due partly to the fact that very limited funds have been spent on agricultural development.

It is obvious that the economy of any country as heavily dependent on the export of a few agricultural products as Malaya will be very much at the mercy of fluctuations in the world demand for, and prices of, these few commodities. And even if more attention should be given to improving and diversifying agricultural production, it does not seem likely that Malaya will become any more self-sufficing in food as long as her population grows at about 3 per cent per year. In fact, as the data given above show, her need for imported food has been growing and seems likely to continue to grow proportionally. Thus Malaya must export more tin, rubber, copra, pineapples, etc., to pay for her food, at a time when natural rubber—by far the most important of her domestic exports—is meeting increasing competition from the synthetic product as well as from the natural rubber produced in other parts of Southeast Asia and in Africa. Her copra is also meeting growing competition from the production of many other areas, and from oil-seed crops, the production of which is not confined to the tropics. Moreover, Malaya's reserves of tin, her second most important export (about one-third as important in value as rubber), are estimated as sufficient to last only fifteen to twenty years if annual exports average 45,000–50,000 tons. Finally, Singapore is encountering increasing competition as a trade and processing center.

INDUSTRY

In 1947 Malaya's secondary industries employed about 210,000 workers (chiefly in Singapore). Classified in five general categories, the numbers and percentages of workers are shown in Table 25 (146, pp. 418, 419).

TABLE 25

NUMBER AND PER CENT OF WORKERS IN SECONDARY INDUSTRIES, MALAYA, 1947

Category	Number (Thousands)	Per Cent
Handicrafts................	56.8	27.0
Processing................	45.5	21.7
Food, drink, and tobacco...	23.8	11.3
Engineering..............	49.0	23.3
Other manufacturing.......	35.0	16.7
Total................	210.1	100.0

To this total might be added a few thousand workers in the building industries, and in gas, water, and electric utilities. It is clear, however, that not more than 10 per cent of the gainfully occupied population is engaged in secondary industries. The workers in the first and third of the above groups are concerned almost entirely with the production of goods for local consumption, and when group five is examined in more detail the same can be said of the workers in that category. Those in group two are engaged chiefly in preparing local agricultural products, and tin which has already been mined, for the export market; those in category four are largely service workers in transportation and in foundries, etc. There is no basic nonagricultural industry aside from tin mining, which normally employs about 40,000 workers, and a small amount of iron ore mining. There is not enough iron ore to justify an integrated steel mill, and the entire output is sold to Japan. Malaya's tin production is also exported, and seems likely to continue to be in the future. As far as is known, Malaya has no other important minerals; there is some coal, but no oil. Hence, there seems to be little likelihood that any basic industry will develop in Malaya.

Further refinements could undoubtedly be made in the processing of rubber and coconuts, and additional types of useful products could probably be manufactured from these domestic products for local consumption; but the installation of the up-to-date equipment needed for such manufactures would make unlikely any rapid increase in the number of workers who could be employed in such industries. As regards the manufacture of goods for export using domestic raw materials (rubber, coconuts, timber), Malaya does not seem to possess any advantage over Ceylon, for example. Moreover, she is probably at a distinct disadvantage, in the long run, in comparison with Indonesia, which has both the raw materials and the fuel for power. Furthermore, Japan is far ahead of all other Asian countries in foreign trade of all kinds, and seems likely to remain ahead for some years. And now China has come with her "political" trade to complicate matters still more.

Even Singapore's eminence as a commercial center for the processing and handling of raw materials from Southeast Asia is more likely to decline than to grow. Nationalism is a factor of increasing importance in determining the direction and extent of economic development everywhere in this region. Every country which produces raw materials intends to refine them at home as far as possible and to use them for home production of needed goods whenever possible, thus reducing manufactured imports. This tendency will make it difficult in the near future for a great commercial center like Singapore to maintain its position in the commerce of the region. Neither can Singapore reasonably hope to manufacture for export many of the kinds of consumption goods it is now making for domestic use, since Malaya's neighbors can soon learn to make such goods for themselves. In regard to the manufacture of light consumption goods for export, Malaya appears to be in exactly the same situation as most of the other underdeveloped countries of Southeast Asia. She does not seem to have any advantage over them in agricultural raw materials which might be used in such manufactures, and she lacks many minerals, as well as the fuel, which some of the others possess. Malaya may have more capital available, and she does have a larger class of experienced businessmen and trained workers of certain kinds; but it is doubtful if these men will be able to build and maintain any considerable markets in those neighboring countries, because the protection of "infant industry" is almost certain to interfere seriously with foreign trade in all of them, whether their economies develop primarily along socialistic or along "free" lines.

Under these conditions, it is difficult to see how Malaya can hope to achieve a substantial improvement in the level of living during the next two or three decades unless the rate of population growth falls off sharply, a prospect for which there is no reasonable hope at present. The situation will be even worse if the new Commonwealth government should prove unable to maintain the relatively stable civil order which has only recently been achieved. Again, as in the other countries of the Indochinese peninsula, the probability that Mainland China will do her best (worst) to disturb the economy of Malaya must be reckoned with in considering the future of this country's economic development.

INDOCHINA

The area formerly known as French Indochina is now divided into four independent countries, each with its own government. Although French Indochina consisted of a colony and four protectorates, it was being developed economically as a single unit. Now, however, each of the four parts into which it has been broken is going its own way economically as well as politically: (1) Vietnam has an area of approximately 66,000 square miles, and is composed principally of what used to be known as Cochin-China and of that part of Annam which lies south of the 17th parallel of north latitude; (2) Viet-Minh (North Vietnam) has an area not greatly different in size (about 60,000 square miles). It is now communist. It consists chiefly of Tongking and that part of Annam which lies north of the 17th parallel of latitude; (3) Cambodia is a kingdom lying west and north of Vietnam and contains about 67,000 square miles; (4) Laos is also a kingdom and lies north of Cambodia and east of Thailand, also having a long border on the east and north with Viet-Minh and on the north with China. It contains about 91,000 square miles.

From the time of the Japanese invasion in 1941 until 1954, but especially since 1946, there has been much turmoil in this area, and its economy has been deteriorating. The military efforts of France to re-establish her position after the war, and the struggle of the Communists to attain control of the entire area as the champions of nationalism against colonial power, were even more disruptive than the Japanese invasion.

From our standpoint, the most significant facts are that the economies of all these countries appear to have retrogressed since 1939 and that the governments now in control cannot yet be considered stable enough to make steady economic progress reasonably probable. But it should be noted that their economic instability arises only in part from the uncertainty of the political intentions of the Communists, who are now in control of Viet-Minh and who are themselves largely controlled by the communist government of China. Another uncertainty in the three "free" countries—Vietnam, Cambodia, and Laos—is the breaking-up of the area into separate political units, none of which has yet had time to develop the political organization and institutions which can provide the basic services essential to further economic development.

Viet-Minh, the communist state in the north, has an area of 60,000 to 65,000 square miles, and had a population of 14.0–14.5 million in 1952, according to Fall (102, October, 1954, pp. 152–55), and of about 13 million according to the United States Department of Commerce (317, Part 1, No. 56-4, p. 3). This area has long had a deficit in its food supply, needing to import around 250,000 tons of rice each year, chiefly from the area now known as Vietnam. However, Viet-Minh possesses a large part of the mineral wealth of the entire area—much of the coal, the iron ore, the phosphates, the zinc, and the lead. Before the war, the exploitation of these mineral resources was very important in the economy of French Indochina. Since the establishment of Viet-Minh as a communist state, no usable data have been available concerning the rehabilitation of its economy. The most reasonable presumption would seem to be that Viet-Minh is encountering much the same troubles as the other three states, and that in some respects she may even be facing greater difficulties because of her regular deficit in food production and the decline in the export of minerals. Besides, much of the fighting with the French took place in Viet-Minh, and the Communists did quite a thorough job of destroying transportation and communications, the mines, and other types of economic enterprise. As regards rehabilitating her economy, the only advantage Viet-Minh has over the three "free" states would appear to lie in the ruthlessness of the communist government in forcing land reform. This may or may not prove to be an advantage in the longer run. Because of the lack of data concerning what has been happening in this communist state, only occasional references will be made to Viet-Minh in the following discussion.

THE "FREE" STATES OF INDOCHINA

Chiefly because the areas now included in Vietnam, Cambodia, and Laos are not the same as the administrative areas recorded in French statistics before the war, it will be impossible to follow the development of the "free" states over a period of time. Our discussion will necessarily be in very general terms, and the data which must be used are quite inconclusive. (See Maps 2, 3a, 3b, and 14.)

Population.—Before the war, the population of French Indochina was increasing at the rate of approximately 14 per cent in a decade (104, Part 1, p. 44). If this rate continued to 1956, the population would then have been approximately 30 million. There has been no census since 1936. The United Nations gave an estimate for Vietnam, including Viet-Minh, of 26 million in 1954; for Cambodia of 4.1 million; and for Laos of 1.4 million (293, 1955, pp. 106–8). This yields a total of 31.5 million for the territory of the former French Indochina, or an increase of a little more than 14 per cent per decade since 1936. Because of the boundary changes mentioned above, these estimates for 1955 cannot be compared with prewar data. But it does not seem unreasonable to assume that the rate of growth was approximately the same in the several portions of Indochina. The United States Department of Commerce has suggested that at the time of partition about 12 million of the total of 25 million went to Vietnam and 13 million to Viet-Minh (317, Part 1, No. 56-4, p. 3), and that the United Nations' estimates for Cambodia and Laos are reasonably satisfactory. On this basis, the three "free" states would have had a population of about 17 million. Since these figures involve considerable guesswork, the total may be off by a million or more, and the allocation of population to the particular states as they are now organized may also be appreciably in error. (See Map 13.)

There have never been any registration data on birth rates and death rates for the whole of Indochina. Before the war some data on births and deaths were published for Cochin-China, the southern portion of what is now called Vietnam. These data showed a birth rate which was slowly rising from 35.5 in 1926–30 to 37.1 in 1936, and a death rate which was declining slowly, but not regularly, from 25.8 in 1926–30 to 24.2 in 1936 (104, Part 1, p. 6). Not much reliance can be placed on these figures. There is not enough difference between the birth rates and death rates just noted to yield the population increase shown by the prewar censuses. Besides, these vital statistics related to only one-fifth or one-fourth of the total population, and there is little doubt that registration, especially of births, was incomplete. About all that can be said is that the population of the different parts of Indochina has probably been increasing at a rate in the range of 1.3 per cent to 1.5 per cent per year; the birth rate is probably in the neighborhood of 40 per 1,000, or a little over, and the death rate in the range of 26–30, varying considerably from year to year.

Agriculture.—The agriculture of the three "free" states consists primarily of the growing of rice. Before the war the exports of rice, largely from Vietnam and Cambodia, often exceeded 1.5 million tons. In 1955 about nine million acres were planted in rice (111, 1956, Part 1, pp. 46–47). Information about the area planted to other crops is extremely meager. Considerable amounts of rubber, copra, and corn (maize) were exported. Since 1954, exports of rice from Vietnam and Cambodia have been small as compared with prewar years, and in 1954 the value of the rubber which Vietnam exported exceeded that of rice. Laos is now just about self-sufficient in rice, but imports some types of foodstuffs and exports some tobacco and coffee. Only Cambodia has exports approximately large enough to balance her imports. A large proportion of the imports of Vietnam and Laos are paid for by the United States, and military aid is given to these countries in large amounts to combat the efforts of communist Viet-Minh to enlarge its area of control.

The United Nations' Economic Survey of Asia and the Far East (303, 1955, pp. 187–91) leaves the impression that Vietnam and Laos are making but slow progress in the rehabilitation of their agriculture. The United States Department of Commerce (317, Part 1, Nos. 56-4 and 55-75) leaves the same impression in its survey of their entire economies. Cambodia appears to be doing somewhat better. Her exports of rice in the past few years have averaged about the same (200,000 tons) as before the war, as have her exports of rubber (17,000–20,000 tons). Cambodia also exports some corn, oil seed, and tobacco. Fishing is an important industry, and fish provide much of the protein in the country's diet. Livestock is also an important part of Cambodia's agriculture.

There is said to be a large amount of undeveloped land of good quality in both Cambodia and Laos. In 1953 the government of Cambodia, in reply to a United Nations questionnaire, said that "approximately 2.1 million hectares [5.2 million acres] are at present cultivated" (287, p. 26). The government of Laos said, in reply to the questionnaire, that "(i) there is no lack of cultivable land; (ii) the density of the population is low; (iii) the majority of the cultivators are owners" (*ibid.*). These countries should be able to provide for a considerable increase in population during the next two or three decades, at a rising level of living. They need more irrigation and flood control works, and they need to improve transport so that it will not only link areas of production with export outlets but also reach into the hinterland where the new land is. Vietnam's prospects for increasing her cultivated land are only fair, however. Her situation in this respect is considerably less favorable than that of Cambodia and Laos. In Vietnam there is great need of land reform if much progress is to be made in agricultural production. A large part of the land is in the hands of noncultivating landlords, or is in large "plantations using modern methods of cultivation" (*ibid.*). In Viet-Minh (communist) the land problem is acute, and land reform has been carried through. The effects of this reform on agricultural production are not at all clear as yet.

In addition to the relatively large amounts of new tillable land available to them, the three "free" states should be able, in the course of two or three decades, to increase substantially the yields per acre of all their important crops. However, the unsettled conditions since 1941 have not given them much chance to inaugurate effective programs for improving their agricultural production. In Cambodia and Laos food production seems to be adequate and, because of the abundance of new land, should remain so for three or four decades. In Vietnam, however, the influx of about 800,000 refugees from communist Viet-Minh, and the disturbances connected with the flight of many large landowners, have resulted in decreased production. The care of these refugees has put a heavy burden on the government. Vietnam has done very little as yet to encourage better farming, although a three-year plan for agriculture is spoken of (317, Part 1, No. 56-4, p. 4). All three countries have plans in which the improvement of agriculture is an important part of the proposed development; in Vietnam, however, making more land available to the farmers and helping them to increase yields are urgent problems.

If the fairly explosive political situation in Vietnam can be controlled by improving total agricultural production substantially within a few years, these three "free" countries should be able to provide a somewhat better living for their growing populations over the next two or three decades. But the *if* is a serious one. Clearly, Cambodia and Laos are too small, vis-à-vis communist Viet-Minh backed by China, to protect themselves and to encourage rapid agricultural expansion at the same time, while continued political turmoil in Vietnam will make agricultural improvement there in the near future very difficult.

Industry.—Vietnam, Laos, and Cambodia appear to have almost none of the minerals most necessary for industrial development—coal, iron ore, bauxite, copper, lead, zinc, etc. Most of the useful minerals in this area are found in Viet-Minh, which also has large deposits of the phosphate needed for manufacturing certain types of fertilizers. Such industry as these three "free" states do have is carried on entirely by hand labor except for the processing of some rice and rubber for export. If any industry is to be established in the near future, it must be confined to light consumption goods made from native raw materials produced by agriculture or in the forests—rubber, hides, cotton, timber, etc. At present these states seem to have very little interest in manufacturing; such expenditures as are being made on economic development, aside from the rather small amount spent on irrigation, are confined largely to improving transportation and rehabilitating the few electric plants.

Economic progress in any sector in these "free" countries is closely related to their attainment of political stability. The population is not increasing as fast as it is in most countries in Southeast Asia, chiefly because health work has not yet become as effective as it is in most of them. However, there is no good reason to assume that the birth rate is significantly lower here than in most of the other countries, and there is no indication of any decline in this rate, nor of any movement which would likely lead to its reduction. If economic conditions improved and health work were expanded, a more rapid increase in population could be expected, but this greater increase could be cared for without too much difficulty during the next two or three decades because there is new land that can be brought into cultivation. The most uncertain factor here is the political situation in relation to Viet-Minh and China. There are reports of Chinese farmers escaping into Laos. These farmers may be bona fide escapees from Communist China, but they may also be fifth columnists infiltrating Laos in preparation for the expansion of Viet-Minh when the time appears favorable. Even now Viet-Minh needs more land for agriculture, and with considerable such land available just across the border the temptation to appropriate it will be increasingly great.

CHAPTER XVI

SOUTHEAST ASIA:

ISLANDS

THE PHILIPPINES

The Philippines consist of a group of about seven thousand islands having a total area of approximately 116,000 square miles. Only thirty of these islands have areas of 100 square miles or more. The Philippines are wholly tropical, extending from about 5° to 19° north of the Equator. Manila, the capital, lies 600 miles southeast of the southern point of the coast of Mainland China and 400 miles south of Taiwan. Like Indonesia, the Philippines are an integral part of Southeast Asia.

POPULATION

Estimates dating back to 1800 indicate that the population grew fairly rapidly during the century preceding the first census, which was taken under United States' auspices in 1903, the increase being from about 1.5 million in 1800 to 7.6 million in 1903. This is a fivefold increase in a century, and would have required an annual average increase of 1.6 per cent. Following the occupation of the islands by the United States the population more than doubled between 1903 and 1939 (16 million), and if the latest estimates are accurate (22.3 million in 1956) it was about three times larger in 1956 than in 1903 (see Map 15).

The estimates for the nineteenth century should not be taken too seriously, but in view of the growth of population in some other islands of this region—notably Java—a fivefold increase in the Philippines during that period is quite possible. The chief contribution of the Spanish occupation during most of the nineteenth century was the maintenance of civil order. With an amount of land that was abundant for the small initial population, this could explain the high rate of growth in spite of the lack of organized health work. Following the occupation of the islands by the United States, health work was established, schools were provided, and export agriculture was developed; as a result, the rate of population growth rose to 2 per cent, or slightly more, per year. A century of growth at this rate (following 1903, when the population was 7.6 million) would result in a population of 55 million in A.D. 2003.

Since 1903 rates of growth calculated from census data rather than from the registration of births and deaths appear the more reliable. The census data are generally believed to be reasonably accurate, while the registration data are known to be seriously deficient. Thus for years

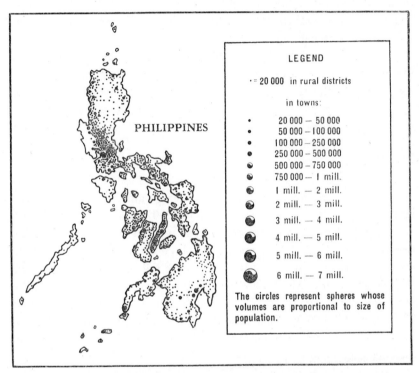

LEGEND

· = 20 000   in rural districts

in towns:

•	20 000 — 50 000
•	50 000 — 100 000
•	100 000 — 250 000
•	250 000 — 500 000
◉	500 000 — 750 000
◉	750 000 — 1 mill.
◉	1 mill. — 2 mill.
◉	2 mill. — 3 mill.
◉	3 mill. — 4 mill.
◉	4 mill. — 5 mill.
◉	5 mill. — 6 mill.
◉	6 mill. — 7 mill.

The circles represent spheres whose volumes are proportional to size of population.

PHILIPPINES

MAP 15.—Population distribution in the Philippines. (Adapted by permission of Dr. Friedrich Burgdörfer and the Heidelberger Akademie der Wissenschaften from *The World Atlas of Population* [Hamburg: Falk-Verlag], copyright 1957 by Heidelberger Akademie der Wissenschaften, Heidelberg, Germany.)

1926–30 the registration data showed a birth rate of 35.2 and a death rate of 19.5, leaving a natural increase of 15.7 (174, 1931–32, pp. 52, 53), or only about 75 per cent of the actual rate of growth between the censuses of 1918 and 1939. In 1953 the registered birth rate was 20.7 and the death rate 8.8, leaving a rate of natural increase of only 11.9 (293, 1956, pp. 617, 641), or only 60 per cent of the rate of growth shown between the censuses of 1939 and 1948 (20.2 per cent in nine years). On the same pages the Economic Commission for Asia and the Far East of the United Nations is given as the authority for a birth rate of 34.2 and a death rate of 9.9 in 1955. Both of these rates may be somewhat too low. However, the natural increase derived from them, 24.3, is about what would be expected from the census increase just cited. It is by no means improbable that the death rate has declined by about one-half since 1930, but it seems doubtful whether there has been any substantial decline in the birth rate in the past two or three decades. Because of the war and the postwar disturbances, the registration of births and deaths may well be much less efficient in recent years than in prewar years.

As would be expected in a mountainous country like the Philippines, the population is concentrated in the level areas along the rivers and the coast. On the smaller islands where the land is tilled intensively, the density of population is very high. On Cebu it was 596 per square mile in 1948; on Bohol it was 351; and on Leyte it was 326. In several of the provinces of Luzon the density rises above 500 (Cavite, 527; Rizal, 749; Pampanga, 504). On the other hand Mindanao, which is almost as large as Luzon (over 36,000 square miles), had a density of only 70 per square mile, in spite of a very large amount of good unused land. The islands with a density of above 300 per square mile in 1948 (census) had a rate of increase below average (20.2 per cent) between the censuses of 1939 and 1948. Three of the larger islands with lower than average density (166 per square mile) gained at rates well above the average: Mindanao, density 70, increase 35.3 per cent; Mindoro, density 43, increase 27.5 per cent; Samar, density 143, increase 38.6 per cent. There are no later data for the different islands and provinces, but some redistribution of population is taking place in spite of the fact that little is being done to help farmers migrate to the less densely settled areas (see Map 16).

Population growth in the Philippines during the next two or three decades seems likely to continue at about the present rate—2 per cent or more per year. Although a reduction in the death rate is still possible, any further decline will be relatively small and rather slow if the crude rate has already fallen to 10–12, as seems quite probable. There is no convincing evidence as yet of any widespread decline in the birth rate. It seems not improbable, however, that the better-educated groups have somewhat lower birth rates than the lower socioeconomic groups and that the practice of family limitation is having some small effect on the national birth rate. It should be remembered that the majority of the Filipino people are Roman Catholics, and most of the others are Moslems. This may tend to delay the adoption of effective practices of

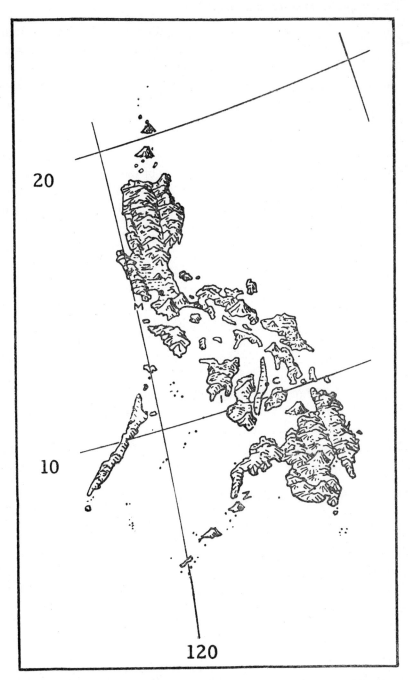

Map 16.—Physiographic map of the Philippines. (Base map a section of the Physiographic Diagram of Asia, © by A. K. Lobeck, reproduced with permission from the Geographical Press, a division of C. S. Hammond & Co.)

contraception as compared with other Asian peoples such as the Indians and the Chinese, whose religion does not definitely oppose such practices. In my opinion, the Roman Catholic church's objection to most contraceptive practices will not prevent their adoption, however, nor will it be the most important factor in delaying the effective practice of contraception. Among any poor agricultural people, the most important factor in delaying the practice of family limitation will be the customs and traditions that have long determined the patterns of family living and reproduction. The religious affiliations of the Filipinos are only an additional obstacle, of unknown importance. It apparently has been of relatively small importance in France for more than a century and in Italy for the past several decades.

AGRICULTURE

In 1939 (there are no later data) Philippine agriculture had a high degree of tenancy: holdings of 12.0 acres and over contained over one-half of all the farm land but made up only 13 per cent of all holdings. Twelve acres is a larger area than can be tilled effectively by the owner if he follows ordinary Philippine agricultural practices. But even these data fail to show adequately the concentration of land in the hands of a few families. Holdings of 25 acres and over contained 33.3 per cent of all farm land but made up only 4.3 per cent of all holdings. In contrast, 71.1 per cent of all holdings contained less than about 7.5 acres, and in the aggregate had only 31.6 per cent of all farm land (287, pp. 27–28). It is not surprising, therefore, to find that in 1939 about one-half of all farmers were tenants or owned only part of the land they tillled.

Philippine agriculture is also highly dependent on commercial crops which are exported after varying degrees of processing. The chief of these are sugar, coconuts (copra, coconut oil, and desiccated coconut), hemp (abaca), pineapples, and tobacco. Before the war these crops occupied about one-half as much land as the food crops for which there is any record of acreage (228, p. 147), or about one-third of the 11 million acres cropped. Data concerning the change in acreage devoted to coconuts since prewar days are not available, but if it is assumed that the acreage in coconuts increased as much as the production of copra between 1934–38 and 1955, it would appear that about 16 million acres were planted to crops in 1955 and that commercial crops constituted a somewhat smaller proportion of the total.[1]

[1] This was calculated from the data on crops (111, 1956, Part 1, pp. 30–120, *passim*), using the assumption just stated.

This estimate of the increase of land in coconuts probably exaggerates the increase in total crop acreage because copra production was probably unusually low in 1934–38, since these were depression years. The fact that the FAO (111, 1956, Part 1, p. 5) reports only 14.7 million acres of "arable land and land under tree crops" in 1953 would also indicate that land under coconuts did not increase as fast as copra production. This smaller figure (14.7 million acres) amounts to an increase in crop lands of about one-third, and seems more reasonable in view of the fact that yields of rice (9 per cent) and of certain other important crops increased during this period, so that an increase of about one-third in cropped land and some increase in yields would result in about the same increase in agricultural production as in population from 1934–38 to 1955. It is of prime interest to our study that the FAO, in this same publication, also reports that about 14 million acres of land are "unused but potentially productive."

Although this figure should probably be classed as a guess rather than as a well-informed estimate based on a survey, it does indicate the general view that a large extension of the tilled area is feasible, although much of the untilled land is almost certainly not as fertile or as cultivable as the land already being tilled. In other words, the basic problem confronting Philippine agriculture for the next two to four decades is not a lack of new land with which to provide food for a rapidly increasing population; the task is rather to establish political, economic, and social organizations that will make possible the effective use of this new land. The existence of this new land, almost as great as the present tilled area, should insure time enough to improve the agricultural extension services and to educate the farmers in better agricultural practices.

Philippine agriculture is still very inefficient, as a few figures will show. The FAO report shows the yield of paddy—unhulled rice—to be about 18 bushels (60 pounds) per acre in the Philippines as compared with 40 bushels in Taiwan and about 41–42 bushels in South Korea. The average yield for the whole of Asia (excluding Mainland China) is reported to be 22.6 bushels per acre. There clearly is room for a large improvement in the yield of the principal food crop. This is also true for most of the other food crops and commercial crops. As regards the expansion of agriculture, therefore, the Philippines resemble more nearly the countries of the Indochinese peninsula than they do India, China, Pakistan, and Ceylon.

However, bringing new land into cultivation and teaching the farmers to use their labor more efficiently will not take place automatically. Many obstacles will be encountered. The chief of these are: (1) the system of large landholdings, combined with the great political power of these landowners; (2) the lack of an effective organization through which the government can acquaint the poor tenant farmers and the young people growing up on the farms in the densely settled areas with the opportunities to be found elsewhere in the islands, and can assist them in establishing new homes; (3) the differences in religion and culture between the people in the more densely settled areas, who are Christian, and the people in Mindanao, where most of the good unused land is to be found, who are Moslem; (4) the lack of transportation facilities; and (5) the reluctance of the poor and ignorant farmers to launch out into strange and unknown regions. It seems highly probable that the most critical of these obstacles for the time being is the political power of the large landowners, who do not want to lose their hold over their tenants. Such a loss would inevitably involve losing much of their own economic and political power. The United Nations report on *Progress in Land Reform* (287, pp. 27–28) indicates that the tenancy situation described above has not changed appreciably since the war.

The second important obstacle which is hindering the more rapid use of new land is the lack of a public authority to assist the farmers in moving to such land. This is probably contrived by the elite governing class and is one of the means by which it delays the social revolution which would follow the relatively easy acquisition of new land by poor tenant farmers and their children.

The cultural and religious differences between the people living in the more densely settled areas and those living in the areas where there is much unused land constitute a very real impediment to migration. But a carefully prepared colonization scheme could reduce these difficulties by settling migrants from the same areas in communities of their own. Such community settlement would also overcome much of the reluctance an individual or a family feels about leaving established homes and friends for an unknown destination among strangers. Furthermore, these planned colonies could provide the facilities and the community institutions to which the people have been accustomed—schools, churches, co-operative societies, transportation, electricity, health services, etc.

In the absence of an earnest effort to help the migrants, it is not surprising that the resettlement of farmers on these new lands has made slow progress, although, as was noted in the section on population, some of the less densely settled islands grew much more rapidly between 1939 and 1948 than the more densely settled. However, it seems reasonably certain that the expansion of crop acreage since 1934–38 has been principally in the already densely settled areas, where only about 60–65 per cent of the land already in holdings (16.5 million acres) was being tilled.

The reports of rapid improvement in agricultural production which have been made year after year since the war are likely to leave an exaggerated impression of progress if one does not keep in mind the fact that a vast amount of agricultural rehabilitation was required merely to restore per capita agricultural production to prewar levels, and that the population is probably increasing by 2 per cent or more per year, which means that there are 450,000 to 500,000 more persons to care for each year.

In the Philippines there seems to be considerable preoccupation with industrial development as opposed to agricultural development, although it is not so great as in some of the other countries in this region. Partly as the result of this growing interest in industry and mining, agricultural production is not improving as rapidly as it might, and diversification of agriculture to provide more adequate animal proteins in the diet is being neglected, while reliance on a few agricultural exports for the exchange with which to buy food is not being reduced very rapidly. In 1954 approximately 10 per cent, and in 1955 approximately 11 per cent, of all imports consisted of condensed and evaporated milk, canned fish, and wheat. Besides, there can be little doubt that a significant proportion of the 30 per cent of all imports not classified in the import data also consisted of foods which were very desirable additions to the diet, but which could be produced at home in the near future if agriculture were properly encouraged.

INDUSTRY

Although the Philippines contain a considerable variety of minerals, they lack some that are very important from the standpoint of industrial development. Estimates of coal reserves run as high as 60 million tons (101, 1940, p. 38), but the actual usable reserves are probably less (283, 1953, p. 194). Most of the reserves are not suitable for coking, but there is believed to be enough coal to support a small iron and steel mill. For other purposes, there is enough coal to last for several decades at least. At present practically all of the coal used in the Philippines is mined there, as compared with a prewar domestic production amounting to only about 10 per cent of the total. No oil has been discovered, but the search for it is going on. In 1955 imports of petroleum products accounted for about 8 per cent of all imports (in value). Water power resources are considerable, but not great enough to provide any large proportion of the electricity that will be needed as industry expands.

One estimate of iron ore reserves in the Philippines (302, 1950, p. 147) places them at about 1.019 billion tons, but only 18 million tons of this are considered presently usable. A more recent estimate raises the reserves to over 1.2 billion tons, but does not specify the amount presently usable (283, 1953, p. 230). The usable ore is being mined at a rate of 1.3 to 1.4 million tons a year for export to Japan. At this rate the better-grade ores will soon be exhausted. Estimates of presently usable ore must recently have been raised still more—although no precise estimates have been found—because the export of ore to Japan continues, and plans for a small steel mill are also going forward.

The Philippines possess considerable reserves of chromite (chiefly refractory), manganese, gold, copper, and silver (*ibid.*, pp. 264, 273, 358, 359). The amounts of these ores mined in any given year depend largely upon their prices in the world market, since practically the entire mineral production is exported—either as ore (iron, chromite, and manganese) or as concentrates (gold, copper, and silver). Lead and zinc are also found, generally in the gold and copper ores (*ibid.*, pp. 360–63). Altogether the principal mineral exports amounted in value to about 6 to 7 per cent of all exports in the years 1954 and 1955 (317, Part 3, No. 56-46, p. 3). The Philippines may possess commercial amounts of other minerals—tungsten, mercury, nickel—but little is known about their reserves or about the feasibility of producing them under present conditions. The quantity and quality of the Philippine mineral reserves do not seem sufficient to justify the hope that their exploitation will ever employ a very large body of workers—a few tens of thousands at most.

Most of the manufactured consumer goods, except those made in the villages in small shops, are still imported. The rate of increase in the volume of domestic-made factory goods, however, is quite high, 12–13 per cent per year, although the amounts produced are still small. Several textile mills have been built and others are under construction; the more complete processing of food products is advancing; several chemical factories have come into operation; and an increasing number of metal products are being produced from imported sheets and shapes. Not surprisingly, manufacturing progress is encountering all the obstacles usually met by underdeveloped countries in this part of the world. There is a serious lack of capital, and the upper economic class does not readily invest in industry because its members have not had experience and training for entrepreneur roles. They are still primarily interested in investment in agriculture and in land. The Chinese, who control a large part of the trade, are likewise inexperienced in industry, but, if permitted, would probably enter industry more readily than the upper-class Filipinos. Education has not encouraged the training of scientists, engineers, and technicians, since there have been few such jobs; besides, they have been considered beneath the dignity of an educated man. About 200,000 students are now enrolled in institutions of higher education and about 600,000 in high schools; there seems to be a growing amount of unemployment among their graduates (102, November, 1957, pp. 166–67).

The basic services essential to all industrial development—transportation, communications, and power—are being improved and extended, but chiefly around Manila and in connection with certain mining operations. As compared with governmental leaders in several other countries in this region, Philippine leaders seem to show less interest in industrial development. The recently prepared over-all plan of economic development allots 48 per cent of all investments to industry, mining, and transportation, as compared with 8.5 per cent to agriculture (*ibid.*, p. 164). About 40 per cent of the total investment is expected to come from public funds. How successfully this plan can be carried out remains to be seen.

Among the factors favorable to rapid development in the Philippines may be mentioned: (1) the familiarity of many Filipinos with the American economy; (2) the lack of suspicion with which the Filipinos accept aid in any form from the "free" world, probably a result of their fifty-year experience as a United States colony; (3) widespread literacy, based on the Western pattern of education as compared with the native pattern among most other Asiatic peoples; (4) large amounts of unused but tillable land and fairly adequate mineral resources; (5) large amounts of aid available from the United States for rehabilitation; (6) a trade treaty with the United States, running to 1974, which should help stabilize export trade while readjustments to world conditions as an independent nation are being made; (7) a reparations agreement with Japan, which should make possible the annual importation, for five years, of a considerable amount of capital goods for which foreign exchange will not be needed.

On the other hand, in addition to the usual difficulties of getting economic development started, there are some special problems for the Philippines. Perhaps these problems may be considered more social than economic, although social difficulties generally create, or are inextricably associated with, economic difficulties. (1) There is a definite class spirit among the elite; they do not wholeheartedly recognize the right of the masses to share fully in economic improvement, and there seems to be comparatively little *noblesse oblige*. Such attitudes are not calculated to produce the best possible leaders for the development of a modern economy. (2) Probably closely associated with the point just mentioned is the great reluctance of the elite and the well-to-do to pay taxes for the common good. (3) The population of the Philippines is growing quite rapidly, more rapidly than that of Indonesia, Indochina, or Burma.

As in the other Asian countries, it seems doubtful whether Philippine industrial plans, even if fully carried out, will create adequate new employment to care for the increase in the labor force. The factories to be established will have the latest labor-saving equipment. Higgins estimates that *open* unemployment is probably increasing now by 50,000 to 70,000 per year, out of 275,000 new entrants into the labor force each year, and that *disguised* unemployment (underemployment) is increasing by 70,000–80,000 per year (*ibid.*, pp. 161–69). Furthermore, much of what is now *disguised* unemployment in the agricultural areas will soon become *open* unemployment in the cities unless, as in China, the migrating youths can be forcibly returned to their families to share the already inadequate food and shelter of the villagers.

In sum, it seems that unless the governing class in the Philippines is prepared to introduce far-reaching land reforms, to sponsor effective work to improve agriculture, to support large resettlement schemes, and to devote much of its energy and means to the development of the industrial sector of the country's economy, little improvement in the life of the masses is to be looked for in the near future. Over a somewhat longer period, internal troubles similar to those encountered after the war are likely to break out again if the economic conditions of the masses are not improved as the national income rises. Finally, and always, the rapid growth of population makes all these economic problems more serious, and ignoring this fact only perpetuates a crisis which then is used as an excuse for neglecting fundamental reforms. The Philippines would appear to be in less immediate danger from direct encroachments by China than the countries of the Indochinese peninsula, but the insurrection following the war shows clearly that communist infiltration and incitements are a constant menace.

INDONESIA

POPULATION AND AREA

Indonesia at present comprises about four-fifths (78.3 per cent) of the prewar Dutch colony called Netherlands India. It has an area of approximately 576,000 square miles (143, p. 20) and a population estimated as 82 million in 1955 (293, 1956, p. 157). The remaining portion of the former Dutch colony, consisting of the western half of New Guinea and some small adjacent islands, is also claimed by Indonesia but is still under Dutch control. The Indonesian name for this area is West Irian. It contains approximately 180,000 square miles and has a population (estimated) of about 700,000 (219, 1956, p. 385). About one-half of the island of Timor, containing about 7,300 square miles and a population of about 450,000, still belongs to Portugal. (For the division of Borneo between Indonesia and the British see the final paragraph in this chapter.) Thus the area under the political control of the government of Indonesia, although only four-fifths as large as Netherlands India, contains over 99 per cent of the total population (see Maps 17 and 18).

The efforts of Indonesia to take West Irian are based on the claim that all Dutch possessions were ceded to the new country in the treaty granting independence. This is a questionable claim. The real reasons, no doubt, for desiring this territory are that there is a very small population in this area, so that the possibilities of resettling Javanese there are large, and that the leaders see an opportunity to gain wider political support by forcing the Dutch to abandon their final foothold in that region. There are now practically no Indonesian Malays in West Irian.

Indonesia is made up of several large islands, or parts of islands, and a great number of small islands (several thousand) lying on both sides of the Equator and extending from the western tip of Sumatra about 3,000 miles eastward. The largest single land mass is the Indonesian portion of Borneo, now called Kalimantan; it has an area of 208,000 square miles and a population of about 3.6 million. Sumatra is second in size, with an area of 183,000 square miles and a population of 11.5

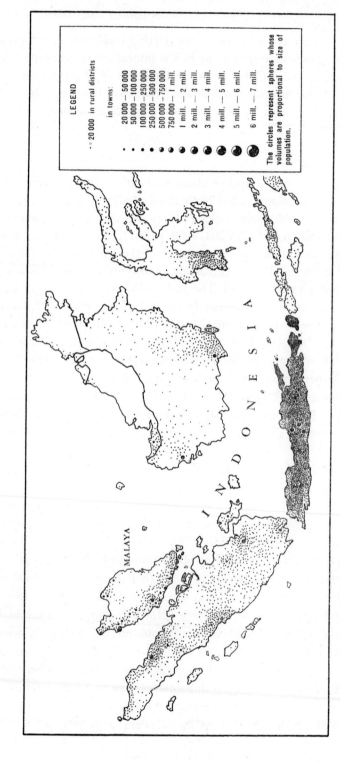

LEGEND

· = 20 000 in rural districts

in towns:

·	20 000 — 50 000
·	50 000 — 100 000
•	100 000 — 250 000
•	250 000 — 500 000
◗	500 000 — 750 000
◗	750 000 — 1 mill.
◗	1 mill. — 2 mill.
◗	2 mill. — 3 mill.
⬤	3 mill. — 4 mill.
⬤	4 mill. — 5 mill.
⬤	5 mill. — 6 mill.
⬤	6 mill. — 7 mill.

The circles represent spheres whose volumes are proportional to size of population.

MALAYA

I N D O N E S I A

million. Other large islands or groups of islands constituting administrative areas are: Celebes, 73,000 square miles and a population of around 6 million; Java, somewhat over 51,000 square miles and a population of 53–54 million; the Lesser Sundas, 28,000 square miles and a population of about 5.1 million; the Moluccas, not including New Guinea (Irian), about 32,000 square miles and a population of perhaps 683,000 (143, p. 20). Timor Archipelago, with an area of about 26,000 square miles, had a population of about 1.2 million in 1941 (219, 1956, p. 439) and of 1.3–1.5 million in 1956.[2]

Of all the islands, Java is by far the most important. It contains about one-eleventh of the area of Indonesia but about two-thirds of the population. The first important European contacts made with the Archipelago were made on the island of Java; not only has it remained the seat of government since it was returned to the Dutch after the Napoleonic Wars, but it has also been the center of the economic development encouraged by the Dutch. Since about 1900 economic activity in the outer islands has become increasingly important, but as yet there is no definite evidence that this more rapid economic development has led to a more rapid population increase in these outer islands than in Java.

The remarkable growth of population in Java since about 1816 has attracted a great deal of attention in recent years. This growth will be described briefly.

Java's population in 1816 is estimated at about 4.5 million (332, p. 14); in 1955 it was estimated at 53–54 million, showing a twelvefold increase in 140 years. This rate of growth is no higher than that estimated for the Philippines during the nineteenth century, but started from a higher base and took place in an area less than one-half as large as the Philippines. If it is assumed that (a) population growth was slow for a few years after 1816 and the population increased to only 5 million by 1825, the rate of increase being quite regular, and that (b) the estimate of 53–54 million in 1955 is reasonably accurate, then the rate of growth has averaged about 1.8 per cent per year during the past 130 years. (For distribution of Java's population see Map 17.)

Vandenbosch gives rates of growth for different periods during the nineteenth century which vary from 1.76 per cent per year in 1845–58

[2] No census has been taken in the territory now included in Indonesia since 1930; unsettled conditions have prevailed ever since 1941. As a consequence, the populations given for recent years, both for particular islands and as a total, must be regarded as approximations only.

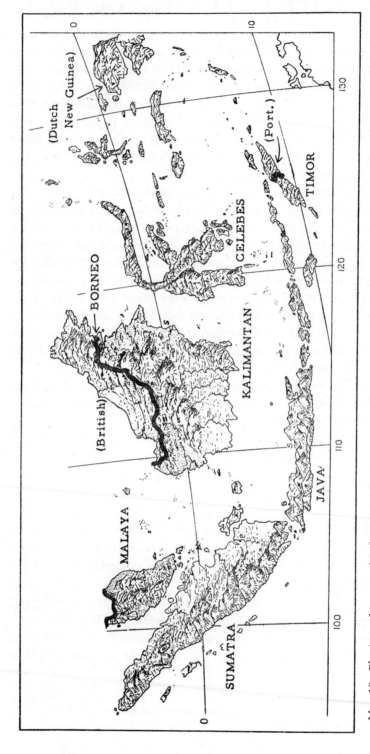

MAP 18.—Physiographic map of Indonesia, Malaya, and Borneo. (Base map a section of the Physiographic Diagram of Asia, © by A. K. Lobeck, reproduced with permission from the Geographical Press, a division of C. S. Hammond & Co.)

to 2.48 per cent in 1815–45, and which average more than 2 per cent between 1815 and 1900. The rates have averaged lower since 1900. The rate dropped to 1.06 per cent (1900–1905), to 0.94 per cent (1905–20), and then rose to 1.73 per cent (1920–30). These data indicate that a fairly rapid growth of population began almost immediately after the re-establishment of Dutch control and that population growth has continued at a high level ever since, although there have been substantial fluctuations from time to time. This pattern of growth is much more probable than a steady rate of growth over such a period of time (see chap. ii).

Considering the small amount of precise information available, the most reasonable explanation for the increase that took place up to about 1900 would appear to be as follows. At the time the Dutch took over control again, a number of native states existed; there were numerous conflicts between them, and much brigandage on the borders. The people had little inducement to extend the tilled area beyond the boundaries where civil order could be maintained. Under renewed Dutch control conflicts between the native states were reduced, and the security of the life and property of the settlers in the fringe areas became more assured. This meant that the area of settlement could be expanded about as rapidly as land was needed to provide for growth in numbers, since, with a population of only about 4.5 or 5.0 million (1815–20), most of the good tillable land in Java was still unused. Improved production of the customary crops through irrigation and better agricultural practices also contributed substantially to the increase of food supply, and the introduction of export crops enabled Java to import increasing amounts of goods from abroad. Thus it would appear that the maintenance of peace, the ease of extending the tilled area, a modest improvement in agricultural practices, and the development of agricultural exports were the principal factors contributing to the unusual growth of Java's population during most of the nineteenth century. The public health services which are now so effectively reducing the death rate in most underdeveloped countries could have had comparatively little influence in Java before 1900. In fact, the decline in the rates of population increase noted above (1900–1920) suggests that life was growing more difficult by 1900, a situation which may have raised the death rate and decreased the margin between the birth rate and the death rate. There is no clear evidence on this point, but it is certainly more reasonable to assume that the fluctuations in the rate of growth during the nineteenth century and the earlier part of the twentieth were due far more to variations in the death rate than to variations in the birth rate.

The recovery of the rate of increase from about 10 per 1,000 (1900–1920) to about 17 per 1,000 (1920–30) may be explained in large part by the improvement of health services after about 1920 and by the increasing ability of the government to provide imports of food in years of local shortage and to mitigate the consequences of droughts by extending irrigation to more and more land. It became increasingly clear in the late 1800's and the early 1900's that Java had a serious population problem. By 1900 the Dutch government had begun to consider migration schemes by which people from Java might be moved to the sparsely settled outer islands.

At present the density of population in Java is between 1,025 and 1,050 per square mile, depending on the estimate of population used. It is highly probable that Java now has a denser population than any other solid block of land in the world of equal size (51,000 square miles). Furthermore, Java has much mountainous land not suitable for cultivation. The rice land that could be flooded amounted to about 8.3 million acres in 1938 (224, p. 54). The amount of land that could be added to this was estimated in 1938 at about 750,000 acres (43, p. 19); if this land had been brought into use at the same rate as new paddy land was added between 1928 and 1938, it would all have been in use by 1948. There is no evidence about what actually happened regarding the use of new land between 1938 and 1948 or since 1948. (For physiography of Java see Map 18; for rainfall see Maps 2, 3*a*, and 3*b*.)

SETTLEMENT SCHEMES

The outer islands have always had relatively sparse populations (see Map 17). Although most of the land in these islands is less fertile than the land in Java, they contain enough good land to accommodate the full annual increase in Java's population, as well as their own increases, for some years, probably for several decades. Indonesia's prime need, therefore, is not for land but for the financial means to carry out resettlement schemes that will appeal to the large numbers of young Javanese who need land.

Before 1930 the Dutch government, although concerned about Java's increasing population, had shown only a mild interest in organized migration. There had been some migration to the outer islands, but most of these migrants intended to work only temporarily on the plantations and did not take their families with them. Some of them worked in the mines and the oil fields and in processing plants, but most of the nonagricultural workers in the outer islands were Chinese. In 1930 only about 825,000 Java-born persons and 1,151,000 people of Javanese ancestry lived in these outer areas (224, p. 189), and agricultural colonists numbered only about 40,000 (43, p. 24)—about 6 to 7 per cent of one year's natural increase in Java.

When the Dutch first tried to move Javanese to the outer islands, they ignored some of the basic cultural factors in Javanese life, and their efforts proved futile. They treated the family as the unit to be dealt with, disregarding the fact that the village is a far more basic social unit in Java than it is among Western peoples. Hence, although the family was given fairly generous financial help, it was not provided with the moral support and the co-operation of other settlers coming from the same or a closely similar community. A family could have such security only if it were settled among people who already had the feeling of belonging to the same group, a village group. Not only were these early attempts very costly, but they had no appeal for the Javanese. In 1930 the population of Java was approximately 41.7 million, and the annual increase, at 17 per 1,000, was about 700,000. The density was a little over 800 per square mile. The size of this annual increase gives a good notion of the volume of migration needed to prevent any increase in population in Java and assure some improvement to living conditions to the migrants.

The depression of the 1930's greatly reduced the value of Java's exports, and it became more difficult to provide the food imports needed to maintain living standards. The population problem became increasingly acute. The program of emigration was reviewed and revised. The importance of keeping groups from the same or neighboring villages together was recognized, a more careful selection of the emigrants was undertaken, and better health protection against typhoid, cholera, dysentery, and malaria was provided. The emigrants were sent out at a time of year when they could help the established colonists with their harvest and thus begin to earn their own keep almost at once. Whenever possible, they were sent out in groups whose members were already known to each other.

This new scheme did not have much time in which to prove its feasibility before the war started, but it was taking hold quite rapidly when the Japanese occupation of Java closed it down. The number of Javanese settlers sent out in 1932 was 7,000; in 1933 it was only between 700 and 800, but rose to over 2,700 in 1934. After that the number went up rapidly to almost 53,000 in 1940 and to about 60,000 in 1941 (224, p. 211). The cost per settler had also been greatly reduced. Before the Japanese occupation it looked as though Java might obtain substantial relief through migration, for once settlement abroad is well begun it snowballs as the settlers let their relatives and friends know about the new opportunities and offer to receive them into an established community.

These settlement schemes do not seem to have been revived on any significant scale since Indonesia gained independence. In fact there are rumors, although unverified, that the net movement of migrants has been from the outer islands to Java. There can be no doubt that Java's population problem is steadily becoming more urgent. This may help explain, in part, the highly unstable political and economic conditions in Java since independence. This instability, and the effort of the Javanese leaders to maintain the highly centralized government inherited from the Dutch, may in turn help explain the political movements in the outer islands aimed at acquiring greater local autonomy. If Sumatra or Borneo or any other of the larger islands possessing lands needed for settlement by the Javanese should become independent, the revival of Javanese migration on a scale sufficient to provide any substantial relief would be more difficult.

If actual starvation can be averted in Java, it is probable that the population of Indonesia will continue to grow 1.5 per cent per year, and it will grow even faster if migration from Java can be organized to remove a large part, say 60–75 per cent, of Java's annual natural increase. Indonesia has abundant land to care for a rapidly growing population for several decades, but at present there is little basis for expecting that an effective scheme for resettling the Javanese will be evolved. As regards the future growth of Indonesia's total population, there is no reasonable hope of a substantial decline in the birth rate within the next three decades. There is no organized movement for birth control, and the official attitude seems to be that there is still plenty of land and therefore no need to give thought to such a matter.

AGRICULTURE

Indonesia's agriculture is of two types: (1) food production and (2) commercial crop production, chiefly for export. Rice is the chief food crop. Since very little information is available regarding agriculture in the outer islands, most of the data used here refer only to Java and

Madura.[3] As was mentioned above, about 8.3 million acres could be flooded for rice in 1938. It was established that another 0.75 million acres could be flooded after proper preparation. Because of the great upheavals since 1941, it is rather unlikely that this last increment has yet been added to the area regularly tilled, but even if it has been added, it means an addition of only about 8 to 9 per cent. A total of 9 million acres would seem to be about all the rice land available on Java. The FAO reports about 10 million acres in rice in 1955. This larger acreage may be accounted for by several factors: (1) The basis on which land cropped more than once a year was reported in the earlier estimate may have been somewhat different from the way such land was reported to the FAO. (2) There may have been some further shift from commercial crops to rice—for example, less sugar cane and more rice. (3) A larger area may have been reclaimed and irrigated since the war than was considered probable in 1938—about 2.5 million acres are said to have been reclaimed (303, 1955, pp. 117, 118). (These last figures apparently apply to the whole of Indonesia.) In any event, it appears that there are now five to six persons per acre of rice land in Java and Madura.

The FAO (111, 1956, p. 26) has calculated indexes of food production in the whole of Indonesia for the three crop years ending in mid-1956, on the basis of prewar production (probably 1934–38) equaling 100. The average food production for the three years preceding mid-1956 is calculated as 110, and for total agricultural production as 119. In the twenty years between 1935 and 1955 the population presumably has grown by about one-third, although this must be regarded as only an approximate figure. There can be no reasonable doubt, however, that in Java the population has grown considerably faster than food production. In the outer islands this probably was not the case, but the data are scanty. Moreover, in the outer islands commercial crops grown on plantations constitute a substantially larger proportion of all agricultural production than they do in Java, so food imports into these islands are larger in proportion to total agricultural production than food imports into Java. It is reasonably certain now that any substantial increase in the acreage of food crops in Java can be accomplished only by taking land out of commercial crops, a process which had been going on for some time before the war and which had resulted in a decline in the amount of food imported into Indonesia, particularly

[3] Madura is a small island off the northeast coast of Java and is generally treated as an integral part of Java.

into Java. This removal of land from commercial crops was partly caused by the loss of export markets during the depression and partly by the greater need for home-produced food. Moreover, increasing proportions of the coconuts and the coconut products were being used domestically, and the area in other food crops that, unlike rice, did not need to be flooded had also been increasing in the prewar years.

On the other hand, there is reason to expect substantial improvement in the yields of the principal food crops in all of Indonesia, once political stability is achieved and an agricultural program is undertaken. Rice yields in Java before the war (1934–38) bore a ratio of 1 to 2.27 to those of Japan, and in Indonesia's best year since the war (1954) her ratio to the best year in Japan (1955) was 1 to 2.28. There is no doubt that Indonesian yields can be raised by the same methods which are being used elsewhere—better seed, more fertilizer, improved methods of tillage, and more adequate irrigation. The above ratios might be reduced to 1:1.5 or 1:1.75 in a decade or so because Java has a naturally fertile soil and a highly dependable rainfall. But such improvement depends upon a stable government, a rising educational level, the availability of funds adequate to develop an efficient agricultural extension service, and a drive toward better living standards among the masses, which does not yet seem to have gained much momentum in Indonesia.

However, if Indonesia remains united, and if she develops a stable government strong enough to make the improvements just listed and also carry out extensive resettlement of the Javanese in the outer islands, the agricultural situation should improve rapidly. Indonesia has more tillable but unused land of good quality in relation to her population than have any of the other countries with which we are concerned here. The fairly rapid use of this land should give Indonesia enough time to introduce control of the birth rate, once her leaders realize that the present rate of population growth cannot continue for more than a few decades without bringing the entire country to the same condition in which Java now finds herself. As yet there is no indication that the leaders realize that the abundance of land they now have will soon become a shortage if the population continues to increase even at 1.5 per cent a year, and that if this rate rises to 2.0 per cent or 2.5 per cent the respite their new land can furnish will be proportionately shortened. An increase of 1.5 per cent per year would lead to a population of approximately 150 million by the end of the century, while an increase of 2.0 per cent a year would raise this to about 190 million. Agricultural resources that can yield an abundance for 82 million are going to be inadequate for the population that is almost certain to come within the next four or five decades.

INDUSTRY

Mineral resources.—Indonesia possesses considerable and varied mineral resources. Although one should not take too seriously the rather frequent claims that Indonesia has *vast* natural resources comparable to those of the United States or the U.S.S.R., there can be no doubt that her resources are adequate to provide for large growth in the non-agricultural sectors of her economy. Estimates of the coal reserves vary from 500 million tons to several billion tons (302, p. 76), and there are great lignite beds in several of the islands. Although there is still some question whether any of the known coal reserves are suitable for coking by the processes currently in use, it is possible that usable metallurgical fuel could be made by mixing the better grades of Indonesian coal with coking coals from China or some other country not too far distant. Indonesia's coal reserves are certainly ample for power purposes for some decades to come.

Indonesia also has fairly large oil resources—as far as is known, the best in Southeast Asia. Before the war, oil production had risen to approximately 8 million tons a year, about three-fourths of which was exported. Production has not yet regained that level, both because of the damage the plants suffered at the hands of the Japanese and because of the nationalistic attitude of the government, which is strongly opposed to the exploitation of Indonesia's resources by foreigners, fearing that such exploitation may raise political complications and may also deplete reserves which will be needed later for the country's economic development. Indonesia does not appear to have any considerable amount of water power.

Indonesia's iron ore resources seem to be large, possibly a billion tons or more (296, p. 304). The largest deposits are of rather low grade and are now classed as "potential," but it is not improbable that they can be used as better beneficiation processes are developed. Indonesia seems capable of developing a modest steel industry, one that could supply at least her own needs. The cost of production, however, is likely to be higher in Indonesia than in India or China.

The tin resources of Indonesia are quite large, and just before the war tin production amounted to about 40,000 tons per year. At that time Indonesia vied with Bolivia for second place as a producer, Malaya holding first place. Almost all of Indonesia's ore was exported for processing. This situation does not seem to have changed significantly since the war, but it is likely that Indonesia will make rather strong efforts to do more tin refining at home. Tin will probably continue to be an important export for some time, since very little of it is likely to be used in Indonesia.

Shortly before the war the production of bauxite began to assume importance (196, p. 209). The known deposits are in the Riouw Islands, off the east coast of Sumatra, and are said to be quite large—20 million tons, containing 50 per cent alumina (102, 1939, p. 145). Other fairly important minerals in Indonesia are sulphur, phosphates (fertilizers), nickel, and manganese. As more thorough exploration is undertaken additional mineral resources will undoubtedly be discovered, some of which will probably be of better quality than those known at present. On the whole, Indonesia seems to possess better mineral resources than most of the other countries of Southeast Asia.

Production by machinery.—Prior to the depression of the 1930's the use of power machinery in Indonesia was confined largely to the plants that processed agricultural products for market—sugar, rubber, spices —the operation of some of the mines, the reduction of a small portion of the tin ore for shipment, the production and refining of petroleum, the operation of the railways and ports, and the generation of electricity on a small scale. In sum, power machinery was used principally by the export industries. The wants of the natives were supplied largely by primitive hand industries; the most notable exception was textiles, a large part of which was imported. On the larger plantations some machinery was being used in cultivation as well as in the processing of the products.

In the 1930 census over 2.2 million persons were classified as employed in industry (208, 1934, pp. 136–39). In 1936 an official estimate placed the number of workers in "large factories" at about 120,000, while the number of full-time handicraft workers was given as 1,535,-000 (246, p. 82). This decline from the total given by the 1930 census is probably explained in some measure by the depressed conditions existing in 1936, which would have been felt most keenly by the workers in "large factories"; but there may also have been a change in classification, reducing the total number of industrial workers.

In 1939 an official estimate classified 300,000 persons as working in industries which used mechanical power. This figure represents a substantial gain over 1936, but there is no way to tell how much of the gain was caused by an increase in the capacity of modern factories and how much by better economic conditions. It is probable, however, that the more active encouragement of industry by the Dutch government after 1930 was beginning to have some effect. This encouragement took several forms. The government gave assistance to small-scale native industries by helping them to train needed workers, by standardizing various types of products, by providing better credit facilities, and by marketing the products of these industries (246, pp. 58, 87, 184). It was hoped that these measures would increase employment and would help native industry to provide some of the goods which could no longer be imported because of the lack of exchange.

Other industries were encouraged by raising tariffs and imposing import quotas. The *Western* industries which the government encouraged were largely light consumers' goods industries such as soap making, the processing of vegetable oils, brewing, the production of electrical goods, cigarettes, and canned foodstuffs—industries which would use domestic raw materials in producing for the domestic market. The weaving of cotton goods by hand was also encouraged quite successfully, as is shown by the increased importation of yarn—from 6,414 tons in 1931 to 21,323 tons in 1939. Some factories financed by foreign capital were also set up: an automobile assembly plant, a tin factory, and several machine and metal-working shops. The generation of electricity was expanded to provide power, which was especially important to small industries that lacked the capital to build power plants of their own.

The Dutch government in Indonesia was no stranger to the operation of economic enterprise. It had long operated many estates, and it had managed the teakwood exploitation, operated coal mines and tin mines, owned and managed the railways and the salt works, and participated in other enterprises such as oil production and refining and bauxite mining. It is not surprising, therefore, that under the depressed conditions of the 1930's the government took the lead in trying to make the country less dependent on its exports of raw materials. The outbreak of war in Europe also made it necessary for Indonesia to become increasingly self-sufficient and encouraged the migration of capitalists and capital to Indonesia. This further encouraged industrial expansion.

The increasing evidence that Japan had plans for conquering and exploiting Indonesia made it even more urgent that she develop industrial capacity in order to resist such encroachment, but by then it was too late to accomplish much. However, plans were formed for the smelting of scrap iron and for the rolling of the steel which this enterprise would produce, and for the establishment of new hydroelectric plants, chemical industries, an aluminum plant, and other industries that would not only be useful for defense but would make the country more self-sufficient in a variety of consumption goods and ultimately in the production of capital goods (246, pp. 83–85; 196, pp. 215–18; 43, pp. 84–85).

It might reasonably have been expected that the impetus which inspired Indonesia's plans for industrial development immediately before the war would have begun to operate again fairly soon after the Japanese were evacuated. This did not happen, because the destruction which accompanied the war was very great and because the war for independence followed almost immediately. Since independence (1948) the government has been plagued by many internal troubles, and it is not clear whether the national unity of Indonesia can be maintained; at the very least, the rebellions in the outer islands have seriously retarded the efforts being made by the central government to put the country's economy on a footing sound enough to insure fairly rapid development during the coming decade or two. At worst, the success of the rebellions, or of some of them, would result in a certain amount of isolation for Java. This, in turn, would make Java's economic problems practically insoluble for some time to come.

For a good many years before the war the proportion of Indonesia's agricultural exports which came from Java had been declining, and by 1940 the proportion originating there had fallen to 40 per cent. In addition, the proportion of mineral exports, chiefly oil and tin, had been growing, and from 1938 to 1940 mineral exports constituted about 30 per cent of all Indonesia's exports. Over 90 per cent of the oil and almost all of the tin came from the outer islands (43, pp. 42–47). Thus the secession of any of the larger of these islands—Sumatra, Borneo, and Celebes—would leave Java in a deplorable situation, while the secession of all three would create havoc. She would be left with almost two-thirds of the total population, almost no new land for agriculture, and only 20–25 per cent of the total exports—possibly 10 per cent more if she were able to hold on to the three small islands close by, which contain practically all of the tin (*ibid.*). Finally, and most importantly, she would lose any chance of large-scale migration to the outer islands.

It appears that Java's population has been and is now growing at about the same rate as the population of the outer islands. If Java's population today is around 54 million (the 1955 estimate is 53–54 million), and if it is growing by 1.5 per cent per year, the annual increase now amounts to over 800,000; even at a rate of 1.2 per cent the increase would be about 650,000 per year, and there is no evidence of any decline in the birth rate.

The situation which would confront Indonesia as a united country is, of course, quite different from that which would confront Java as a separate entity. But even so, Indonesia, because of her postwar troubles, is beset to an even greater degree by the difficulties common to all underdeveloped countries in launching their economic development schemes—lack of capital, lack of trained technicians, an illiterate population, inadequate education facilities, an inexperienced civil service. Up to the present time Indonesia has had little chance to inaugurate an economic program, although a rather ambitious "plan" has been proposed. In addition, the lack of a compact territory, the differences between the economic development in Java and the outer islands, and even the cultural differences between their populations create distinctive problems, and will undoubtedly make political and economic unity more difficult than in most of the other countries.

Indonesia, at present, must be classed with Indochina as so beset with internal political difficulties that any steady or rapid economic development is highly unlikely. How far these internal difficulties are the result of communist influences, of personal ambitions, of cultural differences, of geographic conditions, is by no means clear.

BRITISH COLONIES

There are several small British colonies in Southeast Asia, not thus far mentioned, whose importance, from our standpoint, does not justify giving them more than a word.

Hong Kong.—Hong Kong is a British colony consisting of Hong Kong Island and Kowloon, a territory leased from imperial China in 1890. The entire area contains 391 square miles. Before the war it served chiefly as a commercial center for the assembling and distribution of cargoes bound into and out of Southeast and East Asia, and as a port of call for ships passing up and down the China coast. It has since become an important center for air travel.

As a result of the "liberation" of China by the Communists, many Chinese who were in business in Shanghai, Tientsin, and other coastal cities fled to Hong Kong with as many of their possessions as they could take with them. The textile industry of Hong Kong has increased by leaps and bounds, and many other light consumers' goods industries have sprung up within the last ten years. The population was only about 840,000 in 1931, but it grew very rapidly as the Japanese control of China spread, and by 1941 it was estimated at 1,786,000. It remained near that figure until after 1947, but began to grow rapidly again as the Communists gained control over more and more of the mainland. In 1956 the population was estimated at 2,440,000.

Borneo.—Brunei, North Borneo, and Sarawak, on the large island of Borneo, are also British colonies. In 1955 they contained an estimated population of about 1 million on an area of approximately 79,000 square miles. These areas are comparatively undeveloped both agriculturally and industrially. The chief exports are rubber and oil, with considerable quantities of timber and spices. A much larger population could easily be supported at a greatly improved level of living, but their immigration policies discourage settlement from other areas. There appears to be comparatively little interest in the development of a more efficient economy in these colonies.

CHAPTER XVII

TAIWAN

AND KOREA

TAIWAN

Taiwan (Formosa) is a small and rather mountainous island containing about 13,000 square miles—an area a little larger than the states of Massachusetts and Connecticut combined. It lies about 100 miles off the coast of China, between 21° and 26° north latitude; hence its climate is tropical. Taiwan was under Japanese control from the end of the Sino-Japanese War (1894–95) until the end of World War II. After 1900 the Japanese developed Taiwan's economy as an integral part of that of the Japanese Empire. (See Map 5.)

POPULATION

In 1898 the Japanese estimate of Taiwan's population was 2.6 million. The 1905 census showed a population of 3.0 million—an increase, in seven years, of approximately 400,000, or 15.2 per cent. This increase may be somewhat exaggerated because of an underestimate of the population in 1898. The registration of births and deaths shows that during the period 1906–10 the natural increase was only 8.3 per 1,000, that during 1911–15 it rose to 14.3 per 1,000, and that in 1916–20 it fell to only 9.4 per 1,000 (29, p. 241) (Table 26). These registration data are probably more deficient regarding births than deaths, hence it is probable that the actual rate of natural increase in these years was somewhat higher than the above rates indicate. However, one may very legitimately doubt that the rate of increase in 1898–1905 exceeded 2 per cent per year.

As the registration of births and deaths became more adequate the birth rate showed some increase, probably due to more complete registration, and rose to 45.0 in 1926–30. It did not fall below this level until 1941–43 and 1948–50, and these lower rates may very well have been due to the deterioration of registration in the later years of Japanese

361

control and in the early years of the Nationalist Government. Since 1951 the birth rate has been the highest ever recorded.

I have long regarded the Taiwanese vital statistics which were collected under the Japanese administration after about 1905 as the best data available for any large Chinese population. Most other such data relate to only a few thousands or tens of thousands of people, to short periods of time, and have been gathered under handicaps inevitable in such occasional studies. There is no good reason to believe that the 1905 census (3 million) was in serious error, and the 1940 census (the last census taken under Japanese control) was almost certainly a good

TABLE 26

CRUDE BIRTH AND DEATH RATES AND
RATES OF NATURAL INCREASE,
TAIWAN, 1906–55*

Years	Birth Rate	Death Rate	Natural Increase
1951–55.......	46.3	9.5	36.8
1948–50.......	41.5	12.9	28.6
1941–43.......	42.1	18.5	23.6
1936–40.......	45.4	20.6	24.8
1931–35.......	46.0	21.2	24.8
1926–30.......	45.0	22.1	22.9
1921–25.......	42.8	25.0	17.8
1916–20.......	40.4	31.0	9.4
1911–15.......	42.9	28.6	14.3
1906–10.......	41.7	33.4	8.3

* Source: 293, 1956, pp. 617, 639; 29, p. 24.

census. This 1940 census showed a population of almost 6 million. Thus this Chinese population doubled in thirty-five years, indicating that between 1905 and 1940 the *average* rate of annual growth was about 2 per cent. The rate of increase averaged lower than this between 1905 and 1925, but rose substantially above 2 per cent between 1925 and 1940 (see Table 26).

The most important reason for the difference between these two periods is that before 1925 the death rate, although it had declined somewhat, remained relatively high, averaging well over 30 per 1,000 until 1920; it declined to 25 only in the period 1921–25 as health work became better organized. After that it fell steadily, to 20.6 in 1936–40 and to 18.5 in 1941–43. Since the war Taiwan has joined Japan, Ceylon, and Malaya in establishing new lows for death rates among the Asian peoples. In the last three years for which data are available it averaged only 8.7 per 1,000. Furthermore, there is no evidence as yet of any decline in the birth rate in Taiwan. Since 1951 the lowest natural increase has been 35.8 per 1,000, and the average for 1951–55 was 36.8—a rate which, if it continues, will double the population in twenty-two to twenty-three years. Some of the total increase in population since 1940 must be attributed to the migration of Nationalists to Taiwan, but it appears that far the greater part of the increase from about 6 million in 1940 to 9.9 million at the end of 1956 must be attributed to the excess of births over deaths in the native population (see Table 27).

TABLE 27

POPULATION AND PER CENT CHANGE,
TAIWAN, 1898–1956*

Year	Population	Per Cent Change
1956............	9,863,000	31.9
1950............	7,477,000	19.3
1944............	6,269,949	6.8
1940............	5,872,084	12.7
1935............	5,212,426	13.5
1930............	4,592,537	15.0
1925............	3,993,408	9.2
1920............	3,655,308	5.0
1915............	3,479,922	14.5
1905............	3,039,751	10.5
1900............	2,750,511	5.2
1898............	2,613,433	....

* Source: 1950–56 from 293, 1956, pp. 143, 156, 157; 1905–44 from 267, pp. 2, 3, 27, 157; 1898–1900 from 156, p. 31 (aboriginal savages excepted).

Nothing definite can be said about the future growth of Taiwan's population, of course, but since there is no evidence of any decline in the birth rate it appears likely that the rate of growth, during the next two or three decades at least, will be in the neighborhood of 3 per cent per year, provided the necessities of life can be supplied in about the present per capita amounts. Can Taiwan support a population which by 1980 is quite likely to number about 18 million? Let us look at some other data which will help us assess the situation more intelligently. (See Maps 4 and 5.)

AGRICULTURE

Early in their administration, the Japanese began to organize Taiwan's economy so that it would contribute as much as possible to the economic strength of Japan. As it affected agriculture, this program meant that Japan was interested chiefly in securing imports which would add to her own food supply, both in quantity and quality.

It was officially estimated before the war that because of Taiwan's mountainous character not much over one-fourth of the total area could be tilled (114, p. 43) and that about 24 per cent was already being cultivated. If these estimates were reasonably accurate, there was little basis for expecting much increase in agricultural production from an increase in the tilled area. The estimates of possible increase in crop area varied from about 100,000 acres (114, p. 44) to about 250,000 acres (205). It would appear that the increase in tilled land from 1904 (1,545,000 acres) to 1938 (2,120,000 acres), which amounted to about 37 per cent, had practically exhausted the new land available (114, p. 42). (For rainfall in Taiwan see Maps 2, 3*a*, and 3*b*.)

The area planted to rice increased by about 37 per cent in the twenty-five years between 1910–15 and 1935–39. This extension of the rice area in the prewar years, coupled with improvements resulting from better varieties of seed, the use of more fertilizer, and better tillage practices, more than doubled the production of rice—from an average of 595,000 metric tons of cleaned rice in 1910–1915 to 1,242,000 tons in 1935–40 (340, pp. 316–17). The increase in yield amounted to about 54 per cent. The net exports of cleaned rice from Taiwan increased from an average of 86,000 metric tons in 1910–15 to 621,000 tons in 1935–38. Since the population increased by almost 90 per cent between 1910 and 1940, and since the cleaned rice available to the people of Taiwan increased only from 509,000 tons to 621,000 tons, it is clear that the amount of rice available per capita declined greatly during this time—from approximately 350 pounds per capita per year to 227 pounds. In 1955 the paddy production amounted to 490 pounds per person, or about 343 pounds of cleaned rice—not quite as much as it had been in 1910–15. The export of rice reduces this somewhat, although export no longer takes any considerable part of the total crop.

In 1955 approximately 2,157,000 acres were classed as arable and under tree crops (111, 1956, Part 1, p. 5), a gain of only about 37,000 acres over 1938 in total tilled land, but the area under rice increased from about 1,646,000 acres in 1931–37 to 1,856,000 acres in 1955 (*ibid.*, p. 46). The yield of paddy is reported to have increased from 36.5 bushels per acre in 1931–37 to 39.7 bushels in 1955; these figures would be reduced to about 22.6 and 24.6 bushels, respectively, of cleaned rice, on the basis that cleaned rice amounts to only 62 per cent of the paddy. It would appear, therefore, that there has been an increase of only about 10 per cent in the yield of rice per acre in the last twenty years, assuming that 1955 was a normal year. Actually, this increase of 2 bushels per acre may very well have been due chiefly to the difference in the seasons, since 1955 was an unusually good year in both Japan and China and probably Taiwan also, although no specific statement to that effect has been found. Since very little additional land can be brought into tillage, practically all future gains in total agricultural production must come from improvements in yields. This will not be easy for Taiwan to achieve. Even if Taiwan were able to equal, in the next twenty to twenty-five years, Japan's very best recent yields of rice (50 bushels of cleaned rice per acre), this would only double Taiwan's total production and would only keep pace with the probable increase in her population.

Other crops, as well as livestock, which provide a large part of the proteins in the Taiwanese diet, are already in short supply, and will be desperately needed before twenty years have passed. In the immediate future some of these items will be supplied by gift, but over the longer run they can only be obtained if Taiwan can increase the amount of industrial products she can trade for food, for it is not reasonable to expect that Taiwan can increase her agricultural exports to any appreciable extent. She already exports almost 90 per cent of the sugar produced, most of the pineapples and bananas, and a little rice. These exports are more likely to decline both proportionally and in absolute amount, than to increase, in the course of the next two or three decades.

Taiwan's whole agricultural situation is summed up in the indexes of the FAO (*ibid.*, p. 26). They show the production in 1955 as compared with prewar years. The index for total food production rose to 131 in 1955–56, that is, by 31 per cent since before the war, while the index for total agricultural production rose to 134. At the same time, the population index rose from 100 in 1935–40 to 159 in 1955. Again the point should be emphasized that any future increase in agricultural production must come from increased yields per acre, which become harder and harder to achieve as agriculture reaches higher levels of efficiency. The yields of chief crops of Taiwan are already far above those of most Asian countries.

INDUSTRY

The modern industry developed in Taiwan under Japanese control consisted largely of the processing of agricultural products for export

—sugar refining, rice cleaning and polishing, pineapple canning—and the construction of machine shops, power plants, railways, and harbor facilities essential to the operation of an efficient colonial economy. Taiwan possesses very little mineral wealth, which is not surprising in view of the small area, but the mines and refineries required power and modern machine services. Coal is the most important of Taiwan's minerals and appears to be adequate to the needs of the island for several decades. Like most of the countries of Asia, however, India and China probably excepted, Taiwan seems to lack bituminous coal for coking, as well as iron ore of good quality in workable deposits. There is some petroleum, some sulphur, and some pyrites and copper. But these minerals are not sufficient to support any considerable labor force in mining them, refining them, or using them in the production of consumers' goods (283, *passim;* also 317, Part 1, No. 55-90, *passim*).

Taiwan's industries must necessarily be confined largely to the production for local consumption of goods and services which can use domestic agricultural products as raw materials, or imported raw materials, like cotton, the price of which is small in relation to the price of the finished product. This does not mean that Taiwan will have no foreign trade, even if she remains an isolated political unit. It does mean, however, that Taiwan has no special advantages which will enable her to export any considerable volume of manufactured goods in competition with Japan, China, India, or other Asian countries. For example, there has been a remarkable development in cotton spinning and weaving in Taiwan since the war, a development based on the movement of private enterprises from the mainland similar to the movement from the mainland to Hong Kong. But since Taiwan, like Japan, must import the raw materials for this industry, and since it is unlikely that Taiwan's cotton mills will be as efficient as Japan's for some years, at least until her managers and workmen have gained more experience, and since even now Taiwan must compete with the mills of India and Pakistan for export trade, it seems unlikely that Taiwan can support any large number of workers by her textile exports. The metal and machinery industries have also expanded rapidly since the war, but they have been fostered to a large extent by United States aid, and in any case, they principally serve the army and a small local market. Their further development, like that of the textile mills, would seem to be limited.

The manufacture of cement, for which the raw materials are present in most countries, can no doubt expand considerably in Taiwan, and cement will probably be used widely to economize on the use of steel; but again, Taiwan's export of cement is likely to be small. Taiwan will need rapidly increasing amounts of fertilizer to improve her agricultural production, but the manufacture of fertilizers will not add much employment, and the raw materials will have to be imported.

If Taiwan is considered as an isolated economic unit, there is only one possible conclusion regarding her economic future. She cannot reasonably hope to maintain even her present per capita income for long when outside aid is withdrawn. (At present, living standards in Taiwan are better than in most Asian countries.) Taiwan would find it difficult to maintain this status even if the population were to increase slowly, let us say 1 per cent per year instead of about 3 per cent. It is not at all unlikely that within fifteen to twenty years the death rate will begin to rise sharply, simply because the necessities of life cannot be supplied in amounts sufficient to maintain health. Such economic conditions will furnish fertile ground for a political upheaval, which is almost certain to invite intervention from the mainland, and might lead to a large-scale war.

KOREA

As a colony of Japan before World War II, Korea had an area of 85,000 square miles. It lay approximately between latitudes 34° and 43° north. This would correspond to the latitude of Charleston, South Carolina, on the south, and on the north would reach to about fifty miles above Boston. The climate of Korea, and particularly of the present South Korea, is considerably modified by the country's peninsular position. South Korea, the portion lying south of latitude 38° north, contains about 37,400 square miles. This leaves North Korea, the portion north of the 38th parallel, with about 47,600 square miles (111, 1956, Part 1, p. 5).[1] (See Map 5.)

POPULATION

The 1920 population of prewar Korea was estimated as 16.0 million. There was a very rapid growth between 1920 and 1925 (2.9 per cent

[1] There seems to be considerable disagreement about the exact size of South Korea at the present time. Another publication of the United Nations (293, 1956, p. 144) gives the area as 36,152 square miles; McCune (181, p. 9) gives it as 41,654 square miles; and the United States Department of Commerce (317, Part 1, No. 56-64, p. 1) gives the area as 38,000 square miles. These uncertainties probably arose partly from the vagueness of the "truce line." The figure for North Korea generally seems to be arrived at by subtracting the area of South Korea from 85,000. For South Korea a round figure of 38,000 square miles will be used here.

per year)—so rapid, in fact, for those days when modern health work was only well begun even in the most advanced Western countries, as to make it seem probable that a part of this increase was due to an underestimate of the population in 1920 as compared with a more complete enumeration in 1925 (see Table 28). From 1925 until 1944 the annual rate of growth averaged about 1.33 per cent per year, or 13.3 per 1,000, and the total population reached 25.1 million. If an increase of 1.33 per cent per year had continued until 1949, the total population would have been approximately 26.8 million at the end of that year.

TABLE 28

POPULATION (IN THOUSANDS) AND PER CENT
CHANGE, KOREA, 1910–53*

Year	Population	Per Cent Change
1953	30,000	2.4
1949	29,291	16.7
1944	25,120	3.3
1940	24,326	6.2
1935	22,899	8.7
1930	21,058	7.9
1925	19,523	15.4
1920	16,916	3.9
1915	16,278	22.3
1910	13,313	. . . .

* Source: 1949–53 from 293, 1956, p. 159; other years,
115, pp. 72–73, 76–77. Prewar area.

The United Nations (293, 1956, p. 159) estimated the total population of Korea in 1949 at 29,291,000. This was an increase of almost 4.2 million in five years, or 16.7 per cent, a rate of growth of over 3 per cent per year during the greatly disturbed postwar years. It is larger in absolute numbers by about 2.5 million than the figure which a natural increase of 1.33 per cent per year would produce. Most of this difference is to be accounted for by the repatriation of Koreans after the war. The United States Military Government in Korea reported a total of almost 2.1 million Koreans entering South Korea from October, 1945, to April, 1948. There may also have been some repatriates from North Korea, Manchuria, and the Soviet Far East who did not pass through the regular refugee entry stations along the northern border (the 38th parallel) (167, p. 25). Hence, it seems reasonable to assume that the population of all Korea was in the vicinity of 29–29.5 million at the end of 1949. (For the distribution of Korea's population see Map 4.)

On May 1, 1949, South Korea took a census which showed a population of 20.2 million. If the population of the whole of Korea was 29.3 million at that time, the population of North Korea must have been approximately 9 million. On March 31, 1952, an almost complete census was again taken in South Korea (167, p. 21), which found a population, not including military personnel, of 20.5 million. The United Nations estimate for 1952 is 21.2 million (293, 1956, p. 159); this may include military personnel, although this is not clear. A United Nations estimate for the whole of Korea in 1953 was 30.0 million, and one for South Korea was 21.4 million. This leaves the population of North Korea at about 8.6 million, or somewhat less than it had been in 1949. The data available make it impossible to be more precise regarding the total population of Korea and its distribution between South and North Korea. It is not possible to reconcile the above figures, which would justify an estimate of about 9 million in North Korea in 1956, with the North Korean estimate of 12 million in that year (102, June, 1956, p. 90; see also below).

If the *actual* increase in Korea's population between 1925 and 1940 averaged about 1.33 per cent per year, which seems fairly well established by the censuses, the *natural* increase must certainly have been somewhat higher. The net outward migration to Japan, Manchuria, the Soviet Far East, and China must have been substantial to permit the return of over 2.1 million to South Korea after the war. The natural increase may very well have averaged 1.6 to 1.7 per cent each year. This figure is considerably higher than the difference between the birth rates and the death rates shown by the registration figures gathered under the Japanese administration after 1925, but it accords better with the results of the four censuses taken 1925–1940 and the known emigration. Furthermore, some of this discrepancy between the registration data on births and deaths and the censuses may very well be the result of greater deficiency in the registration of births than of deaths.

Registration data are lacking for the years since 1945. The United Nations (293) gives no birth or death rates except for 1948, and these are manifestly highly deficient. The official Handbook of Korea (1955) contains the statement, "In 1948, a census proved that the birth rate was 1.83 percent and the death rate 0.93 percent, thus lowering the rate of natural increase to 0.92 percent" (167, p. 27). Even if the slight error in subtraction, or in printing, is overlooked, judgment on this statement must be reserved. Such a low birth rate (18.3 per 1,000) for a people still largely agricultural—even allowing for great hardships following the war—seems incredible in the absence of better evidence. Moreover, the assumption of great hardships from 1945 to 1948 makes the death rate of 9.3 per 1,000 even more incredible.

The only thing that can be said with any certainty about Korea's population growth is that it was fairly rapid from the time Japan took control in 1910 until about 1949.

In 1949 South Korea, with 20.2 million people on 38,000 square miles, had a density of about 530 per square mile, or 1.2 acres per person. On the basis of the 1955 census (293, 1956, p. 144) the density would have been about 570 per square mile, or 1.1 acres per person. This is a very dense population for a country in which only about one-fourth of the land is considered tillable because of the mountainous terrain. If the population of North Korea in 1949 was 9.0 million on an area of 47,000 square miles, its density was only about 190 per square mile. (See Map 5.)

If South Korea's population grew from 20.2 million at the end of 1949 to 21.5 million in September, 1955 (about 5.7 years), the rate of growth averaged about 1.1 per cent per year. This period, which included the Korean war, was a time of unusual hardship during which the death rate must have been quite high. A death rate of 14–16 would be low for such a period. Assuming a death rate of 15, the birth rate would have been 26. Such rates seem more likely to be too low than too high, but that there was a difference between them (natural increase) of about 11 per 1,000 of the population even during this period of stress does not seem unreasonable. If the natural increase in South Korea was 11 per 1,000 at such a time, it has almost certainly risen by several points as rehabilitation has taken place and health services have become more efficient. I find myself quite unable to believe that South Korea's birth rate today is not higher than our own (about 25) or that her death rate has not averaged more than two or three points above ours (about 9.5 to 10). As a guess, and assuming that there is not another war in the near future, it would seem reasonable to expect that South Korea's rate of growth will be in the range of 1.2 per cent to 1.5 per cent per year for the next decade at least, and that her population will be in the vicinity of 26–28 million by 1970.

There do not appear to be any data relating to the growth of population in North Korea. The estimate of 12 million in 1956 is much too high, unless the population was about 10.5 million in 1949 instead of 9 million. The latter figure appears the more reasonable estimate, unless there has been a net immigration of perhaps 1.5 million since that time.

There are no data regarding the rate of growth in North Korea on which to base any more precise statement than that North Korea's rate of natural increase is probably in the same range as South Korea's, about 11–13 per 1,000 per year. Like that of South Korea it will probably rise somewhat for several years if there is no war.

AGRICULTURE

South Korea is still chiefly an agricultural country. In 1949 the farm population constituted 71.48 per cent of the total population (109, p. 78). In the census of March 31, 1952, the males engaged in agriculture constituted 64.3 per cent of all males reporting occupations, and the females engaged in agriculture constituted 72.6 per cent of all the females reporting occupations. Over 90 per cent as many females as males were engaged in agriculture (167, pp. 29–30). The farms in South Korea are very small. In 1949 there were 2.47 million farm households, and only 5.07 million acres of land in use—slightly over 2 acres per farm household (109, pp. 77–79). The planted land, however, amounted to 7.1 million acres, or 2.9 acres per household; this difference is due to the fact that about 40 per cent of the land in use was double-cropped. Before the war about 5.6 million acres were in use, and almost one-half of this was double-cropped. Thus the acres planted at that time amounted to about 8.3 million. As late as 1953 the area planted was only 6.7 million acres. South Korea still had a long way to go to attain her prewar level of planting. Moreover, yields had also declined.

Before the war the yield of rice in the whole of Korea had risen steadily, except in bad crop years. In 1940 the index for yield was 170, (1910 = 100), but by 1945 it had fallen to 158. It seems probable that the situation in South Korea is reflected with fair accuracy in these figures, since about two-thirds of prewar Korea's rice was grown in South Korea. Yields of barley, second only to rice in importance (over 90 per cent of the barley is grown in South Korea), did not increase nearly as much as those of rice; nor was the increase consistent enough to eliminate the probability that the increases of 10–20 per cent which took place in some years were due to more favorable weather rather than to better farming. There is some question whether the yields of wheat and soybeans increased between 1910 and 1940, but there is no doubt that the postwar yields of these crops were below prewar yields (167, pp. 140–41).

The food production situation in South Korea may be summed up briefly by a few figures from the United Nations Mission (1953) to that country. In the five years 1937–41 South Korea produced an average of 3,956,000 metric tons of grains, pulses, and potatoes, on a planted food crop area averaging 7.2 million acres. This amounted to slightly over 1,200 pounds per acre. In the five years 1949–53 the average total production of the same crops was 2,953,000 metric tons, or a little over 1,100 pounds per acre (109, p. 85). This is a decline of about one-fourth in the total production, and of 8 to 9 per cent in the average yield, of the principal food crops in South Korea; this decline took place at a time when the repatriation of Koreans from abroad and the influx of refugees from North Korea swelled the population from 16.3 million in April, 1946, to 20.9 million in April, 1948 (109, p. 80). This estimate for 1948 is probably somewhat too high, possibly by 800,000 to 700,000, if the results of the censuses of 1949 and 1952 are accepted.

When the United Nations Mission was in Korea (1953), it estimated that future production of the principal crops (grains, pulses, and potatoes) in South Korea would increase from 2,960,000 metric tons in 1953 to 5,094,000 tons in 1958. These estimates assumed (a) that adequate supplies of fertilizers would be available; (b) that all irrigation systems would be repaired by 1954 and that an additional 86,000 acres of paddy (rice) would be fully irrigated each year; (c) that an additional 37,000 acres of hillside land would be added to the cultivated area each year; and (d) that adequate technical and material aid for rehabilitation would be supplied by the United Nations (109, pp. 81, 82, 85). The latest data available in the FAO Yearbook (111, 1956) indicate that there has been sufficient improvement since the Mission's report to make possible the reduction of food imports. However, the data are unsatisfactory, and a firm judgment of accomplishment will have to be postponed.

As for the immediate outlook, the Mission said that "barring extraordinary destructive events, South Korea could be self-sufficient in food beginning with the Food Year 1956" (109, p. 84). It was felt that favorable weather and adequate fertilizer might make this possible sooner. In the longer view, "it is the opinion of this Mission that in addition to continued improvements in production technics the Korean diet must absorb more and more starches from potatoes, both sweet and white, and less from grains. . . . It is realized that this will necessitate a great deal of education work and the development of better storage and processing facilities for potatoes" (*ibid.*). Clearly, this outlook is discouraging. Population is increasing by perhaps 1.2 to 1.5 per cent per year, and the limit of increase in the tilled area has almost been reached. Of a total of 24.3 million acres in South Korea, only 5.6 million are considered tillable (317, Part 1, No. 56-54, p. 4). If 50 per cent of this tillable land could be double-cropped, the total crop acres would amount to only 8.4 million, or only 0.39 of an acre per person on the basis of the 1955 population. On the basis of 26 million people in 1970, the per capita area would fall to 0.32 of an acre. There is a strong probability that it will be somewhat less. A very large increase in crop yields will be needed to provide even a modest improvement in diet through domestic production.

Much less information is available about North Korea's agriculture. In 1944 North Korea produced only 36 per cent of the rice and less than 7 per cent of the barley, but the larger part (56 per cent) of the wheat, a still larger proportion (over 70 per cent) of the millets and sorghums, and two-thirds to three-fourths of the several types of beans. Its agriculture must have been severely disorganized during World War II, and was disturbed still more by the Korean war (1950–53). The sown area in 1946 was about 4.6 million acres, and it increased to 5.7 million acres in 1949 (102, 1956, p. 87). It decreased again as a result of the Korean war; whether it has yet regained the 1949 level is not clear. In 1954 North Korea's reported grain production was not as high as in 1949.

It appears probable that agricultural rehabilitation in North Korea has been sacrificed to industrial rehabilitation. Furthermore, the collectivization of agriculture has been forced, while only a few state farms have been established. The absence of reliable data on food production and on population makes it impossible to say with certainty what the present food situation is, but the few unsatisfactory data available indicate that it has worsened. Even if it has worsened, the North Koreans may be somewhat better off than the South Koreans, and their food prospects may also be somewhat better.

INDUSTRY

Some nonagricultural industry was developed in Korea while the country was under Japanese control. The Japanese developed Korean industry as they did Manchurian industry, to help make the Japanese Empire a self-sufficient economic unit. Just as the improvement in Korean agriculture was promoted by the Japanese to strengthen their own economy, Korea's industry was developed along lines which would make Japanese industry stronger. The benefits to Korea were substantial, but they were only incidental to her development as a colony. As a consequence, the Korean economy was rather one-sided and unbalanced, and was highly dependent on the economy of Japan. Very little can be said here about Korea's industry, but because of partition it will be well to note briefly the differences in industrial development between South Korea and North Korea.

South Korea has many kinds of minerals, but deposits are small, and the quality of many of them leaves much to be desired. Anthracite coal deposits are estimated at about 615 million tons, and lignite deposits at 80 million tons (283, p. 177). Although these coal deposits are of poor quality, they are South Korea's most important mineral resource. There is no bituminous coal suitable for coking. Coke or coking coal needed for metallurgical work must be imported. Other fairly important minerals are graphite and tungsten. All the important iron ore deposits and most of the hydroelectric potential are found in North Korea.

South Korea, therefore, has no mineral base for the development of heavy industry. As a consequence the industry of South Korea is likely to remain in the "light" class, consisting largely of consumers' goods—cotton textiles, paper and paper products, rubber and canvas shoes, soap, cigarettes, etc. Her industry will include, of course, the production of such building materials as cement, brick, and tiles. If fertilizer for agriculture is produced in South Korea, the raw materials will have to be imported. The few steel products being made are light and simple in construction, bicycles being about the most complex. The vast majority of the manufactured goods South Korea uses is still made in the villages. A growing group of service industries have workshops with power-driven machinery, and have some of the characteristics of factories. The raw materials for practically all such industries—cotton, rubber, steel sheets and shapes, the ingredients for fertilizers—have been imported. Even most of the salt used in Korea in the past came from what is now North Korea.

Since liberation (1945), the political uncertainties, the absence of trade with Japan, and, above all, civil war and a large influx of repatriates have discouraged and retarded the rehabilitation of the few industries that did exist. Besides, the poverty of the country is so great that there is little market for consumers' goods beyond the bare necessities of life, while the defense establishment absorbs so large a part of the government's resources that only very small funds, aside from those supplied by the United States and the United Nations, have been available for rehabilitating either agriculture or industry. Finally, the government appears to have done little to encourage private investment either by Koreans or by foreigners. It seems to prefer public ownership and operation, although it has very scanty means to invest.

On the other hand, with help from the United States and the United Nations, the transportation system is being rehabilitated, and funds have been allocated for new power facilities.

Korea's exports are still very small; in 1955 they were sufficient to pay for only one-fifth to one-fourth of her imports. Aid from the United States makes up most of the difference. In the course of time, South Korea can produce increasing amounts of many types of the goods she now imports, such as textiles, paper, some chemicals, and tools. But the manufacture of most of these goods in even moderate volume will require her to import considerable amounts of raw materials for an indefinite period of time. At the present rate of progress, it will almost certainly be several years before South Korea can supply herself with even the small amounts of consumption goods now being used, and to do even this she will have to increase her exports considerably; and these exports must necessarily consist largely of agricultural products, for which there is little land to spare.

In the meantime the population continues to increase, although not so rapidly as in several of the other Asian countries. As yet the leaders of South Korea do not seem to recognize any connection between continued population growth and the difficulties involved in economic improvement. Under these circumstances the rather gloomy conclusions of the United Nations Mission concerning South Korea's food supply would seem to apply also to the country's prospects for economic improvement through industrialization. Indeed, if outside aid were withdrawn during the next several years—perhaps within the next decade—economic conditions would almost certainly deteriorate, and this would lead to such political instability and insecurity that an authoritarian government, even one imposed from without, might be welcomed by many of the people.

When the whole of Korea was under Japanese control, basic industry and power were developed where it was easiest to do so. Largely because most of the usable mineral and water power resources were found in the northern part of the country, most industrial investment took place there. Like South Korea, North Korea lacks bituminous coal suitable for coking, but she does have much larger amounts of anthracite and lignite than South Korea. North Korea also has rather large deposits of iron ore, those of the Musan area in the northeastern part of the country being estimated at 1,200 million tons. There are also other smaller deposits which the Japanese were in the process of exploiting. There is some copper, but it is mostly of poor quality and rather costly to mine and refine. Graphite and tungsten are also found. Lead, zinc, and manganese were mined in considerable quantities during the war, when costs were less important than production. However, most of these ores are of poor quality, and metal can be produced from them only at prices which are well above world prices. This is true also of the alunite deposits that might be used for the production of aluminum. Before the war the Japanese had developed rather extensive plants for refining most of these minerals, particularly for the use of the better iron ores in small blast furnaces and for the beneficiation of lower-grade ores for export to the refineries and mills of Japan (181, pp. 219–23). North Korea's hydroelectric potential—about 5.9 million kilowatts—is estimated to be about 86 per cent of all such power in Korea (181, pp. 223–24).

The industrial areas under Japanese control lay in the northeast and along the northwest coast. Since the industries were largely confined to the mining and preparing of minerals for shipment to Japan as raw materials, comparatively few finished goods were manufactured in Korea. However, even this preparatory treatment of minerals necessitated the establishment of workshops for repairing and maintaining industrial equipment and for producing certain types of machinery, tools, and other metal products. By 1944, factories or shops engaged in metalworking and in the making of machinery and tools employed over 125,000 workers, and chemical plants employed about 70,000. Both these types of production were located chiefly in North Korea. Together they employed over twice as many workers (81,000) as did the South Korean textile plants (181, p. 225). Other light consumption industries were also located chiefly in South Korea. This industrial development required, of course, considerable development of transportation facilities—railroads, harbors, and some highways.

Independence quite naturally made much of North Korea's industrial capacity useless for the time being because it was organized so largely for the purpose of supplying both raw and semimanufactured materials to Japanese industry. Besides, some of the installations, like those in Manchuria, appear to have been dismantled by the Russians. In any event, whatever was left of North Korean industry after independence, and whatever had been rehabilitated by mid-1950, was pretty thoroughly destroyed in the Korean war.

Shabad's review of North Korea's postwar recovery (102, 1956, pp. 81–91) makes available such information as the communist government has seen fit to supply regarding the rehabilitation of North Korea's economy since 1953. Only a very brief statement of what he found can be given here.

In general, the goal set by the Three-Year Plan was to restore industrial production to 1949 levels by 1956. Official pronouncements claim that this goal was substantially attained, although they admit certain types of production were behind schedule. Electric power production in 1955 was only a little over one-half that of 1949, and the plan called for only 64 per cent restoration by 1956. There probably was no great urgency to increase power production more rapidly, since no power was to be exported to South Korea; before 1948 much of the electric power used in South Korea was generated in North Korea. Coal production in 1955 was only about 60 per cent as great as it had been in 1944, but it was about 83 per cent of what it had been in 1949. Clear evidence concerning the production of nonferrous metals is lacking, and it is almost certain that the goal of 180 per cent of 1949 production was far from being attained. Output of pig iron is said to have been resumed in 1955, but no figures are given regarding actual production. Some steel ingots were produced in 1955, but the statement regarding the amount produced and rolled is so vague that it leaves one wondering whether all of this production did not come from the use of scrap iron, which could be rather quickly resumed on a small scale.

The output of the machinery industry is expressed in monetary units, and also leaves one speculating what the production actually was in 1955 or 1956. Fertilizer production in 1955 was certainly only a tiny fraction of the 403,000 tons produced in 1949, and even the production planned for 1956 was only about one-fifth of the 1949 amount. Cement production in 1955 was said to be 67 per cent of the 1949 amount, and was to be increased to 121 per cent of the 1949 production in 1956. Brick production was reported as twelve times as large in 1955 as it had been in 1949, and was expected to increase by another 40 per cent in 1956 (*ibid.*, pp. 81–91). The railways were said to have been quite fully restored by 1955, although locomotive stock was still so deficient that tonnage moved must have been quite small.

These data on North Korea's industrial recovery leave the impression that rehabilitation efforts had been only partially successful up to 1956 and that the greatest achievements were made in the public services— electricity and transportation—for which there is a reasonably certain market. The production of building materials, such as bricks and cement, also seems to have made rapid progress. Industries that must function as part of an integrated industrial economy in order to operate at all have made less progress because the ancillary facilities which use their products have not yet been restored or developed. Before the war, Korean metal production—both of ferrous and nonferrous metals—found a ready market as an integrated part of the Japanese economy. Today North Korea cannot use her semimanufactured products in any considerable amount at home until her own economy develops the mills and factories to make them into finished products. If trade with Japan were resumed, or if China were to purchase these semimanufactured products, North Korea's heavy industries might be made more productive rather quickly.

Although North Korea has received considerable help from the Soviet Union and its satellites and from China, she has little capital of her own to put into any type of economic development. North Korea also lacks personnel competent to restore quickly the plants that have been destroyed, to say nothing of the trained and experienced people needed to plan, organize, and build the plants and mills which would use North Korea's raw materials and semimanufactured goods. It will take North Korea some years to do this.

Because her mineral resources are fairly adequate and because the exploitation of these resources had already made such progress under Japanese leadership, North Korea appears to be in a much better position than South Korea for developing some basic heavy industry. Even considering the destruction of most of the industrial plants, it cannot be said that North Korea is starting from scratch to the same extent as is South Korea, although the Korean Communists, like the Chinese, would like the world to believe that they have made extraordinary progress. They are probably even more anxious, however, to make their own people believe that Japan was chiefly responsible for the slow industrial development of Korea in the two or three decades preceding World War II. The fact is that North Korea actually has a number of experienced workmen and supervisors who were trained by the Japanese in the extraction and the partial refining of certain metals. Furthermore, the power facilities built by the Japanese only need to be restored, not planned anew.

The land-man ratio seems to be more favorable for the increase of agricultural production in North Korea than in South Korea. How long this will remain true no one can know. If North Korea's population is now 12 million, as is claimed, and if it is increasing more rapidly than that of South Korea, population pressure will soon make the difficulties of economic improvement much greater than they are at present. When that point is reached, it is not improbable that North Korea will become a satellite of China, much as Poland, Czechoslovakia, and Hungary are satellites of the Soviet Union. By that time South Korea will almost certainly be having difficulties in providing herself with adequate food and clothing and, with her scanty mineral resources and her increasingly dense population, will be in even greater economic straits than now. This situation will be made to order for the expansion of communist influence unless there is a very great reorganization of political and economic relations among the "free" nations of the world, resulting in increased opportunities for peoples like the South Koreans to make better use of their labor.

CHAPTER XVIII

POPULATION

PRESSURE

THE NATURE OF POPULATION PRESSURE

As indicated in the summaries of the several chapters, it seems to me that agricultural development in the more densely settled Asian countries will be slower than most of the leaders in these countries expect it to be, and slower than many interested outsiders, like myself, hope it will be. Under certain circumstances a slow increase in food and in other goods might be quite satisfactory; but the leaders of the independence and revolutionary movements in most of these Asian nations have taken great pains to convince as many people as possible that their poverty and distress have arisen chiefly from their exploitation by colonial masters and/or by the capitalists of all nationalities who prevented them from using national resources effectively in national development. As a consequence, some people even among the poor farmers and urban workers, beside larger numbers, especially among those with some education, have come to expect a very rapid improvement in economic conditions as the result of independence.

These people, whose expectations are unlikely to be fulfilled, will form the core of an increasingly larger group who will feel the hardships of their low level of living more keenly than ever before, even though they may actually be living at a better level. This situation will arise first in those countries which are now densely settled and which possess little new land to accommodate an increase in the agricultural population. In the countries still containing a relative abundance of tillable but unused land, this feeling of increasing hardship and poverty can be largely avoided, provided effective efforts are made to settle young farmers on new land which is given or sold to them at about the cost of the improvements needed to render it usable.

The areas in which the feeling of population pressure is most likely to increase rapidly are India, China, Japan, Pakistan, South Korea, Taiwan, and the Indonesian island of Java. Since South Korea, Taiwan, and Ceylon are small countries with comparatively little military power, and since Java is part of a larger country with much unused land, these areas are not likely to try securing greater resources by force. However, the possibility of rash actions by the ruling cliques in South Korea and Taiwan should not be ignored. The general discussion of population pressure here is intended to apply chiefly to the conditions developing in the four larger countries—Japan, India, Pakistan, and China. The probable growth of population pressure in these countries has already been briefly discussed in the summaries attached to individual chapters. Our concern at this point is to describe more fully the general character of *population pressure*.

The *feeling of population pressure* has already been referred to at several points in the preceding discussion. This phrase is used because I do not believe any precise measure of population pressure is possible. The average caloric intake of food per person may be a very good measure of the dietary standards of different peoples and certainly is useful in measuring the relative poverty of peoples; the average per capita consumption of goods and services, both agricultural and non-agricultural, may be a satisfactory measure of the level of living of a people. But the absolute level of consumption does not determine how intensely any people will feel about the inferiority of their level of living. A people must have some standard of comparison before they will be aware of their own poverty and, hence, before they will feel the pressure of population as a motive for supporting national action to relieve this pressure. From the standpoint of creating tensions between nations, it is not absolute poverty that provides people with the strongest motives to support political aggression but the feeling that they do not have enough land or other resources to which they can apply their labor so that *they can live as well as other peoples*. The most intense poverty often does not arouse a people's urge to do something about it even internally (by rebellion or insurrection), to say nothing of creating effective popular support for leaders who want to secure larger resources by aggression against other countries.

There are several reasons why absolute poverty often is not a strong motive for such external aggression. (1) In the poorer Asian nations, where great poverty exists, the people are largely illiterate; they live almost wholly within a very small circle, containing only a few villages, in which their manner of life is much the same as that of their neighbors. Consequently, no significant proportion of the people is aware of any differences in living conditions between themselves and people in other countries, or in other parts of the same country, e.g., in the cities. They are, of course, aware that differences exist between their way of living and that of their landlords, their government officials, and a few villagers who are in somewhat better economic circumstances. But they accept these differences because they are traditional, and only occasionally do they revolt against their local masters. They do not know about and, therefore, are not interested in national differences in levels of living.

(2) Among these poverty-stricken peoples, land is the direct source of practically all the goods they consume. Even the manufactured goods they use are for the most part made in their own village or neighboring market town and are made by hand, chiefly from local agricultural or forest products. Cotton goods are by far the most important type of manufactures made in modern factories and sold in the villages; and often these are still woven in the village, although today chiefly from factory-spun yarns. Since the villagers of the most densely populated countries have seen no unused land that could be brought into tillage by their own labor, except the customary fallows, it never occurs to them that land could be taken from some other people to enlarge their farms or to provide their sons with farms and thus insure them a better living. This attitude that nothing can be done to improve their situation is likely to endure as long as the masses know nothing about how other peoples live and about land elsewhere which is not being used.

(3) The need for resources other than land does not arise as a conscious deprivation as long as nonagricultural production is small and is confined almost entirely to the local fabrication of clothing, home utensils, and farm tools. It is only with modern industrial development that workers become aware that their jobs and improved living conditions depend on securing adequate amounts of many kinds of minerals. When this happens, it also becomes clear to increasing numbers of people that foreign commerce in many types of products is an important source of national income. This industrial and commercial development very naturally leads more and more people to a consideration of the advantages and disadvantages any given country possesses in relation to other countries.

(4) In modern times, the large poverty-stricken countries considered here have not had, until recently, strong enough governments or a large enough economic surplus to enable them to take aggressive action against other countries or even to defend themselves against such action, except when their prospective opponents were smaller, were equally poverty-stricken, or were even less able, politically and eco-

nomically, to mobilize their resources for military purposes. For example, Japan's war with China in 1895 proved to the Japanese that they were no longer too weak to attack in certain directions. As Japan's economic strength increased and her population grew, her needs, at least her *felt* needs, increased and encouraged further aggression. Since World War II, India and China have been gaining slowly in industrial strength. China has already taken military measures which most of the "free" nations consider aggressive, and Pakistan certainly classes India's actions in Kashmir as aggressive.

In several of the largest countries in the Far East there is already a scarcity of land, so that the speed with which agricultural production can be increased depends on how fast an agricultural revolution can be achieved, i.e., on the adoption of new agricultural practices. It is more difficult and takes more time to secure a given increase in total production through an agricultural revolution than it would if young farmers could migrate to land which had not previously been tilled. For nearly a century in India when new irrigation projects were opened for settlement, there has been no great difficulty in securing settlers to work this land. These projects have offered relief to a few communities, but in the area that was India in 1871 the population is now about 85 per cent larger, and the opportunity to secure new land is practically nil. I have talked with farmers in several parts of India who showed much interest in agriculture in America and who asked many pertinent questions about the crops grown, the implements used, the number of acres in a farm, etc. The point which impressed me most was their astonishment—I might almost say their incredulity—that a single farmer could have a farm of the size of the customary family farm in our corn and wheat belts and that one farmer could produce so much grain. They said they needed a little more land but would not know how to farm so much land. The real point of importance for our study, it seems to me, was that they think of the need of a little more land, perhaps an acre or two, as most important in relieving their family's economic problem. How long will it be before these same farmers will begin to think of neighboring unused lands as a possible source of relief for their poverty? Of new farms for their sons? I am not implying that the leaders of India are encouraging this attitude. I am certain they are not and that they have no intention of doing so.

In China, on the other hand, the communist ideology is fundamentally aggressive toward noncommunist peoples. There can be little doubt that if it serves the purposes of the Chinese leaders in their spread of communism, the Chinese farmers will be told that their comparative poverty is a result of being kept by "the imperialists and capitalists" from using land in areas where the population is sparse and that it is their duty to seize this land whenever possible.

It seems inevitable that the peoples in these more crowded countries will become increasingly aware of their comparative poverty. Where this feeling of pressure is encouraged by their governments, its growth will be more rapid than elsewhere, but this deliberate encouragement will not be the primary cause of its growth. This growth is an unavoidable effect of these poverty-stricken peoples coming into contact with a larger world which lives differently. I believe, therefore, that the feeling of population pressure, which may also be thought of as a particular variety of the principle of "relative deprivation," will grow rather rapidly among the peoples of South and East Asia. I also believe that this increased feeling of pressure will create new tensions between nations and that these tensions may lead to aggression, although the form of aggression in some cases may be quite different from that in the past.

A REVIEW OF THE PRINCIPAL MEASURES FOR THE
RELIEF OF POPULATION PRESSURE

The situation regarding the relation between population growth and obtaining a livelihood in South and East Asia is by no means new in human experience. There are, of course, distinctive features in the situation in Asia today which make it different from that with which Malthus (1798) was principally concerned. But the problem of the relief of population pressure, or *the abolition of national poverty*, if one prefers that way of stating our problem today, remains with us. I will consider rather briefly in this chapter several of the more significant measures that have been suggested and discussed over the years for the relief of population pressures, with emphasis on their applicability to the region with which we are particularly concerned.

World population and world food supply.—There has been much discussion of world population and world food supply in the past several years. Two diametrically opposed conclusions regarding the seriousness of the world's food problems have been drawn from considering this problem in terms of world production. There have been those who concluded that when all the factors were taken into account—the amount and quality of the new land available, the determining climatic factors, the erosion losses, the probable increases in yields, etc.—there was no chance that man could produce enough to insure himself a decent living for any considerable period. In contrast, there have been those who believed that there was much more new land available, that the possibilities of increasing production through scientific agriculture were also much greater, and that soil erosion could be arrested rather quickly and cheaply. Such people quite naturally concluded that there was no serious danger of world food shortage in the foreseeable future. My position is that these world approaches are unrealistic and that the real food problems and the real problems of population pressure today are primarily national problems.

But the statement that the food problems of Japan, India, China, etc., are chiefly national does not mean that the world at large need not concern itself with them. These particular problems are highly important to the world as a whole in a number of respects, and a world organization which made international co-operation in economic and political matters easier would be of great value. Nevertheless, the food problems of each country must be solved in large measure by each country working with its own resources. I believe that even if it were possible to show positively that the conclusions of the second group referred to above were valid—that there is no need to be concerned over the possibilities of world food production for a long time to come —such a demonstration would be largely irrelevant to the solution of the practical problems these Asian countries face as they attempt to provide their growing populations with a more abundant and nutritious food supply.

The food problems these countries are trying to solve today are practical problems of the utmost importance. It is of no use to talk of the possibilities of increasing world food production by 50 per cent or 100 per cent under conditions which are relatively ideal but which everyone knows are not likely to materialize within any foreseeable future. Such speculations and calculations contribute nothing to the practical solution of the food problems of the Far East. They are only of theoretical interest in our world today, and will remain so for as long as can be foreseen.

Furthermore, quite aside from the fact that it will take at least several decades to secure the adoption of scientific agricultural practices over a large part of the world, there are many existing social, economic, and political obstacles which effectively prevent the movement of food from the areas where there is now a surplus, and where production might be rapidly increased, to the areas where there is already a deficit and where the need for more and better food is growing rapidly. No reasonable person can assume that these obstacles will be substantially lessened in the near future. *Nationalism* has never been so rampant as it is in the world today. It is quite meaningless, therefore, to talk about world food production and to discuss surpluses, actual and potential, in the United States, Canada, Argentina, Australia, and a few other areas as though they were parts of one surplus that could be made available wherever food is needed. The mere mention of a few changes in social and economic conditions which might *very quickly* lead to a substantial addition to the total food produced in the world, and of the means which would make it possible to transfer this food to the areas where it is urgently needed, will serve to show how impossible it is to transform a potential—or even an actual—increase in world production into an effective increase in supply available to those countries in greatest need.

In a reasonably free economy where land is still fairly abundant, and/or where the farmers have the know-how and the economic means to increase yields, the volume of agricultural production is readily responsive to price variations. For example, assuming normal weather over a period of five or ten years, the United States, Canada, Australia, Argentina, and a few other countries could and would raise their average annual production of wheat and corn by many millions of tons if only one condition were changed: the fixing of the prices of wheat and corn at a level which was attractive to the farmers of these countries. Such a price would no doubt also prove attractive to the farmers in several other countries which might produce smaller surpluses. It would take only a few more years to raise the production of meat and dairy products and of minor products which might be shipped abroad, if their prices were also pegged at a level that made their production profitable to the farmers of these countries. In addition, within a few more years new irrigated lands could be added to the tilled areas in several of these countries, and certain lands, presently marginal, would soon be brought into use if prices promised a good average annual income to the producer over a period of years.

The above discussion has not specifically included increases in agricultural production in the Soviet Union because, in spite of the presence of much land that might be farmed more efficiently and of much new land that might be brought into production quickly through mechanized farming, there seems to have been little increase in the per cap-

ita food supply or in its variety and nutritional quality. The sending of
a few tens of thousands of tons of wheat to India or to Yugoslavia in
times of stress does not prove the existence of a surplus in the Soviet
Union but only the existence of a political situation which made it expedient for the leaders of the Soviet Union to make a show of good
will and to assert that the efficiency of collectivism in agriculture made
this possible. If agricultural production in the Soviet Union has reached
the surplus stage as a regular condition, why should it price the heavy
industrial products it sells to China in terms of tons of pork, peanuts,
soybeans, and other foods high in proteins and fats known to be short
in the Soviet Union? It seems abundantly clear that the incentives offered to Soviet farmers during the past thirty years under collectivism
in agriculture have been insufficient to stimulate any rapid improvement in per capita supplies of agricultural products. Furthermore, some
rather radical changes are now being made in Soviet agricultural organization. It will be several years, however, before anything definite
is known about whether they provide more adequate incentives.

Personally, I have not the least doubt that the fixing of the price of
wheat at a level which insured a good living to the wheat farmers of
the countries mentioned above would add several tens of millions of
tons of wheat to the world's supply in the course of five or ten years;
nor that this increase in production would begin almost at once. (Ten
million short tons amount to approximately 330 million bushels.) Production of other grains, and of many other useful foodstuffs and fibers,
could also be similarly increased. But it should be noted that most of
this hypothetical increase would take place in the more developed
countries where it is not needed to insure a more adequate diet or more
satisfactory clothing. The practical problem then facing the world
would be that of transferring surpluses from the areas of production to
the areas of need. Under the prevailing political and economic conditions, how can these transfers be effected? Let us continue the statement of the hypothetical case.

Obviously the American or Australian farmer cannot give his surplus
wheat away, nor can the Indian, or the Chinese, or the Javanese, or
the Ceylonese who needs it buy it at the price required to insure its
production. Many of the countries of the world now protect their agricultural products by means of tariffs or other trade barriers, and the
countries which might export large amounts of agricultural produce so
protect their industrial products that even if India, or any other country needing food, could export large amounts of manufactured goods

to pay for agricultural produce, these manufactured goods would not be accepted as payment. The drive to become as economically self-sufficing as possible is world-wide; it is more intense now than ever before and shows little tendency to subside. There is no hope that a vast movement of food into the densely settled countries can take place in the foreseeable future under the existing political conditions determining foreign trade. Practically, there is no such thing as a *world food supply*.

However, for the sake of the argument let us assume that the political controls preventing the regular transfer of large amounts of food from areas of production to those of need are swept away. There are still great practical problems of an economic nature to be faced. In order to make our hypothetical example as concrete as possible let us consider in more detail the practical problems involved in the transfer of ten million tons of wheat from areas of production to areas of need. In the first place, this amount of wheat would support, at a bare subsistence level, about fifty million people for one year—about 4 per cent of the people in the more densely settled countries of the region we are concerned with here. As a whole the populations of these countries are now increasing at somewhere between 1.5 and 2.0 per cent annually. It would, therefore, take care of the increase for two to three years at about the present level of consumption, or add about 4 per cent to the per capita consumption of the present population.

In the second place, there are the practical economic problems. Let us assume that this ten million tons of wheat would cost about two dollars a bushel at the local point of shipment, or sixty-five dollars a ton. By the time this wheat was delivered to the user it would cost not less than three dollars a bushel, and probably substantially more. Thus, at least one billion dollars would be needed to handle this transfer.

If the cost added for distribution seems high, let us consider for a moment the logistics problem. These ten million tons would fill 1,000 ships, each of which would carry ten thousand tons and would take the full time of at least 150 ships each year. Ten million tons of wheat would fill about 350,000 American freight cars, and several times as many Asian cars, which would have to be moved an average of several hundred miles in the countries of production and probably an equal distance in the countries of consumption. Many other costs of handling would also be involved in this transfer. It is extremely doubtful whether one dollar per bushel would cover these expenses. Furthermore, there are problems of storing vast quantities of foodstuffs, chiefly grain, to take care of unusual shortages which are almost certain to become much greater, both from the standpoint of finance and logistics, as population continues to increase. Thus even though the transfer of ten million tons of wheat would be quite possible as far as production, financial arrangements, and logistics are concerned, it is almost certain that far more than ten million tons would be needed at times and that any regular transfer of this character would so reduce the death rate that the need for increasing the total amount of food transferred would grow rapidly.

Where is the world organization, or the national organization, which could effect such an operation year after year? Would the United States or any other country be willing, year after year, to underwrite the production of its share of such a surplus and ship it to these less fortunate countries without a *quid pro quo?* And is there any possible *quid pro quo* in our world today? Actually, when Japan sells a few additional million yards of cotton goods in the United States—goods made from raw cotton probably bought in the United States—and uses the exchange thus gained to buy surplus wheat, her exports of cotton cloth are quickly controlled by a "gentleman's agreement," and if this does not reduce imports sufficiently to satisfy the textile interest in the United States, import quotas or higher tariffs are set. A thousand other similar instances, relating to many countries and many products, could be cited to show the practical impossibility of regular trade in foodstuffs with these Asian countries on a scale which would afford them substantial relief.

What I have tried to make clear in this hypothetical case is that there is no such thing in the world as a common supply of food which can be made available where most needed. The world's capacity to produce food will remain largely irrelevant to the practical problem of feeding the people in these countries until perhaps 80 to 90 per cent of the world's people are ready to join in some kind of political and economic organization which can make the world far more of an economic whole than it is now, or seems likely to become within the next several decades. In the meantime, the national food problems of India, China, Japan, Ceylon, etc., are the real food problems of the world, and national efforts to obtain relief are likely to increase tensions between nations to such a degree that the expenditures on defense and probably on actual war will exceed by many times the costs of producing a few more millions of tons of wheat and of distributing them where most needed.

However much we may hope that this kind of world-wide organization will soon come into being, we must face the fact that this *never-never* world is far from being a reality and that even the realization of a very large-scale program for the quick expansion of food production and its distribution to the countries most needing it would not long suffice to meet the needs of the great and crowded countries of Asia. Shortly, all peoples must undertake to control their population growth and to adjust it to the actual conditions in which they live if they are to eat reasonably well and are not to quarrel over the right to eat as well as, or better than, their neighbors.

The reality confronting us demands that we consider to the best of our ability the *probabilities* of developing an adequate food supply in India, China, Japan, and other countries, because each nation actually constitutes to a large extent a closed economic unit. We should not devote our attention to *world population growth* and *world food supply* as a whole but to the more definite problems facing each country. This has been done in preceding chapters with regard to food production, and the conclusions are not very encouraging for the next three or four decades, no matter what the possibilities of world food production may be.

Economic development.—At the present time rapid economic development along modern lines, largely under state control, is the chief hope of those underdeveloped countries most concerned with relieving the poverty of their peoples. It would seem reasonable to assume that expanding production would go far to prevent the rapid growth of the feeling of national poverty, and thus relieve the tensions between nations arising from growing population pressure. The body of this essay has been largely devoted to examining the probability of the early success of these efforts to increase production in the several countries. Nothing can be added here, except to say that I feel forced to conclude that the expansion of production in these underdeveloped countries has thus far been much less rapid than the leaders have expected and also than the foreign friends of these countries hoped it would be. Moreover, I believe the efforts to increase production have been confined too largely to the development of heavy industry and basic services, with the result that they have not had and are not likely to have any appreciable effect on the level of living of the masses in the near future. Besides, the rapid growth of population, primarily as the result of improved health services, is an important factor in preventing a rise in the level of living, i.e., in delaying the rise in the per capita quantity of consumption goods. There is no indication that the policy of concentrating capital and effort on heavy industry is likely to change in the near future.

This matter of economic development and the rapidity with which it may be expected to take place has been discussed in some detail in preceding chapters. Here I will only repeat that I do not believe the evidence now available justifies the expectation that economic development will be sufficiently rapid to prevent a substantial growth of the feeling of population pressure during the next two or three decades.

Migration.—Another means of preventing the growth of dangerous population pressures that has attracted much attention is migration from the more densely populated areas or countries to those areas or countries where there is still a relative abundance of land. In recent years this remedy for population pressure has received less attention than formerly, probably because there is now a wider understanding of the implications of large-scale international migration. Nevertheless, it will be well to examine the possibilities offered by large-scale migration.

Today India's population (including Kashmir) is approaching 400 million, and the yearly increase is probably in the vicinity of 6 million, about 1.5 per cent. If the 1953 census figures for Mainland China are accepted (583 million), and if the rate of increase of 2 per cent per year is used (as is being done officially), China's population is already (mid-1958) in excess of 630 million, and the annual increase is now substantially in excess of 12 million. Pakistan's population is now about 82 or 83 million, and the yearly increase is probably about 1.2 to 1.3 million. Japan's population is now about 92 million and is growing by about 900,000 per year.

The combined population of these four countries now totals about 1,200 million, and the combined annual growth is about 20 million. With the exception of Japan, the death rates in these countries are still quite high by present-day standards. The death rates of India, China, and Pakistan remain relatively high because the customary causes of death—the hardships due to disease and hunger—still operate with considerable vigor. Under these circumstances, the immediate demographic effect of emigration would depend on the scale on which it took place. If the whole of the annual natural increase of about 20 million were removed each year and if this had no harmful effect on production—and it is quite possible that it would not—it would prevent the need to spread the annual production thinner. If annual production for consumption were to increase only by 2 or 3 per cent, it would increase per capita income proportionally. Since 20 million constitutes less than 2 per cent of the population of these countries, and since there is a vast amount of unemployment and underemployment in all these countries, the effect of this volume of migration on production should not only not be serious but might even be beneficial. However, it is as certain as anything of this nature can be that the removal of such a number of people annually would quickly reduce the death rate still more if the emigration were accompanied by a 2 or 3 per cent increase in per capita consumption. Consequently, the annual natural increase would quickly rise above 20 million. Japan would probably be an exception, since her death rate is already low.

If these 20 million emigrants were selected at random, their emigration would have almost no noticeable effect on any particular community, either on a village of 500 or on a city of 1,000,000—8 to 9 fewer persons in the former and about 16,000 to 17,000 in the latter. If all these emigrants were selected each year from a different one-tenth of the communities, it is highly probable that their migration would afford substantial relief to this 10 per cent for several years; but by the time the turn of any community to send out emigrants came again it would have about the same population as before, or even a larger population, living at about the same low level. Whether per capita income would have actually increased would depend upon how fast an economic development had taken place in the country as a whole, for it is reasonably certain that if the people were free to move as they saw fit any marked improvement in living in this 10 per cent of the communities would quickly attract migrants from neighboring communities which had not yet sent out any emigrants.

Our earlier discussion has shown that there is still a considerable amount of unused tillable land on the Indochinese peninsula, enough to give the countries possessing it two or three decades during which they could adjust their population growth to their land and resources. They, at least, have a chance to avoid the more serious problems of overcrowding already being felt in the larger, more populated countries. Indonesia probably possesses the largest amount of unused land to which migrants might go. But Indonesia needs much land for the people in Java who are already badly crowded. The large island of New Guinea (over 300,000 square miles) is also thinly settled. Although only a small part of it is now used for agriculture, its mountainous character will not prevent a relatively large expansion in the culti-

vated area in the future. Approximately equal portions of it are controlled by Australia and the Netherlands. The Philippines also probably
have enough new land to care for their own increase for about a generation or a little longer. There are also some other islands in Tropical
Oceania which are thinly settled. They may contain 40,000 square
miles or more, of which probably one-third to one-half is usable. Madagascar (in the Indian Ocean) is thinly settled, containing perhaps 4.8
million people on about 225,000 square miles. There are also a number
of regions in Africa which are suitable for closer settlement.

These are the principal areas which seem suitable for closer settlement and which also lie fairly close to the crowded peoples of South
and East Asia. Although not even an approximate estimate can be
made regarding the amount of unused but tillable land in these areas,
there is little doubt that it is quite large—amounting possibly to several
hundred thousand or even a million square miles. There is also a strong
probability that thorough geological exploration in these areas would
disclose many large and useful mineral deposits.

The areas noted above are by no means the only ones in the world
on which closer settlement would be feasible. Several countries in
South America have relatively small populations, and many other areas
now occupied by people of European descent could provide ample
room for millions of Asiatics farming in their usual manner. Since there
is still this rather large amount of land which could be used without
depriving indigenous populations of their means of livelihood, it would
seem that large-scale emigration should be considered as a means of
relieving the growing population pressures in South and East Asia.
However, a mere listing of the areas in which population is sparse in
comparison with the amount of tillable land tends to make large-scale
emigration appear a far simpler matter than it actually is.

The emigration of even a few hundred thousand Chinese or Indians
or Pakistanis to the unused lands of the Indochinese peninsula or to
the outer islands of Indonesia would be bitterly opposed by the peoples now living in those regions. Any movement of Asiatics, even if it
involved only a few thousand to New Guinea or to the smaller islands
of Oceania in that general vicinity, would be opposed by Australia and
New Zealand to the full extent of their power. Such a migratory movement could be accomplished only by force. The Indians already have a
foothold in certain parts of Africa—in Natal and Kenya and some
neighboring areas—but the natives there are as much opposed to Indian expansion as they are to continued control by the Europeans. Only

a few tens of thousands of Japanese and Chinese have ever been admitted to South America, and now even the prewar trickle of Japanese has been stopped. *No country in South and East Asia can start large-scale emigration without acquiring actual political control of the area to be colonized, and such control can be achieved only by conquest.*

Before World War II, the opposition to the expansion of Asian peoples into new areas could be—and was—attributed to the European colonial powers. Today it is less easy to hold them responsible, at least with respect to Burma, former French Indochina, Indonesia, and certain regions of Africa. However, the prevention of Asiatic settlement in New Guinea and the larger islands of Oceania can still be charged definitely to the Australians and their allies, and emigration to Madagascar and certain parts of Africa is still controlled by Europeans. There can be no reasonable doubt that as the Asiatic countries, particularly Japan and China, feel growing population pressure, their exclusion from settlement in the Pacific islands will become a source of increasing irritation. Moreover, as long as Australia and New Zealand are themselves thinly settled and are unable to defend themselves against attack by any fairly strong power—to say nothing of defending the large outlying areas of tropical land which Australia now controls—the Asiatic powers will be strongly tempted to expand into these areas by force.

But even if no serious political problems stood in the way of large-scale migration, there are many other obstacles which make such emigration unlikely for at least a decade or two. One of these, which is closely related to the political problem, may be called racial differences—although the anthropologist would consider some of these differences cultural rather than racial. For example, the Chinese are very much disliked in Java and other parts of Indonesia, and in the Philippines. Since they largely control trade and are the local moneylenders, it is felt they are merciless in their exploitation of the native farmers. Some racial differences may well be involved in this antagonism, but the chief factor is undoubtedly the economic power of the Chinese. The Chinese are only a little less disliked by the farmers in most parts of the Indochinese peninsula, although racially the two groups are much alike. The Indians in Burma (most of whom have now returned to India) and in Kenya and neighboring areas who, like the Chinese, are engaged chiefly in commerce, are also thoroughly disliked by the natives. There cannot be the least doubt that as the natives in these areas gain more control over their own affairs they will be even more insistent than the colonial rulers that these *foreign* exploiters be kept out.

Quite apart from political obstacles and the racial or cultural problems which make large-scale emigration from Asia impossible in the near future, the economic and logistics problems involved are equally formidable. Let us examine for a moment the practical aspects of a large emigration movement.

The increase of population in the more densely settled countries is now approximately 20 million annually. The emigration of only one-half of this natural increase would involve moving about ten times as many people as the net movement of immigrants into the United States in the years of the greatest influx preceding World War I. If each ship used to take emigrants abroad were equipped to carry 3,500 at each trip, and if the average round trip took approximately four weeks, with four weeks allowed for maintenance and repair, each ship could deliver 40,000 to 45,000 emigrants per year. Using the larger figure for each ship, it would require about 225 such ships full time, and this is almost certainly an understatement. Eight ships would have to discharge their passengers each day of the year to meet the 10 million total. The actual movement of such a number could probably be provided for, but it would of course be very expensive. Since most of these immigrants would almost certainly be young couples with one or two children, the number of families to be provided for, each day, at 3.5 persons per family, would be close to 8,000, of whom at least four-fifths would be farmers. At four acres per farm family this would mean preparing about 25,000 acres a day for cultivation. But since, under the most favorable circumstances, crops could only be planted twice yearly, it would be necessary to use most of these emigrants as laborers in preparing the land, in building houses and roads and establishing villages, and as laborers on the farms already established, several months before they could begin to cultivate their own land. This would make *large* labor camps necessary—at least one every day.

Again, long before actual emigration could be started, it would be necessary to establish an extensive service in each country to select the emigrants likely to succeed in the new country and to give them a thorough "briefing" regarding the new life they were undertaking. It was the failure to do much of this preparatory work properly that doomed the earlier Dutch schemes to move large numbers of Javanese to the outer islands.

There are many other difficult problems involved in moving such numbers. The services to which the emigrants have been accustomed are few and modest, but even so, preparations would have to be made for the education of the children, for community health services, for religious observances, etc., and, of course, for adequate policing of the new communities; for roads and other transportation, and probably for electricity in the market towns where most of the local manufactures would be located.

Finally, even if 10 million emigrants could be sent out from these countries each year, it would only reduce their rates of growth by about one-half at the beginning and even less later, for it is reasonable to assume that a more rapid reduction in the death rate would follow if emigration really afforded even a small measure of relief from population pressure. At the end of ten years, about 112 million emigrants (including their children) would be living abroad.

The only reasonable conclusion is that emigration on a scale that would afford significant relief to the populations of these four Asian countries is utterly impossible. However, the fact that emigration can never relieve population pressure in these countries does not mean that the growing feeling of national poverty will not lead to attempts by particular countries to secure better opportunities for themselves by conquering some of the less populated areas of the earth. In some respects this danger has increased, because such a large proportion of the earth's population is only now becoming aware of the many thinly settled areas they might use if only they were at liberty to move there. At the same time, the populations of these countries, except Japan, are increasing as never before, and it would be surprising if the masses could not be made to believe that emigration would be an effective means of relieving their poverty.

In one respect, however, migration, even on a modest scale, from the countries of South and East Asia might tend to reduce the international tensions arising from population pressures. I refer to the psychological effect of changing the laws which restrict immigration into all countries, but especially into sparsely settled areas, so that they do not offend the pride of these Asian peoples. Moreover, some experience in actually organizing emigration on even a modest scale, say a few tens of thousands a year, might do more to convince the people in the large and more densely settled countries that emigration will afford no relief than any possible amount of argument. But we must recognize that any change in immigration policy by the "free" countries controlling the sparsely settled islands in the Western Pacific would certainly be interpreted by the Chinese Communists as a trick of the "capitalist" countries intended to delude the people of China into believing they were no longer being discriminated against in the settlement of these areas. In addition, it can be taken for granted that the Chinese Communist view would be vigorously propagated throughout the region.

Foreign trade.—Foreign trade has long been recognized as one of the important means for supporting population and improving its level of living. In the past it was generally some city or small area which depended on foreign trade to any considerable extent. More recently whole nations, some of them quite large—Britain, Japan, Germany—have come to depend more and more on such trade. The importance of foreign trade to Japan and some of the principal difficulties raised by her great dependence on it have been noted in chapter vii.

Britain's pre-eminence in foreign trade for some decades was due to a number of factors which gave her an unusual grip on the world market. Several specific factors may be mentioned: (1) her early development of manufacturing and mining, employing machinery driven by steam power; (2) her possession of an empire within which trade could be carried on largely in her own currency and on her own terms; (3) her virtual monopoly in the export of many types of goods, resulting from her being almost the sole producer and the cheaper producer of them for several decades.

By the time Japan was ready to engage in world trade on a substantial scale she had to meet very stiff competition not only from Britain but from a few other Western countries, except for certain of her luxury goods, and even her export of silk had to meet the competition of Italy and France and, to a lesser degree, of China. However, serious silkworm disease in Europe worked greatly to Japan's advantage in the early years, as did the very rapid expansion of the use of silk in the United States. As her methods of preparing raw silk also rapidly improved she was able to capture and retain a large share of the world's silk trade, which she held up to World War II. The coming of synthetic substitutes for silk has practically destroyed this source of exchange.

Japan had only a small empire, and for nearly all types of machine-made goods exported outside the empire Japan had keen competition. Her chief advantages in expanding her trade consisted in her early development of machine production in comparison with other Asian countries, in her cheap labor, and in her greater knowledge of Asian markets. These advantages enabled her both to produce new types of goods at relatively low prices and to produce many of the types of goods already in use more cheaply than her competitors. Japan may also have had some advantage in transportation costs, but the aid given her exporters by officially sanctioned trade organizations was probably of more importance. Some of these advantages still exist as regards competition with Western countries, especially cheap labor, but as soon as India and China begin to compete in machine products much of this advantage will be lost. This competition is already being felt in cotton textiles, and it will certainly become increasingly difficult for Japan to maintain her present level of trade as these countries establish more modern industry and become more proficient in its operation.

The difficulties of Britain in maintaining an adequate foreign market are too well known to need comment here, and Germany's dependence on such markets is also well known. The fact that foreign trade has *boomed* greatly since World War II has led many people to believe in the possibility of relying on the expansion of this trade for the support of growing populations and rising levels of living. There are conditions under which this might be the case, but the great expansion of foreign trade since World War II seems to me to have a *windfall* character that is not fully appreciated. By this I mean that it is due to unusual circumstances that are not likely to continue and still less likely to be repeated in the future. With the addition of growing competition from India and China, foreign trade is more likely to return to the highly competitive conditions which prevailed before World War II.

In spite of all the improvements in transportation and communication, in spite of the increasing needs of all well-developed countries for many raw materials they either do not possess or cannot produce, or possess and produce only in inadequate amounts, and in spite of a growing realization of the interdependence of the nations of the world upon one another for many goods and services, the strong movement toward autarchy—the economic self-sufficiency of nations—shows no sign of declining. From the standpoint of our study the principal result of this trend toward autarchy is that it is becoming increasingly difficult for any country to rely upon a stable volume of foreign trade for the support of its economy. This uncertainty regarding foreign trade appears likely to increase as the control of trade is used more and more as a political weapon in dealing with other countries. Besides, the internal political necessity of interfering with foreign trade appears to be increasing even in the "free" countries.

It would seem, therefore, that under the circumstances in which we live today the great dependence of any country on foreign trade places it in a highly precarious economic position. This would be true even if the trend toward autarchy merely followed its prewar course, but today the entry of the communist countries into world trade introduces a new and incalculable element of uncertainty. As the communist countries increase their industrial capacity and find how powerful a weapon trade can be in disrupting the economies of the "free" countries it can be assumed that they will use this weapon whenever it is expedient to do so. Moreover, this governmental manipulating of trade can also be used to build up the great dependence of the trade of a "free" country with a communist country, and if such trade is suddenly shut off it can work economic disaster in the "free" country. Today China is in the process of convincing Japanese industrialists and businessmen that a very great market for Japanese goods, both capital goods and consumers' goods, exists in China, and is proposing to pay for these manufactures with iron ore, coking coal, bauxite, etc. Japan greatly needs these raw materials, and the exchange would be highly beneficial to both countries if such trade could be made a regular feature of their economic relations. There is no need here to elaborate on the possibility of disaster to Japan's economy that is involved in becoming increasingly dependent on trade with China under existing conditions. Many similar situations are in the making, and I can see no reason to believe that they will not be exploited to the full in the effort to extend communist influence into the "free" countries as well as into the "uncommitted" countries. This is an important additional reason for doubting whether foreign trade can be relied upon to ease the growing population pressure of the more densely settled Asian countries to any great extent in the foreseeable future.

Population control.—In the long run, in my judgment, the only sure relief for population pressure and the tensions and troubles it creates is population control. I use the phrase *in the long run* because it does not seem reasonable to me to expect the rate of population growth to begin to decline significantly in most of these Asian countries in less than about a generation. I want to make it clear that I am speaking here of the *rate of population growth,* not the *birth rate.* The birth rate may begin to decline in certain areas somewhat sooner, but the rate of population growth will rise as long as the death rate declines faster than the birth rate.

In the long run, man will no doubt learn to adjust his birth rate to his ability to produce the goods needed to provide a decent living, since the alternative to such control must be the return of a high death rate due to hunger and want and disease and probably *hot* war in the not distant future. I am not saying that it is impossible to support a much larger population in these Asian countries at some time in the future and at a better level of living, but I am saying that I do not believe the probable expansion of production and the probable population growth justify an expectation of much improvement in living conditions during the next generation. I am also saying that even a slow but steady improvement in the standard of living will not satisfy these peoples and that, consequently, economic and political tensions resulting from the growing feeling of poverty will increase.

Since I believe that *felt* population pressures will increase significantly in the near future, I am very much concerned that even China and India, in spite of their official approval of contraception, do not seem to be making the great effort necessary to secure its early adoption. If even one-fourth or one-third of the money and effort being used to establish heavy industry and basic services were devoted to educating the masses in the need for birth control, the rate of population growth could almost certainly be reduced in a shorter time than now appears probable, and the level of living could be raised much faster during the next two or three decades than will be possible by following their present plans for depending almost entirely on economic development to achieve this aim. This does not seem to be realized in either India or China.

It is basically this relative indifference to intensive efforts to educate the masses regarding the need to reduce the birth rate at a time when the death rate is declining in an unprecedented manner that has led me to conclude that there is little hope of reducing the rate of population growth for about a generation and that any rise in the level of living great enough to reduce the feeling of population pressure depends even more on the rapid decline of the birth rate than on the rapid improvement of production. This view certainly is not widely accepted either in India or China.

POPULATION PRESSURE AND COMMUNIST PROPAGANDA

At many points in the discussion, attention has been called to the fact that because China is now controlled by the Communists the problems arising from the increasing awareness of population pressure in the Far East are greatly aggravated. This point is so important that specific attention should be given to certain aspects of the communist use of the growing feeling of poverty, even at the risk of repetition.

The Chinese Communists are making full use of the growing feeling of population pressure, of privation in the other Asian countries, both to propagandize for communism and to prepare the way for the subversion of noncommunist governments. If there is one policy of all communist governments under Soviet influence which seems to be firmly settled, it is that the spread of the Soviet type of authoritarian government to more and more peoples must be their foremost task. The means used to do this may be summed up by saying that they exploit every possible grievance of all peoples as resulting from the malevolence and greed of capitalists, whose power for evil can only be eliminated by adopting the Soviet type of communism. The leaders of Communist China have already clearly shown that they accept this view in an extreme form and that they believe their mission to be the elimination of capitalism in Asia by all available means. It can be expected, therefore, that China has only begun to exploit the growing feeling of national poverty in other Asian countries with the object of destroying all noncommunist governments. Their ability to create trouble for these governments should not be underestimated.

There is great hardship among the people in most of these Asian countries, and since this hardship will continue for some years even under the most rapid economic development that can reasonably be expected, the Chinese Communists will not lack for genuine grievances to exploit. The actual hardships being suffered are explained in simple terms which even people with little education can understand and which often are quite convincing, viz., as the consequence of their former colonial status and their exploitation by officials, landlords, money-lenders, and other capitalists. At the same time, exaggerated claims are made over and over again regarding the rapid progress of economic development in China under the Communists.

However inadequate we know this explanation of the poverty of China, or of India, or of Pakistan, or of any other underdeveloped country to be, and however exaggerated we know the claims of progress being made by China to be, we should not underestimate the appeal of such constantly reiterated propaganda to the peoples who have long been striving for independence and who are only now becoming aware of their great relative poverty. Since they have neither any basis in experience nor a sufficient education to examine the soundness of the alleged causes of their poverty and the claims of Communist successes, and since they do know that their own leaders have long been telling them much the same about the abuses of imperialism, it is not surprising that many of them are ready to accept this communist propaganda.

It requires only a little imagination and some knowledge of the actual living conditions in most of these countries to make one realize that the growing feeling of deprivation is a weapon ready-made for the Chinese Communists both in preparing their own people to expand into neighboring noncommunist areas which are rather sparsely settled and also for encouraging many earnest and well-meaning men as well as many frustrated and ambitious men to undertake the subversion of the more moderate governments now in power. The *great* and, I believe, *inevitable* difficulties being encountered in the efforts to improve the economy in most of these underdeveloped countries by evolution rather than revolution will insure the effectiveness of such propaganda for a time at least. For how long a time no one can tell. But it is very difficult to explain to the uneducated and inexperienced people in these poverty-stricken countries the real roots of their poverty—that it is not entirely due to the abuses of past colonialism or to their exploitation by landlords and other capitalists but also to the difficulties of the farmers in improving their crops and, perhaps above all, to the increase in the number of mouths to be fed at a time when the death rate is rapidly declining.

The only way in which the "free" countries of the world can combat this communist propaganda is to assist the moderate governments of the underdeveloped countries in their efforts to improve their economies faster than China is improving hers, while carefully refraining from infringing in any way upon their new rights and privileges as independent peoples. Of course, the success of such efforts is by no means certain.

NUCLEAR WARFARE

Although, at first glance, it may not seem germane to our discussion here, a word must be said about the probable effect of nuclear warfare upon the willingness of leaders everywhere to engage in war to secure larger resources or to satisfy ideological demands. It does not seem credible to most of us that any responsible leader would undertake a conquest *for any reason* if such aggression were likely to result in large-scale retaliation upon his country by the use of nuclear weapons.

If this is assumed to be the case, it would appear that the leaders in any country who had determined to expand either their country's ideological influence or its territory would be forced to seek new means of aggression by which they could gain their ends with a minimum of risk of incurring nuclear reprisal. The only alternative to such an effort would be to make a surprise nuclear attack in the hope of destroying the power or powers likely to retaliate. If it is assumed, as there now seems good reason to do, that the former of these aggressive strategies will be used, it can be seen at once that this situation offers almost unlimited opportunity for mistakes in judgment which may lead directly to a holocaust. This "nibbling" strategy of aggression, already in operation, will almost certainly be preferred for some time to come to direct attack, in spite of the dangers of misjudging the opponents' reaction. A real effort will be made by the communist leaders to make their "nibbling" operations so insignificant in each specific case that they will not provoke nuclear war and yet so important that their power and territory will be constantly expanding.

It is possible, therefore, that with the development of nuclear weapons the expansion of territory by direct conquest will pass out of the picture and that indirect conquest by the subversion of existing noncommunist governments will take its place. This subversion would, of course, be aided by the communist country desiring to expand its power and resources; but since such a "revolution" can often be made to appear as the more or less spontaneous uprising of the indigenous "downtrodden masses," nuclear reprisal against the "foreign" backer of the revolutionists is less likely than if their backer had attacked the established government directly.

The fact that the strategy of subversion and nibbling is now playing such a large role in the expansion of the communist empire may or may not be, in any particular case, the consequence of the fear of reprisal by nuclear weapons; but there can be no doubt that it represents an adjustment of aggressive action to the dangers of nuclear warfare which the "free" world has not yet been able to meet. In our great concern over meeting this new type of aggression we should not lose sight of the fact that the rapidly growing feeling of population pressure in many underdeveloped countries makes this new strategy highly effective.

SELECTED BIBLIOGRAPHY

1. ACKERMAN, EDWARD A. *Japan's Natural Resources and Their Relation to Japan's Economic Future.* Chicago: University of Chicago Press, 1953.
2. ADLER, SOLOMON. *The Chinese Economy.* New York: Monthly Review Press, 1957.
3. AKHTAR, S. M. "The Land Tenure Situation in Pakistan," *Economia internazionale,* VI, No. 4 (November, 1953), 415–24.
4. ALLEN, G. C. "The Concentration of Economic Control in Japan," *Economic Journal,* XLVII, No. 186 (June, 1937), 271–86.
5. ———. *Japan: The Hungry Guest.* New York: E. P. Dutton & Co., 1938.
6. ———. *Japanese Industry: Its Recent Development and Present Condition.* New York: International Secretariat, Institute of Pacific Relations, 1939.
7. ———. *See also* SCHUMPETER (242).
8. ———. "The Present Economic Situation in Japan," *International Affairs,* XXXI, No. 3 (July, 1955), 291–99.
9. ———. *A Short Economic History of Modern Japan, 1867–1937.* London: G. Allen & Unwin Ltd., 1946.
10. ALLEN, G. C., and DONNITHORNE, A. G. *Western Enterprise in Far Eastern Economic Development, China and Japan.* New York: Macmillan Co., 1954.
11. AMANO, FUMIKO Y. *Family Planning Movement in Japan.* Tokyo: Foreign Affairs Association of Japan, 1955.
12. AMERICAN ACADEMY OF POLITICAL AND SOCIAL SCIENCE. *Annals.* Philadelphia. (This contains a number of volumes dealing with various social and economic aspects of life in the countries dealt with in this book. Sometimes an entire number is devoted to a particular country.)
13. AMERICAN GEOGRAPHICAL SOCIETY OF NEW YORK. "Special Publications." New York, 1915——. (An important source of geographical information for all countries.)
14. ANDREWS, JAMES MADISON. *Siam, Second Rural Economic Survey, 1934–1935.* Bangkok: W. H. Murdie (Bangkok Times Press), 1935.
15. ANDRUS, J. RUSSELL. *Burmese Economic Life.* Stanford, Calif.: Stanford University Press, 1947.
16. ANJARIA, J. J. "India's Five Year Plan," *Current History,* XXIV, No. 142 (June, 1953), 321–26.
17. ANSTEY, VERA. "The Colombo Plan: With Special Reference to India and Pakistan," *Economia internazionale,* V, No. 1 (February, 1952), 134–47.

404

18. ———. *The Economic Development of India.* 4th ed. New York: Longmans, Green & Co., 1952.

19. ASAHI, ISOSHI. *The Economic Strength of Japan.* Tokyo: Hokuseido Press, 1939.

20. AUBREY, H. G. "The Role of the State in Economic Development," *American Economic Review,* XLI, No. 2 (May, 1951), 266–73.

21. ———. "Small Industry in Economic Development," *Social Research,* XVIII, No. 3 (September, 1951), 269–312.

22. *Austral-Asiatic Bulletin* (Australian Institute of International Affairs, Victorian Division, Austral-Asiatic Section). Melbourne, April, 1937——.

23. AUSTRALIA BUREAU OF CENSUS AND STATISTICS. *Demography.* Canberra, 1882——.

24. ———. *Official Year Book of the Commonwealth of Australia.* Canberra, 1907——.

25. BAIN, HARRY FOSTER. *Ores and Industry in the Far East.* New York: Council on Foreign Relations, 1933.

26. BAKER, O. E. "Agriculture and the Future of China," *Foreign Affairs,* VI, No. 3 (April, 1928), 483–97.

27. BALOGH, THOMAS. "The Challenge of Totalitarian Planning in Asia," *International Affairs,* XXXI, No. 3 (July, 1955), 300–310.

28. BARBER, MARSHALL A. *A Malariologist in Many Lands.* Lawrence: University of Kansas Press, 1946.

29. BARCLAY, GEORGE W. *Colonial Development and Population in Taiwan.* Princeton,. N.J.: Princeton University Press, 1954.

30. BARNES, J. "Economic Implications of Electrification in Underdeveloped Countries," *Eonomic Development and Cultural Change,* II, No. 5 (June, 1954), 371–79.

31. BEALS, ALAN. "The Government and the Indian Village," *Economic Development and Cultural Change,* II, No. 5 (June, 1954), 397–407.

32. BELSHAW, HORACE. *Population Growth and Levels of Consumption.* London: G. Allen & Unwin Ltd., 1956.

33. BENNETT, M. K. *The World's Food: A Study of the Interrelations of World Population, National Diets, and Food Potentials.* New York: Harper & Bros., 1954.

34. ———. *See also* WICKIZER (340).

35. BERREMAN, GERALD D. *The Philippines: A Survey of Current Social, Economic and Political Conditions.* (Data Paper No. 19.) Ithaca, N.Y.: Cornell University Press, 1956.

36. BISSON, T. A. *Japan in China.* New York: Macmillan Co., 1938.

37. BLACK, JOHN D., and KIEFER, MAXINE E. *Future Food and Agriculture Policy: A Program for the Next Ten Years.* New York: McGraw-Hill Book Co., 1948.

38. BLACKER, C. P. "The Rhythm Method: Two Indian Experiments," Parts I and II, *Eugenics Review,* XLVII, Nos. 2 and 3 (July and October, 1955), 93–105, 163–72.

39. BLANCHARD, FESSENDEN S. *The Textile Industries of China and Japan.* New York: Textile Research Institute, 1944.

40. BORRIE, W. D. *Population Trends and Policies: A Study in Australian and World Demography.* Sydney: Australian Publishing Co., 1948.

41. BOWMAN, ISAIAH. *Limits of Land Settlement.* New York: Council on Foreign Relations, 1937.

42. BRAHMANAND, P. R. See VAKIL (330).

43. BROEK, JAN O. M. *Eonomic Development of the Netherlands Indies.* New York: International Secretariat, Institute of Pacific Relations, 1942.

44. BROWN, JOHN COGGIN, and DEY, A. K. *India's Mineral Wealth: A Guide to the Occurrence and Economics of the Useful Minerals of India.* London: Oxford University Press, 1955.

45. BUCHANAN, NORMAN S., and ELLIS, HOWARD S. *Approaches to Economic Development.* New York: Twentieth Century Fund, 1955.

46. BUCK, JOHN L. *Chinese Farm Economy.* Chicago: University of Chicago Press, 1930.

47. ———. "Fact and Theory about China's Land," *Foreign Affairs*, XXVIII, No. 1 (October, 1949), 92–101.

48. ———. *Land Utilization in China.* Chicago: University of Chicago Press, 1937.

48a. BURGDÖRFER, FRIEDRICH. (ed.). *World Atlas of Population.* Hamburg: Falk-Verlag, 1954.

49. BUTTRICK, JOHN A. See WILLIAMSON (344).

50. CAMBODIA. See INDOCHINA (142); *also* UNITED STATES BUREAU OF FOREIGN COMMERCE (317).

51. CARR-SAUNDERS, A. M. *World Population.* Oxford: Clarendon Press, 1936.

52. CARSTAIRS, G. MORRIS. "Medicine and Faith in Rural Rajasthan," in (223), pp. 107–34.

53. CEYLON, DEPARTMENT OF CENSUS AND STATISTICS. *Census of Ceylon, 1946.* Vol. I, Part I. Colombo: Ceylon Government Press, 1950.

54. ———. *Ceylon Year Book.* Colombo: Government Publications Bureau, 1952–53.

55. CEYLON, MINISTRY OF FINANCE. *Economic and Social Development of Ceylon, 1926–1954.* Colombo: Government Publications Bureau, 1955.

56. ———. *Government Policy in Respect of Private Foreign Investment in Ceylon.* Colombo: Government Publications Bureau, 1955.

57. CEYLON, PLANNING SECRETARIAT. *Six-Year Programme of Investment, 1954/55 to 1959/60.* Colombo: Government Publications Bureau, 1955.

58. CEYLON. See *also* INTERNATIONAL BANK FOR RECONSTRUCTION AND DEVELOPMENT (146).

59. CHANDRASEKARAN, C. *Pilot Study on the Rhythm Method of Family Planning in India.* New York: U.N. Technical Assistance Program, 1954.

60. CHANDRASEKHAR, S. *Empty Lands and Hungry People: An Essay on Population Problems and International Tensions.* New York: Macmillan Co., 1955.

61. ———. *Population and Planned Parenthood in India*. London: G. Allen & Unwin Ltd., 1955.

62. CHEN, TA. "New China's Population Census of 1953 and Its Relations to National Reconstruction and Demographic Research." (Paper presented at the meeting of the International Statistical Institute, Stockholm, August 8–15, 1957.)

63. ———. *Population in Modern China*. Chicago: University of Chicago Press, 1946.

64. CHIAO, CHI-MING. "A Study of the Chinese Population," *Milbank Memorial Fund Quarterly*, XI, No. 4 (October, 1933), 325–41; XII, Nos. 1–3 (January, April, and July, 1934), 85–96, 171–83, 270–82.

65. ———. *See also* THOMPSON (281).

66. CHINA, GOVERNMENT OF THE PEOPLE'S REPUBLIC. *China Reconstructs*. (A journal in English published monthly in Peking.)

67. ———. *People's China*. (A journal in English published semimonthly in Peking.)

68. CHINA. *Handbook on People's China*. Peking: Foreign Languages Press, 1952——.

69. *China Handbook, 1937–1946*. Compiled by the Chinese Ministry of Information. New York: Macmillan Co., 1947.

70. CHINA. *New China News Agency*. (Published in English.)

71. *China Year Book*. Peking: Tientsen Press, 1912——.

72. *China Youth (Chung Kuo Ch'ing Nien)*. (A magazine published in Peking.)

73. CHINA. *See also* U.N., ECONOMIC COMMISSION FOR ASIA AND THE FAR EAST (303, 1955).

74. *China's Women, The New (Hsin Chung Kuo Fu Nu)*. (A magazine published in Peking.)

75. CHOU EN-LAI. An interview in the *Report of the Indian Delegation to China on Agricultural Planning and Techniques*. New Delhi: Ministry of Food and Agriculture, 1956, pp. 22–30.

76. CHRISTIAN, JOHN L. *Modern Burma*. Berkeley and Los Angeles: University of California Press, 1942.

77. CHUNG HUI-LAN. Article published in *Peking Jen Min Jih Pao*, March 17, 1957.

78. CLARK, COLIN. *The Conditions of Economic Progress*. London: Macmillan & Co., 1951.

79. ———. "Population Growth and Living Standards," *International Labour Review*, LXVIII, No. 2 (August, 1953), 99–117.

80. COALE, ANSLEY J., and HOOVER, EDGAR M. *Population Growth and Economic Development in Low Income Countries: A Case Study of India's Prospects*. Princeton, N.J.: Princeton University Press, 1958.

81. CRESSEY, GEORGE B. *Asia's Lands and Peoples*. New York: McGraw-Hill Book Co., 1944.

82. ———. "Changing the Map of China," *Economic Geography*, XXXI, No. 1 (January, 1955), 1–16.

83. CRESSEY, GEORGE B. *Land of the 500 Million: A Geography of China.* New York: McGraw-Hill Book Co., 1955.

84. ———. "The 1953 Census of China," *Far Eastern Quarterly,* XIV, No. 3 (May, 1955), 387.

85. DANDEKAR, V. M., and DANDEKAR, KUMUDINI. *Survey of Fertility and Mortality in Poona District.* Poona: Sangam Press Ltd., 1953.

86. DAVIS, KINGSLEY. *The Population of India and Pakistan.* Princeton, N.J.: Princeton University Press, 1951.

87. *Demographic Yearbook. See* U.N., DEPARTMENT OF ECONOMIC AND SOCIAL AFFAIRS (293).

88. DESAI, M. B. "Agriculture in Second Five-Year Plan," *Indian Journal of Agricultural Economics,* XI (January–March, 1956), 72–76.

89. DE SILVA, DAVID MONTAGUE. *Health Progress in Ceylon: A Survey.* Colombo: Ceylon Government Press, 1956.

90. ———. "Public Health and Sanitation Measures as Factors Affecting Mortality Trends in Ceylon," in (310), I, 411–38.

91. ———. Unpublished paper given to the writer, 1956.

92. DEY, A. K. See BROWN (44).

93. DIETRICH, ETHEL B. "Closing Doors against Japan," *Far Eastern Survey,* VII, No. 16 (August 10, 1938), 181–86.

93a. DOBBY, E. H. G. *Southeast Asia.* London: London University Press, 1950.

94. DONNITHORNE, A. G. *See* ALLEN (10).

95. *Economic Development and Cultural Change.* (This magazine issued by the University of Chicago Press contains articles on many aspects of the interrelations indicated by its title.)

96. ELLIS, HOWARD S. *See* BUCHANAN (45).

97. *Encyclopaedia Britannica.* Chicago: Encyclopaedia Britannica, 1957.

98. *Encyclopaedia Britannica, World Atlas.* Chicago: Encyclopaedia Britannica, 1957.

99. *Far Eastern Economic Review.* (A magazine published in Hong Kong.)

100. *Far Eastern Quarterly: A Review of Eastern Asia and the Adjacent Pacific Islands.* Menasha, Wis.: Far Eastern Association, 1941——.

101. *Far Eastern Review.* New York: 1939——. (Many articles relating to the countries of South and East Asia.)

102. *Far Eastern Survey: A Fortnightly Research Service.* New York: American Council, Institute of Pacific Relations, 1932——. (Excellent short studies on contemporary developments in South and East Asia.)

103. FARLEY, MIRIAM S. *The Problem of Japanese Trade Expansion in the Post-war Situation.* New York: International Secretariat, Institute of Pacific Relations, 1940.

104. FIELD, FREDERICK V. (ed.). *An Economic Survey of the Pacific Area.* Part I: "Population and Land Utilization," by Karl J. Pelzer; Part II: "Transportation," by Katrine R. C. Greene, and "Foreign Trade," by Joseph D. Phillips. New York: International Secretariat, Institute of Pacific Relations, 1941–42.

105. FONG, H. D. *The Post-war Industrialization of China.* Chungking: Nankai Institute of Economics, Nankai University, 1942.
106. FOOD AND AGRICULTURE ORGANIZATION OF THE UNITED NATIONS. *Agriculture in Asia and the Far East: Development and Outlook.* New York: Columbia University Press, 1953.
107. ———. *Agriculture in Asia and the Far East: Report and Working Papers.* Rome: United Nations, 1953.
108. ———. *Problems of Food and Agriculture Expansion in the Far East.* Rome: United Nations, 1955.
109. ———. *Rehabilitation and Development of Agriculture, Forestry, and Fisheries in South Korea.* New York: Columbia University Press, 1954.
110. ———. *Second World Food Survey.* Rome: United Nations, 1952.
111. ———. *Yearbook of Food and Agricultural Statistics, 1947——.* Rome: United Nations, 1947——.
112. FORMOSA. *See* JAPAN (156); *also* TAIWAN (267).
112*a.* GIBBON, EDWARD. *The Decline and Fall of the Roman Empire.* 5 vols. Philadelphia: Porter & Coates, 1880.
112*b.* GINSBURG, NORTON. (ed.). *The Pattern of Asia.* Englewood Cliffs, N.J.: Prentice-Hall, Inc., 1958.
113. GOLDSCHMIDT, WALTER R. "The Interrelations between Cultural Factors and the Acquisition of New Technical Skills," in (126), pp. 135–51.
114. GRAJDANZEV, ANDREW J. *Formosa Today.* New York: International Secretariat, Institute of Pacific Relations, 1942.
115. ———. *Modern Korea.* New York: International Secretariat, Institute of Pacific Relations, 1944.
116. ———. *Statistics of Japanese Agriculture.* New York: International Secretariat, Institute of Pacific Relations, 1941.
117. HANKS, L. M., JR., *et al.* "Diphtheria Immunization in a Thai Community," in (223), pp. 155–85.
118. HART, G. H. C. *Towards Economic Democracy in the Netherlands Indies.* New York: Netherlands and Netherlands Indies Council, Institute of Pacific Relations, 1942.
119. HAYES, SAMUEL P., JR. "Personality and Culture Problems of Point IV," in (126), pp. 203–29.
120. HERSKOVITS, MELVILLE J. "The Problem of Adapting Societies to New Tasks," in (126), pp. 89–112.
121. HIGGINS, BENJAMIN H. "Development Problems in the Philippines: A Comparison with Indonesia," *Far Eastern Survey,* XXVI, No. 11 (November, 1957), 161–69.
122. ———. *Indonesia's Economic Stabilization and Development.* New York: Institute of Pacific Relations, 1957.
123. HIGGINS, BENJAMIN H., and MALENBAUM, WILFRED. *The Problems of Financing Economic Development.* New York: Columbia University Press, 1955.
124. HOOVER, EDGAR M. *See* COALE (80).
125. HOSELITZ, BERT F. "Problems of Adapting and Communicating Modern

Techniques to Less Developed Areas," *Economic Development and Cultural Change,* II, No. 4 (January, 1954), 249–68.

126. HOSELITZ, BERT F. (ed.). *The Progress of Underdeveloped Areas.* Chicago: University of Chicago Press, 1952.

127. HSIA, ROLAND. *Economic Planning in Communist China.* New York: International Secretariat, Institute of Pacific Relations, 1955.

128. HSIEH, CHIANG. "Underemployment in Asia," Parts I and II, *International Labour Review,* LXV, No. 6 (June, 1952), 703–25; LXVI, No. 1 (July, 1952), 30–39.

129. HSU, FRANCIS L. K. "A Cholera Epidemic in a Chinese Town," in (223), pp. 135–54.

130. *Hsueh Hsi (Study).* (Chief ideological magazine of the Chinese Communist party, published in Peking.)

131. HUBBARD, G. E., and BARING, DENZIL. *Eastern Industrialization and Its Effect on the West.* London: Oxford University Press, 1935.

132. *Human Organization.* New York: Society for Applied Anthropology, 1941——. (Contains numerous articles relating to adjustment of culture to economic changes.)

133. ICHIHASHI, YAMATO. *Japanese in the United States.* Stanford, Calif.: Stanford University Press, 1932.

134. INDIA. *Censuses of 1931, 1941* and *1951.* New Delhi: Government of India Press, 1931——.

135. ——. *Report of Indian Delegation to China on Agrarian Cooperatives.* New Delhi: Planning Commission, 1957.

136. INDIA, MINISTRY OF FOOD AND AGRICULTURE. *Report of the Indian Delegation to China on Agricultural and Planning Techniques.* New Delhi: Government of India Press, 1956.

137. INDIA, PLANNING COMMISSION. *First Five Year Plan: People's Edition.* New Delhi: Government of India Press, 1953.

137a. ——. *The New India.* New York: Macmillan Co., 1958.

138. ——. *Report of the Village and Small Scale Industries.* (Second Five-Year Plan.) New Delhi: Government of India Press, 1955.

139. ——. *Second Five Year Plan.* New Delhi: Government of India Press, 1956.

140. ——. *Second Five Year Plan.* (A Draft Outline.) New Delhi: Government of India Press, 1956.

140a. ——. *Study Group on Educated Unemployed.* (Outline Report.) New Delhi: Manager of Publications, 1956.

141. INDIA. *See also* COALE (80).

142. INDOCHINA. "Economic Resources of French Indo-China," *Far Eastern Review,* XXXVI, No. 11 (November, 1940), 401–2.

143. INDONESIA. "The Population of Indonesia," *Ekonomi dan Keauangan Indonesia,* February, 1956.

144. INGRAM, JAMES C. *Economic Change in Thailand since 1850.* Stanford, Calif.: Stanford University Press, 1955.

145. INSTITUTE OF PACIFIC RELATIONS. (Publishes a large amount of material on all Pacific lands as well as *Pacific Affairs* and *Far Eastern Survey*.)

146. INTERNATIONAL BANK FOR RECONSTRUCTION AND DEVELOPMENT. *The Economic Development of Malaya*. Baltimore: Johns Hopkins Press, 1955. (*See also* specific countries.)

147. *Japan Annual*. Tokyo: Institute of World Economy, 1954–55.

148. JAPAN, BANK OF. *Economic Statistics of Japan*. Tokyo: Bank of Japan, 1923——.

149. JAPAN, BUREAU OF STATISTICS. *Résumé statistique de l'Empire du Japon*. Tokyo, 1880——.

150. ——. *Résumé statistique du mouvement de la population de l'Empire du Japon*. Tokyo, 19——?

151. ——. *1955 Population Census of Japan*. Vol. I. Tokyo: Office of the Prime Minister, 1956.

152. JAPAN, DEPARTMENT OF FINANCE. *Financial and Economic Annual of Japan*. Tokyo: Government Printing Office, 1901——.

153. JAPAN, ECONOMIC PLANNING BOARD. *Japanese Economic Statistics Bulletin*. (Monthly.) Tokyo.

154. JAPAN. *Japan in the Beginning of the Twentieth Century*. Tokyo: Imperial Japanese Commission to the Louisiana Purchase Exposition, 1904.

155. *Japan-Manchoukuo Year Book*. Tokyo: Japan-Manchoukuo Year Book Co., 1933——.

156. JAPAN, PROVISIONAL BUREAU OF CENSUS INVESTIGATION OF FORMOSA. *The Special Population Census of Formosa, 1905*. Tokyo: Imperial Printing Bureau, 1909.

157. JAPAN, STATISTICS BUREAU OF THE PRIME MINISTER'S OFFICE. *Statistical Yearbook*. Tokyo: Office of the Prime Minister, 1882——.

158. *The Japan Year Book*. Tokyo: 1906——.

159. JOHNSTON, BRUCE F. "Agricultural Productivity and Economic Development in Japan," *Journal of Political Economy*, LIX, No. 6 (December, 1951), 498–513.

160. KEESING, FELIX M. *The South Seas in the Modern World*. New York: John Day Co., 1945.

161. ——. "Standards of Living among Native Peoples of the Pacific," *Pacific Affairs*, VIII, No. 1 (March, 1935), 21–34.

162. KIEFER, MAXINE E. *See* BLACK (37).

163. KIRBY, E. STUART. *Contemporary China*. Hong Kong: Hong Kong University Press, 1956.

164. ——. "Impressions of Peoples China," *Far Eastern Economic Review*, XX, (January 26, 1956), 113–17.

165. ——. "The People of China: Birth Control for 600,000,000?" *Family Planning* (London), V, No. 2 (July, 1956), 3–8.

166. KITAOKA, JUITSU. *Over-population and Family Planning*. Tokyo: Science Council of Japan, Division of Economics and Commerce, 1957.

167. KOREA. *A Handbook of Korea*. Seoul: Office of Public Information, 1955.

168. KOYA, YOSHIO. "A Study of Induced Abortion in Japan and Its Signifi-

cance," *Milbank Memorial Fund Quarterly*, XXXII, No. 3 (July, 1954), 282–93.

169. KOYA, YOSHIO, *et al.* "A Survey of Health and Demographic Aspects of Reported Female Sterilizations in Four Health Centers of Shizuoka Prefecture, Japan," *Milbank Memorial Fund Quarterly*, XXXIII, No. 4 (October, 1955), 368–92.

170. KUO, PIN-CHIA. *China: New Age and New Outlook.* New York: Alfred A. Knopf, 1956.

171. KUZNETS, SIMON. *Commodity Flow and Capital Formation.* New York: National Bureau of Economic Research, 1938.

172. ——. "International Differences in Income Levels: Some Reflections on Their Causes," *Economic Development and Cultural Change*, II, No. 1 (April, 1953), 3–26.

173. KUZNETS, SIMON, *et al. Economic Growth: Brazil, India, Japan.* (Edited by Simon Kuznets, Wilbert E. Moore, and Joseph J. Spengler.) Durham, N.C.: Duke University Press, 1955.

174. LEAGUE OF NATIONS. *International Statistical Year-Book.* Geneva, 1927——.

175. LEWIS, W. ARTHUR. *The Theory of Economic Growth.* London: G. Allen & Unwin Ltd., 1955.

176. LI TEH-CH'UAN. Speech at Third Session of the Second Chinese People's Political Consultative Conference, March 7, 1957. Published in *Peking Jen Min Jih Pao*, March 8, 1957.

177. LIND, ANDREW W. *Hawaii's People.* Honolulu: University of Hawaii Press, 1955.

178. LING, N. J. "A Sceptical View [of the 1953 Census of Mainland China]." (An unpublished article given to the writer in Hong Kong in November, 1955.) *See also* KIRBY (163).

179. LINTON, RALPH. "Cultural and Personality Factors Affecting Economic Growth," in (126), pp. 73–88.

180. LOCKWOOD, WILLIAM W. *The Economic Development of Japan: Growth and Structural Change.* Princeton, N.J.: Princeton University Press, 1954.

180*a*. LOT, FERDINAND. *The End of the Ancient World and the Beginning of the Middle Ages.* New York: Barnes & Noble, Inc., 1953. (See esp. chap. iv, pp. 55–85.)

181. McCUNE, GEORGE McAFEE. *Korea Today.* Cambridge, Mass.: Harvard University Press, 1950.

182. McCUNE, SHANNON. *Korea's Heritage: A Regional and Social Geography.* Rutand, Vt.: Charles E. Tuttle Co., 1956.

183. MALAYA. *See* INTERNATIONAL BANK FOR RECONSTRUCTION AND DEVELOPMENT (146).

184. MALENBAUM, WILFRED. "India and China: Development Contrasts," *Journal of Political Economy*, LIV, No. 1 (February, 1956), 1–24.

185. ——. *See also* HIGGINS (123).

186. MALLORY, WALTER H. *China: Land of Famine.* New York: American Geographical Society, 1926.

187. *The Manchoukuo Year Book.* Hsinking, Manchoukuo: Manchoukuo Year Book Co., 1942.

188. MANDELBAUM, DAVID G. "Planning and Social Change in India," *Human Organization,* XII, No. 3 (1953), 12.

189. ———. "Technology, Credit and Culture in an Indian Village," *Human Organization,* XI, No. 3 (1952), 28.

190. MARRIOTT, McKIM. "Western Medicine in a Village of Northern India," in (223), pp. 239–68.

191. MATHEN, K. K. "Public Opinion Survey on Certain Aspects of the Population Problem," *Indian Journal of Medical Research,* XLII, No. 4 (October, 1954), 619–34.

192. ———. "A Survey on the Attitude of Men and Women of Calcutta on Certain Aspects of the Population Problem," *Alumni Association Bulletin, All Indian Institute of Hygiene and Public Health,* January, 1954, pp. 32–36.

193. MILBANK MEMORIAL FUND. *The Interrelations of Demographic, Economic, and Social Problems in Selected Underdeveloped Areas.* (Proceedings of a round table at the 1953 Annual Conference.) New York: Milbank Memorial Fund, 1954.

194. MILLER, E. WILLARD. "Mineral Resources of Indo-China," *Economic Geography,* XXII, No. 4 (October, 1946), 268–79.

195. MILLS, LENNOX A. *British Rule in Eastern Asia.* Minneapolis: University of Minnesota Press, 1942.

196. MITCHELL, KATE L. *Industrialization of the Western Pacific.* New York: International Secretariat, Institute of Pacific Relations, 1942.

197. MOORE, FRANK J. "Money-Lenders and Cooperators in India," *Economic Development and Cultural Change,* II, No. 2 (June, 1953), 139–59.

198. ———. "A Note on Rural Debt and Control of Ceremonial Expenditure in India," *Economic Development and Cultural Change,* II, No. 5 (June, 1954), 408–15.

199. MOORE, WILBERT E. *See* KUZNETS (173).

200. MORGAN, THEODORE. "The Economic Development of Ceylon," *Annals of the American Academy of Political and Social Science,* CCCV (May, 1956), 92–100.

201. MORRISON, WILLIAM A. "Attitudes of Males toward Family Planning in a Western Indian Village," *Milbank Memorial Fund Quarterly,* XXXIV, No. 3 (July, 1956), 262–86.

202. MOULTON, HAROLD G. *Japan: An Economic and Financial Appraisal.* Washington, D.C.: Brookings Institution, 1931.

203. MUKERJEE, RADHAKAMAL (ed.). *Economic Problems of Modern India.* 2 vols. London: Macmillan & Co., 1939–41.

204. ———. *Food Planning for Four Hundred Millions.* London: Macmillan & Co., 1938.

205. NASU, SHIROSHI. *Aspects of Japanese Agriculture.* New York: International Secretariat, Institute of Pacific Relations, 1941.

206. ——. *Land Utilization in Japan.* Tokyo: Research Committee of Japanese Council, Institute of Pacific Relations, 1929.

207. NATHAN (ROBERT R.) ASSOCIATES. *An Economic Programme for Korean Reconstruction.* New York: U.N. Korean Reconstruction Agency, 1954.

208. NETHERLANDS EAST INDIES. *Indisch Verslag.* Batavia: Landsdrukkerij, 1916——.

209. NEWELL, WILLIAM H. "A Note on Village Government in the Indian Northern Hill States since Indian Independence," *Economic Development and Cultural Change,* II, No. 5 (June, 1954), 416–19.

210. NEW ZEALAND, CENSUS AND STATISTICS OFFICE. *New Zealand Official Yearbook.* Wellington: Government Printer, 1892——.

211. NEW ZEALAND, DEPARTMENT OF STATISTICS. *Report on the Population, Migration and Building Statistics.* Wellington: Government Printer, 1955–56.

212. NURKSE, RAGNAR. *Problems of Capital Formation in Underdeveloped Countries.* New York: Oxford University Press, 1953.

213. OKASAKI, AYANORI. *A Fertility Survey in Japan of 1952.* Tokyo: Institute of Population Problems, Ministry of Welfare, 1953.

214. OLIVER, DOUGLAS L. *The Pacific Islands.* Cambridge, Mass.: Harvard University Press, 1951.

215. OPLER, MORRIS E. "The Problems of Selective Culture Change," in (126), pp. 126–34.

216. ——. "Problems concerning Official and Popular Participation in Development Projects," *Economic Development and Cultural Change,* II, No. 4 (January, 1954), 269–78.

217. OPLER, MORRIS E., and SINGH, RUDRA D. "Economic, Political and Social Change in a Village of North Central India," *Human Organization,* XI, No.2 (1952), 5–12.

218. *Pacific Affairs: Journal of the International Secretariat.* New York: Institute of Pacific Relations, 1929——. (A quarterly containing valuable book reviews and many comprehensive and objective articles on modern politics and economics.)

219. *Pacific Islands Yearbook.* Sydney, Australia: Pacific Publications Pty., 1932——.

220. *Pakistan.* (An annual report on economic development.) Karachi: Pakistan Publications, 1952–53——.

221. PAKISTAN, OFFICE OF THE CENSUS COMMISSIONER. *First Census of Pakistan, 1951.* Vol. I: *Report and Tables.* Karachi: Manager of Publications, 1952.

222. PATEL, SURENDA J. "Trend of Unit Yields of Foodgrains in India, 1936–50," *Indian Journal of Economics,* XXXIV (July, 1953), 49–59.

223. PAUL, BENJAMIN D. (ed.). *Health, Culture and Community: Case Study of Public Reactions to Health Programs.* New York: Russell Sage Foundation, 1955.

224. PELZER, KARL J. *Pioneer Settlement in the Asiatic Tropics.* New York: Institute of Pacific Relations, 1945.

225. PLANNED PARENTHOOD FEDERATION. *The Fifth International Conference on Planned Parenthood.* (Report of proceedings, October 24–29, 1955, in Tokyo.) London: International Planned Parenthood Federation, 1956.

226. POLITICAL AND ECONOMIC PLANNING. *World Population and Resources.* London: Queen Anne's Gate, 1955.

227. *Population Index.* Princeton, N.J.: Princeton University, School of Public and International Affairs, and the Population Association of America, 1935——. (A quarterly containing much current population information and many articles dealing with the population of different areas.)

228. PORTER, CATHERINE L. *Crisis in the Philippines.* New York: Alfred A. Knopf, 1942.

229. PURCELL, V. W. W. S. *The Chinese in Southeast Asia.* London: Oxford University Press, 1951.

230. RASAPUTRAM, W., and JAYAKODDY, A. T. "Population Problems of Ceylon." (An unpublished report on population problems prepared for the Central Bank of Ceylon, a copy of which was given to the writer in January, 1956.)

231. ROBEQUAIN, CHARLES. *The Economic Development of French Indo-China.* London: Oxford University Press, 1944.

232. ROBERTS, STEPHEN H. *Population Problems of the Pacific.* London: George Routledge & Sons, 1927.

233. ROSEN, GEORGE. "An Examination of Potential Long-run Industrial Development of India and China," *Economic Development and Cultural Change,* II, No. 5 (June, 1954), 357–70.

234. ROSTOW, W. W. *The Process of Economic Growth.* Oxford: Clarendon Press, 1953.

235. ———. *The Prospects for Communist China.* Cambridge, Mass.: Technology Press of Massachusetts Institute of Technology, 1954.

236. ROUSH, G. A. *Strategic Mineral Supplies.* New York: McGraw-Hill Book Co., 1939.

237. ROWE, DAVID NELSON. *China among the Powers.* New York: Harcourt, Brace & Co., 1945.

238. ROYAL INSTITUTE OF INTERNATIONAL AFFAIRS. (In addition to the *Bulletins and Reports* listed here, this institute issues a great deal of other material relating to the western Pacific.) "British Reactions to the War in the Far East, 1941–42." London: Royal Institute of International Affairs, 1942.

239. RUOPP, PHILLIPS. (ed.). *Approaches to Community Development: A Symposium Introductory to Problems and Methods of Village Welfare in Underdeveloped Areas.* The Hague: W. van Howe, 1953.

240. RUSSELL, SIR JOHN E. *World Population and World Food Supplies.* London: G. Allen & Unwin Ltd., 1954.

241. SARKAR, N. K. "A Note on Abridged Life Tables for Ceylon, 1900–1947," *Population Studies,* IV, No. 4 (March, 1951), 439–43.

242. SCHUMPETER, ELIZABETH B. (ed.). *The Industrialization of Japan and Manchoukuo, 1930–1940.* New York: Macmillan Co., 1940. (Contributors: G. C. Allen, E. F. Penrose, M. S. Gordon, and E. B. Schumpeter.)

243. SHABAD, THEODORE. *China's Changing Map: A Political and Economic Geography of the Chinese People's Republic.* New York: F. A. Praeger, 1956.

244. SHAO, LI-TSU. "Chinese People's Political Consultative Conference," *New China News Agency,* March 18, 1957.

245. ———. "A Speech at the National People's Congress," *Peking Jen Min Jih Pao,* September 18, 1954.

246. SHEPHERD, JACK. *Industry in Southeast Asia.* New York: International Secretariat, Institute of Pacific Relations, 1941.

247. SINGH, BALJIT. *Economic Planning in India, 1951–1956.* Bombay: Hind Kitabs, 1955.

247a. ———. *Five Years of Family Planning in the Countryside.* (Monograph No. 6.) Lucknow, India: J. K. Institute, 1958. (Mimeographed.)

248. SINHA, J. N. "Differential Fertility and Family Limitation in an Urban Community of Uttar Pradesh," *Population Studies,* XI, No. 2 (November, 1957), 157–69.

249. SMITH, THOMAS CARLYLE. *Political Change and Industrial Development in Japan: Government Enterprise 1868–1880.* Stanford, Calif.: Stanford University Press, 1955.

250. SOVANI, N. V. *The Social Survey of Kalhapur City.* Part I: *Population and Fertility.* Poona: Gokhale Institute of Politics and Economics, 1948.

251. SOVANI, N. V., and DANDEKAR, KUMUDINI. *Fertility Survey of Nasik, Kolaba and Satara (North) Districts.* Poona: Gokhale Institute of Politics and Economics, 1955.

251a. SPENCER, JOSEPH E. *Asia, East by South: A Cultural Geography.* New York: John Wiley & Sons, 1954.

252. SPENGLER, JOSEPH J. See KUZNETS (173).

253. SPICER, E. H. (ed.). *Human Problems in Technological Change: A Casebook.* New York: Russell Sage Foundation, 1952.

254. STALEY, EUGENE. *The Future of Underdeveloped Countries: Political Implications of Economic Development.* New York: Harper & Bros., 1954.

255. STAMP, L. D. *Asia: A Regional and Economic Geography.* New York: E. P. Dutton & Co., 1938.

256. ———. *Land for Tomorrow: The Underdeveloped World.* Bloomington: Indiana University Press, 1952.

257. STEPANEK, J. E., and PRIEN, C. H. "The Role of Rural Industries in Under-developed Areas," *Pacific Affairs,* XXIII, No. 1 (March, 1950), 65–76.

258. STEWART, OMAR C. "Social Scientists and the Point Four Program," *Human Organization,* IX, No. 3 (1950), 26–27.

259. STRAUS, MURRAY A. "Cultural Factors in the Functioning of Agricultural

Extension in Ceylon," *Rural Sociology*, XVIII, No. 3 (September, 1953), 249–56.

260. STYCOS, J. MAYONE. "Birth Control Clinics in Crowded Puerto Rico," in (223), pp. 189–210.

261. SWEDEN, STATISTISKA CENTRALBYRÅN. *Statistik Arsbok för Sverige*. Stockholm, 1914——.

262. TAEUBER, IRENE B. "Fertility and Research on Fertility in Japan," *Milbank Memorial Fund Quarterly*, XXXIV, No. 2 (April, 1956), 129–49.

263. ——. "Population and Labor Force in the Industrialization of Japan, 1850–1950," in (173), pp. 316–59.

263a. ——. *The Population of Japan*. Princeton, N. J.: Princeton University Press, 1958.

264. ——. "Population Policies in Communist China," *Population Index*, XXII, No. 4 (October, 1956), 261–74.

265. TAEUBER, IRENE B., and BEAL, EDWIN G. "The Dynamics of Population in Japan," *Milbank Memorial Fund Quarterly*, XXII, No. 3 (July, 1944), 222–55.

266. TAEUBER, IRENE B., and ORLEANS, LEO A. "A Note on the Population Statistics of Communist China," *Population Index*, XXII, No. 4 (October, 1956), 274–76.

267. TAIWAN, CHINA. PROVINCIAL GOVERNMENT. *Results of the Seventh Population Census of Taiwan, 1940*. Taiwan: Provincial Government of Taiwan, 1953.

268. TALBOT, PHILLIPS (ed.). *South Asia in the World Today*. Chicago: University of Chicago Press, 1950.

269. TAWNEY, R. H. *Land and Labour in China*. New York: Harcourt, Brace & Co., 1932.

270. TAYLOR, THOMAS GRIFFITH. *Australia*. New York: E. P. Dutton & Co., 1943.

271. ——. *Australia in Its Physiographic and Economic Aspects*. Oxford: Clarendon Press, 1928.

272. THAYER, P. W. (ed.). *Southeast Asia in the Coming World*. Baltimore: Johns Hopkins Press, 1953.

273. THIRUMALAI, S. *Post-war Agricultural Problems and Policies in India*. New York: Institute of Pacific Relations, 1954.

273a. THOMAS, WILLIAM L., JR. (ed.). *Man's Role in Changing the Face of the Earth*. Chicago: University of Chicago Press, 1956.

274. THOMPSON, VIRGINIA. *Postmortem on Malaya*. New York: Macmillan Co., 1943.

275. THOMPSON, WARREN S. *Danger Spots in World Population*. New York: Alfred A. Knopf, 1929.

276. ——. *Plenty of People*. Lancaster, Pa.: Jaques Cattell Press, 1944.

277. ——. *Population: A Study in Malthusianism*. New York: Longmans, Green & Co., 1915.

278. ——. "Population Control and Cultural Change," in WIGGINS, JAMES W.

(ed.), *Interdisciplinary Symposium on Cultural Contact in Underdeveloped Countries*. Atlanta: Emory University Press, 1958.

279. THOMPSON, WARREN S. *Population and Peace in the Pacific*. Chicago: University of Chicago Press, 1946.

280. ——. *Population Problems*. New York: McGraw-Hill Book Co., 1953.

280a. ——. "The Spiral of Population," in (273a), pp. 970–86.

281. THOMPSON, WARREN S., and CHIAO, C. M. *An Experiment in the Registration of Vital Statistics in China*. Oxford, Ohio: Scripps Foundation for Research in Population Problems, 1938.

282. TRAGER, FRANK N. *Toward a Welfare State in Burma: Economic Reconstruction and Development 1948–1954*. New York: International Secretariat, Institute of Pacific Relations, 1954.

282a. TREWARTHA, GLENN T. *Japan: A Physical, Cultural, and Regional Geography*. Madison: University of Wisconsin Press, 1945.

283. UNITED NATIONS, DEPARTMENT OF ECONOMIC AFFAIRS. *Development of Mineral Resources in Asia and the Far East*. Bangkok, 1953.

284. ——. *Measures for the Economic Development of Underdeveloped Countries*. New York, 1951.

285. ——. *Methods of Financing Economic Development in Underdeveloped Countries*. Lake Success, N.Y.: 1949.

286. ——. *Post War Shortages of Food and Coal*. New York: Columbia University Press, 1948.

287. ——. *Progress in Land Reform: An Analysis of Replies by Governments to an United Nations Questionnaire*. New York, 1954.

288. ——. *Recent Changes in Production*. (Supplement to *World Economic Report*.) New York, 1952.

289. ——. *Rural Progress through Cooperatives: The Place of Cooperative Associations in Agricultural Development*. New York, 1954.

290. ——. *A Study of Trade between Asia and Europe*. Geneva, 1953.

291. ——. *World Economic Report, 1951–52*. New York, 1953.

292. ——. *World Iron Ore Resources and Their Utilization: With Special Reference to the Use of Iron Ores in Underdeveloped Areas*. New York: Columbia University Press, 1950.

293. UNITED NATIONS, DEPARTMENT OF ECONOMIC AND SOCIAL AFFAIRS. *Demographic Yearbook, 1948——*. Lake Success and New York, N.Y.

294. ——. *Processes and Problems of Industrialization in Underdeveloped Countries*. New York: Columbia University Press, 1955.

295. ——. *Report on Community Organization and Development in South and Southeast Asia*. New York: Columbia University Press, 1954.

296. ——. *Survey of World Iron Ore Resources: Occurrence, Appraisal and Use*. New York: Columbia University Press, 1955.

297. UNITED NATIONS, DEPARTMENT OF PUBLIC INFORMATION. *Assignment to Everywhere*. Geneva, 1954.

298. ——. "International Aid in Search for Development Funds," *United Nations' Review*, I, No. 4 (October, 1954), 6–12.

299. ——. *Pooling Skills for Human Progress: The Why, What and How of*

United Nations Technical Assistance. New York: Columbia University Press, 1956.

300. UNITED NATIONS, DEPARTMENT OF SOCIAL AFFAIRS. *The Determinants and Consequences of Population Trends: A Summary of the Findings of Studies on the Relationships between Population Changes and Economic and Social Conditions.* New York, 1953.

301. ———. *Preliminary Report on the World Social Situation: With Special Reference to Standards of Living.* New York: Columbia University Press, 1952.

302. UNITED NATIONS, ECONOMIC COMMISSION FOR ASIA AND THE FAR EAST. *Coal and Iron Ore Resources of Asia and the Far East.* Bangkok, 1952. (Also publishes *Coal and Iron Ore Studies.*)

303. ———. *Economic Survey of Asia and the Far East, 1949——.* New York and Bangkok.

304. ———. *Mining Development in Asia and the Far East, 1954/55.* New York, 1955.

305. ———. *Mobilization of Domestic Capital: Report and Documents of the Second Working Party of Experts.* Bangkok, 1953.

306. ———. *Rural Electrification.* New York, 1954.

307. UNITED NATIONS, ECONOMIC AND SOCIAL COUNCIL. *Instability in Export Markets of Underdeveloped Countries.* New York: Columbia University Press, 1952.

308. UNITED NATIONS, FOOD AND AGRICULTURAL ORGANIZATION. *See* FOOD AND AGRICULTURAL ORGANIZATION OF UNITED NATIONS, (106) through (111).

309. UNITED NATIONS, SECRETARIAT STATISTICAL OFFICE. *Statistical Yearbook, 1948–56.* Lake Success, N.Y.

310. UNITED NATIONS, WORLD POPULATION CONFERENCE. *Proceedings of the World Population Conference, 1954.* 6 vols. New York, 1955–57.

311. UNITED STATES, AMERICAN CONSULATE GENERAL, HONG KONG. *Survey of China Mainland Press,* No. 1, November 1, 1950. (Published several times a week.)

312. UNITED STATES BUREAU OF THE CENSUS. *International Population Reports.* (Series P-91, No. 3, June, 1956.)

313. ———. *Statistical Abstract of the United States, 1878——.* Washington, D.C.: Government Printing Office, 1879——.

314. ———. *United States Census of Agriculture, 1950, Territories and Possessions.* Vol. I, Part 34. Washington, D.C.: Government Printing Office, 1952.

315. ———. *United States Census of Population, 1950, Hawaii.* Washington, D.C.: Government Printing Office, 1952.

316. UNITED STATES BUREAU OF THE CENSUS and WYNNE, WALLER, JR. *The Population of Manchuria.* Washington, D.C.: Government Printing Office, 1958.

317. UNITED STATES BUREAU OF FOREIGN COMMERCE. *World Trade Infor-*

mation Service: Economic Reports. (Contains much up-to-date information on the economy of different countries.)

318. UNITED STATES DEPARTMENT OF AGRICULTURE, FOREIGN AGRICULTURAL SERVICE. *Foreign Agriculture Circular.* (FATP Series.) (Contains much information regarding agricultural conditions in foreign countries.)

319. UNITED STATES DEPARTMENT OF INTERIOR, BUREAU OF MINES. *Mineral Resources of China.* Washington, D.C.: Government Printing Office, 1948.

320. ———. *Mineral Resources of Japan.* Washington, D.C.: Government Printing Office, 1945.

321. ———. *Minerals Yearbook Review.* Washington, D.C.: Government Printing Office, 1933——.

322. UNITED STATES DEPARTMENT OF STATE. *Economic Problems in Asia.* Washington, D.C.: Government Printing Office, 1956.

323. ———. *Economic Survey Mission to the Philippines.* Washington, D.C.: Government Printing Office, 1950.

324. ———. *Indochina: The War in Viet-Nam, Cambodia and Laos: Background.* Washington, D.C.: Government Printing Office, 1953.

325. ———. *Thailand: Background.* Washington, D.C.: Government Printing Office, 1956.

326. ———. *The Union of Burma: Background.* Washington, D.C.: Government Printing Office, 1955.

327. UNITED STATES, PRESIDENT'S MATERIALS POLICY COMMISSION. *Resources for Freedom.* Washington, D.C.: Government Printing Office, 1952.

328. VAILE, ROLAND S. "Southeast Asia in World Economics," in MILLS, LENNOX A. (ed.), *The New World of Southeast Asia.* Minneapolis: University of Minnesota Press, 1949, pp. 343–70.

329. VAKIL, C. N. *Economic Consequences of Divided India: A Study of the Economy of India and Pakistan.* Bombay: Vora & Co., 1950.

330. VAKIL, C. N., and BRAHMANAND, P. R. *Planning for an Expanding Economy.* Bombay: Vora & Co., 1956.

331. VANDENBOSCH, AMRY. "Ceylon—Progress in Asia," *Current History,* XIX, No. 110 (October, 1950), 206–9.

332. ———. *The Dutch East Indies.* Berkeley: University of California Press, 1942.

333. VAN DER KROEF, JULIUS M. "Economic Origins of Indonesian Nationalism," in (268), pp. 188–93.

334. ———. "Entrepreneur and Middle Class in Indonesia," *Economic Development and Cultural Change,* II, No. 4 (January, 1954), 297–325.

335. ———. "Social Conflict and Minority Aspirations in Indonesia," *American Journal of Sociology,* LV, No. 5 (March, 1950), 450–63.

336. WALKER, RICHARD LEWIS. *China under Communism: The First Five Years.* New Haven: Yale University Press, 1955.

337. WANG, KUNG-PING. "The Mineral Situation in the Far East," *Mining Engineering,* November, 1951.

338. WANG, KUNG-PING, and READ, THOMAS T. "Controlling Factors in

China's Coal Development," *Pacific Affairs,* XIX, No. 2 (June, 1946), 165–81.

339. WATNICK, MORRIS. "The Appeal of Communism to the Underdeveloped Peoples," in (126), pp. 152–72.

340. WICKIZER, V. D., and BENNETT, M. K. *The Rice Economy of Monsoon Asia.* Stanford University, Calif.: Food Research Institute, 1941.

341. WILKINSON, H. L. *The World's Population Problems and a White Australia.* London: P. S. King & Son, 1930.

342. WILLCOX, WALTER F. (ed.). *International Migrations.* 2 vols. New York: National Bureau of Economic Research, 1929–31.

343. ———. *Studies in American Demography.* Ithaca, N.Y.: Cornell University Press, 1940.

344. WILLIAMSON, HAROLD F., and BUTTRICK, JOHN A. (eds.). *Economic Development: Principles and Patterns.* New York: Prentice-Hall, 1954.

345. WILLNER, A. R. "The Foreign Expert in Indonesia: Problems of Adjustability and Contribution," *Economic Development and Cultural Change,* II, No. 1 (April, 1953), 71–80.

346. WOLF, CHARLES, JR. "Institutions and Economic Development," *American Economic Review,* XLV (December, 1955), 867–83.

347. WORLD POPULATION CONFERENCE. *See* UNITED NATIONS (310).

348. WU, YUAN-LI. *An Economic Survey of Communist China.* New York: Bookman Associates, 1956.

349. WYNNE, WALLER, JR. *See* UNITED STATES BUREAU OF THE CENSUS (316).

350. YAMASAKI, KAKUJIRO, and OGAWA, GOTARO. *The Effect of the World War upon the Commerce and Industry of Japan.* New Haven: Yale University Press, 1929.

351. YEARBOOK OF FOOD AND AGRICULTURE STATISTICS. *See* FOOD AND AGRICULTURE ORGANIZATION OF THE UNITED NATIONS (111).

352. ZINKIN, TAYA. *India Changes.* New York: Oxford University Press, 1958.

INDEX

[Page references to tables, figures, and maps are indicated by *italics;* numbers in parentheses refer to the Bibliography.]